OUT OF LOVE FOR MY KIN

OUT OF LOVE
FOR MY KIN

Aristocratic Family
Life in the Lands
of the Loire,
1000–1200

AMY LIVINGSTONE

CORNELL UNIVERSITY PRESS

Ithaca and London

First published 2010 by Cornell University Press

Printed in the United States of America

Library of Congress Cataloging-in-Publication Data

Livingstone, Amy, 1961–
  Out of love for my kin : aristocratic family life in the lands of the Loire, 1000-1200 / Amy Livingstone.
      p. cm.
  Includes bibliographical references and index.
  ISBN 978-0-8014-4841-6 (cloth : alk. paper)
  1. Aristocracy (Social class)—France—Loire River Valley—History—To 1500.   2. Families—France—Loire River Valley—History—To 1500.   3. Kinship—France—History—Loire River Valley—History—To 1500.   4. Loire River Valley (France)—Social life and customs.   5. France—Social life and customs—To 1328.   I. Title.
    HT653.F7L58   2010
    305.5'209445—dc22   2009039909

Cornell University Press strives to use environmentally responsible suppliers and materials to the fullest extent possible in the publishing of its books. Such materials include vegetable-based, low-VOC inks and acid-free papers that are recycled, totally chlorine-free, or partly composed of nonwood fibers. For further information, visit our website at www.cornellpress.cornell.edu.

Cloth printing   10 9 8 7 6 5 4 3 2 1

For Carol and Frank Livingstone
Beloved parents and treasured friends

✖ CONTENTS

❦ ACKNOWLEDGMENTS

All historians are indebted to the help and guidance of archivists and librarians, and I am no different. This book could not have been completed without the aid of the capable staff of several archives and libraries. I wish to thank the archivists and librarians at the Archives départementales d'Eure-et-Loir, the Archives départementales de Loir-et-Cher, the Archives départementales de Maine-et-Loire, the Bibliothèque nationale de France, and the Buhr Library and the Harlan Hatcher Library at the University of Michigan; the staff of the Rare Books Room of the Waldo Library at Western Michigan University; and the librarians of the Thomas Library at Wittenberg University.

As with raising a child, so too, it takes a village to help one write a book. Many people have provided support and encouragement for this project over the years. First, I would like to thank my teachers, the late Richard E. Sullivan and Emily Z. Tabuteau. Both contributed greatly to my development as a scholar, teacher, and member of the academy. André Chédeville provided invaluable guidance during my research year in France and after. My students, past and present, have helped me examine my own ideas about the past more closely. Many medievalist colleagues have also provided valuable feedback on dimensions of this work. I would like to thank Constance Bouchard, Theodore Evergates, Kimberly LoPrete, Fredric Cheyette, George Beech, Robert Berkhofer, Richard Kaiser, Adam Davis, Jonathan Lyon, Constance Berman, Charlotte Newman Goldy, the late Jo Ann McNamara, Louis Haas, and Mark Angelos for their suggestions and insights. Thanks also to those colleagues who read portions of the manuscript: Linda Mitchell, Tammy Proctor, James Huffman, Brenda Bertrand, Christian Raffensperger, and Molly Wood. Pastor Anders Tune kindly helped me identify and understand passages of scripture in the charters. Jim Scott lent his skill in polishing the genealogical charts. The book is better for their comments and contributions.

Wittenberg University has been generous both in allowing me the time to work on this book and in providing financial support. I have also benefited from having several faculty-research aides—Courtney Smith Chung, Erin

Waltz, Corey McOsker, Alison Gaughenbaugh, and Whitney Yount—who have been enormously helpful with this project. I am blessed with wonderful Wittenberg colleagues who have expressed interest in and support for a topic that is far removed from their own interests and vocations. Leanne Wierenga has lent her expertise in French to this project in many ways, from reading poems in Old French to proofing correspondence. Mary Jo Zembar has been a trusted source for much-needed professional and publishing advice. Warm thanks go to the Wittenberg History Department—including the ever-gracious Margaret DeButy—who have cheered me on and offered advice along the way. Finally, a special thank-you to Rachel Tune and Jennifer Oldstone-Moore for their friendship and for helping me balance life with professional responsibilities.

Since this is a work about family, it is only appropriate that I thank my own. My husband, Gordon Thompson, drew the maps for the book and provided technical support. This book would likely not have made it into print without his expertise, patience, and unflinching support. To my sons, Samuel and William Thompson, many thanks for your enthusiasm for history and most especially for your understanding on those occasions when a research trip meant I could not be there for you at home. To our "Paris family," Josef and Isa Konvitz, profound gratitude for the warm hospitality, sage advice, and encouragement over the years.

Sadly, several people who left an imprint on this project did not live to see its completion. Richard E. Sullivan taught me much about how to do history but also how to make history interesting and make people care about it. The late Thomas Amos, director of the Rare Books Collection at Waldo Library at Western Michigan University, provided support—both bibliographical and personal—on several research trips to visit the Waldo Library's excellent collection of nineteenth-century French cartularies. My uncle Ernst Goldschmidt gave me my first book by Georges Duby and unknowingly set me on a journey that has become my career. Though my parents, Frank and Carol Livingstone, are now both deceased, their spirits were ever-present companions while I completed this book. My father introduced me to the life of a scholar and was always willing to offer an anthropological perspective on medieval families. My mother was my intrepid traveling companion on many trips through the lands of the Loire. Many of the questions I address in this book are questions she asked during those trips. For their support, encouragement, and pride in my accomplishments, this book is lovingly dedicated to them.

ABBREVIATIONS

AD	*Archives départementales*
AESC	*Annales: Economies, sociétés, civilisations*
AHR	*American Historical Review*
BNF	Bibliothèque nationale de France
Bonneval	*Cartulaire de l'abbaye de Saint-Florent de Bonneval*
CMPD	*Cartulaire de Marmoutier pour le Dunois*
CSVM	*Cartulaire de Saint-Vincent du Mans*
CTV	*Cartulaire de l'abbaye cardinale de la Trinité de Vendôme*
CV	*Chartes Vendômoises*
Gondon	*Cartulaire de Saint-Gondon-sur-Loire*
Jean	*Cartulaire de Saint-Jean-en-Vallée*
Josaphat	*Cartulaire de Notre-Dame de Josaphat*
MB	*Marmoutier, cartulaire Blésois*
MM	*Cartulaire manceau de Marmoutier*
MP	*Cartulaire de Marmoutier pour La Perche*
MSAEL	*Mémoires de la société archéologique d'Eure-et-Loir*
MV	*Cartulaire Marmoutier pour le Vendômois*
NDDC	*Cartulaire de Notre-Dame de Chartres d'après les cartulaires et les titres originaux*
Père	*Cartulaire de Saint-Père de Chartres*
RHDF	*Revue d'histoire de droit français et étranger*
SD	*Saint-Denis de Nogent-le-Rotrou*
Tiron	*Cartulaire de la Sainte-Trinité de Tiron*

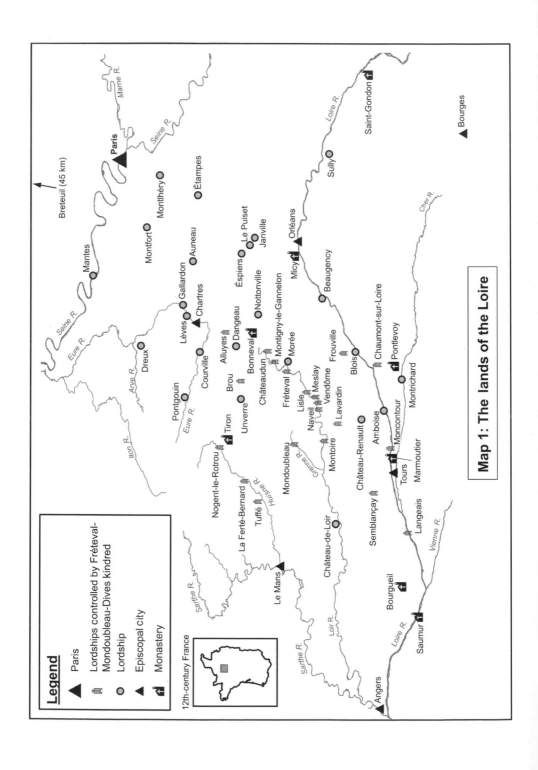

Map 1: The lands of the Loire

Legend

- Paris
- Lordships controlled by Fréteval-Mondoubleau-Dives kindred
- Lordship
- Episcopal city
- Monastery

12th-century France

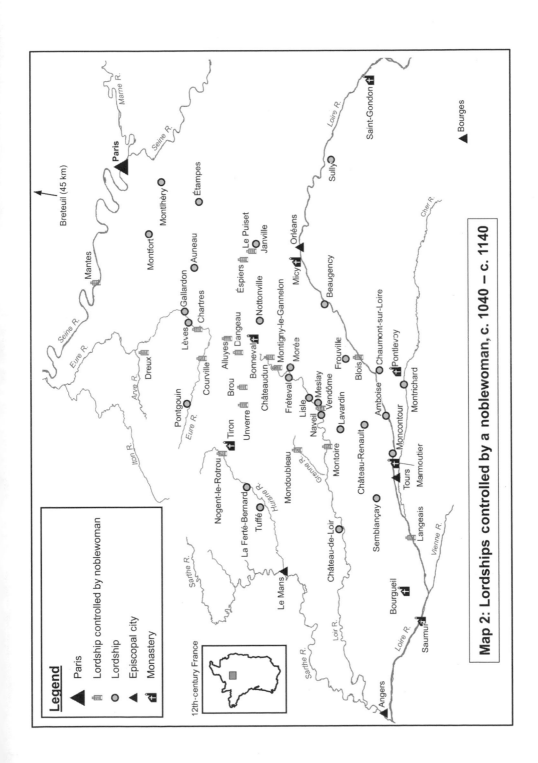

Map 2: Lordships controlled by a noblewoman, c. 1040 – c. 1140

Legend

▲ Paris

🏛 Lordship controlled by noblewoman

● Lordship

▲ Episcopal city

🏰 Monastery

12th-century France

Breteuil (45 km)

Marne R.

Seine R.

Paris

Montfort

Montlhéry

Étampes

Mantes

Seine R.

Eure R.

Arve R.

Dreux

Pontgouin

Eure R.

Iton R.

Gallardon

Lèves

Chartres

Courville

Tiron

Unverre

Brou

Alluyes

Dangeau

Bonneval

Châteaudun

Espiers

Le Puiset

Janville

Nottonville

Montigny-le-Gannelon

Morée

Fréteval

Lisle

Naveil

Meslay

Vendôme

Lavardin

Frouville

Blois

Micy

Orléans

Beaugency

Sully

Saint-Gondon

Loire R.

Bourges

Cher R.

Chaumont-sur-Loire

Pontlevoy

Amboise

Moncontour

Montrichard

Château-Renault

Montoire

Mondoubleau

Cisne R.

Nogent-le-Rotrou

La Ferté-Bernard

Tuffé

Huisne R.

Sarthe R.

Le Mans

Château-de-Loir

Semblançay

Tours

Marmoutier

Langeais

Vienne R.

Bourgueil

Saumur

Loire R.

Loir R.

Sarthe R.

Angers

❧ OUT OF LOVE FOR MY KIN

Introduction

Aristocrats and Their Families

In the year 1102, records tell us, Adelina and Walter Minter and their children rode across the town of Chartres, passing under the shadow of the cathedral and traveling east through the winding streets and alleys of the market district to the abbey of St. Père. Upon arriving at the monastery, they proceeded to the chapter house, where they arranged to give property to the brothers.

During their long marriage, Walter and Adelina had added to their joint inheritances by purchasing extensive properties, including fiefs, vineyards, land, houses, mills, and wine presses, thus giving them the means to make not only that original donation in 1102 to St. Père but also several more later on. After Walter died, Adelina and her six children continued working together to make profits from the original properties and to acquire additional wealth. As the children matured and eventually left the family home, each received a portion of the patrimony as well as what had been added to the family coffers. Three of Adelina and Walter's children married, two joined religious orders, and one son remained a bachelor. Once the earthly affairs of her family were settled, Adelina turned to the care of souls. She made a third donation to St. Père, this time to benefit her own immortal soul and Walter's. This generous benefaction was made with her children's assent, which they gave of their own free will, and in the presence of the bishop and other powerful men of the region.[1]

The experience of the Minter family and the details of these property arrangements give us important information about the family life of medieval elites. The grant of 1102 shows that Adelina was her husband's partner in making the transaction. The document's use of plural verbs makes the point that Adelina and Walter possessed and acquired the properties together and donated them together. Under the widow Adelina's watchful eye, the Minter family managed its property as a group, with each child having a share in family resources. They cooperated in deciding which property would be used to endow those siblings who entered the church and they all agreed on which properties would be used to commemorate their father and benefit their parents' souls. In short, we are left with the distinct impression that Adelina and Walter valued all of their children, that each child enjoyed a portion of family holdings, that the family took care in arranging the future of its members, and that women were influential and important members of the family. That is, the Minters acted as many modern Western families do.

In this book, I will argue that the Minter family organization represents the norm rather than the exception among the aristocratic families of the lands of the Loire. I posit that an ethos of inclusivity lay at the center of aristocratic family life, meaning that medieval aristocratic families cared about their members. As a consequence, these families put in place strategies, practices, and behaviors aimed at including a range of relatives in family life and providing for them. Indeed, this care—and in some cases outright affection—for family members is recorded in the documents themselves, as many a nobleman and woman made pious benefactions "out of love for my kin." Inclusivity was at play in aristocratic family dynamics in three significant ways.

First, medieval elites conceptualized their family broadly and did not give primacy to one line of descent. As is evident in the Minter family, both maternal and paternal kin were important and recognized, thus making aristocratic families collateral.[2] Inclusivity is also apparent in aristocrats' recognition of

---

1. *Cartulaire de Saint-Père de Chartres,* vol. 2, no. 9, pp. 407–8 (hereafter, *Père*). For additional discussion of this family, see Chédeville, *Chartres et ses campagnes,* pp. 476–79.

2. A word about terminology and kinship patterns. *Patrilineage* represents a family configuration that has preference for the male line, particularly that of the firstborn son, over all others. *Cognatic kinship* refers to a kinship system that recognizes both the maternal and paternal lines. "Collateral" or "bilateral" are terms also used to refer to cognatic kinship. *Agnatic,* in contrast, describes a reckoning of kin that follows only the male line and can be roughly synonymous with patrilineal. *Horizontal* and *vertical* are applied to kinship configurations in order to describe the type of kinship. Horizontal suggests a broad reckoning of kinship and the rights of kin. Vertical indicates a more lineal descent and can mean that rights to property are reserved for only those of one line. *Natal* refers to kin by

a wide range of kin and in the ways that medieval elite interacted with their kin throughout their lives. Second, far from adhering to one monolithic form of family structure or inheritance, the aristocracy of the Loire region implemented a variety of practices. Indeed, the ways in which the Minter family functioned represent only one strand of the intricate tapestry that was aristocratic family experience. Other families fashioned different ways of providing for children and managing their resources. Third, the many roles that women played as influential members of their family demonstrate that they were not excluded from family decisions or made powerless by a system that invested authority solely in men. Furthermore, the notions that marriage was exclusively repressive and violent for women, that parents did not love their children, and that elites viewed their kin as their chief competitors would have been puzzling to many of the nobles of the Loire region. For most families were bound together by affection and experienced family interactions in generally positive ways.

In arguing that the private life of the nobility rested upon an ethos of inclusivity I challenge an older model that asserts that aristocrats implemented a family dynamic aimed at supporting only the line of the eldest son to the exclusion, and detriment, of other kin. Such a family structure was adopted in the eleventh century, so this model asserts, and represented a departure from previous practice as family dynamics shifted from inclusion to exclusion.[3] Yet, as I will argue in the pages to come, the family practices of the twelfth-century Minters and their contemporaries did not differ significantly from those of their predecessors. An underlying theme of this book is that there was no fundamental shift in family structure during the period under examination, the eleventh through twelfth centuries.[4] Although families

---

birth. In contrast, *affinal* relatives are those related through marriage. Perhaps not surprisingly, kinship patterns shape inheritance practices. *Primogeniture,* or the inheritance by the firstborn son, often (but not always) accompanies a patrilineal-kinship organization. Partible, impartible, and shared also refer to inheritance strategies. *Partible* means that all children receive a share of family holdings. *Impartible* is the opposite, where inheritance is not split among heirs and is often, but not always, associated with patrilineage. Much in the way that primogeniture and patrilineage usually go together, so too cognatic kinship often appears in families practicing partible inheritance.

3. Georges Duby, while the most recognized proponent of this model, actually based his vision of aristocratic family life on the work of Karl Schmid. See Duby, *Medieval Marriage; The Knight the Lady and the Priest;* the essays collected in *The Chivalrous Society* and *Love and Marriage in the Middle Ages;* "Women and Power"; "Communal Living"; Duby and Braunstein, "Solitude"; Schmid, "Zur Problematik von Familie, Sippe und Geschlect, Haus und Dynastie beim mittelalterlichen Adel"; and "The Structure of the Nobility in the Earlier Middle Ages." For a recent analysis of the intersections between French and German scholarship, see Bernhard Jussen, "Famille et parenté."

4. Given the significant political, legal, economic, and cultural differences between the early and central Middle Ages, historians assumed that family structure and inheritance must also differ radically between these two eras. Yet scholars have more recently come to recognize the continuities

adjusted their inheritance patterns over time, there was not a mass abandonment of one system of inheritance or family structure for another. Indeed, the forms prevalent from the early Middle Ages never went out of fashion in the lands of the Loire, leading one to the conclusion that the nobles of this region would have been very comfortable in the families of their great-grandparents. While elegant in its simplicity, a model of patrilineage, primogeniture, and patriarchy does not accurately describe the family experience of the aristocracy of the lands of the Loire.

The region of the Loire is ideally suited for an analysis of aristocratic life. First, it is rich in documentary evidence, as I will discuss below. Second, the area between the Seine and Loire rivers held an important place in the French Middle Ages. It was this region that provided a seedbed for developing the lines of dependency between lords and vassals. Castles came to dot the landscape as these mighty lords asserted their power. It was here that the French kings tested their mettle as they began their centralization of France. A study of the aristocratic families of this area can thus contribute much to the general contours of French medieval history. By providing a comprehensive analysis of aristocratic lives from birth to death, this book will reconstruct how medieval aristocratic families functioned. The evidence offered adds new and different voices to the narrative that enriches our understanding of the lives of medieval aristocrats not only in the lands of the Loire but also throughout medieval Europe.

The Sources

Literary sources, including chivalric romances and *gesta,* or songs of deeds, have been invaluable to historians seeking to depict aristocratic private life.[5] This study will likewise recognize the valid insights such sources can provide as they set the stage and the cultural backdrop against which aristocratic lives were played, for while the story line and characters might have been imagined, the world in which they are placed can be useful for reconstructing the context of the lives of medieval nobles. However, because the goal here is to

---

between these two time periods. See Jane Martindale, "The French Aristocracy in the Early Middle Ages: A Reappraisal"; Constance B. Bouchard, "The Origins of the French Nobility: A Reassessment"; Dominique Barthélemy, "La mutation féodale a-t-elle eu lieu?"; Jeffrey A. Bowman, *Shifting Landmarks;* and Richard E. Sullivan, "The Carolingian Age." The scholarship on the medieval family has been affected by this larger trend in medieval historiography.

5. John W. Baldwin, *Aristocratic Life in Medieval France;* Georges Duby, *William Marshal* and *Women of the Twelfth Century: Volume I;* C. Stephen Jaeger, *The Origins of Courtliness* and *Ennobling Love;* R. Howard Bloch, *Medieval Misogyny and the Invention of Western Romantic Love;* and Stephen D. White, "The Discourse of Inheritance in Twelfth-Century France."

reconstruct the lives of actual individuals who lived in the lands of the Loire, the main body of evidence will be the surviving documents from the region. Charters recording the transfer of property are rich in detail and plentiful for the Loire region. They allow us to observe aristocratic behavior, piece together individual lives and experiences, and establish which relationships were important within and among these elite families.[6] While some original charters do remain from the ecclesiastical houses of the lands of the Loire, many are what are called "cartulary copies." Cartularies were books of charters assembled by the monks to help them better manage—and defend—their estates.[7] The evidentiary base for this examination of aristocratic private life will rely on both published and unpublished charters for the communities of St. Père of Chartres, St. Trinité of Vendôme, Marmoutier, St. Jean-en-Vallée, Notre Dame de Josaphat, Notre Dame de Chartres, St. Florentin de Bonneval, the priory of St. Gondon, St. Avit of Châteaudun, St. Trinité of Tiron, St. Vincent of Le Mans, and St. Denis of Nogent-le-Rotrou.

Obituaries from these ecclesiastical foundations are also useful in reconstructing aristocratic life. The monks carefully recorded the names of those patrons who were to be included in their prayers, usually on the anniversary of the layperson's death. While charters and obituaries are valuable to understanding noble life, they are limited by the fact that both tend to provide only a snapshot of a noble person's life or death, making it difficult—although not impossible—to know the events leading up to or following the event recorded. In many lucky cases there are series of charters dealing with a particular grant or contestation, thus making it possible to flesh out more of the details. Furthermore, while some elites might appear in a charter only once or twice, many participated in charters throughout the course of their lives. By piecing together evidence from literally hundreds of such documents, a relatively complete picture of aristocratic life emerges. As well as connecting nobles to each other, charters also contain nuggets of detail that are useful in restoring the more personal and affective dimensions of medieval life. The charters from central France can sometimes be "loquacious" and provide

---

6. Several recent studies have used charters and legal sources to write biographies and prosopographies of nobles. See Bernard S. Bachrach, *Fulk Nerra;* Bruno Lemesle, *La société aristocratique dans le Haut-Maine (XIe XIIe siècles);* W. Scott Jessee, *Robert the Burgundian and the Counts of Anjou;* Fredric L. Cheyette, *Ermengard of Narbonne and the World of the Troubadours;* Linda E. Mitchell, *Portraits of Medieval Women;* Erin L. Jordan, *Women, Power and Religious Patronage in the Middle Ages;* Theodore Evergates, *The Aristocracy of the County of Champagne, 1100–1300;* and Kimberly A. LoPrete, *Adela of Blois.*

7. For an in-depth analysis of the construction and use of the cartularies, see Robert F. Berkhofer III, *Day of Reckoning.* The analysis of the cartulary of St. Père is particularly useful. See pp. 30–32, 69–70, 80, 86–88, 116–17. For Marmoutier, see Dominique Barthélemy, "Note sur les cartulaires de Marmoutier (Touraine) au XIe siècle," pp. 247–60.

windows into how nobles felt about each other and their reactions to certain life events.

In order to have a well-rounded view of aristocratic private life, however, it is necessary to supplement the charter evidence with other sources. Chronicles are full of details and insights that add flesh to the evidence found in the charters. Those that provide information on individual nobles living in the lands of the Loire include Orderic Vitalis' lively narrative of the history of the Anglo-Norman world, the *Chronica de Gestis Consulum Andegavorum,* the *Gesta Ambaziensium Dominorum,* Abbot Suger's historical narrative, *Deeds of Louis the Fat,* and Lambert of Ardres' *The History of the Counts of Guines and Lords of Ardres.*[8] In addition to chronicles, other narrative sources offer valuable insight into aristocratic life in general. Memoirs, particularly those of Guibert of Nogent and Peter Abelard,[9] record the life experiences of two male aristocrats and are useful for this study. Letters, saints' lives, and other treatises written by the intellectual elite of the lands of the Loire are yet another group of sources to be mined for information. Owing to the illustrious cathedral school at Chartres, the Loire region produced and was home to several accomplished clerical reformers and intellectuals, with Bishop Ivo of Chartres perhaps the best known. In addition to producing theological works, Ivo also left behind a hefty correspondence. Particularly relevant to this study are his letters to the aristocracy advising them on their choice of spouses. Ivo's eleventh-century predecessor Fulbert of Chartres similarly enjoyed the respect of his clerical peers as well as the medieval aristocracy, who sought his advice on a range of issues. Many letters of Abbot Geoffrey of Vendôme also survive and provide information about aristocratic life in the lands of the Loire. Bernard of Angers, a cleric educated at the cathedral school of Chartres, compiled the miracles of St. Foy of Conques. While St. Foy herself lived far from the region of the Loire, it is reasonable to assume that Bernard's insights about the saint were shaped by his own life experience. Blending these sources with the charter evidence allows for a fairly thorough and engaging reconstruction of aristocratic private life.

---

8. Chroniclers often had a particular point to make when they crafted their account of events. Politics, secular and ecclesiastical, could affect how they recorded the past. For a discussion of how such issues shaped the *Gesta Ambaziensium Dominorum* and *The Deeds of Louis the Fat,* see LoPrete, *Adela of Blois,* pp. 36–39 and 223–30 respectively.

9. Both Peter Abelard and Guibert of Nogent were indirectly related to the aristocracy of the Chartrain. Heloise, Peter's lover and wife, may have been related to the vicedominal family of Chartres—a family that will figure in this study. Guibert, moreover, was distantly related to the vicecomital family of Chartres.

Building the Argument

The first section of this book examines the heart of aristocratic life: the family. The book begins in chapter 1 by setting the backdrop against which the noble born of the Loire region lived their lives and interacted with their family, friends, and foes. Focused discussion of aristocratic life starts—just as the life experiences of the elites themselves did—with family. In chapter 2 the life course of medieval aristocrats is laid out with particular attention to the family relationships they fostered during each life stage. Delving deeper into the personal dynamics of individual families, chapter 3 considers the lives and experiences of a particular kindred. I argue that members of this kindred played meaningful roles in each other's lives and provided support at key moments in the aristocratic life cycle. The combined evidence of these two chapters illustrates the broad embrace of aristocratic family life. Building upon this theme, inheritance is the subject of chapter 4. This chapter turns to the question of how family relationships were interwoven with the dispersal of property and how noble families managed their resources. The myriad strategies that aristocratic families employed in distributing their holdings so as to furnish support for their members provide proof of the inclusive nature of aristocratic family life.

Marriage was a critical moment in both the life of the individual elite and his or her family. The next section of the book takes up this important topic. Chapter 5 considers the property arrangements that accompanied marriage and asserts that these arrangements were a reflection of the high status that noblewomen enjoyed in their family in particular and medieval society in general. In the next chapter, chapter 6, I look at some of the practical questions surrounding marriage, such as, at what age did nobles marry? How often did they marry? How long did their marriages last, and what did medieval people think about marriage? The answers to these questions provide context for understanding the emotional bonds between husbands and wives. While some aristocratic couples in the lands of the Loire undoubtedly did not get along well, the vast majority seem to have been content in their marriage. Chapter 7 continues this line of questioning by examining the ways in which husbands and wives were partners as lords and as heads of their family.

Continuing the discussion of the nexus between property and family, the final chapter explores how strands connecting family and friends were interwoven with property in the context of disputes. Throughout their lives, aristocrats were drawn into disputes concerning who had a claim to property. What compelled nobles to contest gifts made by their kith and kin?

Chapter 8 unwinds the tangled threads that led aristocrats to dispute gifts and argues that many nobles used property contestation as a means of asserting their place in their family. Indeed many contestations can be read as artifacts of the broad and inclusive nature of aristocratic family life. Finally, the book concludes with an overview of aristocratic family life in France, considering the broader implications of the experiences of elites of the Loire region for those living elsewhere in medieval Europe.

❧ CHAPTER 1

The Lands of the Loire, 1000–1200

Adelina and Walter Minter lived their lives, raised their children, and died in the lands of the Loire. To understand the complexities of family life and the forces that shaped it, and why Adelina and Walter and their neighbors made the choices that they did, the physical, political, and social backdrop needs to be sketched out.

The Physical Setting

Let us start with the stage on which these families lived their lives: the land, the territory. What geographical area does the term "the lands of the Loire" actually cover? For the purposes of this study, it encompasses the territories of the Chartrain, the Beauce, the Blésois, the Vendômois, the Perche and the Touraine (see map 1). It is perhaps best to conceptualize this geographic area roughly as an isosceles triangle with the western corner of the triangle anchored at the city of Tours, the eastern corner at Beaugency, and the pinnacle of the triangle situated to the north in the town of Chartres. Topographically, this region is quite diverse. The city of Chartres itself sits high above the plain of the Beauce, a region of rich soils that turn golden in the summer months as the wheat fields ripen. Stretching down to the Loire River, the land alternates between flat fields and undulating hills. Due west of Chartres, the wheat fields give way to the more hilly and remote region of the Perche, known for its dense forests and wild game. Proceeding to the south, the land flattens out into the rich alluvial fields of the Loire River valley. Rivers are an important feature of this region. The Eure, Loir, Huisne, Cher, and many other tributaries flow into the Loire River, providing medieval people with not only a means of transportation but also an important resource to be exploited.

The families that are the focus of this book held property in this topographically diverse and rather amorphous geographical region. Since nobles used land to increase their wealth and to forge important political ties, they were not constrained by geopolitical boundaries in their quest for power and recognition. Indeed, families benefited from having contacts with as many powerful territorial lords as possible.

The territories of the Loire region provided medieval elites with important resources; chief among them was property. Property was the engine that powered the medieval aristocracy. At the same time it provided the basics of food, goods, support, and a place to live, it could also garner opportunities for status, wealth, and power. Property could make friends and create enemies. The power networks of the Middle Ages hinged upon the control of property, the general adage being the more property one controlled, the more powerful one was. It could also be employed to enhance an individual's or a family's status through grants to other powerful people in return for services—a process known as subinfeudation—and to patronize ecclesiastical houses. Where people ranked in society depended upon their relationship to property: Did they control it directly? Did they hold it from another lord or lords? What did they do in return for the property? Did they inherit the property or was it originally granted to them? While property could secure all of these benefits, a lack or loss of property could undermine all of these relationships and potentially threaten the status of an individual or a family. The stakes in disputes over the control of property were high, causing tension and potentially unraveling these carefully constructed and fostered relationships. So how did medieval elites go about creating and maintaining such networks?

Land and Power: Political Developments

The period from roughly 1000 to 1140 witnessed the coalescence of several discrete territories into the counties of Blois-Chartres, Anjou, and the Perche—a process which affected the lives of nobles and in which they played an important part.[1] While the details of the development of the individual

---

1. From the late tenth century through the mid-thirteenth century, the county of Blois-Chartres was unified and controlled by a descendant of the founder of the comital house, Thibaut

counties differ, the general contours of disparate lands transforming into a discrete political entity were essentially the same. For the elites who are the focus of this book, the political evolution of Blois-Chartres was particularly significant. As well as a political narrative, the development of this county is also a story of the successes, failures, and luck of individuals.

The turbulence of the tenth century provided the seedbed from which the families that would come to control the lands of the Loire emerged. By the tenth century, the empire of Charlemagne had been torn apart by competing claims to titles and territories. This internal instability was compounded by the appearance of deadly invaders from three directions: the Mediterranean on the south, the lands to the east of the Carolingian world, and the Vikings from the north. The Vikings in particular had a devastating effect on the tenuous central powers of Western Europe, with their invasions causing weak monarchical powers to become weaker; thus they provided local warriors with the opportunity of creating their own seats of power. Against this backdrop, Thibaut l'Ancien, the ancestor and possible founder of the Chartrain comital family (the family of the counts of Chartres), appeared in the historical record.[2] While much about Thibaut l'Ancien remains obscure, we can reasonably assert that he gained his power base, which was centered around Tours, through his skills as an exceptional warrior. It is also possible that Thibaut, like many of his peers, was related to the Carolingian nobility, most likely through his mother.

The comital family's connection to a Carolingian lineage was established by the next count of Blois-Chartres, Thibaut le Tricheur, or the Trickster, who may have been the son of Thibaut l'Ancien (see appendix, chart 1). This count took as his wife Letgard, the daughter of the count of Vermandois and a direct descendant of Charlemagne.[3] Letgard was also related to the Capetians, the future royal family of France; Hugh Capet, the first king of the Capetian dynasty, was her first cousin. Association with the Capetians allowed the power and influence of the fledgling comital family to grow

the Trickster. By 1240, however, the county was split between the two daughters of Count Thibaut V. His two daughters, Margaret and Isabelle, became the countesses of Blois and Chartres respectively when their nephew Thibaut VI died of leprosy without heirs. After his death, the counties remained divided throughout the medieval period.

2. Thibaut l'Ancien does not appear in any of the charters. Rather, most information about him has been gleaned from secondary sources. Much about Thibaut remains shrouded in uncertainty, however, and scholars disagree over his origins, when he lived, and his relationship to other elite families of the era. See André Chédeville, *Chartres et ses campagnes*, p. 252; Jacques Depoin, "Etudes préparatoires à l'histoire des grandes familles palatines III; F. Lesueur, *Thibaut le Tricheur, comte de Blois, de Tours et de Chartres au Xème siècle*, p. 64; Léonce Lex, *Eudes, comte de Blois, de Tours, de Chartres, et de Meaux, (995–1037) et son frère Thibaut (994–1004)*," p. 16; Ferdinand Lot, "L'origine de Thibaut le Tricheur"; and René Merlet, "Les Comtes de Chartres, Châteaudun, et Blois au IXe et Xe siècles."

3. Lesueur, *Thibaut le Tricheur*, p. 174.

significantly. The experiences of Thibaut l'Ancien and Thibaut the Trickster suggest continuity with the aristocracy of the Carolingian era contrary to the rupture between the aristocracies of the central Middle Ages and Carolingian centuries postulated by Marc Bloch.[4] Like those in other parts of *Francia,* the comital and seigneurial families of the lands of the Loire were founded by new men who gained power through their ability to swing a sword and women from established and prestigious families with roots in the Carolingian nobility.[5]

Thibaut the Trickster inherited a power base upon the death of Thibaut l'Ancien centered in the mid-Loire region and added to it by gaining control of Chartres, Blois, and Bourges, thus laying the foundations upon which his descendants and successors Odo I, Odo II, Thibaut III, and Thibaut IV would build. As the early counts of Blois-Chartres were securing and extending their power, other powerful men were doing the same. Most immediate for the comital house of Chartres was the expansion of the counts of Anjou. Tensions between these houses were inevitable as both attempted to carve out their power base in the region of the Loire valley. Odo I, like his father, was faced with the Angevin threat and dealt with it in a similar fashion: he cultivated a close relationship with his royal relatives, the Capetians. For further protection, Odo also created a network of castellans to help protect his lands from the Angevins.[6] Odo I met with an untimely death in battle around 995, however, leaving a widow with minor sons. To maintain the position of the comital house, his wife, Countess Bertha, followed the policy set by her predecessors of close alliance with the Capetians but with a slightly different twist. Bertha not only allied herself politically with the line of Hugh the Great but also married his grandson, Robert the Pious. Regardless of whether the marriage was the product of

---

4. Marc Bloch, *Feudal Society,* vol. 2, pp. 283–86. Bloch saw the nobility changing from that of a warrior class whose function was to fight to a legal class. For a different take on how the function of the nobility changed during the Middle Ages, see Timothy Reuter, "Nobles and Others." Thomas Bisson considers what made princes and "nobles" noble and finds that deeds were an important way of making up for a less-than-illustrious birth. See Thomas N. Bisson, "Princely Nobility in an Age of Ambition (1050–1150)."

5. Research from other regions within the old Carolingian empire has established the continuity of descent from the Carolingian nobility through the female line. See Georges Duby, *The Chivalrous Society,* pp. 59–80, 88–93, 94–111, 158–70, 178–85; Léopold Génicot, *La noblesse dans l'Occident médiévale* and "La noblesse du Moyen Âge dans l'ancienne 'Francie'"; Martindale, "The French Aristocracy in the Early Middle Ages"; Bouchard, "The Origins of the French Nobility"; Thomas N. Bisson, "The 'Feudal Revolution'" and "Nobility and Family in Medieval France"; and John Freed, "Reflections on the Medieval German Nobility."

6. For example, Odo I installed the lords of Fréteval on the border with Vendôme. Similarly, the lords of Alluyes, also located in the west, owed allegiance to the counts of Blois-Chartres.

political expediency or a *grande passion,*[7] King Robert shortly organized a successful campaign against Anjou and restored Tours to Bertha and her sons. Complications with Robert and Bertha's alliance emerged, however, and Robert eventually repudiated Bertha on the grounds of consanguinity.[8] The culminating effect of Bertha's dismissal was tension between the comital and royal families.

Beginning around 1010, Odo II battled against both the king and the Angevin count.[9] When Odo II died in 1037 fighting for his right to the kingdom of Burgundy, which he claimed through his mother,[10] he left a vast territorial base that was divided between his two sons. The elder, Stephen, received the Champenois lands that Odo II had inherited through his grandmother,[11] and Thibaut III, the second son, inherited the patrimonial lands of Blois, Chartres, and Tours, along with the traditional enemies of the house of Chartres. Unfortunately, Thibaut III was not as successful in protecting the county from these foes as his predecessors. In 1044 Tours was lost to the counts of Anjou, and Thibaut III suffered the humiliation of capture and imprisonment by the Angevins. Aggressions between the counts of Chartres and Anjou continued into the 1060s as Thibaut tried to regain the jewel of his territorial crown.

The wars between Chartres and Anjou were important to the development of the noble families of the mid-Loire region. In addition to the families that had supported Thibaut III's father and grandfather, new men

---

7. Scholars have interpreted this alliance in various ways. Jan Dhondt went so far as to suggest that Bertha seduced Robert into marriage to provide stability to her county and defense against Anjou. Jan Dhondt, "Sept femmes et un trio de rois," p. 42. Lex, *Eudes, comte de Blois,* p. 21.

8. Bertha and Robert's marriage violated ecclesiastical principles of kinship on two levels. This couple was related in the prohibited degrees of kinship and their relation was further complicated through ties of fictive kinship as Robert had stood as godfather to Odo I and Bertha's children.

9. Before Robert's remarriage in 1002, Bertha's son Odo II had been supportive of the king and participated with him in his war against Otto William of Burgundy. Lex, *Eudes, comte de Blois,* p. 35.

10. Jean Dunbabin, *France in the Making,* p. 192.

11. An additional point of friction with the king was Odo II's inheritance of Champagne from his grandmother's family. Adding Champagne to the areas already controlled by Odo II extended the dominion of the Chartrain counts from Tours to Troyes and surrounded the royal demesne. Not surprisingly, King Robert did all he could to prevent Odo's receipt of this territory. Odo grew impatient with the king and complained to Bishop Fulbert of Chartres that the king was usurping lands from him that belonged to him through inheritance. With the mediation of the duke of Normandy, these lands eventually passed to the Count of Blois-Chartres. Fulbert of Chartres, *Letters and Poems,* no. 86, pp. 152–55. See also Louis Halphen "La lettre d'Odo II de Blois de roi Robert." For a discussion of Bishop Fulbert's political life, see Josephine M. Faulk, "Bishop Fulbert of Chartres (1006–1028)." For Bishop Fulbert's contributions to the intellectual life of the Middle Ages, see Michel Rouche, ed., *Fulbert de Chartres: Précurseur de l'Europe médiévale?*

also appear as comital vassals.[12] The ongoing disputes ensured that men of military skill continued to be rewarded by counts and lords alike with land. As comital vassals subinfeudated, or created clients by granting out their land in fiefs, their status and power ascended. Relations between Chartrain count and king deterioriated because of the monarch's support of the Angevins, to the point where the count was absent from royal acts. Yet more lords of the lands of the Loire began to appear in the kings' transactions, an indication of the power that these families were coming to command.[13] The inclusion of comital vassals in royal acts was hardly coincidental but rather a sign of their growing power and in some cases independence from both count and king.

The absence of the viscounts of the region in the retinue of the count is also suggestive of vassalic independence. Bishop Fulbert of Chartres, for example, had to appeal to the king to prevent the viscount of Châteaudun from erecting adulterine castles (castles built without approval of a lord) throughout the Chartrain. The bishop threatened to place the diocese under interdict and "go somewhere into exile" if King Robert II did not intervene.[14] By the tenure of Thibaut III, viscounts were conspicuously missing from comital acts, and the viscount of Chartres, in particular, became a disruptive force within the region.[15] But lords of every status were a potential source of disarray. Between 1038 and 1048, several local seigneurs violently

---

12. The viscount of Blois, the lord of Fréteval, the lord of Montigny, and the vidames of Chartres affirmed grants made by the count, as well as having Thibaut III consent to their donations. For Viscount Gelduin of Chartres, see *Cartulaire de Notre-Dame de Chartres d'après les cartulaires et les titres originaux,* eds. E. du Lépinois and Lucien Merlet, vol. 1, no. 14, pp. 89–91, and no. 18, pp. 95–96 (hereafter, *NDDC*) and *Père,* vol. 1, no. 31, p. 158. The lord of Fréteval acted in charters for Marmoutier; see *Cartulaire de Marmoutier pour le Dunois,* no. 5, pp. 5–6, and no. 35, p. 33 (hereafter, *CMPD*); *NDDC,* vol. 1, no. 14, pp. 89–91. The Lord of Montigny and the vidame of Chartres appear in *CMPD,* no. 35, p. 33. The "new" men included Gaulsen of Chartres, *NDDC,* vol. 1, no. 14, pp. 89–91; the lord of Courville and Guarner Oculo Canis, *CMPD,* no. 35, p. 33. The Dangeaus made a donation in *CMPD,* no. 25, p. 26; a member of the Borrellus family witnessed, *CMPD,* no. 40, pp. 37–38.

13. For instance, the Montigny family had Henri I's approval of their donation of the priory of St. Hilaire-sur-Yerre; *Catalogue des Actes de Henri Ier, roi de France,* no. 71, pp. 72–73. Similarly, Henri's successor affirmed a gift made by the Fréteval family. *Recueil des actes de Philippe Ier, roi de France (1059–1108),* no. 69, pp. 176–77. Lords from the Chartrain also participated in royal charters. In 1078 Hervé of Gallardon witnessed Philippe I's royal gift; *Recueil des acts de Philippe Ier,* no. 92, pp. 236–37.

14. Fulbert of Chartres, *Letters and Poems,* no. 100, pp. 181–83.

15. Although Viscount Hugh I of Chartres witnessed several acts for the king, he also waged war against the king and captured many of the king's vassals. Charles Cuissard, "Les seigneurs du Puiset (980–1789)," pp. 337–39; *Recueil des actes de Philippe Ier,* no. 37, pp. 107–109; no. 43, pp. 120–23; no. 50, pp. 134–37; no. 52, pp. 140–42; no. 53, pp. 142–44. On April 2, 1080, Maurice, the son of Joscelin of Rotundard, was preparing to go to the aid of Viscount Hugh II of Chartres, whose castle was being besieged by the king—no doubt in response to the viscount's own aggressions; *Cartulaire de l'abbaye cardinale de la Trinité de Vendôme,* vol. 1, no. 290, pp. 444–46 (hereafter, *CTV*).

asserted their claim to certain dues from the market at Chamars by disrupt-ing the marketplace.[16] Yet in spite of the competition for power and the vio-lence associated with it, the lords of western France did provide stability and security—perhaps more than they are usually credited with.[17]

In 1089 Thibaut III's son Stephen succeeded his father as count of the Chartrain. While his rule as count was cut short by his departure on Cru-sade in 1096, followed by his death at Ramla in 1103, his joint tenure with his wife Adela represented another pivotal moment in the history of the region. Once Stephen left on Crusade, Adela took sole control of the family holdings and offices. The daughter of William the Conqueror, Adela was well suited to the task of managing the Chartrain. At a time when French monarchical power was resurgent, Adela maintained the independence of the county. While her policies were distinctively pro-Anglo-Norman in support of her brother, King Henry I of England, she was able to negotiate a deli-cate balance with the kings of France. Although the borders of the county did not see expansion under the supervision of Adela, the autonomy of the counts of Chartres was maintained, and she implemented an alliance system that extended the power of both her natal and affinal families.[18]

Starting in 1109, Adela's son Thibaut IV began to assume more responsi-bility for the family holdings, yet Adela remained a force in comital policies and actions far into the second decade of the twelfth century.[19] The internal and external problems that had tormented Adela and Thibaut IV's predeces-sors continued. The viscount of Chartres, Hugh III, frequently challenged the authority of the count as well as that of the king. In 1111 Thibaut IV joined King Louis VI in condemning Viscount Hugh III to the forfeiture of his property and successfully besieged his castle at Le Puiset, which was subsequently dismantled and burned.[20] Unfortunately their success in this venture ultimately resulted in estrangement between count and king.[21] The

---

16. *CMPD* no. 28, p. 29.

17. Jessee, *Robert the Burgundian;* Bachrach, *Fulk Nerra;* Barthélemy, "La mutation féodale a-t-elle eu lieu?"; Bowman, *Shifting Landmarks;* and Richard E. Barton, *Lordship in the County of Maine, c. 890–1160.* Jean Dunbabin has also challenged the interpretation of weak monarchical power under the early Capetians and their poor lordship; see "What's In a Name? Philip, King of France." Recently, Thomas Bisson has offered a new way of interpreting the political developments of the central Middle Ages; see *The Crisis of the Twelfth Century.*

18. Kimberly A. LoPrete, "The Anglo-Norman Card of Adela of Blois"; and *Adela of Blois,* pp. 118–231.

19. LoPrete, *Adela of Blois,* pp. 304–418.

20. Achille Luchaire, *Louis VI le Gros: Annales de sa vie et de son règne (1081–1137),* no. 114, pp. 61–62.

21. The precipitating event would seem to have been disagreement over the chateau of Le Puiset. After the first siege, Thibaut petitioned Louis to raise a fortress at Allaines, located close to Le Puiset.

years spanning 1115 and 1130 saw continued tension. The Chartrain felt royal wrath in 1119 when the king burned parts of Chartres in retaliation for Thibaut IV's imprisonment of the count of Nevers, and again in 1132 when the town of Bonneval, with the exception of the monastery, was similarly set ablaze.

The 1130s saw relations between the count of Chartres and the King improve. This may have been due in part to events spawned by the sinking of the White Ship in 1120. During a routine crossing from Normandy to England, the White Ship, which was carrying the heir to the English throne as well as children of many prominent Anglo-Norman families, sank in a storm. A dynastic crisis ensued since Henry I had no legitimate sons (he did have several bastard sons) and in 1135 he died without male issue. Henry I had designated his daughter, Mathilda, as the next monarch, but Count Thibaut's elder brother, Stephen, challenged his cousin for the throne of England. This action had serious consequences for the region of the Loire for in challenging Mathilda, Stephen was also challenging the house of Anjou. Mathilda's second husband and the father of her son—the future King Henry II—was Count Geoffrey of Anjou. The contest for England drew in the counts and aristocratic families of west central France. Thibaut may have realized the increased dangers to the lands of the Loire that his brother's quest for the English crown posed and sought to protect himself by allying with the monarch. If he improved relations with the king, Thibaut could hope that the eastern border of his territories might remain free from threat—so he would be fighting a "one front" war instead of being ringed in by his enemies. The bonds of alliance and friendship tenuously created by Louis VI and Thibaut IV were strengthened in the next generation. Adela, Thibaut IV's daughter, became the third wife of King Louis VII. Thibaut IV's sons, Count Henry of Troyes and Thibaut V, each married a daughter of Louis VII and Eleanor of Aquitaine. In addition to these alliances, the count of Chartres was also given political power by the king when, in 1154, Count Thibaut V was made seneschal of France, an honor that he enjoyed until his death in 1191.[22]

Perhaps fearing comital power, Louis refused, which provoked Thibaut to ally himself with the Rochefort family in open rebellion against Louis VI and to join his uncle, King Henry I of England, on his military expedition to France. Abbott Suger, *Vie de Louis VI,* p. 70. Tensions escalated in 1112 when Viscount Hugh III of Chartres rebuilt the fortress at Le Puiset with the aid of Thibaut and Henry I. A battle ensued at Le Puiset, and the chateau fell to the king. The viscount was disinherited, and a wounded and defeated Thibaut IV was granted safe passage back to Chartres. Luchaire, *Louis VI,* no. 134, pp. 70–72.

22. Marcel Pacaut, *Louis VII et son royaume,* p. 112.

The changing relationship between king and count reflects important changes in the nature of power that were occurring in the twelfth century. Under the guidance of kings such as Louis VI, Louis VII, and most particularly under Philip Augustus, monarchical power increased dramatically. Instead of resisting royal power, many counts, lords, and dukes were co-opted by the expanding monarchy. These men, like Thibaut V, assumed important offices and positions of power in the realm.

What had begun in the early eleventh century as an amorphous collection of personal estates had developed into a well-defined political entity by the first quarter of the twelfth century. Through war, conquest, flexibility, subinfeudation, marriage, and their own acumen, the comital family of Chartres secured a position of power and influence within medieval France.

Land and Power: The Church

As immediate to medieval elites as the ebb and flow of political power was their relationship with the church. First and foremost, the church and the clergy offered spiritual salvation.[23] Patronage provided the faithful with a means of gaining a place in heaven. Humble knights and powerful dukes alike made gifts to the church to benefit their souls as well as those of their ancestors, relatives, and progeny. Because elites gave land, revenues, tithes, rights, buildings, rivers, and woods to the church, they often shared possession or use of these properties with the clergy. Some elites even held their lands directly from a prelate or monastery.

Family was another place where the secular and sacred intersected. The monks, nuns, abbots, priors, bishops, canons, priests, and archdeacons of the medieval church were all aristocrats. Although the Benedictine Rule, which nearly all of the monasteries in the region followed, stated that monks were to abandon all ties to the secular world, the sources demonstrate the clergy's continued association with and attachment to their biological families. Control of ecclesiastical offices also allowed elite families to extend their power and status.[24] In many areas of Western Europe, families established

---

23. For analysis of these relationships, see Megan McLaughlin, *Consorting with Saints* and Michel Lauwers, ed., *La mémoire des ancêtres, le souci des morts.*

24. For the Angevin bishoprics, see Steven Fanning, *A Bishop and His World before the Gregorian Reform;* "From *Miles* to *Episcopus*"; "Family and Episcopal Election 900–1050 and the Case of Hubert of Angers (1006–1047)"; and "Les origines familiales de Vulgrin." See also Jean Gaudemet, "Recherches sur l'épiscopat médiévale en France." William Ziezulewicz has researched the abbots of the region of the Loire; see "Abbatial Elections at Saint-Florent de Saumur (ca. 950–1118)" and "From Serf to Abbot." See also Bernard Bachrach, "Robert of Blois."

ecclesiastical dynasties that dominated bishoprics, archbishoprics, and, to a lesser degree, monastic offices.[25]

While the counts of Chartres were creating a polity and the kings of France resurrecting their power, the church also underwent an important period of transformation. After the dissolution of the Carolingian empire, religious authority fell under the control of the warrior aristocracy in much the same way as political power did. At the heart of the problems plaguing the feudal church—so the reformers believed—was secular interference. Attempts were made in the tenth century to respond to these problems, as evident in the development of Cluniac monasticism in Burgundy. But the call for reform grew louder in the next century as dedicated clerics set about reforming the church.

The severity of abuse and corruption within the church varied throughout Europe, and corruption may not have been as widespread as the reformers have led us to believe.[26] Indeed the comital family of Chartres supported reform of the church instead of using ecclesiastical placements as a means to extend their power. When the abbey of Marmoutier was destroyed by the Normans, Count Odo I restored the monastery and, in return for his generosity, the monks elevated him to lay abbot. Odo I supported reform and in 985 or 986 removed the secular canons, replaced them with Cluniac monks,[27] and insisted on the autonomy of the abbot from secular influences.[28] Like his father, Odo II was a supporter of monastic reform. He favored the elevation of Albert, a product of the cathedral school and dedicated to the independence of the abbey from lay control, as abbot.[29] Count Stephen and Countess Adela similarly supported Ivo, one of the most famous of church reformers, as Bishop of Chartres.[30]

---

25. The usual practice was for uncles to designate their nephews (usually their sister's son) as their successor. Constance B. Bouchard, *Sword, Miter, and Cloister;* "The Geographical, Social and Ecclesiastical Origins of the Bishops of Auxerre and Sens in the Central Middle Ages"; and *Spirituality and Administration and the Role of the Bishop in Twelfth-Century Auxerre;* Gui Devailly, "Les grandes familles et l'épiscopat dans l'ouest de France et les pays de la Loire"; and Thomas Head, *Hagiography and the Cult of the Saints in the Diocese of Orléans, 800–1200,* pp. 214–15, 227–28.

26. For an overview of the reform movement in the region of the Loire, see Jean-Hervé Foulon, *Église et réforme au Moyen Âge.* For other areas, see Augustin Fliché, "Premiers résultats d'un enquête sur la réforme grégorienne dans le diocèse français de Narbonne" and *La réforme grégorienne;* Jacques Choux, *L'épiscopat de Pibon (1064–1107);* and Jacques Boussard, "Les évêques en Neustrie avant la réforme grégorienne (950–1050 environ)."

27. Sharon Farmer, *Communities of Saint Martin,* pp. 67–68. Odo I was married to Bertha of Burgundy. It is possible that he was exposed to Cluniac reform through her.

28. Oliver Guillot, *Le comte d'Anjou et son entourage au XIe siècle,* vol. 1, pp. 173–74.

29. Farmer, *Communities of St. Martin,* pp. 68–70.

30. LoPrete, *Adela of Blois,* pp. 235–37.

Reformation of existing houses and the founding of new ecclesiastical communities were also central to the reform movement. Around the year 1100, five monastic foundations dominated the mid-Loire and had done so for centuries: St. Florentin at Bonneval, Marmoutier, St. Trinité in Vendôme, St. Père of Chartres, and St. Vincent du Mans (see map 1). The twelfth century saw the number of houses in the Loire region expand dramatically.[31] In 1099 the abbey of St. Jean-en-Vallée was reformed through the joint efforts of Bishop Ivo and Countess Adela.[32] The support and patronage of the Lèves family brought about the establishment of the Abbey of Notre Dame de Josaphat a few kilometers northwest of the city of Chartres in Lèves. There were also several important foundations in the western lands of the Loire patronized by local aristocratic families. The abbey of St. Denis, for example, was established in the eleventh century by the counts of the Perche at their family seat of Nogent-le-Rotrou. In the early twelfth century the preacher and ascetic Bernard of Tiron hoped to create a house of monks near Nogent-le-Rotrou, with the support of Count Rotrou of the Perche.[33] The dowager countess objected, however, on the grounds that another monastery so close to St. Denis would be detrimental to the community of Cluniac monks living there. Bernard's reformed abbey was subsequently placed a considerable distance to the east of Nogent-le-Rotrou at Tiron. As a result of the reform movement of the eleventh and twelfth centuries, the elites of the lands of the Loire had a wider choice of houses to patronize. While many families continued to make donations to the older houses, they also supported the newly reformed or established houses. It was against this religious and political backdrop that the aristocratic families of the lands of the Loire lived their lives.

---

31. There were few religious foundations for women in the region, and they were established later than the traditional houses of St. Père and Marmoutier. For the purposes of this study, we are dealing nearly exclusively with male religious. For discussion of the experience of religious women of central and western France, see Penelope Johnson, *Equal in Monastic Profession* and Bruce Venarde, *Women's Monasticism and Medieval Society.*

32. *Cartulaire de Saint-Jean-en-Vallée de Chartres,* no. 1, pp. 2–3 (hereafter, *Jean*). The abbey of St. Jean-en-Vallée had been founded originally by Odo II around 1028. For further discussion, see the editor's introduction, *Jean,* pp. v–xxxii. In addition to reformed monastic foundations, elites in the Chartrain also supported Templar foundations, exemplars of a new kind of spirituality, in the region. See chapter 7, note 121 for examples.

33. See Bernard Beck, *Saint Bernard de Tiron, l'ermite, le moine et le monde.* Bernard was attracted to the Perche as a place for his foundation because it was less developed than other regions of France. Indeed, much of the Perche was still forested and unsettled at the beginning of the twelfth century. For a discussion of the establishment of Tiron and its growth, see Ruth H. Cline, "The Congregation of Tiron in the Twelfth Century."

The Aristocratic Families of the Lands of the Loire

Now that the stage has been set, it is time to meet the main actors: the elites of the lands of the Loire. Who were these noble families who dominated this region?

Like the comital family of Chartres, the aristocracy of the Loire region was made up of both "old" and "new" families. The "old" families were those who could trace their origins back to the Carolingian nobility. Co-existing and intermarrying with these families were those whose entry into the aristocracy was based upon their service, or the service of one of their ancestors, to the king, count, or duke. Men who were known for their strength instead of their birth gained entrance into the elite through their alliances with women from established families. The two types or strata of elites were thus fused, making a class that consisted of those who held their position by blood and those who held power through their ability to shed it.[34]

This pattern holds for all levels of the landed elites of the mid-Loire.[35] It may not be surprising that counts were able to secure alliances with the Carolingian aristocracy, but this practice was not confined to them. Viscounts and lords who owed their power and fame to their strong sword arm also found wives among prominent families of the region.

The viscounts of Châteaudun were one of the most powerful families of the eleventh- and twelfth-century Loire region (see appendix, chart 2). Viscount Geoffrey I was the first viscount to appear consistently in the charter evidence and may have been descended from the Carolingian count of Maine.[36] Yet the extant documents portray Geoffrey as a warrior and plunderer rather than a Carolingian aristocrat. His wife, Hildegard, however, was a member of a well-established and socially prominent Tourangeau family. Testimony to its prominence is evident in the fact that two vicecomital

---

34. This view of the origins of the medieval aristocracy has been borne out in research from various parts of France. For Burgundy, see the work of Constance Bouchard, cited in note 25 above; Guy Devailly, *Le Berry du Xe siècle au milieu du XIIIe siècle;* Michel Bur, *La formation du comté Champagne, v. 950–1150;* Theodore Evergates, *Feudal Society in the Baillage of Troyes under the Counts of Champagne, 1152–1284* and "Nobles and Knights in Twelfth-Century France"; Dominique Barthé-lemy, *La société dans le comté de Vendôme de l'an mil au XIVe siècle* and "Castles, Barons, and Vavassors in the Vendômois and Neighboring Regions in the Eleventh and Twelfth Centuries"; Oliver Guillot, *Le comté d'Anjou et son entourage;* George T. Beech, *A Rural Society in Medieval France;* Bruno Lemesle, *La société aristocratique dans le Haut-Maine (XIe-XIIe siècles);* Kathleen Hapgood Thompson, *Power and Border Lordship in Medieval France;* Richard Barton, *Lordship in the County of Maine.*

35. Jacques Boussard, "L'origine des familles seigneuriales dans la région de la Loire moyenne"; André Chédeville, *Chartres et ses campagnes,* pp. 250–68.

36. Boussard, "L'origine des familles seigneuriales," 310–11.

families sought alliances with them.[37] Geoffrey I of Châteaudun pursued marriages with well-established families for his children as well. The marriages of Geoffrey's daughters reflect an interesting shift in geographical orientation. Instead of seeking spouses from prestigious families in the Touraine, Geoffrey made alliances with families whose seats of power and interest lay north of the Loire valley. One daughter married into the Micy family, which gave the family connections with the influential Bellême family whose power base was located in Maine and Normandy. Another daughter, Melisend, was allied with what would become the comital family of the Perche. Geoffrey may have again been seeking to make a connection to an old Carolingian family, since descent from a daughter of Charlemagne has been suggested for the Percheron comital house.[38] Melisend and Geoffrey's son, Geoffrey II, succeeded to the vicecomital office and powers as well as those associated with his father's family in the Perche. The marriage of newly emerged warriors into older, more socially prestigious families with roots in the old Carolingian elites lent them legitimacy to establish themselves as the new, powerful lords of the lands of the Loire.

Like viscounts and counts, men of the rank of lord also sought alliance with women with more impressive backgrounds than their own. William Gouet was such a warrior. He was invested by the count of Blois-Chartres with extensive lands in the western part of the Chartrain. These were strategically placed lordships for the count since they guarded the western boundary of his domain from his aggressive Norman neighbors. William Gouet had much to recommend him as a lord, including his military skill and also his knowledge of things Norman, for according to the Anglo-Norman historian Orderic Vitalis, William was entangled in Norman politics. So much so that his son and successor, William II Gouet, and their vassal, Girogius of Courville, became the victims of one of the infamous Mabel Talvas' poisoning plots.[39] While William I Gouet was familiar with the politics of

---

37. The vicecomital houses at Blois and Châteaudun both married into this family. Hildegard's sister Gerberge and her husband Gelduin, who was likely the lord of Saumur, were the parents of Viscount Hervé of Blois. The importance of connection to Gerberge, Gelduin, and Hildegard is evident in the naming practices of later generations. Viscount Hervé I named two of his children (Gelduin and Gerberge respectively) after his parents, thus recalling their connection to the region of the Touraine and their family connections. Boussard, "L'origine des familles seigneuriales," 310–13.

38. Marc A. P. Oeillet des Murs, *Histoire des comtes du Perche de la famille des Rotrou de 943 à 1231,* pp. 59–67. Kathleen Hapgood Thompson suggests a new twist to this theory for the origins of the house of Rotrou. See *Power and Border Lordship,* pp. 29–31. Thompson also offers reconstruction for the origins of the viscounts of Châteaudun that is different from mine. See pp. 195–99.

39. Orderic Vitalis, *The Ecclesiastical History,* vol. 2, pp. 123–24. Mabel was part of the prominent Bêlleme family. She was notorious for her scheming and plotting against people she perceived as

Normandy, he does not appear to have held any lands there. Instead, he made his way to the lands of the Loire where his abilities and experience made him an ideal candidate for a lordship on the unstable, yet crucial, western fringes of the county. William successfully established a lordship and founded a line of lords that extended into the thirteenth century (see appendix, chart 5).[40] Yet in spite of the count's confidence in his military prowess, William was lacking in social standing.

To rectify this weakness, he married Mahild, the daughter of Lord Walter of Alluyes and Brou, whose family had been established in the Chartrain since the late tenth century.[41] In 1024, Mahild's father, Walter, was invested with lands by the count to reward his service against the counts of Anjou. The alliance between Mahild of Alluyes and William of Gouet created a strong and extensive territorial power. Mahild brought the lordships of Alluyes and Brou to the marriage, which, combined with the Gouet fiefs of Authon, La Bazoche-Gouet, and others, resulted in an extensive patrimony. William gained lands through his marriage to Mahild, but he also gained something more intangible and important for an interloper from Normandy: social status and connection with a family that had been a presence in the region for several generations.

William Gouet's contemporary Ingelbald Brito shared a similar life experience. As his cognomen indicates, Ingelbald came from Brittany—a province far to the west of the mid-Loire.[42] Like William Gouet, Ingelbald seems to have been drawn to the region in an attempt to seek his fortune

---

rivals or threats to her power. William and Girogius were unintended victims in her plot to poison Arnold of Échauffour, a member of the rival Giroie family.

40. The Alluyes-Gouet family's continued patronage of St. Vincent of Le Mans indicates that the family maintained an interest in and connection to the territory west of the Chartrain—the lands from which one of the founders of their line had sprung. For further discussion of this family, see Kathleen Hapgood Thompson, "The Formation of the County of Perche."

41. In 985 Hugh of Alluyes witnessed a donation to St. Père of Chartres as part of the retinue of the count of Chartres and was most likely his vassal. *Père* vol. 1, no. 18, pp. 77–80. Also acting in this charter was Henri, the duke of France. Hugh's inclusion among such illustrious personages suggests that he enjoyed considerable prominence in the region. The founder of this house, Guicher, was also a participant in the transactions of St. Père. E. Lefevre, "Notice sur la baronnie d'Alluyes," believes that Walter of Alluyes and Hugh of Alluyes were the sons of Guicher. Since the span of one generation separates Hugh's act of 985 and Walter's investment with the tower at Alluyes, it would seem more likely that the Hugh who appears in the charter of 985 was Walter's father rather than his brother.

42. Ingelbald Brito may have come to the Vendômois and Chartrain as a result of the marriage of Count Odo II's daughter Bertha to the count of Brittany. It seems unlikely, however, that he was part of a retinue of the count of Brittany, since there is no reference to this in the sources. It seems more probable that the alliance may have made it easier or more common for men from Brittany to settle in the region of their countess's birth.

(see appendix, charts 9 and 11). Around 1050 Ingelbald began to appear in the transactions of some of the most powerful men of the Vendômois. His entrée into this circle was not due to his family but rather his usefulness to powerful men. In particular, Ingelbald was associated with Fulcher Dives, who controlled important lordships surrounding Vendôme and was allied through blood and politics to some of the most influential families of the region. Ingelbald Brito, like William Gouet, was an outsider. To establish himself in the power structure of the region, as well as to garner friends and fiefs, he married Hildiard-Domitilla, the daughter of Fulcher Dives. This marriage transformed Ingelbald from an outlier to a member of the inner circle that wielded power and influence in the region.

Although some families in the lands of the Loire could claim descent from Carolingian families, most based their power through their service and talent rather than their birth. Robert of Moncontour was one such man. In 1080, Robert dictated to a monk of St. Trinité of Vendôme what was, for all intents and purposes, his last will and testament. Recounting his possessions, he stated that many of his honors came through his "hard and long labor in this world" in the conquest of such properties. Other properties, he says, he held "justly" through a lord.[43] The life experience of this *miles,* or knight, indicates that the ability to fight was necessary in order to secure properties for himself and also to establish his family. The vicecomital family of Chartres also used such skills to their advantage. This family owed its position and office entirely to the function of their ancestors as officers of the count and as trustworthy warriors.[44] The office of viscount of Chartres was first established in the tenth century, but the progenitor of the vicecomital line that would control the office throughout the Middle Ages is first recorded in the 1030s in a Marmoutier charter.[45] Viscount Gelduin seems to have come from the region of the Beauvaisis (to the northwest of Paris), where his family controlled the lordship of Breteuil, which he and his heirs would continue to hold. Why Gelduin moved to the land of the Loire remains

43. *CTV,* vol. 1, no. 299, pp. 455–60. Robert held other properties through maternal and paternal inheritance.

44. Chédeville, *Chartres et ses campagnes,* p. 259. Chédeville asserts that this family had its roots in service rather than blood. Other scholars have tried—unsuccessfully, I think—to connect the viscounts of Chartres with the Carolingian aristocracy. Boussard, "L'origine des familles seigneuriales," 310–11; Adolphe de Dion, "Le Puiset aux XIe et XIIe siècles," 1–3; and Cuissard, "Les seigneurs du Puiset," pp. 323, 326–27.

45. Cuissard, "Les seigneurs du Puiset," 323ff.; *CMPD,* no. 21, pp. 21–22. Gelduin and his kinsmen Fulcher do appear in the charters of the late tenth century. They witnessed and signed charters for Countess Letgard and Bishop Odo. See *Père,* vol. 1, no. 8, pp. 63–65; no. 17, pp. 75–76; no. 1, pp. 81–83; no. 15, pp. 74; no. 18, pp. 77–79.

unclear. Like William Gouet and Ingelbald Brito, he may have been attracted by promises of land in the Chartrain or recruited by the counts of Chartres into their service.

Acquisition of offices provided another means for elites to gain power and to center dynasties. Around the middle of the tenth century, a warrior named Gautier was appointed by Count Odo I as his provisor of foodstuffs and other supplies for the area around Tours.[46] Gautier's son Ganelon succeeded him as provisor but also secured other properties and offices that reinforced his status (see appendix, chart 6). Ganelon inherited the lordship of Montigny from his cousin Hugh. He was also appointed to an important ecclesiastical office—that of treasurer of the cathedral of Tours and the collegial church of St. Martin.[47] Like others of the lands of the Loire, this family seems to have had Tourangeaux roots, which is apparent in its nearly exclusive patronage of Marmoutier. Unlike some of their noble neighbors, the Montignys held lands from the Count of Anjou—a relationship that is made apparent in a donation charter of the church of St. Hilaire-sur-Yerre where Count Thibaut III of Blois-Chartres, King Henri I of France, and Count Geoffrey Martel of Anjou were all listed as Ganelon's lords. Given the proximity of Montigny to Angevin lands, and the Tourangeaux origins of the family, it is not surprising that the lord of Montigny was bound to the count of Anjou, as well as that of Blois-Chartres.

The vidames of Chartres also gained power through their monopoly of an office. In contrast to other lords in the region, the vidames owed their allegiance to an ecclesiastical lord: the bishop of Chartres. Early in the tenth century, the bishop created the office of vidame, or vice-lord (*vicedominus*), to manage and protect his holdings. Unlike the secular warlords, the bishops were powerless against the Vikings and Normans. So they secured a defender. While the vicedominal office was somewhat different from others, the vidames similarly acquired it through their capabilities rather than their birth. The first reference to a vidame occurs in a charter from St. Père datable from 930 when Vidame Giroard was listed as one of the *fideles,* or

---

46. Chédeville, *Chartres et ses campagnes,* pp. 255–58; *CMPD,* pp. xviii–xxiii. Gautier was a bit over zealous in gathering food, for the abbot of Marmoutier complained vigorously to the count that Gautier and his nephew were seizing too much from church lands.

47. Jacques Boussard, "Le trésorier de Saint-Martin de Tours"; and Quentin Griffiths, "The Capetian Kings and St. Martin of Tours." While Ganelon was the first lord of Montigny whose acts are extant, the charters indicate that his family had controlled this lordship for at least two generations (see appendix, chart 6). A charter from 1042/44 records that Ganelon I gave the church of St. Hilaire-sur-Yerre to Marmoutier for the souls of his "relatives" Raher of Montigny and his son Hugh, from whom he had inherited the lordship. AD Eure-et-Loir, H 2429. See also *CMPD,* no. 22, p. 23.

supporters of the bishop, but the family that would dominate this office for several generations gained control in the mid-eleventh century when Vidame Hugh of Chartres appears in the charters (see appendix, chart 4).[48] By the end of this century, the office had become a hereditary possession when Hugh's sons claimed the title and its corresponding lands. While the vidames of Chartres originated as officers of the bishop, they held property and owed service to secular lords.[49] Yet unlike any other elite family in the region, the vidames based their power and position upon their service to the bishop.[50]

In addition to the families who held office or controlled castles, there were many others who did not hold formal titles. Sometimes they carried geographic designators, such as Salomon of Fréteval or Emmeline of Châteaudun. But they were clearly not the primary lord of these places. Other elites were only referenced by their first name. Since the pool of names used for elites was rather limited (there could, for example, be two siblings with the same name), sobriquets were often used. These names could be based upon physical characteristics (Odo the Red, Warin with a Beard, Big Alice) or personal peculiarities (Adelard Who Bites Eels, Guido Who Does Not Drink Wine). There were also lesser noble families that adopted cognomens, such as Diabolus, Magonis, Desredatus, and Caules. The elites of this rank clearly held land and were often bound to greater lords through ties of dependence. Unfortunately, because many appear only sporadically in the charters, it is sometimes difficult to fill in their family background or trace them beyond one generation.[51] Most likely, they were warriors who were rewarded with lands and fiefs by lords who were in need of their skills.

While it is easy to lump all landholding elites into one group or "class," this would be far too simplistic.[52] The nobility of the central Middle Ages (1000–1200 CE) was not a static group. With few exceptions, however, those families who were in power in the eleventh century continued to dominate the region far into the twelfth. The most powerful families of the

---

48. *Père,* vol. 1, no. 1, pp. 19–25.

49. The vidames were the vassals of the counts as well as of the lords of Alluyes-Brou.

50. As a reflection of this, the charters record that the early transactions of this family concerned the transfer of primarily ecclesiastical property: *Père,* vol. 1, no. 88, pp. 212–13 and *CMPD,* no. 35, p. 33, for example.

51. In some cases these families held land and their elite status only tenuously. As a consequence, it is not possible to trace them multigenerationally. These were the elites most at risk and most susceptible to economic or political changes.

52. Many scholars recognize such differences among the nobility; Barthélemy, *La société dans le comté de Vendôme,* pp. 507–13; 615–20 and "Castles, Barons, and Vavassors," pp. 56–88; Evergates, "Nobles and Knights in Twelfth-Century France," pp. 11–35; and Reuter, "Nobles and Others," pp. 87–98.

county, the viscounts and counts, were established at the end of the tenth century and could trace their origins back to the Carolingians through the maternal line. The beginning of the eleventh century witnessed the emergence of "new men" who were given lordships, castles, offices, and fiefs in return for their military prowess. Throughout the century, more vassals were created by these lords, establishing yet another sector within the elite of the Loire region. The twelfth century saw new noble families emerge, based again on their service and skill rather than their descent from illustrious ancestors. The aristocracy of the lands of the Loire thus ranged in status from knights who held modest lands to families who controlled significant portions of west central France. Economic, social, and political standing varied among these families and affected their family dynamics and uses of property. To assume that families with such disparate backgrounds, realities, and experiences used property in the same way, or that their family pattern conformed to one model, would be misguided.

Conclusion

The centuries from 1000 to 1200 witnessed dramatic changes and developments. The elites living in the lands of the Loire saw a collection of lands that had once been the personal possessions of the counts transformed into a political polity. Castles were erected throughout the region as military defenses and expressions of the power of their lords. Families that would continue to control these edifices throughout this period emerged, intermarried, and built political alliances through the granting of land and exchange of oaths. The church underwent an important period of reform and revitalization. As part of this movement, new ecclesiastical communities were founded and older establishments reformed. In response to a call from the pope, the noblemen left the lands of the Loire to go on Crusade.

Throughout this historical ebb and flow, family life remained a constant. Nobles could depend on their family for political, physical, emotional, and spiritual support. Now that the stage has been set, it is time to turn from the general situation in the eleventh- and twelfth-century lands of the Loire to the actual life and family experiences of the noble born who called the region home.

CHAPTER 2

Aristocratic Family Life

What did family mean to the elites of the Loire region? There were many layers to "family" in the medieval world. Family was of immense importance to medieval people since a person's standing in society was determined by his or her family and that individual's place in it. But "family" also connoted relationships and affective ties. The conjugal unit of parents and children provided the focus of most noble families,[1] but extended kin, including grandparents, aunts, uncles, and cousins, also played key roles in the lives of the noble born. An aristocrat's concept of family stretched out to include "relatives," affinal as well as natal kin, and reached back to "ancestors" of previous generations.[2] Family relationships were dynamic. Elites interacted with various family members at different times in their lives, and their "family" expanded—as a result of marriages and births—and contracted through the loss of relatives.

---

1. Evergates, *Aristocracy of the County of Champagne,* pp. 88–89; John S. Moore, "The Anglo-Norman Family." Moore finds that the average household consisted of parents and their children, with noble households averaging four to five members.

2. This is evident in the language employed to describe such family relationships. See Anita Guerreau-Jalabert, "La désignation des relations et des groupes de parenté en Latin médiévale." Pierre Bauduin finds that the terminology used by Norman chroniclers to describe family was neither fixed nor monolithic. Pierre Bauduin, "Désigner les parents," p. 72.

By outlining each life stage of medieval elites, this chapter will set out family interactions among the aristocrats of the lands of the Loire. What will emerge is an interpretation of family life that has much in common with the family structures envisioned for the early medieval world.[3] Aristocratic families of this region remained collateral, recognized the rights of women, found their kin to be supportive, and were not organized around an ethos of exclusion. Indeed, inclusivity was at the heart of family life.

Life Stages: Childhood and Youth

In the early stages of life, parents and siblings, as well as wet nurses and other servants, made up the circle of a young child's life. As the experience of Queen Mathilda's grandchildren in the following account indicates, siblings could often be playmates—as well as the apple of their grandmother's eye.

> As the venerable Mathilda seated herself at the royal banquet table next to Queen Adelheid, the young ones ran about nearby absorbed in their childish games. Then Henry, who was particularly beloved by God's holy one, approached the royal table, and gazed lovingly at his illustrious grandmother, crawled up into her lap in hopes of a kiss from her. The venerable queen happily picked him and hugged him close.[4]

But the long reproductive life of a medieval woman could also mean that her children might be quite far apart in age. Take, for instance, the family of Hubert Magonis. At the same time that Hubert and his wife were arranging the marriage of one daughter, they still had a very small child at home, who was referred to by the diminutive "Agnete" and was labeled a "minor" in the charter.[5] Like many modern families, medieval aristocrats

---

3. Some have challenged the notion of this horizontal and extended kinship as characteristic of family life in the early Middle Ages. See Alexander Callender Murray, *Germanic Kinship Structure*. In contrast to Duby, Constance Bouchard argues that the practice of organizing lineages patrilineally dates back to the Carolingians and long before the twelfth century. See Bouchard, "The Carolingian Creation of a Model of Patrilineage" and "Family Structure and Family Consciousness among the Aristocracy in the Ninth through Eleventh Centuries." Paul Fouracre questions whether there was ever a time when nobles' lands were not partitioned. See Fouracre, "The Origins of the Nobility in Francia," p. 22. Isabelle Réal challenges the idea that inheritance was shared equally among siblings and that the early Middle Ages were a "golden age" for women. "Représentations et pratiques des relations fraternelles dans la société franque du haut Moyen Age (VIe–IXe siècles)," pp. 83–88. Although aspects of the Schmid model have been questioned, a definitive and comprehensive refutation remains to be offered.

4. Sean Gilsdorf, trans., *Queenship and Sanctity*, p. 115.

5. AD Loir-et-Cher, 16 H 105. See also *CMPD*, no. 87, pp. 177–78; no. 90, pp. 179–81; no. 91, p. 181.

could have families from two different marriages, which usually meant a substantial age difference between the children of the two alliances. Hugh Guernonatus, for example, had two grown sons who acted with him when he made a gift before leaving with his eldest son to fight in the Holy Land. The other son was charged with protecting the gift, which was made for "the soul of their mother," while his father and brother were gone. At the very end of the charter, "Astho the boy, the son of Hugh Guernonatus and another wife," consented to the transaction and was given two *solidi*[6] as a countergift.[7] Astho was clearly still a child, in contrast to his half-brothers who, respectively, were going to the Holy Land and assuming responsibility for protecting family interests.

Nurses were of particular importance to elite children and were remembered by their young charges later in their lives. "Young Lady Mary of Esternay," from Champagne, left one pound "to the wet nurse who nourished her."[8] In the lands of the Loire, nurses were also involved in the family life of their young charges. When Godefred, the young son of Fulco of Patay, quitclaimed his right to certain of his father's properties, his nurse witnessed his quitclaim and received a cash countergift for her participation.[9] Tutors of young children also appear in the charters. For example, Durand, the tutor of the young viscount of Châteaudun, witnessed a gift for his patron.[10]

In addition to family retainers, young elites would have become acquainted with their extended kin early in life. Because donors required the consent of a wide range of kin, relatives oftentimes traveled to be present when gifts

---

6. A word of explanation about medieval coinage. Medieval currency consisted only of coins and was broken down as follows: A *denarius* (plural *denarii*) was a penny. A *solidus*, or the plural *solidi*, was a shilling and equaled twelve *denarii*. *Libra* (*libri*) was a pound and equivalent to twenty shillings. Pennies only were minted as coins, with *solidi* and *libri* functioning only as units of calculation. Coinage was not standardized during this period. Rather individual cities and rulers minted their own coins. Often the provenance of the coins are described in the documents, such as "ten pounds of coin from Paris" or "two *denarii* from Tours."

7. AD Loir-et-Cher, 16 H 118. See also *CMPD*, no. 152, p. 141. Hugh Guernonatus was the provost of Blois and accompanied Count Stephen on the First Crusade; LoPrete, *Adela of Blois,* p. 76, 94.

8. Theodore Evergates, ed. and trans., *Feudal Society in Medieval France,* p. 73.

9. *CTV,* vol. 2, no. 513, pp. 337–42. The question of whether aristocratic women nursed their children has been the subject of considerable debate. The charters from the lands of the Loire suggest that women both nursed their children (see the charter referenced in note 16) and, as the cited charter indicates, secured wet nurses. Although the data is limited, it would appear that the decision about nursing was driven by personal preference.

10. *Cartulaire de l'abbaye de Saint-Vincent du Mans,* no. 197, p. 124 (hereafter, *CSVM*). Durand also witnessed a gift to the abbey of Tiron: *Cartulaire de l'abbaye de la Sainte-Trinité de Tiron,* vol. 1, nos. 152 and 153, p. 176 (hereafter, *Tiron*). For an example of a woman with a tutor, see Evergates, *Feudal Society,* p. 64.

were made.[11] Young elites accompanied their parents and visited the homes of their kin as well as local monastic houses. Large groups of extended relatives were often present as families gathered for important events such as marriages, baptisms, and deaths, in addition to transfers of property. As a result, cousins, aunts, uncles, and grandparents were familiar faces to noble children. Noble born boys and girls began participating in family transactions at a very young age. Take, for instance, Pagan and Mathilda, the young children of Viscount Hugh II of Châteaudun. They approved and witnessed their father's quitclaim even though they "were not yet Christian." Further proof of Pagan's extreme youth is the fact that his nurse appears in the transaction.[12] The children of the lord of Château-Gontier and Château-Renault also consented when their father abandoned his claim to comital property. While the sons were of age, their sister Milesend was "only a child."[13] Consent of such young children posed certain legal complications, however.[14] Contestations could easily be grounded in assertions that a noble had consented to a gift when too young to be fully cognizant of the implications of the alienation. Therefore, it was in the interest of nobles and monks to devise strategies to address such potentially sticky situations. When three brothers made a gift shortly after the death of their father, their brother Salomon was a "boy" at the time of the gift and thus unable to consent. Several years later, however, the monks gave Salomon (now presumably of age) a measure of grain in return for his approval of the gift.[15] A charter from Marmoutier proves just how young children could be when called upon to consent to a transfer of property. In 1130, when Rainald of Mondeiaco settled a dispute with Marmoutier, his sister, Amelina, and all of her children gave their consent to the quitclaim. The names of Amelina's children were listed in the body of the charter, and at the very end we learn that one daughter, Hildeberg, was still a baby. "All should know that Hildeberg, minor daughter of Amelina sister of

---

11. Historians generally concur that consent indicates that the consenter likely had a potential claim to the property in question (or at least they, the donors, or the monks believed they had a claim). Barbara Rosenwein, *To Be the Neighbor of St. Peter,* pp. 49–77; Stephen D. White, *Custom, Kinship and Gifts to Saints,* pp. 140–42; Emily Z. Tabuteau, *Transfers of Property in Eleventh-Century Norman Law,* pp. 170–95; Constance B. Bouchard, *Holy Entrepreneurs,* pp. 136–42; Bowman, *Shifting Landmarks,* pp. 47–52; Joanna Drell, *Kinship and Conquest,* pp. 98–112; Lemesle, *La société aristocratique dans le Haut-Maine,* pp. 114–17.

12. *CMPD,* no. 141, pp. 131–32.

13. *MB,* no. 42, p. 55.

14. Although canon law established the age of consent at eight, there seems to have been no fixed age at which children began consenting to gifts. See Evergates, *Aristocracy in the County of Champagne,* p. 92. For canonical prescriptions on the age of consent, see James Brundage, *Law, Sex, and Christian Society in Medieval Europe,* p. 38.

15. AD Loir-et-Cher, 16 H 80.

Rainald, listed above with the six other [children], was still in a cradle at the time of the gift and her mother was [still] nursing her."[16] Rights to property and participation in family transactions started at a very young age indeed. To redress the problem of securing the approval of such a young child to the resolution, her mother confirmed the gift for her. While not extant, it is possible that once she assumed her majority (or even older), Hildeberg, like Salomon, personally confirmed the quitclaim and gift.

Parents and Children

Recovering the experience of medieval children is challenging. Sources that are concerned with children directly are few and far between. While they do not specifically address childhood, the charters do furnish some glimpses into the parent-child relationship. One way to uncover relationships among elites is through analysis of donations to the church and in particular on whose be-half they were made. Such benefactions were serious business for they were made with the hope of achieving salvation and saving souls from the depths of hell—a horror that was believed to be real—and was graphically depicted on the tympana of the surrounding churches and cathedrals. Parents made arrangements for the care of their children's souls. So frequently are children and parents named as the recipients of the spiritual benefits of such gifts that their inclusion is almost formulaic: donations were made for "my soul, those of my spouse, and my children." Yet some charters transcend the formulaic. Particularly poignant is an eleventh-century act that shows the grief of me-dieval parents at the death of their children.

> Hamelin of Langeais and his wife Helvisa, daughter of Odo of Dubel-lus, by divine grace they had a son named Walter, beloved of God, a fine example of a young boy. When from the present rapture of this secular world he was called to God at seven years, concerned with the state of his soul, and made vehemently sad by his absence, trying to make amends for his sins.... His parents made a gift to the monks... [includ-ing] one arpent [of land] worth four *denarii* to be used to [provide candles] to illuminate the altar of Christ. Helvisa gave and accepted the benefit of our prayers from the hand of the prior, and then placed a branch into the hand of the prior, and then placed this symbol of

---

16. AD Loir-et-Cher, 21 H 69. See also *Cartulaire de Marmoutier pour le Vendômois,* no. 36, pp. 331–32 (hereafter, *MV*).

the gift on the altar of St. Trinité. Done in Vendôme 26 days after the death of the boy.[17]

This is a gem of a charter for it provides wonderful insight into the affective lives of medieval aristocrats. The medieval household has been frequently characterized as patriarchal and cold,[18] but this document presents a different picture. Here we have a grieving family, suffering much from the loss of their child. "Concerned for his soul and trying to make amends for his sins," they did what, in their social context, was the most caring thing for their dead child: they made a gift on behalf of his eternal soul. A mere three weeks after Walter's death, his mother and father traveled to Vendôme to make this gift upon the altar; it is a gift particularly fitting for a young child if one imagines that children throughout the ages have been afraid of the dark. His parents may have also found some comfort in the idea of an eternal light to commemorate one whose life had been snuffed out so early.

Nor were Hamelin and Helvisa the only grieving parents recorded in the charters.[19] In the mid-twelfth century Juliana of Pray lost her young daughter Guitberg. At the time of her death, Guitberg's mother and brother had been excommunicated because of their *calumnia* (a disagreement over possession of property) with the monks of St. Trinité.[20] The death of her daughter, however, made Dame Juliana "believe in the power of Ultimate divinity... so that groaning and weeping with her son Peter," she abandoned her previous claim to the property.[21] Wracked by guilt and physically debilitated by

---

17. *CTV,* vol. 2, no. 326, pp. 37–38.

18. Interestingly, modern scholars' interpretations of the ills of premodern childhood seem to stem from their reading of Jean-Jacques Rousseau's *Emile*. This treatise was written to encourage parents to educate their children, and Rousseau consciously overplayed what he thought was "wrong" with current parental practices. Scholars, such as Lawrence Stone, Lloyd DeMause, and Edward Shorter, seem to have interpreted Rousseau's exaggerations as reality. I am grateful to Richard Wilson for drawing this to my attention. This disaffected interpretation of family life and childhood has been disproved. For a point-by-point refutation of the "proofs" used to support this cold-hearted interpretation of family life, see Linda Pollock, *Forgotten Children;* Pierre Riché and Danièle Alexandre-Bidon, *L'enfance au moyen âge;* Robert Fossier, ed., *La petite enfance dans l'Europe médiévale et moderne*. For an overview of the historiography of childhood, see Barbara A. Hanawalt, "Medievalists and the Study of Childhood."

19. *CMPD,* no. 132, pp. 122–23. Agnes of Marly was similarly compelled by the death of her son to make a gift to the monks of Marmoutier to provide for his soul.

20. The monks describe claims made to their property as *calumnia,* which is the root for the modern word, calumny, meaning to bring slanderous or false accusations. The monks characterized all claims made to their property as unjust or spurious, so it is difficult to determine if this was always the case. I chose to use the word *calumnia* to refer to claims, just and unjust, since it is how these actions were described in the charters. But when a claim is denoted as *calumnia,* we should not rush to any assumptions about its merit.

21. *CTV,* vol. 2, no. 532, pp. 375–77.

grief, Juliana—like Hamelin and Helvisa—made a gift to save her child from the possible perils of the afterlife. While she could not protect her from the wrath of God in this life, this grieving mother, believing that her actions had cost her daughter's life, ensured that her daughter's immortal soul would be safe.

Chronicles support what the charters reveal. King Louis the Fat and his queen, Adelaide, similarly mourned the death of their son Philip. Suger remarks that not even Homer could describe the grief that befell these parents and the nation at the death of this young man. Louis himself "grieved mournfully and cursed his wretched life because he was the one who survived."[22] Count Fulk of Anjou was recorded as loving his youngest son very deeply because he was born in his old age.[23] One can easily envision the older gentleman laughing at his young son's antics and scenes of filial affection as the young boy looked after his aging father. These fathers clearly regarded their progeny with affection and did not view them as disposable or mere pawns to advance their ambition.

The evidence from the Loire region also suggests a different role for aristocratic mothers than has been previously suggested. Because the aristocracy of the eleventh and twelfth centuries was essentially a military elite, it has been assumed that mothers had little to do with the acculturation of their warrior sons (see map 2). The picture that emerges from the charters and chronicles of this region is at odds with such a characterization, however. Mothers exercised their influence on their sons directly. "A certain young boy, named Magnelin, gave to us at Viviers one *carrucata* of land, which his mother encouraged him to give," so he could become a monk.[24] Here we have a mother encouraging her son to make a pious donation to the church. Perhaps it was also her influence that led Magnelin to enter the monastery. Mothers, and even grandmothers, directed the spiritual instruction of their young sons. Guibert of Nogent provides ample testimony to his mother's role in his own religious development—an experience he had in common with other men of his class. Hildegard Franca, we are told, assumed the practical role of educating her young grandson by "[teaching] him Holy Scripture when he was a small boy."[25] Like Hildegard, Countess Adela also "carefully

---

22. Abbot Suger, *The Deeds of Louis the Fat,* pp. 149–50.

23. *Chronica de Gestis Consulum Andegavorum,* p. 37.

24. *CTV,* vol. 1, no. 34, pp. 54–55. The gift also provided for Magnelin's soul as well as for the souls of his parents.

25. *Père,* vol. 1, no. 99, p. 221. For discussion of the role of grandparents in the lives of medieval elites in England, see Joel T. Rosenthal, *Old Age in Late Medieval England.*

educated her sons in the defense of holy church."[26] The tutors who appear in the charters were also quite likely hired by mothers.[27]

The bellicosity of aristocratic society meant that noblemen were frequently absent. Not only were they drawn away from home and hearth by military campaigns but there were long absences also due to capture.[28] While wars ravaged the region, taking many noblemen of the lands of the Loire away from home, their wives stepped in to assume control of their family. As a consequence, women exercised a powerful influence over their children. When Fulcher of Meslay, who is described in the charter as "*puer*" and "*infans*" (meaning he was so young he was likely unable to speak), sold land to the monks, his mother consented to the alienation. Although the charter intimates that Fulcher arranged the sale, this seems highly improbable given his youth. More realistically, his mother was the one who brokered the exchange and was likely acting as his guardian.[29] Mothers were not remote figures to their noble sons. Rather they aided in their education and guided them toward manhood.

Aunts and Uncles

As the child reached adolescence, the familial focus shifted and broadened to include more contact with extended kin. Aunts and uncles, in particular, played important roles in the acculturation of young elites.[30] Male children

---

26. Orderic Vitalis, *Ecclesiastical History,* vol. 6, pp. 42–43.

27. For discussion of the mother's role in the education of her children, see Kimberly A. LoPrete, "Adela of Blois as Mother and Countess"; and Lois L. Huneycutt, "Public Lives, Private Ties." The frequent association of women with books in medieval imagery suggests they played a key role in educating their children. See Susan Groag Bell, "Medieval Women Book Owners," pp. 149–87. Some fathers also oversaw their sons' education. Peter Abelard's father was concerned that his children be educated. See Peter Abelard, *Letters of Abelard and Heloise,* p. 57. Count Eustace II of Boulogne "infused" all of his children with the love of learning. But he took care to have his sons also well educated in martial skills. Lambert of Ardres, *The History of the Counts of Guines and Lords of Ardres,* p. 71. For a discussion of medieval fatherhood, see David Herlihy, *Medieval Households,* pp. 127–30.

28. See *CTV,* vol. 2, no. 391, pp. 141–42; *Marmoutier-Cartulaire blésois,* no. 42, p. 55 (hereafter, *MB*) for examples.

29. AD Eure-et-Loir, H 2350. His mother, moreover, was Fulcher's only adult relative appearing in the charter.

30. Uncles are often referred to as *avunculi* in the charters. See *Père,* vol. 2, no. 21, pp. 531—32 and *Cartulaire de Notre-Dame de Josaphat,* vol. 1, no. 212, pp. 257–58 (hereafter, *Josaphat*). It is difficult to determine whether these were their mother's or father's brothers. Sometimes *patruus* was used to indicate a maternal uncle, yet this practice is not consistent, and in some cases *patruus* was used to refer to a paternal relative. As with relatives in general, it would seem that there was little concern over whether or not the uncle was the brother of the father or mother. This suggests that *both* lines were important to the family and that kinship was figured collaterally. No emphasis or preference was placed upon descendants from the paternal line. For a discussion of the terminology applied

were sent at a relatively early age to be trained as knights, although sometimes this training occurred at home. The fostering process generally took place under the guidance of an uncle, many times a maternal uncle.[31] While uncles have long been recognized as instrumental in orchestrating the careers of clerics, lay uncles have something of a different reputation.[32] The popularity in legend of the "evil uncle" who plots and schemes to usurp his nephew's rightful inheritance is second only to the "evil stepmother." Were uncles really so diabolical? The evidence suggests not.

To be fostered, a child would move to his uncle's home where he would be trained in the art of war.[33] Fostering also exposed the warrior-in-training to the other aspects of maintaining and extending power, such as the management of resources and the more-subtle skills of negotiation, tactics, and diplomacy. Preparing for the warrior life carried certain risks and sometimes resulted in tragedy. In 1152, Vulgrin, the young son of Henric Brunellus, was fatally wounded by an arrow as he was "being trained in the weapons of knighthood (*miles probates armis*)."[34] While the charter recording Vulgrin's death is not explicit as to where he was being trained, the participation of his uncle and cousins in the donation indicates he was being fostered with them. Another young eleventh-century nobleman similarly found himself under the watchful eye of his uncle. Evidence of young Matthew's fostering comes down to us through a dispute. Sometime before 1070, a priest wished to make a gift to St. Trinité of Vendôme. Matthew disputed this gift,

to kin, see Anita Guerreau-Jalabert, "La désignation des relations et des groupes de parenté" and "La parenté dans l'Europe médiévale et moderne." Anthropology has shaped how historians have approached medieval family life, and many scholars now reject the idea of patrilineage in favor of a collateral organization for the aristocratic family. Régine Le Jan, *Famille et pouvoir dans le monde franc (VIIe-Xe siècle);* Anita Guerreau-Jalabert, Régine Le Jan, and Joseph Morsel, "De l'histoire de la famille à l'anthropologie de la parenté"; Jussen, "Famille et parenté."

31. See Marjorie Chibnall, "The Empress Matilda and Her Sons," p. 284, and LoPrete, "Adela of Blois as Mother and Countess," pp. 319 and 322, for examples of the roles that uncles played in the lives of the medieval elite. See also John Freed, *Noble Bondsmen,* esp. pp. 104–13; Constance B. Bouchard, *"Strong of Body, Brave and Noble,"* pp. 77–78. In contrast, Evergates has found no evidence of fostering among the thirteenth-century nobility of Champagne; *Aristocracy in the County of Champagne,* pp. 152–53.

32. Bouchard, *Sword, Miter, and Cloister,* pp. 79–84; Boussard, "Les évêques en Neustrie avant la réforme grégorienne," pp. 161–96; Madeleine Dillay, "Le régime de l'église privée du XIe au XIIe siècle dans l'Anjou, le Maine et la Touraine"; Fanning, *A Bishop and His World,* pp. 19–44 and "Family and Episcopal Election"; Head, *Hagiography and the Cult of the Saints,* pp. 220–35.

33. Daughters were also sent to relatives' homes to be acculturated. See Barbara Hanawalt, "Female Networks for Fostering Lady Lisle's Daughters" and Mitchell, *Portraits of Medieval Women,* in particular pp. 11–28 for the lives of the de Ferrers sisters, and pp. 29–42 for the relationship between Maud de Quency and her daughter.

34. *CTV,* vol. 2, no. 540, pp. 387–88.

however, because he had not authorized the original sale of the property. At the time of the sale, Matthew was described as "under the tutelage" of his uncle Odo and abiding at "his [Odo's] home."[35]

Chronicle evidence confirms what the charters indicate about the close relationship between aristocrats and the children of their siblings. Lisois of Amboise was a powerful noble whose star was on the rise in the Loire valley during the eleventh century. He was a faithful supporter of Count Fulk Nerra of Anjou, but he became the lord of Amboise—an important defensive spot on the Loire River—through his marriage to Hersend. Hersend had led an interesting life by the time of her marriage to Lisois. Her father had been a trusted vassal of the Angevin count, who, along with his brother, protected Amboise from the predations of the counts of Blois-Chartres. When Hersend's father died, his brother Sulpice—who was also the treasurer of St. Martin in Tours and apparently unmarried—assumed the guardianship of his nephew and two nieces. Sulpice feared for the safety of his young charges and acted swiftly to move them to the stone keep at the castle of Amboise. Later, after the immediate threat to their safety had passed, Sulpice arranged their futures. The elder daughter married Lisois, with whom she founded the seigneurial family of Amboise. Her sister married an important noble from Bourges and received a part of the patrimony as her dowry. Robert, Sulpice's nephew, inherited his father's original lands.[36]

At a time of political instability, Sulpice acted first to protect his nephew and nieces and later to ally them with families that would continue to provide for their security and ensure them a place among the powerful families of the region. Shortly after arranging the marriages of his nieces and ensuring his nephew was installed on his lordship, Sulpice died. Hersend and her siblings owed their very lives to Sulpice. While some uncles did take advantage of their young charges, most did not. Rather, they acted like Sulpice, who did everything in his power to protect and advance his nieces and nephews. Given the constant warfare and shifting of alliances common in the Loire region at this time, Sulpice could easily have displaced his wards and taken the land for himself. A sense of honor and responsibility, if not affection, did not allow for such a course of action for this noble uncle, however.

---

35. *CTV,* vol. 2, no. 210, p. 342. As an adult, Matthew contested the transaction based on his lack of consent. The matter was investigated, and the verdict accorded with Matthew's account. The priest had to forfeit the disputed property, much to his displeasure.

36. *Gesta Ambaziensium dominorum,* pp. 83–86. For the political circumstances of these alliances, see Bachrach, *Fulk Nerra,* pp. 184–89.

Sulpice's support and fostering of his brother's children established a tradition of family solidarity in the Amboise family that continued into the generation of his grandnieces and grandnephews. Hersend and Lisois had five children. Their eldest son, Sulpice—who was named for his great uncle—died while his children were still young. Before his death, however, Sulpice's brother Lisois swore an oath to support his nephew Hugh's control of the family patrimony and retainers. After Sulpice's death, the count of Vendôme tried to wrest certain holdings from young Hugh. Uncle Lisois, along with his friend Hugh of Alluyes, came to this young nobleman's aid.[37] For two generations of the seigneurial family of Amboise, uncles assumed responsibility for their nieces and nephews. In this family, uncles were far from the scheming and greedy characters often found in medieval literature. Instead, these men assumed the role of surrogate father to their young orphaned nieces and nephews. They protected and defended both the children themselves and their property rights.

Uncles also lent their assistance in legal matters. At some point in the first four decades of the eleventh century, a salt marsh traded hands. When one of the actors needed clarification of who controlled what parts of the property he had granted to the church, he brought his uncle to court, whose testimony settled the problem once and for all.[38] Uncles were useful witnesses since they could recall how property had been divided or how it had passed from one generation to the next. Nephews could provide the same assistance to their uncles. When a noble named Walter was on his deathbed, he made a gift to Marmoutier. Among those approving and witnessing this benefaction was his nephew Ulric. Walter's heirs eventually disputed the gift, and the monks called Ulric to testify to his uncle's gift: "[When] another of his [Walter's] heirs, from counsel of the count and malicious spirit contested the gift, they called the nephew Ulric of Frideburg, who stated the monks were in the right."[39] Ulric, although he had a right to his uncle's property, could be counted upon to testify to what his uncle had provided. Noblemen even solicited the help and support of uncles of illegitimate birth. In the 1060s, when Wicher was compensated by the count of Anjou for his loss of properties brought on by comital warfare, his bastard uncle Lethbert witnessed and guaranteed Wicher's quitclaim against other properties.[40] In some cases,

37. *Gesta Ambaziensium dominorum*, p. 98.

38. *MB*, no. 25, pp. 30–31. Elizabeth van Houts finds that uncles were particularly sought out to help settle family matters. *Memory and Gender in Medieval Europe, 900–1200*, pp. 28–39.

39. *MB*, no. 26, pp. 32–33.

40. *MB*, no. 40, pp. 51–54; no. 86, pp. 94–95.

young nobles inherited property from their uncles. Early in the twelfth century, William of Ferrières gave property to the church, "first and foremost for the soul of my uncle, from whose fief this [property] came."[41] William made this gift to honor the man who had left him the property. The bonds forged between young elites and their uncles were further tempered as the nieces and nephews reached adulthood.

Like uncles, aunts could play formative roles in the lives of young elites. Although less frequently, young men were also sent to the households of aunts, where they would be put into service. This was the case of Robert the Burgundian, an important lord of Anjou who had many dealings with the noble families of the mid-Loire. In the 1040s, Robert, who was the son of the count of Nevers, was sent to his Aunt Agnes, the countess of Anjou. Through the patronage of this woman and her husband, Robert gained his lordships and eventually became one of the most powerful lords of Anjou.[42] William of La Porcherie may also have been fostered in the house of a female relative. William was the nephew of Viscountess Helvisa of Châteaudun and witnessed charters for his uncle, the viscount, indicating that William may have been living with this couple and thus likely fostered at the home of his aunt.[43]

Attachments between nephews and aunts could run quite deep. When the aunt of St. William of Norwich heard that her nephew was dead, "she bewailed the nephew whom she had so greatly loved."[44] Lambert of Ardres relates the story of how a young Count Arnold of Flanders took in his pregnant aunt and raised her son. Arnold "took care of Ardulf [his cousin] and his mother in every way" and stood as godfather to this infant. The count also insured Ardulf's military training and invested him with lands from his own patrimony.[45] The life experience of Guibert of Nogent's mother provides a counterexample to this main theme, however. Shortly after the death of her husband, her husband's nephew tried to compel her to remarry.

---

41. *CSVM*, no. 648, p. 374. William of Ferrières was married to Vicedomina Elizabeth of Chartres.

42. Jessee, *Robert the Burgundian and the Counts of Anjou*, pp. 26–52.

43. *Tiron*, vol. 1, no. 185, pp. 207–8. Blanche of Navarre also offered her illegitimate nephew the opportunity of service at her court. Theodore Evergates, "Aristocratic Women in the County of Champagne," 83. Queen Blanche of Castile also fostered her nephew at the royal court. Miriam Shadis, "Blanche of Castile and Facinger's 'Medieval Queenship,'" p. 143.

44. Thomas Head, *Medieval Hagiography*, p. 530.

45. Lambert of Ardres, *The History of the Counts of Guines and Lords of Ardres*, pp. 61–62. Count Arnold's aunt, Elftrude, had a liaison with Siefried, who "pined with great love" for her. Although the events that Lambert relates were in the past, he imbues them with his own contemporary perspective.

She withstood the pressure, but clearly her relationship with her nephew was adversarial. The fact that a nephew was such a prominent force in this noblewoman's life does, however, support the premise that nephews played an important role in aristocratic families.[46]

In the romantic literature of the time, aunts played key parts, which suggests they were familiar—if not important—kin to noble children. In Marie de France's *lai, Guigemar,* the young heroine is assisted by her niece, who is pivotal in the romance.[47] She is the matchmaker for the two lovers and helps to facilitate their budding romance. In the *Deux Amanz,* another of Marie's *lais,* the aunt of the love-struck lady aids the lovers against the outraged father.[48] The literary evidence embroiders upon what the charters suggest: aunts were familiar and supportive kin.

For those children destined for religious life, family ties also shaped their lives. Children were often placed in religious houses where their aunts, uncles, cousins, or siblings had taken vows.[49] Hildegard Franca's young illegitimate grandson, for example, was placed in a religious house where his grandfather and another of his relatives were already serving God.[50] The case of the boy Gaufred is somewhat unusual. His father was a chaplain, either to a seigneurial house or a dependency of St. Martin, and when he decided to join the monks of St. Florent, he arranged for his young son to take orders there as well.[51] Relatives were invaluable to shaping the future of young elites in the church.[52] Guibert of Nogent remarked that he owed his placement in a certain ecclesiastical office to the pious influence of his mother and the more pragmatic intercession of his kin.[53] Uncles could be particularly helpful in arranging ecclesiastical careers or placements for their nephews.

---

46. John F. Benton, *Self and Society in Medieval France,* p. 71.

47. Robert Hanning and Joan Ferrante, trans. and eds., *The Lais of Marie de France,* pp. 37–38.

48. Hanning and Ferrante, *The Lais of Marie de France,* p. 130.

49. In addition to joining houses where they had relatives, family ties also played a role in "conversions" to the monastic life. Joachim Wollasch argues that at key moments of religious reform, groups of family members converted. Such conversions reflect the cooperative nature of the family and, as Wollasch argues, demonstrate the concern that family members had for the spiritual well-being of their kin. Joachim Wollasch, "Parenté noble et monachisme réformateur."

50. *Père,* vol. 1, no. 99, pp. 221–22.

51. AD Maine-et-Loire, H 3107. Lemesle's analysis of the entrance of nobles in Maine into the church contradicts the assumption that most joined the religious orders as young children. He finds the majority of nobles entered as adults. His interpretation of the gifting of children to the church, however, follows Duby's assertion that sons were placed into the church to limit their claims on the patrimony. Lemesle, *La société aristocratique dans le Haut-Maine,* pp. 85–94.

52. Bouchard, *Sword, Miter, and Cloister,* pp. 48–64; See also Joseph Lynch, *Simonical Entry into Religious Life from 1000–1200,* pp. 25–50.

53. Benton, *Self and Society,* pp. 51, 83, 97.

In the mid-twelfth century, Gauslen of Lèves succeeded his uncle as bishop of Chartres. While Gauslen earned his office on his own merits, his uncle, Bishop Geoffrey, certainly helped guide and perhaps promote his nephew's career. On a more modest scale, Herbert the priest secured property, which had been previously claimed by the lord of Lavardin, so that his nephew could become a monk at Marmoutier.[54] Likewise, another priest, as he was approaching the end of his life, arranged for his two young nieces to become nuns at the convent of St. Avit.[55] The entrance of nieces and nephews into religious communities where their aunt or uncle was in charge was so much a part of medieval aristocratic life that it was reflected in the romantic literature of the time. In the *lai Le Fresne,* the heroine is abandoned by her mother and left at a local nunnery. The abbess is so taken with child that she vows to raise Le Fresne as her niece.[56] Apparently the presence of nieces at convents was commonplace. Uncles and aunts were not remote relatives but were frequently called upon to play the role of surrogate parent, or at the very least, career advocate.

Aristocratic children often entered religious life at a fairly young age. In the early eleventh century, Leulfus arranged for his young son (*puerela*) Walter to join the monks of St. Florent of Saumur.[57] The daughter of Fulco also joined a religious community as a young girl. Yet she continued to be in her family's thoughts for her father remembered her in a gift that he made sometime after she entered the convent.[58] Even though children entered the church at a young age, they continued to participate in family transactions. Ursio of Fréteval's daughter, Berta (who was named for her mother) became a nun at St. Avit of Châteaudun. When her father, mother, and siblings acted to renounce their rights to certain of their possessions, the monks sent envoys to secure her consent at St. Avit.[59] An ecclesiastical career was the fate of some children of the noble born. Ties to family—indeed daily interactions with relatives—were an important part of these children's lives. Parents did not place their sons and daughters in monasteries or nunneries because they viewed them as extraneous or "second class." Having a child in the church

---

54. *MB,* no. 10, p. 17.
55. AD Eure-et-Loir, H 4333.
56. Hanning and Ferrante, *Lais of Marie de France,* p. 78.
57. AD Maine-et-Loire, H 3497.
58. AD Eure-et-Loir, H 4288.
59. *Chartes Vendômoises,* edited by Charles Métais, no. 82, pp. 106–10 (hereafter, *CV*). Several noble families had relatives who were prestigious clerics. For example, Stephen, the son of Vicedomina Helisend and Vicedominus Guerric became the abbot of St. Jean-en-Vallée. Ada of Touraille, kinswoman to the viscounts of Châteaudun became a prioress of St. Avit. See note 76, chapter 3, for discussion of this noblewoman.

served the family in a variety of ways, including providing spiritual intercession and association with the holy. Moreover, some children were clearly
disposed to the life of a monk or nun. Remember the children of Walter
and Adelina Minter who took their vows because they were drawn to the
spiritual life.

Life Stages: Adulthood

Husbands and Wives

Marriage—either to a person or, in the case of a nun, to God—represented
the transition from youth to adulthood for most of the noble born. Marital
alliances were made to benefit the family through social or political advancement. Consequently, when a child reached marriageable age, kin played a
key role in finding a suitable mate.[60] Acquisition of allies was of vital importance to medieval elites. Not surprisingly, families arranged marriages with
families whose lands, and hence interests, bordered on their own. Take the
Fréteval family, for instance. In the course of three generations, this family
married into the vicecomital house of Châteaudun and the seigneurial families of Mondoubleau, Frouville, La Ferté, and Montigny, all of whom held
lands that abutted the Fréteval patrimony (see map 1). Marriage into other
families increased the kin base of an elite family, but also its power network.

Because medieval marriages were arranged by noble families to best suit
their socio-political agendas or to bolster family economics, neither future
husbands nor future wives had much say, beyond either granting or with-
holding their consent, in deciding who they would marry. Guibert of Nogent's discussion of his own parents' union makes it clear that neither of
them had any input into selecting their prospective spouse. It does seem that
widows had more control over whom they would marry or if they would
remarry at all, as Guibert of Nogent's mother exemplifies. After the death of
Guibert's father, she was pressured by her affinal kin to remarry. She cleverly

---

60. While most elites did not marry until they were in their late teens, many were betrothed
quite early. To enter into marriage, canon lawyers insisted that the child needed to be eight, which
was considered the age when a child had "reason" enough to aid in determining his/her future.
Brundage, *Law, Sex, and Christian Society,* p. 38. While children might enter into an agreement or
contract to marry at some future date, the actual marriage was not consummated until several years
later. The charters from the Loire region indicate that the women who are acting as married women
appear to be women and not young girls. For discussion of marital demographics, see chapter 6 and
Evergates, *Aristocracy in the County of Champagne,* pp. 142–44. RaGena C. DeAragon also examines
the age at marriage and the length of the marriages of sixty-eight Anglo-Norman dowager countesses in "Dowager Countesses, 1069–1230."

outmaneuvered them, however, and opted not to remarry but to follow her religious vocation into the church.[61]

Chronicles and letters of the eleventh and twelfth century are often cited as evidence of how ill-suited some medieval aristocratic couples were. During the eleventh century, the clergy attempted to establish certain guidelines for marriage. As one of the most learned and respected clerics of his generation, Bishop Fulbert of Chartres was consulted on certain issues pertaining to marriage. It is through Fulbert's correspondence that we learn of the marriage of Galeran of Meulan. Galeran, like many others, wrote to Fulbert concerning his marriage. His wife, it seems, had run away. Citing the incompatibility of their marriage, she did not wish to return to her husband. Galeran complained that he would be forced to commit adultery if she did not return. He asked Fulbert to compel his spouse to come home. The bishop, however, was reluctant to do so because Galeran "hates her so and so unto her death."[62] In contrast, chronicle evidence provides examples of loving or happy marriages. Orderic Vitalis tells of many affectionate couples, with wives longing for their husbands' return.[63] Even Abbot Suger characterized aristocratic marriage as emotionally invested. When Guy of La Roche-Guyon was assassinated at the behest of his kinsmen, his wife,

> struck dumb at seeing this, . . . tore her cheeks and hair with wifely fury. She ran over to her husband and, caring nothing for death, tumbled down and covered him with her body. "Me," she said, "Behead me, you vilest of butchers, I am the most miserable wretch that should die." Having thrown herself on top of her husband, she received blows and wounds inflicted by the swordsmen. "Dearest spouse, what wrongs did you these men? Weren't this son-in-law and father-in-law inseparable friends? What is this madness? You people are complete maniacs." Twisting her by the hair, they dragged her away struggling as best they could, for she was stabbed and wounded over nearly her whole body. . . . While the murderers roamed about gnashing their teeth, the woman lay on the floor and, lifting up her piteous head, looked upon the mutilated body of her husband. In an outburst of love which her weakness hardly allowed, she slid along like a snake, dragging her own completely bloody body up beside the lifeless corpse. As if he were alive, she gave him as many sweet kisses as she could.[64]

---

61. Benton, *Self and Society in Medieval France,* p. 71.

62. Fulbert of Chartres, *Letters and Poems of Fulbert of Chartres,* letter 93, pp. 168–70.

63. Orderic Vitalis, *Ecclesiastical History,* vol. 2, pp. 219–21.

64. Abbot Suger, *The Deeds of Louis the Fat,* pp. 77–78. As part of his message that that the king was responsible for establishing political order, Suger plays up the violence of aristocratic family

This example is even more extraordinary given the fact that Guy's assassins were his wife's brothers, meaning that this noblewoman stood up for her husband against her natal family.

The charters also reveal that most aristocratic marriages at the very least functioned smoothly, whether or not generating genuine affection. Yet some do provide glimpses of something more. Ansold the Knight acted with his "beloved" wife to make a gift to the abbey of St. Père.[65] Ivo gave the garden next to the mill "for his wife, who was infirmed."[66] Here we have a husband making a gift to help his ailing wife, which is certainly evidence of affection or care between spouses. Wives, in turn, acted out of affection for their spouses. Agnes of Montigny was compelled "out of love for her husband" to donate property to Marmoutier.[67] Given the fact that some aristocratic marriages could last several decades,[68] it is perhaps not surprising that husbands and wives came to genuinely care about each other.

Arrangements made after the death of spouses confirm the existence of abiding conjugal affection.[69] Demographics and the realities of a life dedicated to war shaped these donation practices, for wives tended to outlive their husbands and therefore arranged postmortem gifts for them.[70] There are, however, a few examples of husbands who survived their wives and made gifts on their behalf.[71] In 1135, Boellus of Beaugency was concerned for his wife's immortal soul. He arranged that certain of his properties be transferred to the monks to provide for his wife's burial with the monks.[72] The count of Maine was in somewhat more urgent circumstances when he made a benefaction for his spouse. His countess was gravely ill, and the count hurriedly traveled to a priory of Marmoutier to make a gift for her soul.[73] In general, noble husbands

---

members toward each other and the instability of aristocratic family life. Aristocratic families were Louis VI's chief impediment to controlling France. As a result, Suger shows how Louis used his might for good and for the benefit of the weak, in contrast to the aristocrats who used their strength in wanton acts of violence—intra- and extrafamilial.

65. *Père,* vol. 1, no. 16, p. 241.

66. *Père,* vol. 2, no. 12, p. 477. Ivo's mother, Roscia, and brother Tronellus consented to the gift at the court of Lady Eustachia of Brou.

67. *CMPD,* no. 97, pp. 90–91.

68. The marriages of Mahild of Alluyes, for example, seem to have lasted for approximately fifteen years each. Her daughter-in-law, Eustachia of Gouet, may have been married for fifty years. This long-lived match only ended upon the death of her husband. Similarly, Agnes of Montigny was married to Odo of Vallières for approximately twenty-five years. See chapter 6, table 1.

69. *Cartulaire du prieuré bénédictin de Saint-Gondon-sur-Loire (866–1172) tire des archives de l'abbaye de Saint-Florent près Saumur,* no. 21, pp. 42–43 (hereafter, *Gondon*).

70. *Père,* vol. 1, no. 67, p. 193; *Jean,* no. 7, p. 14.

71. For examples of this, see *MB,* no. 31, p. 37. Heliand of Fréteval made a similar arrangement for his wife; AD Loir-et-Cher, 16 H 87.

72. *CTV,* vol. 2, no. 476, p. 279.

73. *Cartulaire manceau de Marmoutier,* vol. 1, no. 9, pp. 127–28 (hereafter, *MM*).

did not wait until the last moment to arrange pious gifts for their wives—although the countess may have been quite young and in the bloom of good health when she was taken ill. Most men tended to provide for their wives' spiritual health while they were still alive.[74] Ingelbald Brito, for instance, "gave to St. Trinité and all the servants of God in the same place, certain land... for the good of his soul and that of his wife Hildiard [-Domitilla]."[75]

Once they were married, the familial ties of individual nobles expanded considerably. Although as married people elites became part of another kin group, they still remained connected to their natal kin. The tendency of women to survive their husbands meant that a woman had a somewhat different relationship with her kin and to the property that bound her to them. Because some noble-born women married more than once, balancing their family considerations—and managing their property—was complicated indeed. When sometime before 1080, Adelina made a gift to St. Père, she specified that the gift was for her second husband Rodbert, "and for the health of her [sic] soul, as well as the soul of my father Ingenulf, and also John, my first husband... I concede this *vicaria,* which I hold from my relatives by law or custom."[76] The concern and connection that Adelina felt for her first husband continued into her second marriage, even though she refers to her second husband Rodbert as "most illustrious" and characterizes the marriage as "noble." As the example of Adelina illustrates, remarriage did not terminate the connection—through land or affection—with a previous spouse's family. Widows often received life estates and dowers that lasted the entirety of their lives regardless of whether they remarried, so their interests remained intersected with those of their affinal kin. Hence, a woman's in-laws and her children had a vested interest in how the widow managed her lands. As she was dying, Hildegard, the wife of Ansold of Mongerville, gave land to St. Père that had been given to her in dower by her first husband. Her son

---

74. Husbands frequently made gifts on behalf of their children and other relatives in addition to themselves and their spouses. Sometime before 1030, Hugo Pirarius, his wife Ledgard, and their son Fulco restored lands belonging to a cell of St. Père of Chartres to benefit all of their souls (*Père,* vol. 1, no. 57, pp. 182–83.) Similarly, when another Hugh made a donation, he specified that the gift was to benefit the souls of his relatives, his wife, and his children, as well as his own (*CMPD,* no. 29, pp. 29–30.) The inclusion of children was clearly dictated by the life stage at which many elite men made pious gifts. Most made these gifts while they were married and when their children were still relatively young. Provisions made for a family, as opposed to solely for a spouse, should be read not as a man's lack of affection for his wife but rather a difference in life stage and life experience.

75. *CTV,* vol. 1, no. 273, pp. 424–25. It appears that this woman preferred the name "Domitilla" to her given name of Hildiard/Hildegard. Consequently, she will be referred to as "Domitilla" throughout. For a discussion of her adoption of the name "Domitilla," see chapter 7.

76. *Père,* vol. 1, no. 38, pp. 165–66.

Pagan, his wife, and their children all consented to the gift, as did Hildegard's lord.[77] But sometime later, another son, Joscelin of Mongerville, disputed the gift:

> The mother of Joscelin of Mongerville held certain land at Boisville, which her first husband, Radulf (who was not the father of Joscelin) gave to her, so that she could do whatever she wished with the land, giving it or selling it. When she was dying, she gave to St. Peter for the soul of her husband, who had given it to her, and for herself, but Joscelin contradicted this and made a false claim; so that an appeal for justice was made to us; there the judgment was that nothing from these lands belonged to him, and that it was not from his patrimony. He, however, did not cease his claim and did many bad things to us; for these actions he was excommunicated. However, through the will of God, he was led to penitence, came to us in his bare feet, confessing his sins, and recognized the injustice of his claim.[78]

Joscelin's attempt to claim land given to his mother in dower by her first husband reflects the various and potential claims to family property. Even though Hildegard was dead, her son by another marriage was making claim to lands given to her decades earlier. The issue was so complex and hotly contested that a *placitum,* or a court to hear the case, was called. Unfortunately the details of the *placitum* are not extant in the charter. The charter records only the finding that Joscelin had no claim to the land. Many years after the original grant, and even though Hildegard's first husband was dead, property provided a bond between Hildegard and her affinal kin that persisted throughout her lifetime and even after her death.

Parents and Siblings

The relationships that had shaped the lives of the noble born as children continued to have meaning for them as adults. What can we determine about the relationship between grown children and their parents? At the end of the eleventh century, Harduin of Adrestiaco made arrangements to give a church to the abbey of St. Trinité in Vendôme.[79] Before the transaction could be completed, however, Harduin died on pilgrimage to Jerusalem.

---

77. *Père,* vol. 2, no. 31, p. 425.
78. *Père,* vol. 1, no. 58, p. 453.
79. *CTV,* vol. 2, no. 306, pp. 11–12.

His son, "who was the equal of Harduin," followed through on his father's wishes and gave the church to the monks. The future of Harduin's soul was imperiled by his untimely death because he had been unable to complete the gift. Acting out of concern for his father, whose torment his son could undoubtedly envision thanks to vivid sermons and sculptural programs, his son ensured that the transaction took place. To spare his parent this suffering and to secure a place for him among the elect, this son also supplemented the original gift with additional lands.[80]

The concern for one another's souls that both parents and children evinced indicates a family life based on care and affection rather than cold patriarchy. Children frequently made gifts for the benefit of their parents' souls. "Since he [their father] was now close to death," the children of Gislebert of Ruga Vasselorum made a gift of extensive properties and revenues to the monks of St. Trinité in Vendôme to ensure he would be buried with the monks.[81] Burial with the monks was a privilege, one that these children were anxious to claim for their ailing parent. Securing spiritual benefits was an important way of providing for souls, but it also was a way of formalizing relationships with the monks. Sometime about 1067, Rainald and his wife Hildeberg made a gift to the same monks on behalf of their own souls, those of their children, and those of Hildeberg's family, specifically her father, her mother, and her brother.[82] Over a century later, Philip of Montoire and his sister Lucie gave all that they held in revenue from certain lands to benefit the soul of their mother. But their gift included one further requirement: every year on the feast day of John the Baptist, the monks were to pay Philip, Lucie, and her husband five *solidi* to commemorate their mother's piety and to remind the community of the relationship between this family and the monks.[83] Children orchestrated their benefactions in such a way to continuously remind their kin, friends, and neighbors of their parents' piety and the donors' relationship to these relatives.

Maternal influence continued as children came of age. Mothers, for example, encouraged their adult sons to make peace with the church. Some

---

80. Medieval children mourned their parents. For specific examples, see Tracy Chapman Hamilton, "Queenship and Kinship in the French *Bible moralisée*," p. 179; Huneycutt, "Public Lives, Private Ties," p. 302. See also Gilsdorf, *Queenship and Sanctity*, pp. 84–87.

81. *CTV*, vol. 1, no. 136, pp. 241–43. Convincing parents to convert to the religious life also reflects the affection and concern that children had for their parents. Wollasch, "Parenté noble et monachisme réformateur," 8–12.

82. *MB*, no. 45, p. 59. For a discussion of kinship and commemoration, see Drell, *Kinship and Conquest*, pp. 125–46.

83. *CTV*, vol. 2, no. 615, pp. 491–92.

were successful, like Philippa of Courville. Others, Vicedomina Helisend of Chartres among them, could not get their sons to atone for their actions against the monks.[84] After the death of Vicedominus Guerric, Helisend made a gift for his soul to St. Père. To his mother's distress, Helisend's son Hugh claimed part of the gift and seized it from the monks. In spite of her attempts to have him return it, Hugh possessed the property until his death. Helisend remained undeterred, however, and arranged a generous gift so that the monks would forgive and forget Hugh's unjust seizure of their property. Sons and mothers also acted together to make donations and resolve disputes. Berlay and his mother, for instance, reached an agreement with the monks of Marmoutier concerning their possession of a furnace at Chamars.[85] Mothers also felt free to advise their grown sons. Elizabeth, the mother of Lord Sulpice II of Amboise and Chaumont, chided her son for not consulting her as he planned to engage many powerful lords, including the count of Blois, in battle. She wisely predicted he would have trouble defeating this host. Sulpice replied, defensively, that he too had many strong vassals. Unfortunately, things did not go well for Sulpice, and he was eventually imprisoned at Châteaudun.[86] Sulpice clearly should have listened to his mother. His failure to take her advice, however, does not detract from the fact that mothers offered advice and acted as counselors to their sons throughout childhood and even into adulthood.[87]

In spite of such interactions, the role of mothers has been often overlooked. Part of the reason for this may lay with the extant charters themselves, which can obscure the activities of women in aristocratic society. Take, for example, two charters recording a donation made by the Legedoctus

---

84. *Père,* vol. 2, no. 55, p. 562. Women frequently acted as peacemakers between their male relatives and the church. For just a few examples, see Sharon Farmer, "Persuasive Voices"; Lois L. Huneycutt, "Intercession and the High-Medieval Queen"; Chibnall, "The Empress Matilda and Her Sons"; Miriam Shadis, "Berenguela of Castile's Political Motherhood."

85. AD Eure-et-Loir, H 2271. Interestingly, Berlay is referred to as the "nephew of William," which may be a reference to his mother's brother. Perhaps Berlay's father had died while Berlay was very young, and like many of his contemporaries he was fostered at the home of this maternal uncle. He may have chosen to identify himself with the man who raised him as opposed to his biological father. Praxedis, the mother of Gelduin the knight, witnessed and signed a charter with her son at the end of the eleventh century; AD Loir-et-Cher, 16 H 119.

86. *Gesta Ambaziensium dominorum,* pp. 126–29. The editors note that Elizabeth's speech was composed of various bits of classical literature, although they are not able to identify the particular sources. Elizabeth's advice should not be dismissed as a simple trope, however. While the author may have used classical sources, the fact that he portrayed a mother as giving her son such advice indicates that his audience would have been familiar with and accepting of a mother advising her son.

87. See John Carmi Parsons and Bonnie Wheeler, eds., *Medieval Mothering;* LoPrete, *Adela of Blois,* pp. 126–28; Clarissa Atkinson, *The Oldest Vocation;* Lois L. Huneycutt, *Matilda of Scotland.*

family. "Let it be known by all posterity, that Helvisa Legedocta gave to St. Martin the tithes from the church of St. John of Chamars, except [those] from bread and wine, and three arpents of land in the cemetery. To this her son Robert [and many clerics and her other children] consented."[88] The transaction took place in Helvisa's house and her lord, the viscount of Châteaudun, approved the transfer. Yet a later episcopal confirmation recorded the act differently. Bishop Ivo confirmed that the tithes pertaining to the church known as St. John of Chamars were given by Robert Legedoctus and his mother, Helvisa.[89] The episcopal document clearly casts the transaction in a different light from the original grant, relegating Helvisa to the role of a supporting character as opposed to her true role in the gift as main actor. For whatever reasons, the scribe (or bishop himself) chose to make Robert the donor. It is certainly possible that many other documents suffered a similar sort of redaction and may account for, or certainly contribute to, the skewed model of women's experience as one of repression and powerlessness.[90] What the original charter reveals, and reinforces, is the important role that mothers played in the lives of their sons. Here we have a woman making a gift to benefit her soul and the souls of her family, with the support and consent of her grown children. From childhood to adulthood, sons' lives were intertwined with the lives of their mothers. Mothers were not pale creatures relegated to the towers of castles, far from the activity of aristocratic life. No indeed, they were an integral part of their children's lives.

The lives of sisters and brothers intersected from birth to death.[91] Bonds between siblings have been characterized as one of the most powerful of medieval society.[92] As children they played together or were schooled together. As adults, siblings relied on each other for support and assistance. Siblings could count upon their brothers and sisters to foster their children and assume responsibility for them in case of their demise. Aid in times of

---

88. AD Eure-et-Loir, H 2268. Helvisa's other children also consented to the grant, although the section confirming their approval comes at the bottom of the charter. This might suggest that Robert had some special claim to the property in question. Perhaps it was to be his inheritance. Perhaps he was the eldest child—although none of the acts designate him so. Or perhaps it was a scribal convenience.

89. AD Eure-et-Loir, H 2268.

90. Scholars working on other regions of medieval France have detected similar scribal practices that ultimately result in an underreporting of women in the charters. See Elisabeth Carpentier, "La place des femmes dans les plus anciennes chartes poitevins"; and Jean Gay, "Remarques sur l'évolution de la pratique contractuelle en Champagne méridionale (XIIe-XIXe siècle)."

91. LoPrete, "Adela of Blois as Mother and Countess," pp. 314–18; Huneycutt, "Public Lives, Private Ties," pp. 303–8; Ralph V. Turner, "Eleanor of Aquitaine and Her Children"; Susanna Greer Fein, "Maternity in Aelred of Rievaulx's Letter to His Sister," pp. 139–56.

92. Riché and Alexandre-Bidon, *L'enfance au Moyen Age,* p. 118.

trouble was another feature of the sibling relationship—particularly when one sibling was under attack. The family of the lords of Amboise banded together to fight off an attack by the count of Anjou.[93] The faction of the Rochefort and Montmorency families similarly came together to fight King Louis the Fat. Gifts made for the soul of a sibling also attest to this enduring connection.[94]

Sometimes donations for siblings were made in tragic circumstances. In the mid-twelfth century, Bernard of Dangeau was involved in a dispute with a priory of St. Trinité of Vendôme over a winepress. The monks claimed that it belonged to them, but Bernard insisted that it was his. Bernard was so angry and certain of his claim that he seized the winepress and took it to his castle. Shortly after these events, tragedy struck. Bernard's brother, Thibaut, had a "sinister accident": he drowned in the Loir River. Bernard interpreted this event as a sign of God's displeasure over his behavior concerning the winepress. Besieged by guilt, he immediately conceded the property to the prior and swore that neither he nor his successors would make any claim to it. To commemorate his brother, Bernard agreed to pay a certain tax on the anniversary of Thibaut's death.[95] Bernard clearly did not regard Thibaut's death casually. Even if the monastic scribe tailored these events to make a point about those who usurped property from the church, Thibaut's role in the drama as the recipient of divine wrath indicates that a brother's death would have meaning for Bernard and compel him to resolve the matter.

About a hundred years before, in the mid-eleventh century, Peter of Montigny also experienced the tragic loss of a sibling—although in entirely different circumstances (see appendix, chart 9). His brother Guido became gravely ill. Peter asked Brother Tetbald, a monk from Marmoutier who was known as an experienced healer, to try to help his ailing brother.[96] Guido was transported to Marmoutier so he could receive the monk's ministrations, and Peter visited him there at least twice.[97] Sadly, although Guido lingered, he did

---

93. *Gesta Ambaziensium dominorum,* p. 91. Jacqueline Hoareau argues that sisters in particular could count on their brothers to defend their honor and to seek vengeance when their honor was impugned. Jacqueline Hoareau, "Meu d'amour naturelle... Défendre l'honneur de sa sœur à la fin du Moyen Âge."

94. When their brother Stephen died, Robert, Hubert, and their sister Ada ensured that property given for his soul was conveyed to the abbey of St. Père. *Père,* no. 153, p. 367.

95. *CTV,* vol. 2, no. 546, pp. 395–96.

96. Countess Adela also arranged medical care for her sickly son. LoPrete, "Adela of Blois as Mother and Countess," p. 318. So too did Queen Mathilda of Germany; Gilsdorf, *Queenship and Sanctity,* p. 109.

97. Other relatives, including an aunt, uncle, and cousins, also visited Guido as he lingered in the monastery. AD Loir-et-Cher, 16 H 118, no. 6.

not get better. As he approached death, he took the habit and was eventually buried in the monastery.[98] The death of Guido had a profound effect on Peter. He soon decided to build a stone chapel at the priory of Marmoutier at Villeberfol to honor his brother—a significant undertaking.[99] To realize this goal, Peter needed to muster his resources—including selling off properties to gain the revenues necessary to build the chapel. The chapel was constructed and then donated to Marmoutier to memorialize Guido. Peter, moreover, assumed responsibility for Guido's minor children. Clearly these two brothers were quite close. Peter commemorated his brother not only by making pious gifts but also by ensuring that his brother's memory lived on in the chapel that the monks would use to celebrate God.

Some brothers even elected to grow old together and they retired from the world as monks. As Hameric Chanard approached the end of his life and was plagued by infirmities, he petitioned to become a monk at St. Père where his brother was abbot. Hameric presumably lived out his days as he had begun them: in the company of his brother.[100] The bond between brothers, in some cases, even transcended death. Lisois of Amboise requested to be buried next to his brother.[101] But brothers will be brothers, even in the Middle Ages. When his brother made a gift to Marmoutier's priory of Daumeray, Gaufred "cared more for avarice than his brother's soul" and prevented the monks from claiming the donation for more than two years.[102]

The relationship with sisters was also important for the noble born. Recall the significant role that aunts and nieces serve in the romances of the day. Sisters' care for their siblings is revealed in their gifts. Donations made on behalf of siblings indicate that noblewomen maintained a bond with their brothers and sisters after marriage.[103] Consider the experience of Nivelon, the son of Warin. Sometime in the 1060s, Nivelon got into a dispute over a portion of a church with the monks of Marmoutier. After some negotiation, Nivelon agreed to sell his portion to the church. Significantly, this compromise was reached at the "court of [Nivelon's] sister." Nivelon's sister was married, but her position as wife and member of another family did not prevent her from playing a role in her brother's reconciliation with Marmoutier.[104] Moreover,

---

98. *CMPD,* no. 118, p. 112.

99. AD Loir-et-Cher, 16 H 118, no. 7.

100. *Père,* vol. 2, no. 162, pp. 373–74.

101. *Gesta Ambaziensium dominorum,* p. 100.

102. AD Maine-et-Loire, 39 H 2.

103. Mitchell, *Portraits of Medieval Women,* pp. 11–28.

104. Countess Adela played a similar role in reconciling her brother, Henry I, with the archbishop of Canterbury. LoPrete, *Adela of Blois,* pp. 170–78.

it was declared at this court that "none of [Nivelon's] kin would have a right to what he had sold to the monks." That such a declaration took place at his sister's court was hardly coincidental: as Nivelon's sister, she, and subsequently her heirs, could make legitimate claim to his property.[105] Ties to natal kin and property thus persisted after noblewomen joined another family through marriage. But so, too, did affection and concern. Sulpice of Amboise died while at his sister's home. He apparently had become ill while at the court of the count of Anjou.[106] He may have been staying at his sister Sibilla's home because it was convenient, but sibling affection could also have been a reason. Perhaps he and Sibilla had been particularly close as children. Perhaps Sulpice felt she was best able to nurse him back to health. Whatever his motivation, Sulpice chose to be with his sister in the final hours of his life. The bonds forged between brother and sister, in this case, seem to be as strong as those between brothers.

As well as their "legitimate" siblings, aristocrats also had relationships with their bastard brothers.[107] Families apparently did not attach any stigma to illegitimate birth. Fulcrad of Vendôme described himself as "son of Gauslen the Bastard" in transactions. Presumably if being a bastard were something that brought with it second-class status within the family or nullified a claim to property de facto, Fulcrad would not have designated himself so.[108] The charters also provide clear evidence that bastards did exercise some right to family holdings. In 1066 Haimeric made a gift to the church of Sts. Gervase and Protase of land. Witnessing the gift, and thereby providing his tacit approval, was Haimeric's bastard brother Gaufred.[109] A similar situation is found in the family of the lords of Dangeau. When Herlebald of Dangeau wished to donate half of the church associated with his castle, his brother Odo consented. But Rainard Brisard, Odo and Herlebald's bastard brother, witnessed this gift as well as a later gift by Odo.[110] What can be gleaned about the experience of bastards from these two accounts? Being a bastard did not mean you were excluded from transactions concerning family holdings. Indeed, like cousins

---

105. AD Loir-et-Cher, 16 H 118. See also *CMPD,* no. 123, pp. 115–16.

106. *Gesta Ambaziensium dominorum,* p. 96.

107. Interestingly, the charters contain no references to illegitimate female kin. Presumably there were girls who were bastards, but they either do not appear in the charters or are not designated as illegitimate in the sources.

108. AD Loir-et-Cher, 16 H 118. It may be that Fulcrad was also illegitimate himself or that in some charters he was referred to in a sort of shorthand as "Fulcrad Bastard." See AD Loir-et-Cher, 16 H 84.

109. AD Eure-et-Loir, H 2308.

110. AD Eure-et-Loir, H 2514. Hoareau finds that bastards played an important role in families seeking vengeance on behalf of women. Hoareau, "Meu d'amour naturelle," pp. 191–92.

and other kin, illegitimate children—the male children, at any rate—took part in the dispersal of family holdings. The noble born clearly knew their bastard siblings. In some cases, they may have been raised with them.

Did bastards get a share of family property? This is a more difficult question to answer. Clearly, they were thought to have a right to it since monks and relatives secured their consent to the alienation of property. But it is also possible they received some sort of property or support. A case brought before the bishop of Le Mans corroborates this view. At the very end of the eleventh century, a gift made by Gausbert Pirarius was disputed by "a certain youth named Gaufred, who says he was the bastard of Morin, Gausbert's brother."[111] Gaufred claimed that his father had accepted the property in exchange from Gausbert Pirarius. To settle the matter, the bishop examined many nobles, and only one was able to corroborate Gaufred's story. The others responded that the property had been held without a claim for over thirty years, proof that Morin had not held it and that Gaufred did not have a claim. Appearing to hear this resolution were Morin's cousin Bernard and "a certain woman who said she was the daughter of Gausbert" and hence Gaufred's cousin. This contestation reveals much about the experience of noble bastards. Even though illegitimate, Gaufred expected he would receive property from his father. Like legitimate progeny, this bastard believed he had a right to family land and took his case to court. The response of the bishop is also telling. He did not dismiss the case outright simply because Gaufred was a bastard. Rather he followed procedure and interrogated witnesses in an attempt to get to the bottom of the matter. As in resolutions concerning legitimate offspring, the bishop made sure that those who might have a potential interest in or claim to the property in question were present to hear the findings of the court. All in all, the case of Gaufred the bastard suggests that illegitimate progeny were part of the mainstream of family life. Like those born on the right side of the blanket, they could expect to inherit property from their fathers, and if some impediment to this inheritance appeared, they were able to have their complaint heard.

A dense web of family relationships and interconnections gave shape to the lives of elites. While their relationship with their siblings was but one strand of this intricately woven tapestry, it was an important one. The households

---

111. *CSVM* no. 74, pp. 54–55. For another example of bastards participating in family transactions, see AD Eure-et-Loir H 2280 and H 2275. The attitudes toward bastards in the lands of the Loire are found in other places in the medieval world. Lemesle finds that bastards in Maine both had a claim to family lands and inherited family property; *La société aristocratique dans le Haut-Maine,* pp. 121–22. Drell argues that bastards were treated little differently from their legitimate siblings in Salerno; *Kinship and Conquest,* p. 102.

of brothers and sisters were places that children were fostered, trained, and educated. Elites depended upon their siblings to help them reconcile with the church, contest alienations of property, or refute such contestations. Siblings could also be called upon for protection or defense in times of war. Brothers and sisters also argued, disputed, and ended up on different sides of political fences. But to suggest such interactions represent the totality of sibling relationships is clearly not accurate.

Interactions with Extended Kin

Relatives and extended kin played pragmatic roles in aristocratic family life. Cousins, for instance, assisted their relatives in many ways. In the first half of the eleventh century, Hamelin of Langeais murdered a cousin of the count of Anjou. The count was angered and sought justice for his kinsman's death. He called a *judicum* where it was decreed that Hamelin would forfeit all that he held from the count—a stiff penalty.[112] That the count could not let his cousin's murder go unpunished is an ethos that resonates with the early medieval practice of feuding.[113] Hamelin appealed to his kin to intercede on his behalf with the count. A compromise was reached, and instead of giving up all that he held from the count, Hamelin forfeited two mills. The tale of Hamelin and the count demonstrates how nobles depended upon their extended kin for support and intercession. Salomon of Lavardin helped out his cousin, Sulpice of Amboise, at a particularly critical moment. Caught up in the political fallout concerning control of the county of Anjou, Sulpice found himself imprisoned by the count of Anjou. Salomon rode to the rescue to sweep Sulpice to safety.[114] These two cases demonstrate how effective and dependable cousins could be when dealing with politically charged scenarios. In a time of political turbulence, nobles could count on their kin.

Elites also called on their kin to guarantee their gifts and pledges. Guarantors were charged with ensuring that the donor abided by the terms of the agreement, a responsibility reminiscent of what was expected of kin in the early Middle Ages. In the 1120s, Jean of Étampes gave to St. Jean-en-Vallée all that he held in fief. His brothers and cousins promised, along with Jean, to defend this donation against all claims. Moreover, the cousins acted as

---

112. *CTV,* vol. 1, no. 16, pp. 34–35.

113. Réal, "Représentations et pratiques des relations fraternelles," pp. 74–76, 88–93; Reuter, "Nobles and Others"; Aline G. Hornaday, "Early Medieval Kinship Structures as Social and Political Controls."

114. *Gesta Ambaziensium dominorum,* p. 93.

oath-swearers to the gift, meaning that they would be certain that Jean and his brothers stood by the agreement.[115] About ten years later, Ivo of Porte Morard fulfilled a similar function for his kinsman Chotard. Along with his wife, son, and nephew, Chotard had disputed St. Père's control of a measure of land. When this group of kin eventually agreed to abandon their claim, Ivo, "to augment the monks' security," gave his pledge that the property would remain uncontested and in their possession.[116] Chotard could clearly depend on Ivo to back up his own promise to the monks, thus leading to his reconciliation with the church. Nor was this the sole instance of these relatives providing their support to one another. When their kinsman died on Crusade, Ivo, Chotard, and his son Hubert collectively seized the property that he had given to the church before he left for the East. Eventually, Ivo and his cousins relinquished this property, as well as any future claim they might have, and together they swore to defend the gift against all unjust claims. Such ties between cousins complemented the close relationships between siblings, creating a dynamic family network.

Relationships with cousins could also stem from close ties to uncles. Indeed, Ivo of Porte Morard's relationship with his cousins seems to have been the result of the relationship he had with his uncle. Ivo's family was filled with crusading fervor sometime around 1120, and the charters from St. Père indicate that Ivo, his brother, and his cousin all made plans to go to the Holy Land.[117] Presumably to raise cash for his trip, Ivo sold property to the monks. To satisfy that the property was free from claim, Ivo's uncle and another cousin provided their pledges.[118] The aristocrats of the lands of the Loire could count upon a range of kin to come to their assistance in this way.

Gifts on Behalf of Kin

Gifts played an important role in medieval society. Pious donations, in particular, provide a dependable marker of which individuals were important enough to the medieval aristocracy to merit benefaction. Aristocrats commonly made gifts for their relatives. Indeed, 20 percent of gifts where the recipient of spiritual benefits of the donation was made clear were made for the health of souls of "relatives." This concern for the spiritual well-being of

---

115. *Jean,* no. 36, pp. 22–23.
116. *Père,* vol. 2, no. 12, p. 410.
117. While the charters indicate that Ivo and his brother Henry had intended to go to Jerusalem, there is no evidence to suggest that they actually went.
118. *Père,* vol. 2, no. 127, p. 349.

"relatives" was not newly manifest in the twelfth century. Rather, making a donation on behalf of "relatives" was a practice that carried over from previous centuries. The continuity of this practice affirms that no radical shift or transformation in family structure took place in the eleventh century.

Benefactions for relations could be straightforward, such as when, around 1070, Mahild of Alluyes donated land next to the cemetery of the church of St. Germain for the benefit of her soul as well as the souls of her two husbands, William and Geoffrey, and her children.[119] She also specified that the gift provide for the parents of her husbands, her affinal kin. In this single grant, Mahild took care of the souls of her immediate and extended family that spanned at least three generations and included affinal as well as nuclear kin.

Such gifts go beyond pro forma bequests for kin and demonstrate a genuine concern for the immortal souls of relatives—living and deceased. This concern is made particularly clear in the restoration of ecclesiastical property. Starting in the middle of the eleventh century, churchmen warned nobles that their possession of churches, tithes, and other ecclesiastical appurtenances was evil and went against God. Throughout the century, church councils decreed that lay possession of ecclesiastical property would result in anathema and excommunication.[120] The warnings and threats of eternal damnation offered by the clergy eventually penetrated the consciousness of the aristocracy, and they restored churches and tithes to the church.[121] In his

---

119. *Père,* vol. 1, no. 67, p. 193.

120. In 1056 the church council held at Toulouse declared that possession of churches by the laity was unjust and characterized lay possession of such holdings as usurpation. Four years later, another church council met at Tours and reaffirmed the spirit of the prohibitions passed at Toulouse. The Council at Clermont in 1095 ruled against secular possession of tithes and declared that if nobles or their heirs usurped church property or contested donations, they would be denied the sacred offices. *Sacrorum Consiliorum nova et amplissima collectio,* vol. 19, pp. 847–50; vol. 20, pp. 816–19. These proclamations were brought home to the aristocracy of the lands of the Loire. For example, Bishop Ivo of Chartres placed Nivelon and Ursio of Fréteval under divine interdiction for their "malefactions" against the abbey of St. Trinité of Vendôme sometime between 1102 and 1115. See also *Regesta Pontificum Romanorum ab condita ecclesia ad annum post Christum natum 1198,* vol. 1, p. 797. For the impact of reform on the lands of the Loire, see Foulon, *Église et réforme au Moyen Âge,* pp. 64–67, 125–36, 173–89, 494–501.

121. Lester Little, *Benedictine Maledictions,* pp. 20–26, 131–43. For discussion of ecclesiastical restorations, see André Chédeville, "Les restitutions d'églises en faveur de l'abbaye de Saint-Vincent"; William Ziezulewicz, "'Restored' Churches in the Fisc of St. Florent de Saumur (1021–1118)." C. Van de Kieft examines one of these "private churches" to illustrate the various rights that the lay patron—in this case, Count Geoffrey Martel of Anjou—exercised over a church associated with the abbey of St. Trinité of Vendôme. C. Van de Kieft, "Une église privée de l'abbaye de la Trinité de Vendôme au XIe siècle." For the impact of the Gregorian reform movement on the aristocracy, see Wollasch, "Parenté noble et monachisme réformateur" and Jean-Hervé Foulon, "Stratégies lignagères et réforme ecclésiastique."

restoration of ecclesiastical property, Simon of Islou-sur-Dampierre stated, "I have listened to the words of many wise men, which God has shown me to be true, namely that I realize that it is unjust for the laity and against the well-being of their souls for them to hold the property of the church which belongs to the servants of the church."[122] A common feature of such restorations was the specification that the gift benefit the relatives of the donor as well as the donor himself or herself. While the twelfth-century nobility recognized their possession of churches and the like as against God's law, their ancestors, from whom many inherited or received such property, had not. So when restoring ecclesiastical property, donors took care to ensure that their relatives' souls were redeemed. In 1107, for instance, Denis Pagan gave his half of a church not only for the good of his soul but also for the benefit of his ancestors "from whom he possessed this inheritance."[123] The fact that elites took care to provide for the souls of their ancestors and relatives who they believed had held church property against God's law and whom they could envisage "burning in the fires of damnation" shows concern about extended family even though the donor might never have met or known the relatives in question. Long-dead relatives were certainly removed from the daily lives of medieval elites, but these kin mattered to noblemen and noblewomen. Such ties through blood and property were important enough for the noble born to merit salvation through pious gifts or restorations.

Nobles had many reasons for seeking association with their relatives. Around 950, Teduin gave the monks of St. Père alods (property not bound by feudal obligation) that he held by right through his mother (*ex jure materno*) to remit the sins of his father, his mother, and his relatives.[124] The donation acknowledged Teduin's descent from a broad kin group and demonstrated his concern for the souls of his extended family as well as those of his parents. But it also reinforced how and from whom Teduin received his land. Here family connections and claims to land intersected. Another tenth-century act reflects a similar practice. In 965 Teodfred generously gave a church to St. Père. His lord, Count Walter of Dreux, affirmed the gift. Both Teodfred and Walter specified that the gift of the church was on behalf of the souls of their relatives. Count Walter wanted the gift, in particular, to benefit the soul of his direct predecessor, Count Landric.[125] Walter had a special reason for calling attention to his relationship with this count. Walter did not gain the

---

122. *Père,* vol. 2, no. 61, pp. 565–66.
123. *Père,* vol. 2, no. 53, pp. 509–10.
124. *Père,* vol. 1, no. 6, pp. 89–90.
125. *Père,* vol. 1, no. 1, pp. 55–56.

county of Dreux from his own family. Rather it came to him through his marriage to Landric's daughter. By using the general *parentes* to describe the kin from whom he made the gift, Walter accomplished two goals: he highlighted his association with the comital family and provided for the souls of his own extended kin.

As the gift by Count Walter of Dreux suggests, donations for the souls of extended kin could be triggered by a desire to reinforce connection to a particular relative or kin group. Such was the case for Hugh and Richeld of Château-Vallière. The second half of the eleventh century was a period of warfare between the counts of Blois-Chartres and Anjou. Just as the hostilities began, this couple made a gift for the souls of their ancestors and specified that their names be recorded in the monks' martyrology.[126] Concerned with what the results might be of the wars between the counts, Hugh and Richeld took steps to ensure the spiritual well-being of their immediate and extended family, specifically Richeld's parents, from whom they had inherited the lordship. But the gift—particularly the writing down of their names in the martyrology—served an additional purpose. Recording the names of their predecessors in the martyrology affirmed the relationship between this couple and their children and the previous lords, thus providing proof of their legitimate claim to the land. Hugh and Richeld's children witnessed the charter. Their son, Hugh, was still a small boy, however. This couple's actions were clearly motivated by a desire to be sure that their own and their young children's claim to the lordship would go unchallenged. As they knew well, aggressions between these two counts could—and did— have drastic consequences for the elites of the region. Lordships, castles, and property changed hands. By making a gift that recorded their relationship to their ancestors, this couple effectively sought to ensure their continued possession of family lands.

As it turned out, Hugh and Richeld's concern was well founded for Hugh was taken captive and held in Blois by the count of Chartres.[127] While the charter does not provide the details surrounding Hugh's imprisonment, it does indicate that Richeld intended to visit him there, perhaps to negotiate the terms of his release. Before she left the Vendômois, however, Richeld first stopped at the abbey of St. Trinité. There she confirmed all of the gifts that

---

126. *CTV,* vol. 1, no. 242, pp. 382–85. Hugh sought further association with the monks by requesting to be buried with them.

127. Hugh's holdings were located in the Vendômois, which makes it likely that he was fighting for the Angevins and captured by the Chartrain side. This would account for his imprisonment in Blois, one of the strongholds of the counts of Chartres.

had been made previously to the monks from her husband's lands. Then she made her own gift from "those properties which she held from her relatives, by right of inheritance" *(jure patrimonium).*[128] Richeld was clearly concerned about her husband. Thus prompted, she secured the support of the monks and God. By making her gift and invoking her connection to relatives, she demonstrated publicly her legitimate possession of the property and reiterated her relationship to the land. Donations were made in public in front of witnesses, including Richeld's brother-in-law, the monks, the abbot, and several local noblemen. Facing a time of hardship and political upheaval, Richeld reminded friend and foe of her connection to her relatives and her right—and her children's right—to these lands. Aristocrats from the tenth through the twelfth century sought association with their extended kin for a variety of reasons. This broad configuration of kin continued as a prominent feature of aristocratic family life through the eleventh and twelfth centuries.

Conclusion

Sometime between 1119 and 1128, young Simon Turre was attending the court of Count Thibaut IV of Chartres. During this visit, Simon was struck down by the "gravest and incurable weakness." Simon lingered for many days, confined to his bed, in the house of his sister Isabel and his brother-in-law, William Ansold. Time passed, and Simon did not improve, so he appealed to the monks of St. Père for aid and even took refuge with them—perhaps in the hopes that their ministrations, spiritual and physical, might help him. To provide for his support, this young nobleman gave land that he held through inheritance. William and Isabel were reluctant to allow the property to be transferred to the monks, however. Count Thibaut and Andre of Baudement, the count's seneschal *and* Simon's kinsman, brought their influence to bear, and this couple dismissed their claim to the property.[129]

Simon died two years later, and all the parties with an interest in the land (William and Isabel as well as the kin from whom Simon held the land in fief plus the count and his seneschal) appeared before the bishop of Chartres to confirm the original grant and abandon their claim to it. Joining their parents in consenting were William and Isabel's "small sons." André of Baudement secured the consent of "all of Simon's relatives" (*propinqui*) and resolved a conflict with another of Simon's kinsmen, who was reticent to have the donated properties pass from family control.

---

128. *CTV,* vol. 2, no. 305, pp. 10–11.
129. *Père,* vol. 2, no. 53, pp. 446–49.

Simon's sad tale encapsulates much about family life for the aristocrats of the lands of the Loire. For one thing, Simon was staying with his sister while doing business with the count, indicating that siblings maintained contact with each other as adults. Isabel's experience, in particular, refutes the long-held notion that women severed ties to their natal family upon marriage. When Simon became ill, it was his sister who likely took care of him until he moved to the monastery. André of Baudement also acted on his cousin's behalf, making sure that objections to his gift were smoothed over. Clearly these kin were unable or unwilling to oppose their powerful kinsman, who could bring the authority of his office and his association with the count to bear on uncooperative parties.

Ironically, Simon's death allows a glimpse into life among the medieval elite. His family did everything in their power to restore him to health. While his sister and brother-in-law initially resisted the alienation of Simon's inheritance, after his death they willingly conceded the gift and even donated some of their own property to benefit Simon's soul. His lingering illness and eventual death caused sadness among Simon's family and friends, who did what they could to ease his suffering and provide for his care. Simon's experiences demonstrate that the ties of kinship were inclusive and broadly configured among the nobility of the Loire region. When combined with the description of life at Queen Mathilda's court quoted at the outset of this chapter, a family life based on care and affection emerges. Perhaps like Queen Mathilda's grandchildren, Simon and Isabel had cavorted around the dinner table as children. As an adult, then, Simon could count upon his family—immediate and extended—to come to his aid and support. Simon's life and the other lives analyzed here indicate that family patterns were based on the idea of inclusiveness.

The experiences relayed thus far are gleaned from a wide range and variety of noble families. Let us now turn our attention to one kindred group for a more in-depth examination of what family life was like for members of one particular collective of kin.

CHAPTER 3

Aristocratic Family Life Writ Small

The Fréteval, Mondoubleau, and Dives Kindred

Living to the west of the Chartrain, according to Bernard of Angers, was a nobleman who had all anyone could ask for: status, wealth, happiness, a beloved spouse, and many children to whose care and upbringing he devoted his life. Sadly, this happy life did not remain untouched by tragedy, for one by one his children died. Struck through with profound grief and sadness, this father withdrew completely into himself. When word of the death of the last remaining child reached relatives and neighbors, they rushed to this couple's side to provide what comfort they could. But the parents were beyond comfort and seemed to slide more deeply into their grief. Finally, the gathered kin and friends suggested that they all pray to St. Foy for a miracle. In the midst of their collective entreaty, the boy's lifeless body began to breathe and was restored to life.[1]

With the exception of this episode of a miraculous raising-from-the-dead, the families of the lords of Fréteval and Mondoubleau and the descendants of Fulcher Dives experienced family life in much the same way as Bernard of Angers described for this unnamed noble family.[2] The lives of these men

---

1. Bernard of Angers, *The Book of St. Foy,* p. 239.

2. The Fréteval, Mondoubleau, and Dives kindred consists of approximately two hundred individuals over the span of nearly two centuries. In other words, while the terms "kindred" and "family" may be used, this is a large sample of elites.

and women were drawn together through birth, marriage, and death. Family gathered to mourn the dead, but they also came together to celebrate life and provide assistance and support to their kin.

The goal of this chapter is to tease out the threads that connected each of these families, to understand how individual lives were interwoven, and to examine relationships between family members. The experiences of those of the Fréteval-Mondoubleau-Dives kindred will also test the key hypotheses offered by scholars concerning the shape, ethos, and inner workings of the medieval aristocratic family by asking questions such as: Did families privilege one line or individual to the detriment of others? Were extended kin effectively pruned from the family tree? Were women and younger sons seen as extraneous and relegated to powerlessness? Discussion will begin with an examination of each family's origins and how they came to be related to each other. Focus will then shift to consideration of individual connections and relationships among the members of the kindred.

Families and Alliances

The families that made up the Fréteval-Mondoubleau-Dives kindred came from roots planted along the banks of the Loire in the first third of the eleventh century (see map 1). The men and women who founded these families, moreover, established dynasties that would control these territories far into the thirteenth century. Marriages between these families and the resultant births combined with existing members to create a dense and complex web of family relationships (see appendix, chart 7). Because the Fréteval family in many ways is the center from which these interconnections radiate, it provides the starting point for analysis.

The name Fréteval derives from the Latin *fracta valles,* meaning "broken valley." The chateau at Fréteval is indeed situated upon a rocky promontory overlooking the Loir River valley below. Nivelon I of Fréteval was a dedicated supporter of the count of Chartres during his wars with the Angevins. In appreciation for his service, Nivelon was granted a lordship situated between two emerging comital powers. As a result, the Fréteval lords were connected to the neighboring counts of Vendôme, while sustaining their allegiance to the Chartrain comital house. They also cultivated ties with other elite families to their south. In 1033 Nivelon attended the court of the count of Vendôme along with Odo of Mondoubleau, Fulcher Dives, Ingelbald Brito, and Nithard of Montoire.[3]

---

3. *CTV,* vol. 1, no. 10, pp. 25–26.

To solidify and expand their power, the scions of these families allied themselves through marriage. Nivelon's two sons married daughters of Odo Dubellus of Mondoubleau, and Odo himself was married to the daughter of Nithard of Montoire. Some connections had already been forged by the time of this transaction, for Fulcher Dives was Odo's maternal grandfather and Ingelbald Brito was Odo's cousin by marriage (see appendix, charts 8, 9, and 10). The insertion of the Frétevals into these alliances put in place kinship ties that defined these families for generations to come.

In spite of their interests in the Vendômois, Nivelon I's son, Lord Fulcher of Fréteval, chose to marry a woman from an important family of the Chartrain: Hildeberg Gouet, the daughter of William I Gouet and Mahild of Alluyes. Like the Frétevals, the Alluyes-Gouet family was bound through vassalage to the counts of Chartres.[4] Alliance through the marriage of their children appealed to these comrades-in-arms. The match benefited the lords of Fréteval, for Hildeberg's family was well established in the area, which would have been important to a recently established lord. Hildeberg's continued use of her natal cognomen, Gouet, throughout her marriage confirms the importance of this union to the family and this noblewoman's lineage.[5] The patriline did not dominate in this family.[6]

The next generation of the Fréteval family was pivotal for the expansion of this noble house (see appendix, chart 8). Fulcher and Hildeberg married their children to several of the most prominent families of the Chartrain, again seeking alliances north of the Loire. Nivelon II, their eldest son,[7] married Eustachia, who seems to have come from a comital or vicecomital family (perhaps that of Dammartin). The next son, Hamelin, married the widow of the lord of Montigny, a seigneurial family that had its roots in the Carolingian era, which counted a treasurer for the canons at Tours and a provisor for

---

4. In 1024, for example, Nivelon witnessed a gift by Count Odo II to Walter. *Père,* vol. 1, no. 5, pp. 96–97.

5. *CMPD,* no. 9, pp. 10–11. Association with the Gouet line continued. Early in the twelfth century, Fulcher's son Nivelon II and his grandson Ursio witnessed a gift by Hildeberg's brother William Gouet II and his family to the monastery of St. Père of Chartres. See *Père,* vol. 2, no. 8, pp. 475–76. Around 1117, Nivelon II and Ursio witnessed for William Gouet II concerning the disposition of property at Montmirail. See *Tiron,* vol. 1, no. 12, p. 27. The relationship founded in the eleventh century by two brothers-in-arms continued into the second half of the twelfth century as Lord Nivelon II, his son Ursio, and William Gouet III witnessed Count Thibaut IV's resolution of a dispute that he had with St. Trinité over land at Boisseau. AD Eure-et-Loir, H 2275.

6. See Constance B. Bouchard, "Patterns of Women's Names in Royal Lineages," and "The Migration of Women's Names"; David Herlihy, "Land, Family and Women in Continental Europe, 701–1200." For a "woman's view" of patrilineage, see Bouchard, "Family Structure and Family Consciousness among the Aristocracy in the Ninth through Eleventh Centuries."

7. *CTV* vol. 2, no. 330, pp. 45–46 indicates Nivelon II was the eldest son of Fulcher.

the count of Chartres among its members. Fulcher and Hildeberg's daughter Agnes made a prestigious match with the Viscount Hugh II of Châteaudun and, after she married, Agnes adopted the name "Comitissa" as a way of underscoring her connection to this highly placed family. Another daughter, Hildeberg, was named for her mother, thereby providing a connection to the Alluyes-Gouets. She married a local lord, Bernard of La Ferté.[8] Bernard's kin had long been associates of the Fréteval family. Moreover, the La Fertés held land with a Fréteval relative, Hamelin of Langeais, making it likely that these kin recommended Bernard as a suitable match for a Fréteval daughter.[9] Another daughter, Pagana, married another local lord, Pagan of Frouville.

Like their Fréteval cousins, the seigneurial family at Mondoubleau was establishing and extending its power from 1020 to 1050 (see appendix, chart 10). Unlike the Frétevals, the lords of Mondoubleau held property in the county of Maine and owed allegiance to that count as well as the count of Chartres.[10] The house of Mondoubleau was founded by Hugh, who was married to Adela, the daughter of Fulcher Dives of Vendôme and Adela of Bezai.[11] "Mondoubleau" derives from the Latin *Mons Dublellus,* and this lordship,

---

8. *CSVM,* nos. 181 and 182, pp. 112–14. The founder of the La Ferté family was Gauslen Norman, whose cognomen suggests he originally came from Normandy. Two of his several sons, Hugh and Bernard, appear prominently in the charters. Holdings at Tuffé linked the La Ferté and Mondoubleau families. Early in the eleventh century, Hugh of Mondoubleau gave all that he held in Tuffé to found the church of St. Mary there. But the Mondoubleau family continued to hold land near or in Tuffé, for Hugh's granddaughter Helvisa-Adierna and her husband Hamelin of Langeais gave additional properties there later in the eleventh century. Nearly a century after the original gift had been made, the lords of Mondoubleau continued to assert their rights over Tuffé, for early in the twelfth century, Pagan of Mondoubleau (Helvisa-Adierna's son from her first marriage) had to recognize that his right over the powers of the *ban,* or rights of lordship over Tuffé, was unjust: *CSVM,* no. 192, p. 121. The lords of La Ferté exercised some right to Tuffé—they may have held it in fief from the lords of Mondoubleau, for Hugh of La Ferté approved the gift made by Hamelin and Helvisa-Adierna (no. 181). Hugh's brother, Bernard La Ferté (who eventually married Hildeberg, the daughter of Fulcher of Fréteval), contested what his brother had given. He was able to come to a reconciliation with the monks, however (no. 182) and confirmed the gift. These associations make it likely that the Mondoubleau relatives may have thought him a suitable husband for one of Fulcher of Fréteval's daughters.

9. Pierre Petot suggests that in the region of the Touraine, family played an important role in the marriage and guardianship of children. In particular he notes that it was the family, not the feudal lord, who determined suitable mates and attributes this to the strength of family in the lands of the Loire. Pierre Petot, "Le mariage des vassales."

10. Lemesle, *La société aristocratique dans le Haut-Maine,* pp. 238–40.

11. The Mondoubleau family figures in Barthélemy's study of the Vendômois and Lemesle's analysis of the aristocracy of Maine. They reach somewhat different conclusions about this family, however. Barthélemy, *La société dans le comté de Vendôme,* pp. 340–42, 345–47, 571–74; Lemesle, *La société aristocratique dans le Haut-Maine,* pp. 123 and 236–42. For discussion of Mondoubleau patronage of St. Trinité of Vendôme, see Penelope Johnson, *Prayer, Patronage and Power,* pp. 86, 88, 90, and 192.

like that of Fréteval, was situated on a hill overlooking a river. Hugh was succeeded as lord by his son Odo, who ruled the seigneury from about 1040 to 1056. The charters provide a glimpse into Odo's personality, for in documenting the resolution of a conflict this sometime-generous donor to the church was described as "more concerned about money than his soul, for his concession accepted six pounds from Poitiers from the Lord Abbot Odric."[12]

Odo died while his son, Hugh, was still a child. Until Hugh came of age, the lordship was under the supervision of Odo's brother. Sadly, young Hugh died shortly after assuming the lordship for himself. After his death, Hugh's sister, Helvisa-Adierna, and her husband Hamelin of Langeais inherited the lordship of Mondoubleau (see map 2). By the end of the eleventh century, Pagan, Helvisa-Adierna's child from her first marriage to a son of the house of Fréteval, had assumed control. Pagan, who was named for his father, continued to be connected to a wide network of kin. Pagan was married and had two daughters who would eventually inherit the lordship. One daughter, Guitberg, married Bartholomew of Vendôme, and they had only one child, a daughter.[13] Pagan's other daughter, Helvisa (who was clearly named for her grandmother), married the viscount of Châteaudun, and her son Pagan eventually succeeded his grandfather as lord of Mondoubleau (see appendix, chart 11).

The Dives family appears to have been established in the Vendômois earlier than their Fréteval or Mondoubleau kin (see appendix, charts 9 and 11). Fulcher Dives, the founder of this family, came from the area around Vendôme and was associated with the counts of Vendôme early in the eleventh century.[14] Fulcher married Adela of Bezai, a woman of some significance and considerable property. Her brother was Robert, lord of Moncontour located

---

12. *CTV*, vol. 1, no. 74, pp. 135–37.

13. She and her husband witnessed and participated in one of her father's grants. AD Loir-et-Cher, 16 H 105. See also *CMPD*, no. 79, pp. 62–63. Sometime around 1100, Pagan witnessed a gift to Marmoutier made by his cousin Nivelon II of Fréteval. Appearing with Pagan was his son-in-law, Bartholomew of Vendôme. Bartholomew of Vendôme was the grandson of Ingelbald Brito and Domitilla. Bartholomew's father was Geoffrey Pagan of Vendôme, and he had three brothers (Vulgrin, Geoffrey, and Ingelbald) and a sister, Maria.

14. It has been assumed that "Dives" referred to Fulcher's wealth ("Dives" is Latin for wealth). It could also be a geographic cognomen, as there is a region in southern Anjou called "Dives." Given that many of the families traced their origins back to the Touraine, "Dives" could just as easily reference where Fulcher came from as opposed to his wealth. Fulcher Dives and his kin have been studied by other scholars as well, although with slight differences in the reckoning of their genealogy. Barthélemy, *La société dans le comté de Vendôme*, pp. 308–11; White, *Custom, Kinship and Gifts to Saints*, pp. 58–71; Fanning, "From *Miles* to *Episcopus*," 9–30; "Les origines familiales de Vulgrin," 243–55; Johnson, *Prayer, Patronage and Power*, pp. 44, 78–79, 88.

to the southwest of Vendôme, an indicator that Adela too had her origins close to Vendôme. This couple was an important patron of the newly established abbey of St. Trinité of Vendôme. Adela was a particularly generous patron and gave many properties to these monks.

Fulcher and Adela had four children, and the lives of two are traceable from the charters. Fulcher II adopted the surname of "Turre" or "de Turre," perhaps after a stone tower erected on his property, and he succeeded to many of his parents' holdings as well as control of the family seat in or near Vendôme. He married Hildiard, about whom little is known, and had several children. The lives and descendants of three of these offspring are recoverable, and their interactions will be discussed below. Fulcher II's sister, Adela, married Hugh of Mondoubleau, and it was from this union that all future lords of Mondoubleau sprang. The Dives kindred was vast and connected to many of the influential families of the Vendômois and mid-Loire region.

Politics and marriage connected the Fréteval, Mondoubleau, and Dives families. Now that we know the contours of these families, what roles did specific kin play in the lives of these elites? How did family shape and affect the lives of these noble-born men and women?

Family Life in the Eleventh Century

Parents and Siblings

Interactions with immediate family were important to the Dives family. Fulcher II Turre was unusually close to his daughter Domitilla's family. Domitilla was married to Ingelbald Brito around 1060, and they had several children.[15] Recall that Ingelbald came from outside the region and that this marriage provided him with an extensive and well-placed network of local kin. Domitilla and her family were "from the castle of Vendôme," and they made gifts at her father's court.[16] One of Ingelbald and Domitilla's sons, Vulgrin, frequently appeared with his grandfather as a witness to various transactions between 1084 and 1086. While it is difficult to establish the date of Vulgrin's birth, it is certainly possible that he was installed at his grandfather's court where he could be schooled in the ways of power and lordship. Instead of fostering Vulgrin with an uncle, his parents may have elected to send him to his grandfather. Fulcher was a prominent man, well respected by cloister

---

15. Although Domitilla started life as Hildiard, she took on the name "Domitilla" as an adult. Since Domitilla was evidently the name she preferred, I refer to her by this name. For discussion of the reasons behind her adoption of this name, see chapter 7.

16. *CTV*, vol. 1, no. 272, pp. 423–24.

and castle, as evident in his role as counselor to those involved in disputes.[17] Who was better able to prepare Vulgrin to assume control of his territorial and political responsibilities as a member of the Dives clan than his experienced, powerful, and well-respected grandsire?

Like other elites, those of the Fréteval-Mondoubleau-Dives kindred were close to their siblings as both children and adults. Sometime around 1040, the Fréteval family was forced to defend their lordship, for in spite of Nivelon I's associations with Countess Agnes of Vendôme, the count of Anjou's sister, her brother attacked Fréteval. Nivelon's eldest son, Pagan, died defending his home. A younger son, Fulcher, left the spiritual life and became the lord of Fréteval.[18] Fulcher was successful in protecting the lordship and depended upon his surviving brothers for support. Early in his tenure as lord, Fulcher reached an agreement with the monks of Marmoutier over what he held in Chamars. When his father, Nivelon, had been lord, the monks charged that he had taken and occupied part of the *burgus* of this village. Fulcher recognized that he held this property unjustly and transferred it to the monks. His two brothers, Girard and Nivelon Pagan, approved the gift and swore that it should be in the control of the monks. Even though all had established their own households, ties and claims to the patrimony bound these siblings. Fulcher could count on his brothers to assist in his effort to make peace with the monks. In addition to his legitimate siblings, Fulcher's bastard brother Milo witnessed the gift as well (thereby giving his tacit consent). Milo was still regarded as part of the family with some claim to property—like the bastard son of Morin discussed in the previous chapter. The Frétevals did not adhere to a linear configuration of family, but rather they embraced the claims of all siblings, legitimate and illegitimate, and included them in their family life.[19]

Cooperation and interaction among Fréteval siblings continued into the next generation. When sometime between 1072 and 1084 their sire (Fulcher) wished to retire from the secular life, he made a gift to Marmoutier at his

---

17. *CTV,* vol. 1, no. 255, pp. 403–4; vol. 1, no. 179, 309–10; vol. 1, no. 218, pp. 350–52; vol. 2, no. 329, pp. 43–45; vol. 2, no. 302, pp. 7–9.

18. *Père,* vol. 1, no. 1, pp. 24–25. It was somewhat unusual for children to leave the church once they had joined the clerical order. Fulcher's parents may have felt uneasy about this, since both made generous gifts to St. Père. Ermengard gave jewelry and all that pertained to the church of St. Lubin to the monks. Fulcher affirmed his wife's gift but asked that he be able to enjoy the use of them while he lived. He requested to become a monk and promised that the lands would then revert to the monks. AD Eure-et-Loir, H 570. For a somewhat similar case, see Fanning, "From *Miles* to *Episcopus.*"

19. Milo and Hugh also witnessed *CMPD,* no. 9, pp. 10–11. For a discussion of bastards, see Barthélemy, *La société dans le comté de Vendôme,* pp. 536–40.

house at Chartres and was allowed to join the order. His children, Nivelon, Hamelin, Comitissa, and Pagana, consented to the act.[20] These brothers and sisters continued their support of their brother as Nivelon II succeeded their father as lord. When Nivelon II abandoned rights to land and a mill, his brother-in-law Viscount Hugh II of Châteaudun witnessed the agreement for him.[21] But siblings did more than consent to the alienation of property. Hugh's wife, Comitissa, played an important role in repairing her brother's relationship with the monks of Marmoutier.

Nivelon II and the monks were at odds over who had certain rights to construct dwellings for craftsmen and merchants at Francheville (a newly established settlement), as well as who controlled certain dues owed by these people. "Through the counsel and assent of his [Nivelon's] sister Comitissa," an agreement was reached.[22] Comitissa acted as envoy between her brother and the monks. Noblewomen were frequently called upon to act as mediators between the clergy and their male kin. As benefactors and defenders of the church, viscountesses enjoyed the friendship of the monks.[23] Nivelon clearly respected his sister since he called upon her for assistance and then acted on her counsel to resolve things with the monks. The common experiences of childhood could forge important relationships between siblings that lasted for the remainder of their lives.

As lord of Fréteval, Nivelon II seems to have had a special need for such intercession since his interactions with the local ecclesiastical houses were particularly contentious. In June of 1087, Nivelon was in trouble with the monks of St. Trinité of Vendôme. They accused him of falsely claiming land from them. The language of the charter is quite strong and depicts Nivelon as an instrument of the devil sent to torment the monks. The dispute was settled, however, when the monks paid Nivelon a cash gift.[24] The settlement was arranged at the castle of Montigny with the consent of Nivelon's wife, Eustachia, and all of his siblings. But why would a lord of Fréteval settle a dispute at Montigny? Moreover, why had all of the Fréteval siblings congregated there? To witness the marriage of Hamelin to Adela of

---

20. *CMPD,* no. 86, p. 76. Hildeberg, Fulcher's wife, must have predeceased him since she does not appear in the charter. As his wife, she would be required to give her consent in order for him to become a monk.

21. *MB,* no. 46, pp. 58–59.

22. AD Loir-et-Cher, 16 H 105. See also *MB,* no. 44, pp. 56–57. The interactions of the Fréteval siblings, as well as of their Mondoubleau and Dives kin, seem to resemble what Isabelle Réal has found among the elites of the Frankish world. Réal, "Représentations et pratiques des relations fraternelles."

23. For further discussion of this, see chapter 7.

24. *CTV,* vol. 2, no. 330, pp. 45–46.

Montigny.[25] Maybe Hamelin, like Comitissa, had persuaded his brother to resolve his conflict with the monks in order to create peace in time for the celebration of his marriage. Perhaps Hamelin's bride, Adela, insisted that her future brother-in-law resolve his issues with the monks. There are many possible scenarios to account for Nivelon's accord. But at the very least, the charter records continued association and gathering of siblings throughout their lives, to witness marriages, deaths, and to help each other atone for their actions and make peace with God's earthly representatives, just as Bernard of Angers described in the account of noble family life that opens this chapter.

Although he married into the Montigny family, Hamelin continued to act very much as a Fréteval.[26] Even while lord of Montigny, Hamelin's descent from the house of Fréteval was emphasized, and he was referred to as "Lord Hamelin of Montigny, the son of Fulcher, son of Nivelon." Hamelin felt no need to identify exclusively with his newly acquired lordship. It has been argued that men who married heiresses associated themselves with their wife's family to justify their control of the lordship and their status as lord.[27] Hamelin clearly experienced no compunction to do so. Like his brother, Hamelin also remained close to his siblings. His nephew Robert Flagellus (his sister Pagana's son) witnessed Hamelin's resolution with the monks. This nephew seems to have been in residence at Montigny for he witnessed later confirmations of this grant.

Perhaps to atone for his frequent usurpations and other bad behavior toward the church, Nivelon joined the First Crusade. In 1096 he began making preparations and, like many other crusaders, Nivelon felt the need to make gifts for his soul before leaving on the perilous journey east.[28] A variety of kin appear in these acts, but most interestingly were his sister Hildeberg's sons. As lord of Fréteval, Nivelon held extensive rights to the forest of the

---

25. This charter from 1087 is the earliest evidence of the marriage of Hamelin and Adela. The charters after this date portray Hamelin and Adela as lords of Montigny. Adela's daughter from her first marriage, Agnes, witnessed the grant as well. She, as her mother's heir, could have some claim on the property of the Fréteval family.

26. Hamelin witnessed his brother's abandonment of his right to property in Fridigmantellum in the presence of the count and countess of Blois-Chartres at Chartres. See AD Loir-et-Cher, 16 H 105. Like his brother and father, Hamelin acted violently toward the church. Specifically, the monks of Marmoutier stated that he had forcefully evicted some of the monk's men from the mill at Matresemita. *CMPD,* no. 61, pp. 53–54.

27. Duby, "Youth in Aristocratic Society," pp. 101–3.

28. For a discussion of the First Crusaders in general, see Jonathan Riley-Smith, *The First Crusaders, 1095–1131,* pp. 106–43. For Nivelon's personal experience, see pp. 62, 71–72, 88, 112–15, 122, 138, and 215.

Long Forest. Nivelon's lords, Count Stephen and Countess Adela, had made extensive gifts from their holdings in this forest to the monks of Marmoutier. Yet the lords of Fréteval were reluctant to allow this property to pass from their possession. Before he departed for Jerusalem, however, Nivelon granted what he controlled in these woods, with the consent of his minor son Ursio.[29] In return for his consent, Ursio received a scarlet tunic. Nivelon's sister Hildeberg of La Ferté's sons also witnessed on his behalf. The youngest son, Bernard, and Ursio were of a similar age since Bernard received a countergift of a pair of red shoes for his consent. Nivelon's relationship with the La Ferté family seems to have been close. Bernard frequently witnessed for his uncle and may have been living with Nivelon and his family.[30]

Like their kinsman Peter of Montigny (see chapter 2), other men and women of the Fréteval-Mondoubleau-Dives kindred arranged commemoration for their brothers and sisters. Young Hugh of Mondoubleau played a special part in the life of his sister, Helvisa-Adierna. Shortly after his death, Helvisa-Adierna and her husband Hamelin of Langeais made a gift to the monks of St. Vincent of Le Mans. We know from the charter that Hugh was buried in the cloister of the monks, and his sister and her family gave all that they held from the churches of St. Mary of Tuffé and St. Mary of Mondoubleau to commemorate him.[31] This was a very generous gift and an important one. The donation certainly reflected concern for the soul of Helvisa-Adierna's young brother, but it also reinforced the connection that this family had with young Hugh—for they succeeded him as the lords of Mondoubleau.[32] Commemoration in this case served a double purpose: to provide for the spiritual health of a loved one and to reinforce the connection between the new lords and the previous one.

The relationship between Hugh and Helvisa-Adierna's father, Odo, and his brother, Hugh of Mondoubleau, was apparently also quite close. Sometime in the first half of the eleventh century, Odo and his brother Hugh, the archdeacon, made a donation of a church to the abbey of St. Trinité (see appendix, chart 10). These brothers acted together to make the gift (the charter

---

29. He is called Urseto—"little Ursio"—in the charter, an indication of his youth.

30. Bernard's brothers were clearly older than he was, although Bernard succeeded his father as lord of La Ferté. He married a woman named Julianna and had several children. AD Eure-et-Loir, H 1422 and H 2271.

31. Like Helvisa-Adierna, Countess Ermengard of Blois-Chartres saw that her husband's body, which had been seriously damaged during his last battle, was taken to Marmoutier and buried alongside his father in the abbey church. Elizabeth van Houts has found that women in particular were responsible for seeing to the burial of their male kin. *Memory and Gender*, pp. 94–95.

32. *CSVM,* no. 175, pp. 105–8.

uses the plural *donaverunt*), indicating that they both held this land and that Odo and Hugh had shared inheritance of this part of the patrimony.[33] Odo and his wife named their only son after Hugh, which suggests a particularly affectionate relationship between the brothers. Archdeacon Hugh may also have acted as godfather to his nephew, since children frequently took the name of their spiritual sponsor.[34] It seems clear that Odo also trusted Hugh because he and his wife appointed Hugh guardian of their minor children.[35]

The fraternal bond between Odo and Hugh provided a foundation for the relationship between uncle and nephew. A charter from 1075 records Odo's son Hugh's first and only gift as an adult and provides additional insight into the interactions between uncle and nephew.

> After becoming an adult, Hugh, the son of Odo Dubellus, accepted into his own hands the honors of his father, [and] gave to God and St. Trinité, for his soul, his father, and his uncle, that is Hugh the archdeacon, that which he accepted as his honor, namely all of the tithes from the honors of Mondoubleau, namely pasturage, woods, hunting, honey and comb from the bees, and all that he holds in tithe from the mill.[36]

The gift was made at the court of the Count of Anjou, where his uncle Hugh requested the honor for his nephew in front of the whole court and the men associated with the lordship of Mondoubleau. Uncle Hugh was clearly acting on his nephew's behalf in securing the honor from the count and ensuring that it would become his by right. Uncle and nephew acted together in asking for the monks' prayers, in authorizing the gift in front of the entire chapter, and in placing a symbol of the gift upon the altar of the monastery. Hugh thus fulfilled his role as trusted guardian and surrogate father by guiding his young nephew through the process of becoming lord and receiving his honor. The relationship between this uncle and nephew is certainly at odds with some of the more vivid literary examples, such as

---

33. *CTV,* vol. 1, no. 21, pp. 41–42.

34. Joseph H. Lynch, *Godparents and Kinship in Early Medieval Europe,* pp. 172–73; Louis Haas, "Social Connections between Parents and Godparents in Late Medieval Yorkshire"; Hanawalt, *Growing Up in Medieval London,* pp. 46–51.

35. In 1058 the Mondoubleau family appeared at the court of Count Geoffrey Martel of Anjou to approve a sale between one of their vassals and the abbey of St. Trinité in Vendôme. The "children of Odo Dubellus" acted with their uncle in giving their approval of this gift. *CTV,* vol. 1, no. 118, pp. 212–14. Two other Mondoubleau uncles also acted to confirm and witness the gift: Gaufred and Adam, a monk at St. Trinité.

36. *CTV,* vol. 1, no. 250, pp. 394–96.

Raoul de Cambrai or Tristan, who were clearly in conflict with their uncles.[37] Archdeacon Hugh, moreover, had children of his own and could have been tempted to usurp his nephew's inheritance to benefit his own progeny.[38] But this did not occur. Like Sulpice of Amboise, Hugh acted as support and nurturer for his young ward. Young Hugh regarded his uncle as a second father for he made the gift to benefit not only his own soul but also his father's and his uncle's—the man who gave him life, and the man who guided him to manhood. Moreover, two other uncles helped with this transaction. Because Hugh was shortly departing on a trip, "it was through his two uncles, Adam and [Gaufred] the monk," that the gift was transferred into the patrimony of the monastery. In young Hugh of Mondoubleau's experience, his father's brothers were particularly important and supportive kin.

Uncles played another important role in family life: they were the repositories of family memories.[39] In 1096 two brothers, who were vassals of the lords of Fréteval, sold and donated property that pertained to the castle of Fréteval. Lord Nivelon and Hamelin consented to the gifts. But a problem arose when the boundaries between the Fréteval lands and those of their vassals were not recalled. So Nivelon sent for his uncle Girard, who was currently at Hamelin's home of Montigny, to have him attest to the property divisions. As a senior member of the family, Girard could be counted upon to remember previous gifts, where the property pertaining to the lordship of Fréteval ended, and what property made up the fief of these two vassal brothers. Girard's residence at Montigny is also intriguing. Hamelin may have asked his uncle to look after the lordship while he traveled to the monastery of Marmoutier. Or perhaps Girard lived with Hamelin. Either is possible. What is clear from this charter, however, is that extended relatives were important members of the Fréteval family.

Fulcher II Turre enjoyed a particularly close relationship with his maternal uncle, Robert of Moncontour (see appendix, chart 9). His frequent appearance in transactions with Robert of Moncontour suggests that Fulcher was being fostered in Robert's household. Fulcher and Robert also shared control of property. In 1061 these kinsmen had a disagreement with the house of Marmoutier about their joint possession of land in Villeberfol. A resolution with the monks was soon reached when these two elites accepted

---

37. Bouchard, "*Strong of Body, Brave and Noble,*" p. 77.

38. *CSVM,* no. 180, pp. 109–11. Two of Archdeacon Hugh's sons gave their consent to the alienation of certain portions of their "benefices" made by their grandfather for the support of St. Mary of Mondoubleau. A third son, Odo the deacon, also signed the charter.

39. Van Houts, *Memory and Gender,* pp. 29–37.

countergifts from the monks in return for their abandoning their right to the property.[40] Robert and Fulcher's joint control of property was the result of Fulcher's inheritance through his mother.[41] But did their close relationship stem solely from their mutual interest in property?

Fulcher's ongoing relationship with Robert of Moncontour could be dismissed as resulting from his expectation of inheriting from his uncle. Two acts datable from 1081 and 1098 respectively suggest that this was not the whole story, however. In 1081 Robert of Moncontour made a generous gift to St. Trinité for his soul and those of his relatives, consisting of extensive property, rights, and dues.[42] Yet sometime later, Robert's son Bertran contested the donation.[43] Thus we know from Bertran's dispute that Robert of Moncontour had children of his own, and that his special relationship with his nephew Fulcher Turre was not based solely on his potential claim to his uncle's land.[44] Robert and Fulcher enjoyed a long association, one likely based on affection—perhaps as a result of Fulcher's fostering in Robert's household—or at least shared interests. Fulcher Turre was one of the most powerful men of the Vendômois, as was his uncle Robert. They associated with the same people, had the same allies, and owed allegiance to the same lords—as well as being kinsmen. As a result, the lives of nephew and uncle were intertwined for over thirty years.

---

40. AD Loir-et-Cher, 16 H 118; *CMPD,* no. 126, pp. 117–18.

41. To settle their claim with the monks, these men journeyed to the court of the count of Vendôme. Traveling with them were several of Fulcher's other kin, specifically his grandson Peter of Montigny, his son-in-law Ingelbald Brito, and Ingelbald's son Vulgrin, all of whom consented to the quitclaim. Of the many present at the comital court, why were these men chosen to participate in the resolution? These witnesses were selected because of their relationship with Fulcher as well as their distant, but nonetheless potential, claim to the disputed property. Even though he was married and had children and grandchildren of his own, Fulcher still maintained contact with his maternal relatives. Indeed, Fulcher witnessed six acts with his uncle Robert, further proof of his contact with Robert and association with this kin group. See *CTV,* vol. 1, no. 95, pp. 171–74; vol. 1, no. 249, pp. 393–94; vol. 1, no. 281, pp. 437–38; vol. 1, no. 285, pp. 442–43; vol. 1, no. 295, pp. 450–51; vol. 2, no. 347, pp. 86–87.

42. AD Loir-et-Cher, 21 H 69. Fulcher Turre was present in the chapter house when Robert made the gift and "praised" the benefaction as well. Fulcher's grandson Vulgrin was also there and consented to the gift. See also 16 H 118, no. 9.

43. AD Loir-et-Cher, 21 H 69, no. 4. See also *CTV,* vol. 2, no. 361, pp. 105–7. This family's remuneration was exceedingly generous. Bertran himself received 1800 *solidi* of *denarii,* a hefty countergift, which might suggest that the monks realized that Bertran had a legitimate gripe about their control of this property—which they had controlled for seventeen years. Such a generous countergift could have been an attempt to atone for this. Since Bertran was on his way to the Crusade, and financing such a journey was terrifically expensive—in particular finding sufficient cash—their countergift may have been aimed at helping a crusader on his way to fight the infidel.

44. Nor was Bertran Robert's only child, since the charter designates him as *"primogenitus,"* indicating that he was the firstborn of several sons and/or daughters.

As was the case for their grandfather Fulcher, connections with their uncles also shaped the lives of the progeny of Ingelbald Brito and Domitilla (see appendix, chart 11). One son, Vulgrin, was named for his maternal uncle. Another son, Fulcher, became a monk and in 1076 was placed at Chartres so that he would be close to his uncle and receive the benefit of his uncle's patronage or guidance. The uncle-nephew relationship was clearly important in determining Fulcher's ecclesiastical future and in securing his success in his selected career.[45] Secular uncles were also important to members of the Dives-Turre kin. Robert of Lisle made a gift for his uncle Bartholomew so that his uncle could be buried with honor with the monks at St. Trinité in Vendôme.[46] Two other uncles, along with Robert's brother and mother, acted with him to secure the gift. A few years later, the monks threatened to deny burial rights to another of Robert's uncles unless he abandoned his claim to certain properties.[47] Robert was apparently quite close to his uncles. He arranged their burial with the monks and was pained by the thought of one of them being denied this privilege. Moreover, the charter recording Robert's benefaction on behalf of Bartholomew says that this uncle died at Lisle. Either this uncle lived with Robert or was visiting him at the time of his death. In either case, the experience of Robert of Lisle further reiterates the close, indeed affectionate, bond that existed between uncles and nephews.

Extended Kin

In addition to siblings and uncles, extended kin such as cousins was also familiar to the members of the Fréteval-Mondoubleau-Dives kindred. Relatives from both the maternal and paternal lines appear in transactions. Odo and Hugh of Mondoubleau had their maternal uncle Rainald of Turre witness one of their gifts. Ingelbald Brito, their first cousin, also stood as witness for them. Nithard of Montoire, who would either become Odo's father-in-law or was his father-in-law by the time of the donation, was also present.

---

45. Four sons of Ingelbald and Domitilla appear in the charters: Vulgrin, Fulcher, Geoffrey Pagan, and Hugh of Losdon. Of the four, only three appear with any frequency. While Vulgrin's life is somewhat recoverable through his relationship with his grandfather, he disappears from view about 1090. A gift by his mother, Domitilla, dated about 1096 was made for the souls of both her husband and son, so it is possible Vulgrin died in the 1090s. Perhaps he, like many of his generation, went on Crusade. Fulcher appears in charters as a cleric, "the son of Domitilla," on occasion. Hugh may have inherited property at Losdon and have gone by a different cognomen. The Geoffrey Pagan line does continue, and his sons appear in the charters. One of his sons, Bartholomew, married the daughter of Pagan of Mondoubleau (see appendix, charts 11 and 13).

46. *CTV,* vol. 2, no. 541, p. 389.

47. *CTV,* vol. 2, no. 564, pp. 427–28.

Maternal kin aided Odo and Hugh in this donation, as well as appearing in other transactions.[48] The vicecomital family of Châteaudun also maintained close relationships with their extended kin.[49] Cousins, maternal and paternal, were frequent participants in the vicecomital charters. Clearly kinship was figured collaterally in these families.[50]

The life experience of Pagan of Mondoubleau illustrates the depth of the bond between cousins. Pagan was the son of Helvisa-Adierna of Mondoubleau and Pagan of Fréteval. After his mother remarried (to Hamelin of Langeais), Pagan remained with her and appeared with his mother, stepfather, and stepsiblings in several donations.[51] But by around 1080, some changes had taken place in Pagan's life. The resolution of a dispute holds some interesting clues. It seems that Pagan had recently returned to Mondoubleau, indicating he had been residing elsewhere for some time.[52] Moreover, the monks granted Pagan a horse as a countergift in recognition of his quitclaim. Gifts of horses were appropriate gifts for young men just about to enter the ranks of knighthood. Combined with the reference to Pagan's return to Mondoubleau, it would seem that he was being trained as a warrior, perhaps at the court of his maternal aunt, Fredescind of Semblançay. His cousin, Herluin, was about the same age, and they likely trained together.

As adults, the foster brothers became brothers-in-arms.[53] At the end of the eleventh century, Pagan made a gift to St. Vincent of Le Mans. The charter begins, "Repay all of your debts; pay tribute to whom you owe tribute; love those you love." To whom did Pagan owe a debt? To whom did he owe tribute? Whom did he love? His cousin Herluin. For the charter tells us that during a heated battle, Herluin sacrificed his own life to save his cousin. "Since I am unable to restore his corporal body to life," Pagan said, he wished to ensure that his beloved cousin would enjoy eternal life and eternal peace. With the consent of Herluin's brother, mother, and his own wife and daughter, Pagan gave extensive properties for his cousin. Pagan remembered

---

48. *CTV,* vol. 1, no. 118, pp. 212–14.

49. See *CMPD,* no. 177, p. 169; *CMPD,* no. 94, pp. 84–85; *Tiron,* vol. 1, no. 153, p. 176; vol. 1, no. 87, pp. 107–8; vol. 1, no. 109, pp. 129–30; vol. 1, no. 185, pp. 207–8; *Josaphat,* vol. 1, no. 59, pp. 81–82.

50. Bouchard, "The Bosonids" and "The Migration of Women's Names in the Upper Nobility"; van Houts, *Memory and Gender,* pp. 85–92. Through analysis of the language used to describe kin, Anita Guerreau-Jalabert finds no evidence of the use of "agnatic" to describe kinship descent. She asserts that medieval families were fundamentally cognatic. Guerreau-Jalabert, "La désignation des relations," p. 90.

51. *CSVM,* nos. 175 and 178, pp. 105–9.

52. *CSVM,* no. 179, p. 109.

53. *CSVM,* no. 179, p. 109.

his cousin because of the affection he felt for him and the ultimate sacrifice
Herluin had made on his behalf. Although Herluin's mother had left the immediate vicinity of Mondoubleau and Fréteval when she married the lord of
Semblançay, she kept in touch with her natal family and her sister in particular.[54] By the time they were grown, these men were emotionally connected.
Indeed, one was willing to sacrifice his life for the other—a true testament to
their bond as both kin and comrades-in-arms.[55]

To conclude the discussion of family life in the eleventh century, we will
end where we began, with the Fréteval family. As Lord Nivelon II prepared for departure with the First Crusade, he sought to make amends with
the church. In addition to the monks of Marmoutier and St. Trinité of
Vendôme, Nivelon had also aggrieved the brothers of St. Père of Chartres
by claiming rights which "he did not hold through ancient custom,... but
rather since the time of his father... through the tyranny of usurpation." To
atone for this grievance, and for the redemption of his soul, he abandoned
his claim. Nivelon's son Ursio and "certain of [Nivelon's] relatives" approved
the resolution with the monks and the quitclaim.[56] Moreover, a curse or
malediction included in the charter promised suffering with Dathan and
Abiron, who were damned because they led a rebellion against Moses, for
any of Nivelon's descendants or relatives who might be inclined to dispute
the gift. Nivelon, his son Ursio, his brother Hamelin, his sisters Comitissa
and Pagana, and his brother-in-law the Viscount of Châteaudun, all signed
the charter with a cross.

This charter encapsulates the familial reality of the Fréteval family, as well
as that of many of their contemporaries and kin, at the end of the eleventh
century. As the foregoing discussion indicates, extended kin were not distant
or unfamiliar figures for the Frétevals. Rather, they were people with whom
they had contact all their life. They saw each other often and played significant and enduring roles in each other's lives. Nephews, cousins, aunts, and
uncles could be depended on for help, intercession, protection, and guidance.
In particular, the relationship among Nivelon, Hamelin, and their sisters appears to have been quite close. They looked to each other for advice and fostered one another's sons in their homes. Uncles, as demonstrated by Nivelon,

---

54. This was a second marriage for Fredescind. She was married first to Nivelon Pagan of
Fréteval, with whom she had Nivelon Pagan II. After his death, she married a man with ties to the
Touraine. Her other son, Ernulf, was the lord of Semblançay, which may indicate that he inherited
this title and land from his father.

55. Given that Pagan refers to Herluin as *servitium*, it is possible that Herluin may have been
Pagan's vassal.

56. *Père*, vol. 2, no. 36, pp. 428–29.

Hamelin, and Girard, were prominent figures in the lives of these elites. They could be counted on to fill a variety of roles. Cousins were also important kin. They witnessed transactions, provided oaths, gave their tacit support to each other's gifts, and, in at least one case, died defending another cousin.

Continuity of Kinship: The Eleventh to the Twelfth Century

The twelfth century witnessed profound changes as the economy shifted from one based on gifts to one based on currency and profit. Moreover, the aristocracy itself changed. They lost much of the warrior ethos and were "civilized" by the notions of chivalry and Christian knighthood. The relationship between king and noble also transformed. Kings became more powerful and extended their authority over once virtually independent counties, lordships, and duchies. The Fréteval-Mondoubleau-Dives kin group provides a testing ground for whether or not family life transformed in the face of these challenges and new realities.

The evidence from the eleventh century confirmed the mutual dependency of kin. Using literary topoi as a kind of reality check for aristocratic family life and focusing on the family dramas among the very pinnacle of the aristocracy, scholars point to uncles taking over inheritances and brothers and cousins preying on each other's lands as evidence that such relationships became more predatory in the twelfth century.[57] Tension between the Fréteval family and their vicecomital kin would seem to confirm such an interpretation.

Sometime in 1136, Viscount Geoffrey III was imprisoned by his cousin Lord Ursio at his castle at Fréteval. With Geoffrey imprisoned, his family rallied. His son, Hugh, and his wife, Helvisa, assumed control of the lordship. His brother-in-law, the count of Vendôme, and his son came to Châteaudun to lend their support. Having a count in residence would certainly serve as a deterrent to anyone thinking about taking advantage of the viscount's misfortune. Gifts continued to be made and property managed, as is clear by Hugh's confirmation of a gift to Tiron. It was arranged that Hugh would travel to the abbey to finalize the gift while Helvisa would remain at Châteaudun, maintaining a presence at their family seat. Accompanying young Hugh was their neighbor, the viscount of Chartres. The participation of this fellow viscount was unprecedented in the transactions of the Châteaudun

---

57. Stephen D. White, "Inheritances and Legal Arguments in Western France, 1050–1150"; "The Discourse of Inheritance in Twelfth-Century France"; Bouchard, *"Strong of Body, Brave and Noble,"* p. 73; Duby, "Youth in Aristocratic Society."

family. His presence at the confirmation suggests that he, too, was lending his support. As in Bernard of Angers's chronicle account, kin and neighbors converged to help this family.

Unfortunately, the sources remain frustratingly silent as to why the viscount spent several months locked up in his cousin's keep.[58] But the action was probably politically motivated. War between the Anglo-Normans and the French kings was waged throughout the lands of the Loire. Ursio may have taken exception to Geoffrey's political affiliation. Regrettably, we will probably never know the details behind this story. But what may appear at first glance as evidence of a shift in the character of kinship actually provides proof to the contrary. Yes, one cousin imprisoned another, but other kin came to assist and support the family during this trying time. Moreover, the viscountess and her son clearly were able to manage and defend their family's holdings. For better or for worse, cousins clearly affected the course of each other's lives.

To appreciate fully all the hues and textures of family life, we need to step back and examine the many different ways that relatives within the Fréteval-Mondoubleau-Dives kin group interacted in the twelfth century. To do this, various families will be presented as case studies to highlight important facets of aristocratic family life (see map 1 and appendix, chart 7).

The Frétevals: The Persistence of the Collateral Family

At the outset of the century, Nivelon II of Fréteval was in the Holy Land taking part in the First Crusade. During his absence, his son Ursio came of age. In 1108, a monastic scribe of Marmoutier recorded that Ursio, "who was now a knight *(miles),* came to our house at Chamars, and there he conceded to God and Holy Martin and [his] monks, that which we hold from the fief of his father, and from his [fief]."[59] Confirmations of property given previously by fathers, mothers, and other kin were quite common once young elites attained their majority. Ursio's entrance into adulthood and knighthood was marked in another way. In return for this confirmation, Ursio received a horse, which his uncle Pagan of Frouville had given to the monks for this purpose. A horse was an appropriate, indeed generous, gift for a young

---

58. *Tiron,* vol. 1, no. 215, pp. 242–43.

59. AD Loir-et-Cher, 16 H 77, no. 4. See also *CMPD,* no. 164, p. 155. Fréteval holdings at Chamars were particularly contentious. Nivelon II had many disagreements with the monks of Marmoutier over his rights. Both the lords of Fréteval and the viscounts of Châteaudun disputed the monks' possession of it. See AD Eure-et-Loir, H 2270 and H 2272.

man who had just earned his spurs and entered the realm of knighthood. His uncle, who had probably acted as Ursio's guardian during Nivelon's absence, assumed the role of father by recognizing the occasion of his nephew's graduation from childhood to adulthood. In this way, Pagan was playing the same role in Ursio's life as Nivelon had played in fostering Bernard of La Ferté. In this family, paternal uncles in particular took an active part in the lives of their young nephews—especially when fathers were absent.

The bonds forged with kin when Ursio was a child followed him into adulthood. While Fréteval cousins and uncles played important roles in Ursio's life, so, too, did a new group of affinal kin. In 1115, Ursio and his father, Nivelon, were in serious trouble. They had been excommunicated by the pope because of certain "damnations and inflictions" they had perpetrated against the monks of St. Trinité of Vendôme.[60] In 1122, father and son finally appeared before the monks at their chapter house.[61] By this point, Ursio was married to Berta, a daughter of the Dives house. Witnessing the resolution were many of his affinal kin: Ursio's father-in-law, Jeremy of Lisle, who was the son of Fulcher Turre, as well as Ursio's brothers-in-law, Rainald Turre and Bartholomew, and Vulgrin, Ursio's first cousin by marriage. Unlike their Fréteval kin, the Dives clan had had a friendly relationship with the ecclesiastical foundations of the region. Moreover, the founders of this family, Fulcher Dives and Adela of Bezai, had been important patrons of this very monastery, and their son, Fulcher II, had acted as the monks' advocate on several occasions. Such a reputation and longstanding relationship would have made them ideal to witness this Fréteval attempt to repair relations with the monastery at Vendôme. Furthermore, since this reconciliation took place early in Ursio's marriage, it was a perfect time to celebrate this newly formed relationship between two powerful families. Resolutions, gifts, and quitclaims were public events. The proceedings took place in front of the secular and religious community and would serve to remind all of the important bonds that tied elite families, not only to each other, but also to the holy church.[62]

---

60. This sentence did not seem to have much effect on these two noblemen, since it took seven years for them to be restored to the monks' good graces. *CTV,* vol. 2, no. 429, pp. 202–3. Abbot Geoffrey of Vendôme wrote to Bishop Geoffrey of Chartres in 1119 about the misbehavior of Ursio, Nivelon II, and Pagan of Frouville (whom Geoffrey erroneously identifies as Nivelon's brother). *Oeuvres,* letter 159, pp. 352–53. Nor was this the first time Nivelon and Ursio had been the focus Geoffrey's ire. Between 1107 and 1110, Abbot Geoffrey of Vendôme wrote to Bishop Ivo of Chartres complaining about the injuries this father and son had done to his abbey. *Oeuvres,* letters 94 and 95, pp. 177–81.

61. *CTV,* vol. 2, no. 439, pp. 217–18.

62. Rosenwein, *To Be the Neighbor of St. Peter,* p. 75; Tabuteau, *Transfers of Property,* pp. 119–26.

From around 1122 onward, Lisle relatives became frequent participants in Ursio's acts. Sometime between 1130 and the end of his life, this lord of Fréteval gave what he held from two closes in the precinct of a church.[63] The gift was made for his own soul but also for the souls of his *parentes* (relatives), and many of Ursio's *parentes,* both natal and affinal, participated in the grant. To prevent any false claims to the property or any disputes, the monks insisted on having Ursio's family consent to the donation. Several monks accompanied Ursio to Fréteval, where Berta, his wife, and his sons and daughters as well as his daughter-in-law Agatha consented to and confirmed the gift. Jeremy of Lisle, Ursio's father-in-law, was visiting Fréteval at this time, for he stood as witness to these confirmations.[64] Berta maintained contact with her family after her marriage and even entertained them at the castle of Fréteval.[65]

Alliance with the Lisle family added to an already extended network of kin upon which Ursio and his family could rely. The selection of names for Ursio and Berta's children provided a living tie to Berta's family and illustrates that they conceptualized family and kinship cognatically. Eight children survived infancy: Nivelon, Hamelin, Philip, Fulcher, Rainald, Berta, Hersend, and Comitissa.[66] Two of their sons were named for Ursio's father and uncle (Nivelon and Hamelin). Yet two others carried the names of Dives kin: Rainald was named for Berta of Lisle's brother, and Fulcher was probably named for her illustrious progenitors, Fulcher Turre and Fulcher Dives (her grandfather and great-grandfather respectively). Philip was the odd man out and carried a name unknown to both kin groups (he was likely named after the French king or perhaps for Louis VI's brother). Equal division of names between Fréteval and Dives relatives is apparent in the denomination of their female offspring as well. One daughter was named after Ursio's aunt, Viscountess Comitissa of Châteaudun, while another was named after Berta's aunt, Hersend of Montigny. The third was named for her mother, Berta. Maternal and paternal kin alike played significant roles in the lives of elites. This is a reality that is confirmed by, and reflected in, Ursio and Berta's choice of names for their children.

---

63. *Père,* vol. 2, no. 150, pp. 364–65.

64. Moreover, when Ursio made his gift at the chapter house, his cousin Hamelin Flagellus witnessed. So, too, did Pagan of Frouville, Ursio's first cousin.

65. *Père,* vol. 2, no. 22, pp. 481–83. Shared interest in property, as well as kinship, tied these two families together. Sometime between 1115 and 1130, Ursio of Fréteval made a gift of what he held at Bois Ruffin and Arrou to the monks of St. Père, with the exception of what his father-in-law, Jeremy of Lisle, had already given to the monks of Tiron. See *Tiron,* vol. 1, no. 5, p. 16 and vol. 1, no. 130, p. 156 for conflicts over which monastic house controlled these lands.

66. *CMPD,* no. 182, pp. 172–73.

The Frouvilles: The Importance of Cousins

The addition of the Lisle relatives to the Fréteval kindred did not diminish the participation of other kin in the lives of the Frétevals. On the contrary, Frouville and La Ferté cousins were frequent participants (see appendix, chart 8). Pagan of Frouville and his son Robert, for example, figured prominently in Ursio's life before his marriage and continued to do so afterward.[67] Ursio's association with Frouville kin, however, was not surprising since Pagan of Frouville had helped guide Ursio to manhood. This nobleman also appears to have enjoyed a close relationship with his cousin Robert for they were frequent associates.[68] Significantly, Robert's son Philip was often present at Ursio's court and witnessed his transactions, evidence that Ursio might have been fostering young Philip as he himself had been fostered and protected by a Frouville uncle.[69] Another Frouville cousin who appeared on Ursio's behalf was Hamelin Flagellus.[70] He witnessed two of Uriso's grants to St. Père of Chartres made between 1135 and 1149. Hamelin appears to have been associated with the monks since he is frequently included among the clerical witnesses for St. Père. His relationship with the monks would have made him a useful associate for his Fréteval cousin.[71]

Reciprocally, it was to his Fréteval kin that Pagan II of Frouville turned for assistance in 1129. A potential problem arose when he arranged to exchange some properties with the abbey of Tiron. Pagan's "heirs" were all still young children. Ursio of Fréteval, Pagan's cousin, agreed to "freely and faithfully defend [the lands] against all invaders...and guarantee the property against all claims."[72] Another kinsman, the viscount of Châteaudun, similarly lent his support. Because this property pertained to the viscount's fief, he and his wife and children consented. They also lent their lordly, and familial, support in another way: it was at their court at Châteaudun that these arrangements were made and formalized. By holding these proceedings at the vicecomital court, the viscount's support—as both lord and kinsman—was made public.

---

67. For example, when Ursio traveled to Marmoutier to reaffirm one of his gifts in front of the monks, his uncle Pagan and his cousin joined him and witnessed the confirmation for him. Pagan of Frouville also witnessed Ursio's quitclaim to Tiron at the end of his life, probably around 1146. *Tiron,* vol. 2, no. 290, p. 59.

68. *Tiron* vol. 2, no. 267, pp. 35–37, and vol. 1, no. 127, pp. 149–52.

69. *Père,* vol. 2, no. 22, pp. 481–83.

70. While Hamelin was clearly a member of the Frouville kindred, as evident in his use of the cognomen Flagellus, it is difficult to establish his precise place in the family. He was either the son of Pagan of Frouville or of Pagan's son Robert Flagellus.

71. *Père,* vol. 2, nos. 150 and 151, pp. 364–66.

72. *Tiron,* vol. 1, no. 117, p. 136; vol. 1, no. 109, pp. 129–30.

Not only would Ursio of Fréteval act to protect the interests of the monks and Pagan's children, so too would their vicecomital kin. The children, however, did not make the journey to Châteaudun. Their consent, and their acceptance of countergifts, took place at Fréteval—which was, again, another strategic move on the part of Pagan and his kin. These children were publicly associated with their protector, Ursio of Fréteval, and the physical safety his fortress could provide. In one transaction, Pagan telegraphed the support his children would receive from their powerful cousins.

The Vicecomital Family of Châteaudun: Lordship and Kinship

The adoption of patrilineage and primogeniture has been ascribed to lords' need to streamline which vassals held fiefs from them. As the case above demonstrates, the bonds of kinship could and did overlap with those of lordship and vassalage. This was particularly true for the Fréteval's vicecomital cousins at Châteaudun (see appendix, chart 2). Because so many elites held their land, directly or indirectly, from the viscounts, the intersection of kinship and lordship was common. Sometime in the first two decades of the twelfth century, for instance, Viscount Geoffrey III confirmed a gift by "a certain of his knights, who had served him many times and who was a kinsman of his wife Helvisa, named Ernulf of Semblançay."[73] The vicecomital couple had good reason to remember Ernulf for he was the brother of Herluin who had given his life in battle to save Viscountess Helvisa's father. The viscount and viscountess gladly affirmed their kinsman and vassal's gift. Even though Ernulf's mother had moved further south upon her marriage to the lord of Semblançay over fifty years before, her family still retained an interest in land in Mondoubleau for Ernulf's gift consisted of land from "among Mondoubleau" and a property that was "in front of the castle, next to the house of the lepers." Connections to land and kin stretched back and out over the generations to include cousins, grandfathers, and even great-aunts. As early as the beginning of the eleventh century, the viscounts and lords of Mondoubleau had been tied together through bonds of vassalage.[74] Over the generations, relationships through marriage and blood strengthened these political ties.

Later in the twelfth century, Viscount Hugh III, the son of Viscountess Helvisa and Viscount Geoffrey III, was similarly bound to Ada of Touraille by

---

73. *CSVM,* no. 198, pp. 124–25. Ernulf granted these properties in *CSVM,* no. 197, p. 124. He was apparently close to death for he had taken the habit of a monk. His entrance into the religious life was quite recent since his squire Hervé witnessed the gift.

74. AD Loir-et-Cher, 16 H 80.

both kinship and vassalage. In 1187, Viscount Hugh, his brother Pagan,[75] his wife, and children made a gift of what "Ada of Touraille, who is bound to me by lines of consanguinity, freely and completely possesses" to the nuns of St. Avit.[76] Earlier Hugh had arranged that Ada would enjoy control of land in the territory of St. Avit for her lifetime. Yet in other transactions, it is clear that Ada was a vassal of the viscounts of Châteaudun.[77] While Ada's precise relationship to the viscount is unsure, the charter demonstrates that the viscount took care to ensure the support of his kinswoman. Further, the bonds of vassalage continued to overlap with those of kinship without an attempt to organize either into a strictly primogenitary or patrilineal pattern—as indicated by the fact that Ada of Touraille, a *woman,* held a fief.

The Dives Descendants: The Power of Women

Corresponding with the presumption that families assumed a more lineal form in the twelfth century is the belief that women's power and importance diminished in that century. The experience of Guitberg, the wife of Bartholomew of Vendôme, daughter of Pagan of Mondoubleau and great-great-granddaughter of Fulcher Dives would seem to confirm this interpretation.

In sharp contrast to her Fréteval-Mondoubleau-Dives kinswomen, Guitberg does not appear in many charters, nor was she closely associated with her natal kin. Indeed, once she was married, with the exception of confirming one of her father's gifts around 1108, she disappears (see appendix, charts 11 and 13).[78] Guitberg's relatives played virtually no role in her life or that of

---

75. Early in the thirteenth century, Viscount Geoffrey's son would confirm what his uncle Pagan had given to the nunnery of St. Avit. See AD Eure-et-Loir, H 4332.

76. AD Eure-et-Loir, H 4545. The identity of Ada of Touraille is somewhat mysterious. One possibility is that she could be Aia, the wife of Pagan of Mondoubleau, about whom little is known beyond her name. This would have made her the maternal grandmother of these men, so they were certainly bound to her by "ties of consanguinity." But this would seem a rather close relative to be referred to so vaguely. Guerreau-Jalabert identifies *consanguinitae* as corresponding roughly to *cognati,* meaning the people with whom the person shared descent and thus were too closely related to marry. More broadly, it could refer to the relatives "less immediate than the parents, brothers and sisters, and the children." Guerreau-Jalabert, "La désignation des relations," 79–81. The gifts to the nunnery of St. Avit could account for Aia/Ada's lack of participation in family charters: she could have become a nun. The charters from St. Avit bear out that Ada was one of their order and was even prominent among the nuns of St. Avit. She held the office of cantor and then prioress. See *CV,* no. 116, pp. 149–50; no. 123, pp. 156–57; no. 127, pp. 169–70. The above scenario for Ada's relationship with the vicounts of Châteaudun would fit this definition of *consanguinitae* given by Guerreau-Jalabert.

77. AD Eure-et-Loir, H 4557.

78. AD Loir-et-Cher, 16 H 105. See also *CMPD,* no. 79, pp. 62–63. Even when she approved her father's benefaction to Marmoutier, she was not present when he made the gift at Vendôme.

her young daughter, although it is difficult to gauge if this is the result of her choice, her circumstance, or the capriciousness of documents' survival.

Her husband, Bartholomew, on the other hand, was a frequent participant in Guitberg's natal family's charters. He witnessed the transactions for his brother-in-law Viscount Geoffrey III of Châteaudun and also lent his assistance to his nephew on several occasions.[79] For example, when his nephew Pagan made a gift to the monks, Bartholomew aided in determining the boundaries of the lands entailed in the gift.[80] Indeed, Bartholomew was quite close to his affinal family for he and his brother-in-law Viscount Geoffrey became brothers-in-arms when they went on Crusade together.

Bartholomew's involvement in his affinal family did not cause him to neglect his own natal kin, however. He made his first appearance in the sources in 1101 when he approved the purchase by his uncles of certain church properties—which they then donated to the church to benefit the soul of their mother, Domitilla.[81] Like his grandparents and great-grandparents before him, Bartholomew was a generous patron of the church. Between 1116 and 1146 he made two extensive grants to create a community of monks of the abbey of Marmoutier in the Perche to benefit his soul and those of his ancestors. Just before he was planning to depart on the Second Crusade, Bartholomew revisited this gift. Apparently no community of religious had been established. Bartholomew was understandably concerned about this, and thinking it was due to the fact that there was not enough property to support a proper community, he gave more land, rights, and revenues. His brothers Ingelbald (who eventually became the archbishop of Tours) and Vulgrin and his sister Domina Maria and her husband and children were all present when he arranged these grants and consented to them.[82] Neither his daughter nor his wife Guitberg appeared in these transactions, however, nor did any of his affinal kin.

As Bartholomew prepared to go on Crusade, he turned his lands over to his daughter and her husband and stated they would inherit his holdings should he not return. Sadly, Bartholomew seems to have died either en route to or in the Holy Land. Gosbert took control of his father-in-law's properties

---

Rather, she affirmed the gift when she and her husband—and her husband's kin—traveled to the abbey of Marmoutier.

79. *Tiron,* vol. 1, no. 78, p. 98.

80. *Tiron,* vol. 1, no. 157, p. 180. See van Houts, *Memory and Gender,* pp. 29–30.

81. *MV,* no. 187, pp. 266–68.

82. AD Eure-et-Loir, H 2302. See also *CMPD,* no. 170, pp. 160–61; no. 183, pp. 173–75. Bartholomew also made a gift to Tiron about the same time. Only his sister and his brother-in-law took part in the transaction.

and confirmed gifts and agreements his predecessors had made with the monks. His wife, Adeled, consented to this and was given a silver cup as a countergift.[83]

During Bartholomew's lifetime, patrilineal seems to be the best description of his family interactions and the role—or perhaps more accurately, nonrole—of his wife. This lasted only for Bartholomew's lifetime, however, as Adeled joined her husband, Gosbert, as partner in the management of their lands and holdings, as an episcopal confirmation illustrates. Gosbert and Adeled together donated considerable properties pertaining to the church of St. Gilderic. Consenting to these alienations were Adeled's paternal aunt, Domina Maria of Lavardin, and her cousin John, her uncle Vulgrin, his wife, and several of his children.[84] Moreover, Maria consented at Vendôme, but Vulgrin witnessed Gosbert and Adeled's original gift at Boschet and his sister's confirmation at Vendôme.[85]

The virtual absence of Guitberg from the documents certainly suggests that this woman, at least, was not very powerful or that her right to property was diminished. Yet in the next generation this trend toward powerlessness was reversed. Why? It is difficult to say. This seeming "triumph of patrilineage" could be explained by the survival of certain documents and the loss of others, but an argument based on silence is neither very compelling nor good history. Perhaps the answer lies in one or more of the other intangibles, such as personalities and life experience. Guitberg may have been unwell and confined to bed. She could have been uninterested in the management of family properties. Maybe she hated her natal kin. Perhaps Bartholomew was a tyrant and did not want his wife involved and kept her shut in the castle. While all of the scenarios are speculative, what we do know is that Guitberg's daughter experienced life in a very different way. She was an active participant in the management of family lands with her husband. Moreover, Bartholomew's sister, Maria, was also a partner to her husband. Indeed, her prominence and power are evident in the use of the term *domina* in the charters. The experiences of these three women indicate the importance of evaluating the totality of women's lives before assuming a wholesale shift in the powers, rights, and positions they enjoyed in aristocratic society.

---

83. *CTV,* vol. 2, no. 524, pp. 360–63.
84. AD Eure-et-Loir, H 2305.
85. AD Eure-et-Loir, H 2305.

Conclusion

Sometime around 1146, when Ursio of Fréteval was "ill to the point of death," he sought to make restitution with St. Trinité of Vendôme. He admitted "the many bad things he had done" and "publicly confessed his misdeeds." In doing so, Ursio was trying to set his son and successor on the right track with the monks and establish a positive relationship between them. As a father, Ursio felt compelled to help his son avoid his progenitors' mistakes. Ursio's cousin and lifelong companion, Pagan of Frouville, joined with his sons to witness and affirm this resolution. Pagan had been a part of Ursio's life from childhood to the grave. This close connection between the two families would continue under Ursio's sons.[86] A couple of years after Ursio's death, a dispute developed concerning land he had allowed one of his vassals to give to the monks of St. Trinité. Ursio's *primogenitus,* Nivelon, had also approved the agreement. Sadly, Nivelon followed his father in death shortly after becoming lord of Fréteval. His brother Hamelin succeeded him and worked with the abbot to resolve the conflict. Hamelin agreed to what his father and brother had affirmed, and at his court he "recogniz[ed] the justness of his father [and] promised to defend the agreement with the monks. And so this would remain in perpetuity, the seal of his father, which he now had as his own, he pressed into the charter."[87] The faithful Pagan of Frouville and his son Robert stood witness to these acts.

Like their peers so vividly brought to life by Bernard of Angers, the members of the Fréteval-Mondoubleau-Dives kindred depended on their kin for support. All sorts of relatives played significant roles in the lives of these aristocrats. Sisters, brothers, uncles, aunts, nephews, nieces, and cousins could be relied on to foster young children, act as guardians, confirm gifts, mediate disputes, and attest to the terms of donations. Even when the eldest son inherited the title of lord, his siblings continued to share in family holdings and exercise a right to the patrimony. Aristocratic women, moreover, were not second-class citizens; rather, they were fully vested members of their family. They exercised a right to property and used their influence to aid their relatives in many ways.

The men and women of the Fréteval-Mondoubleau-Dives kindred did not see their relatives as expendable or as threats to their own existence.

---

86. *CTV,* vol. 2, no. 492, pp. 312–13.
87. *CTV,* vol. 2, no. 513, pp. 337–42.

Instead, they counted on their immediate and extended family to help them survive chaotic times and prosper in times of peace. Nor was family life cold, detached, or impersonal. Parents loved their children. Brothers loved and cared for their siblings and their siblings' children. Cousins died for cousins. Certainly relatives squabbled over land, but to assume that these actions indicate that families preyed on each other's holdings and viewed each other as fierce rivals is to do these people a disservice. Given the tangled skein of kinship and property, perhaps it is not surprising that kin asserted their rights to each other's lands.

Intimately tied to kinship and family structure was property. Both here and in the previous chapter, I have argued that elite families of the lands of the Loire configured their kin broadly and inclusively. What implications would such kinship practices have for the disposition of family resources?

CHAPTER 4

Inheritance

Diversity and Continuity

Lambert of Ardres, reflecting upon the inheritance practices of the nobility, recorded that Count Arnulf of Boulogne "distributed his land proportionally to his three sons according to how well they loved him, what their pursuits were, and how suitable their love and pursuits were." William of Ponthieu, Lambert tells us, did the same:

> Now since William had four sons, he gave the land that is now called Ponthieu, as the most worthy and excellent part of his dominion, to the most worthy, the firstborn, because with glorious eagerness he took pleasure, as regards knighthood, in weapons and horses. To the second, because he devoted his spirit to the pursuit of the hunting occupation and said that nothing was any fun or pleasure without dogs, he gave arboreal woodlands...as fief and domain. To the third, because he was devoted to agriculture and the gathering and preserving of crops, William gave Thérouanne...as a perpetual fief. And then, not least, William decided to give the fourth....Guines, because he gave his whole attention to raising cattle and sheep and the land, partly hilly, is covered with little woods and thickets, and also has pasturelands and watery expanses of marshland.[1]

---

1. Lambert of Ardres, *History of the Counts of Guines and Lords of Ardres,* pp. 63–64. It appears that Lambert may have invented this "William of Ponthieu" or at least confused him with someone else

William parceled out his property to suit the personalities and interests of his sons. He knew his sons well enough to recognize their preferences and he gave considerable thought as to how best endow his children. The nobles of the lands of the Loire exhibited the same care for their children. Some families followed William of Ponthieu's example and practiced partible inheritance, others collective inheritance, and still others invested their family holdings in one heir. Individual circumstance and family need dictated the dispersal of family resources rather than a dedication to the idea that one method of distribution was in some way superior to all others.[2] Inheritance was thus diverse, fluid, and far from monolithic.[3] This diversity is evident in the several differing, but sometimes overlapping, modes of inheritance used by the nobility of the lands of the Loire: collective, impartible, partible, and primogenitary.[4]

The reluctance to abandon a patrilineal interpretation perhaps stems from the sources themselves. Historians have found the charters full of male donors, whom they characterize as the undisputed and sole lords of noble patrimonies. But is this really an accurate understanding of how noble families managed and dispersed their holdings? The extant transactions of the lords of Courville and Beaugency can serve as both corrective and cautionary tale.

Between 1025 and 1048, Ivo, the first lord of Courville, granted a church to Marmoutier.[5] At first glance, this act would seem to be prototypical of

---

(Lambert of Ardres, p. 64, n. 69). Whether or not William was real, Lambert relays this division of property matter-of-factly, indicating it would not have been surprising to his audience that noblemen divided their patrimonies to support all of their sons. Nor was Lambert criticizing the practice. Interestingly, Lambert's writings were the foundation on which Duby built much of his interpretation of aristocratic family life. See his *Medieval Marriage* and *The Knight, the Lady and the Priest*.

2. Cédric Jeanneau has found a multiplicity of inheritance practices at work in Poitou. See "Émergence et affirmation des familles seigneuriales à la frontière des grandes principautés territoriales" and "Liens adelphes et héritage. Une solution originale en Poitou aux XIe et XIIe siècles." Historians have looked to anthropological models to help them examine inheritance in the Middle Ages. Florian Mazel, "Monographie familiale aristocratique et analyse historique."

3. White, *Custom, Kinship and Gifts to Saints,* pp. 86–130; Tabuteau, *Transfers of Property,* pp. 170–95; Bowman, *Shifting Landmarks,* pp. 47–52; Drell, *Kinship and Conquest;* Amy Livingstone, "Diversity and Continuity"; Michel Nassiet, "La monographie familiale à la fin du Moyen Âge."

4. Guerreau-Jalabert, "La désignation des relations et des groupes de parenté en Latin médiéval"; "La parenté dans l'Europe médiévale et moderne." David Herlihy acknowledged there were two types of inheritance and family structure: the *consorteria* and dynastic lineage. In the *consorteria,* heirs collectively controlled the patrimony. However, Herlihy argues that such configurations were to be found only among the elites of commercial centers. Dynastic lineage, according to Herlihy, where titles and lands were passed only through one line, were characteristic of "feudal" Europe—meaning the north. *Medieval Households,* pp. 88–92. Although Anita Guerreau-Jalabert has demonstrated that aristocratic families were collateral, scholars still describe family organization in linear—often patrilinear—terms. For example, Pierre-Yves Laffont, "Réflexions méthodologiques sur un corpus de monographies familiales."

5. AD Eure-et-Loir, H 2308. See also, *CMPD,* no. 109, pp. 100–101.

the solitary male disposing of his property as he pleased—behavior consonant with primogeniture and patriarchy. But further investigation reveals nuances. While the lord of Courville made the gift, his wife, children, and brothers consented to the grant and acted in the charter with him. If Ivo was absolute lord of his demesne, why would he require their consent? Ivo recognized these kin had a right to the property in question, as did the bishop of Chartres, who included a warning against any kin that might potentially make a claim. Shortly after this act, Ivo confirmed a donation made by one of his vassals. The four sons of the lord of Courville appeared with their father in this act, and their vassal described his fief as belonging to the dominion of lord Ivo and his sons. No one son was designated as Ivo's heir here or in any other act.[6] Although the extant documents do indicate that Ivo's son Girogius followed his father as lord, Girogius's brothers continued to appear in his charters.[7] While the eldest son inherited the title and lordship of Courville, his brothers continued to have a right to family lands and to exercise lordship.

The absence of women in these two acts could be read as evidence that they were somehow restricted in this primogenitary form of inheritance. But such an interpretation would be at odds with all of the evidence from the Courville family in which women, in fact, played quite important roles. Philippa of Courville, the wife of Girogius, became the guardian of their minor children when her husband died, even though Girogius had *five* brothers who could have taken over the responsibility of the estates and progeny. The notion that wives were outsiders and viewed with suspicion by their husband's family is not supported by this example. Instead, the charters make it clear that Philippa enjoyed the same powers as lord that her husband and father-in-law had. When she and her son Ivo gave the *ban,* or authority over a village, she stated she gave that "which we hold from our predecessors [as lord of Courville], namely Ivo [her father-in-law] and Girogius [her husband]."[8] Philippa continued to be influential even when her son came of age. Sometime between 1109 and 1129, Ivo refused to abandon certain customs that his parents had levied on the abbey of St. Père. Philippa, who was on her deathbed, called her son to her and exhorted him to give up

---

6. AD Loir-et-Cher, 16 H 118. See also *CMPD,* no. 108, p. 100. For additional charters concerning the Courville family, see *CMPD,* no. 22, pp. 22–24; no. 35, p. 33; no. 103, p. 96; no. 107, pp. 98–99; no. 109, pp. 99–100, no. 110, pp. 100–102; no. 138, pp. 127–29. Jeanneau has found instances of lordships being shared by sons in Poitou. See "Liens adelphes et héritage," pp. 95–105.

7. AD Eure-et-Loir, H 2237. When Girogius gave the church of St. Nicholas of Courville to Marmoutier, two of his brothers acted with him. See also *Jean,* no. 2, pp. 1–2.

8. AD Eure-et-Loir, H 201. See also, *Père,* vol. 2, no. 43, pp. 499–500. For a more complete translation of this charter, see chapter 7, p. 187.

these customs. Ivo eventually followed his mother's advice and gave them to the monks.[9]

The seigneurial family of Courville holds some important lessons for investigating aristocratic inheritance. While this family, like others, invested the eldest son with the title and honors, other siblings were not forgotten or abandoned. Their rights to family holdings were recognized, and it is likely that they received a portion of the patrimony. Women, who were supposed to be marginalized and repressed when eldest sons inherited, were important members of this family and wielded considerable influence. One must read beyond the first line of the charter and weigh all the evidence. Surviving data from one family can make it difficult to develop a singular or consistent model for inheritance. But the behavior of donors seems inconsistent only if one assumes that one mode of inheritance was practiced. Consider the Beaugency family.

In the mid-twelfth century, Lord Lancelin II was involved in many disputes with the church over his possession of certain properties and rights. In one transaction, Lancelin appeared with his kinsman, sons, and brothers in quitclaiming what they claimed together from the monks of St. Trinité.[10] But a few years later, Lancelin acted alone in arranging a settlement with the bishop of Orléans.[11] Nor was this the first time Lancelin acted independently: before he succeeded his brother as lord, he had arranged resolutions to conflicts on his own as both disputant and as the lord of the person bringing the contestation. Hence, one act suggests that the Beaugency family shared control of certain properties. Yet in others, a lack of kin in the grant suggests that relatives did not have a right to other holdings. But still another implies division of the patrimony between two sons. Analysis of Beaugency family transactions reveals that lords frequently acted with their kin but also individually—a pattern Lancelin shared with his peers.[12]

This evidence points to the impact of particular circumstance, life stage, and other factors in unraveling the tangle of aristocratic inheritance. The

---

9. *Père,* vol. 2, no. 46, pp. 502–3. Ivo initially did not heed his mother's advice and "followed the heart of a youth." He later repented his actions and was reconciled with the monks. After Philippa and Ivo, possession of the lordship of Courville passed out of this family. In charters from the twelfth century, Nivelon, the lord of Meslay, is also designated as the lord of Courville. See AD Eure-et-Loir, H 1417 and H 1422.

10. *CTV,* vol. 2, no. 548, p. 399.

11. *CTV,* vol. 2, no. 569, pp. 434–35.

12. Such inconsistency can be baffling and makes it difficult to fit these actions into a monolithic model of inheritance or property rights. Fulcher Turre, for example, sometimes acted alone to resolve conflicts, but in other cases he appeared with a full spectrum of kin. *CTV,* vol. 1, no. 206, pp. 395–98; *MV,* no. 105, pp. 163–65.

possibility that different family holdings may have been bound by different rights, claims, and potential rights also emerges perforce. Just this handful of charters indicates a multiplicity of strategies of inheritance and control of property. The Beaugency charters suggest that the elite of the Loire region practiced both partible and impartible inheritance *at the same time*. In some cases, families shared inheritance of resources, thus favoring a model of impartible inheritance—at least for a portion of family property. Others may have invested not all, but key parts, of the patrimony in the patriline; still others clearly divided property among their heirs.[13] A multiplicity of options was open to aristocratic families to allow them to adjust their inheritance practices to best suit their family's individual circumstance.

Collective Control of Property: Indivisible Inheritance?

Continuity of Kindreds

The early Middle Ages have been portrayed, and generally accepted, as a time when an extended model of family structure prevailed in concert with an inheritance structure where children received support.[14] The documents from the Loire region contain many examples of exactly this open, extended family system—but with a nuance. Instead of dividing the patrimony—which is an assumed feature of a broad and expansive kinship network—these families

---

13. Nor were the elite of the lands of the Loire unique in the flexibility and diversity of inheritance practices. Evergates finds a model of the aristocratic "family viewed through the prism of patrilineage-primogeniture-patrimony" insupportable. *The Aristocracy in the County of Champagne,* p. 119. For Maine in the central Middle Ages, Lemesle characterizes family structure and inheritance as supple. *La société aristocratique dans le Haut-Maine,* p. 111–12. Jeanneau suggests that inheritance practices differed between seigneurial and vicecomital families in the frontier regions of Poitou. "Émergence et affirmation des familles seigneuriales," pp. 161–87. Scholars working in other parts of Europe have found similar flexibility in inheritance. Drell's analysis of the nobility of Norman Salerno in *Kinship and Conquest* demonstrates a wide array of inheritance practices and choices, including both partibility and primogeniture. The work of Jonathan Lyon, Stephanie Mooers Christelow, and Kathleen Hapgood Thompson has seriously challenged the notion that noble families were concerned with the male line to the exclusion of all other kin and casts further doubt on the dominance of patrilineage and primogeniture. See Lyon, "Cooperation, Compromise and Conflict Avoidance"; Stephanie Mooers Christelow, "The Division of Inheritance and the Provision of Non-Inheriting Offspring among the Anglo-Norman Elite"; Kathleen Hapgood Thompson, *Power and Border Lordship in Medieval France* and "Dowry and Inheritance Patterns." See also Amy Livingstone, "Kith and Kin."

14. This could mean that an heir would receive a share of the property, thus adhering to partible inheritance. In other cases, families did not divide their resources but shared them as a group. While the patrimony was not divided, the aim of this form of impartible inheritance was to provide support for a wide range of kin, in contrast to the use of impartible inheritance with patrilineage where the inheritance passed only to the firstborn son.

adhered to impartible inheritance. While impartibility would seem to signal the primogenitary model and its characteristic restrictions, the evidence suggests that the underlying premise of collective inheritance of the patrimony was not to exclude relatives but to provide support for many.

Did features consistent with what scholars have identified as the characteristics of early medieval family life persist into the eleventh century, precisely the era when radical "revolutions" in family structure were thought to take place? Yes. Analysis of a database consisting of a total of five hundred separate acts shows that 15 percent were grants made by collectives of family and kin in the eleventh and twelfth centuries, making collective inheritance a regular option for aristocratic inheritance.[15]

Around 1050, for example, five brothers and two nephews together sold one measure of land. The charter uses plural verbs, indicating that this collective of kin both "held" the land and "sold" the land as a group.[16] Their children, moreover, as demonstrated by the participation of two nephews, exercised a claim to the property as well—presumably through the claim of inheritance. Groups of sisters also acted together to control land and make donations. Two sisters, along with one of their husbands, donated property to St. Trinité. Once again the charter uses plural verbs to record this act.[17]

Kindreds of elite landholders also operated in the twelfth century. A grant made to the abbey of Tiron is particularly instructive. Around 1127, Hugo of Lièvreville, his mother, Maria, and his *cognatus* Herbert Guitum placed all of their land in mortgage to the monks. Significantly, the property at Lièvreville is designated as *feodum,* or fief.[18] Indeed, Bardulf of Galardun and his wife Helvisa "from whose fief the aforementioned land" pertained, consented to the transaction. The transfer of property closes with the original

---

15. This charter database is constructed from five hundred separate acts datable between 1000 and 1200 that are relevant to the aristocracy of the lands of the Loire from the cartularies of St. Trinité in Vendôme and St. Père and the charters from Marmoutier for Le Dunois, the Vendômois, and the Perche. Acts were included based on if they involved nobles from the mid-Loire region. The program used was Microsoft Excel, and various attributes of the charters were designated for sorting. The type of transaction (gift, sale, confirmation, resolution), the sex of the donor, the family status of the donor (father, mother, son, daughter, etc.), and those who consented, witnessed, or signed the donation were established as separate data fields. Other basic information such as the monastic house and the date and place of the transaction was also noted. These data fields make it possible to track certain characteristics, like the frequency with which men appeared individually as donors, or how often husbands and wives acted together to make a gift, or how many gifts resulted in disputes. Geographical and personal names were also recorded, making it possible to call up all acts involving one family or member of a family, thus providing a scope of activity for individual elites.

16. *CMPD,* no. 101, pp. 93–94.

17. *CTV,* vol. 1, no. 291, p. 446. This group also acted jointly to place a symbol of the gift upon the altar of the monks' church to consecrate the gift.

18. *Tiron,* vol. 1, no. 86, pp. 106–7. For another example of property held in fief by two cousins, see AD Eure-et-Loir, H 3451.

donors (Hugo, Maria, and Herbert) joining with even more kin to swear to observe the terms of their agreement, and the additional kin were granted countergifts for their consent and participation.[19] What conclusions can we draw? In some families extended kin shared control of property and thus shared the revenues and support generated by it. Collectives of kin also controlled feudal property, that is, land that required some sort of military obligation. This is particularly significant since it has been suggested that lords insisted that feudal holdings be held by and passed through the line of the eldest male. This preference, in fact, has been depicted as the catalyst for the change to primogeniture and patrilineage. Finally, the right that Maria had to the land as one of its controllers, and that Helvisa had as one of its lords, is proof that women were not marginalized. Rather, they shared control and the incumbent obligations enjoyed by male property holders.

The experience of Hugo of Lièvreville's family could be dismissed as an exception but for the many other examples of such collectives controlling and dispersing property among the twelfth-century elite of the Loire region. For example, Hugo of Monte-Bernardo, Roschus of Beaugency, his sister's husband, his wife's brother, their wives, and sons all gave up their right to the tithes from the animals they had falsely claimed from Tiron's priory of Cintry.[20] Like the grant by Hugo of Lièvreville, the disputed tithes were described as *feodum,* and their lord gave his consent to the resolution and even placed a knife upon the altar to symbolize the end of the hostilities between the monks and his vassals. How so many people exploited such properties is not clear. Each family unit or member might have enjoyed a particular portion, as suggested by Hugo of Lièvreville's grant.[21]

The close bond between nephew and uncle evident in the lives of the noble born was both complemented and reinforced by the shared control of property. In 1140, William of Plessis made a donation "of what I hold in fief... which came to me from my uncle Girard, who was without heirs and thus made me the heir to the aforementioned fiefs."[22] Evidently Girard

---

19. Countergifts were small gifts rewarded to donors, consenters, and witnesses in recognition of their donation. These gifts served as a security measure for the gift (the monks could remind people at a later date that they had received a countergift if they disputed the gift). Countergifts in most cases suggest that the recipient had some claim to the transferred property. See Tabuteau, *Transfers of Property,* pp. 115–19, 133, and 147; Bouchard, *Holy Entrepreneurs,* pp. 87–93.

20. *Tiron,* vol. 1, no. 205, pp. 232–33. While Roschus is acting with a group of his immediate and extended kin, the relationship between him and Hugo of Monte-Bernard is not clear.

21. AD Eure-et-Loir, H 3260. Barthélemy and Jeanneau also find evidence of collectives acting together. See *La société dans le comté de Vendôme,* pp. 528–30 and "Liens adelphes et héritage," pp. 100, 104–5.

22. *Tiron,* vol. 2, no. 238, pp. 11–12. Not only did William's father and brothers concede his gift and acceptance of a cash gift from the monks, they also promised to defend the gifts from all

and William developed a special relationship since William was eventually chosen as Girard's heir. It is even possible that William was fostered with his uncle Girard in preparation for him one day assuming control of his uncle's lands. As brothers, Girard and William's father were bound by blood ties but also by property since each inherited half of the family holdings at Choudri and Ozoir.[23] The closeness between brothers transcended their generation when Girard adopted one of his nephews as his heir.

In other families, uncles and adult nephews controlled property jointly. Gosbert of Boschet and his nephew, Herbert, for instance, became entangled in a dispute with the monks of St. Vincent of Le Mans sometime in the twelfth century over control of appurtenances associated with a church. Gosbert and Herbert claimed they were theirs by right of inheritance. The monks insisted their community possessed them because Gosbert's brother had exchanged them for other property. A plea was taken to the bishop's court, where Gosbert and Herbert freely and quietly dismissed their claim to this property and recognized that neither they nor their heirs would have a further claim to the land.[24] This contestation is interesting because it reveals several important points about inheritance and relationships between uncles and nephew. Since Gosbert and his nephew, Herbert, are labeled "*coadjutores,*" they brought the suit together. Both believed they had a right to the church through inheritance. Their association in this action also suggests that Herbert was under Gosbert's tutelage. Indeed, Gosbert may have been acting on behalf of his ward to ensure that he received his proper inheritance.

Nuclear Family

Nuclear families, as well as collectives of more distant kin, shared property:

> In the festival of the Holy Trinity, Matthew and Agrippa and their mother Guitberg, wife of Hugo Grippe, gave . . . land and . . . pasture at

---

false claims. This was not the first time these kin had played such a role in gifts. When William's uncle Girard had arranged a gift about fifteen years earlier, his brother Pagan II (William's father) stood as guarantor. The paths of these brothers intersected throughout their lives as they witnessed each other's transactions and participated in acts of their kin. Both Pagan and Girard witnessed their cousin Ursio's reconciliation with the monks of Tiron in 1146. *Tiron,* vol. 2, no. 290, p. 59. Pagan II of Frouville had two other brothers, Robert and Peter, who gave their consent to his quitclaim of property at Villeberfol in 1131. Pagan abandoned his right to this property at Count Thibaut V's court. His nephew Gosbert witnessed the accord. AD Loir-et-Cher, 16 H 118, no. 20.

23. *Tiron,* vol. 1, no. 117, p. 137.

24. *CSVM,* no. 132, p. 85. Apparently Gosbert's brother had entered religious life, and once the dispute was settled, he became a monk. It is possible that Gosbert's brother may have left his young son in his brother's care when he became a monk.

Rodon… to Holy Trinity of Vendôme.… All the monks saw them put the gift on the altar, which they [the monks] accepted… and by authority of the monastery they accepted into their prayers Agrippa and her mother, but Matthew they refused because he was excommunicated.[25]

In this intriguing charter, a mother and her two children act to give what they hold in Rodon to St. Trinité of Vendôme. The gift-giving ceremony, with the placement of a symbol of the gift on the altar in front of monastic witnesses, provides further evidence of their solidarity. Such rituals established the commitment of those who placed the symbol. Breaking a covenant that had been sacramentalized on the altar would be tantamount to breaking faith with God and the saints, and divine retribution would be sure to follow. Family togetherness broke down, however, when it came to the granting of spiritual countergifts. Agrippa and Guitberg were welcomed into the monks' prayers, but Matthew was not because he had been excommunicated. Typically, the charter does not tell us *why* Matthew had incurred this sentence, but given the actions of his peers, it is not difficult to speculate what might have been the reason.[26] Nuclear kin frequently participated in ecclesiastical benefactions by consenting to donations, witnessing, receiving countergifts, or confirming what had been given. What differentiates the grant by Guitberg and her children is that they act *together* as donors, as compared to a donor making a grant "with" or "with the consent of" immediate family.[27] For the Grippe family, all its members were donors of the property.

Like their neighbors and peers, the families of the Fréteval-Mondoubleau-Dives kindred also controlled many of their properties collectively, as a charter recording the donation by Ingelbald Brito, his wife, Domitilla, and their three sons illustrates. On September 6, 1070, this family donated "what they had through inheritance from their predecessors in the forest which is called Chatenay."[28] The language of this charter is quite clear: this family holds this property collectively and had inherited it as a group from their predecessors. The collectivity of possession and of the grant itself was reinforced by the

---

25. *CTV*, vol. 1, no. 135, pp. 339–40. As in other charters, the plural of the verb was used to signify that all the family held this land together. There was another son, but he was absent from this charter. Perhaps the land in question did not pertain to his part of the patrimony.

26. Barbara Rosenwein, Thomas F. Head, and Sharon Farmer, "The Monks and Their Enemies," pp. 764–96.

27. For example: "Gislebert of Ruga Vasselorum, *with* his wife and sons and daughters, for his soul." *CTV*, vol. 1, no. 136, pp. 241–43 (emphasis added). For an original charter for this family, see AD Eure-et-Loir, H 500.

28. *CTV*, vol. 1, no. 218, pp. 350–52.

placement of "the gift with their own hands upon the altar, in the plain view of all of their *fideles.*" The monks further affirmed that this property was controlled by this family group by writing all of their names in their martyrology and promising to pray for *all* of their souls. A charter from about twenty years earlier indicates that Domitilla and her family were following family precedent in their collective control of family holdings. Fulcher Dives, Domitilla's grandfather, and his wife, Adela, and their two sons gave an alod that was described as pertaining to "our jurisdiction," an indication that these people shared control of the legal obligations and rights of this territory as well.[29]

Siblings

Siblings also held property jointly. Two brothers, Hugh the archdeacon and Odo of Mondoubleau (the grandsons of Fulcher Dives), donated the church of St. Bienheuré to St. Trinité of Vendôme.[30] Both Odo and Hugh signed the charter, and several of their kin witnessed the gift for them. Nearly 125 years later, the descendants of these men continued to share possession of property among brothers. Yet family structure appears somewhat modified. Or was it?

> Let all the present and future know that two certain *juvenes* of Lisle, one was a cleric named Bartholomew, and the other named William was a layman and the *primogenitus,* both came into the chapterhouse of Vendôme with their friends, and they gave [what] they hold from the same church in fief…to God and the monks of Vendôme. William who was first born, sent a book to Prior Hugh in the chapterhouse, which was witnessed by [these] monks. So that the gift would remain firm and no one could bring a claim or quarrel, both the brothers placed [a symbol] upon the altar of the Lord.[31]

Here we have two brothers giving property possessed jointly and in fief, a practice that seems very much in keeping with what their predecessors were doing a century earlier. There were some subtle transformations, however. William, who was a layman, was identified as the eldest, and he clearly plays

---

29. *MV,* no. 130, pp. 225–26.

30. *CTV,* vol. 1, no. 21, pp. 41–42. They made the gift with the consent of their lords, Count Geoffrey and Countess Agnes. This gift was also confirmed in *CTV,* vol. 1, no. 46, pp. 99–100.

31. *CTV,* vol. 2, no. 571, pp. 436–37.

an additional role in securing the gift by giving a book to the prior. Some would find it significant that Bartholomew was a cleric and would suggest he was placed in the church in an attempt to reduce the number of claims to the patrimony.[32] But these assertions of change must be balanced against other evidence. First, it is clear that the brothers each have a claim to the property and are acting *together* to make the gift. William's place as firstborn did not supersede his younger sibling's possession of and right to family holdings. Moreover, the brothers acted together to consecrate the gift to prevent any possible disputes to their donation. Second, the Dives family, of which the lords of Lisle were a branch, had a long-established practice of placing sons in the church. So Bartholomew becoming a cleric can be as easily ascribed to family tradition as to a strategy to preserve limited resources. William's designation as *primogenitus* may be significant in that it suggests a new concern with birth order, but it does not herald a completely new form of family structure or inheritance practice.[33] When all of the evidence is weighed and placed in the context of this particular family, it is clear that the family practice of shared inheritance had continued and that the same basic family structure was still in place.

The neighbors of these brothers would have been familiar with the practice of siblings sharing possession of property for the charters of the Loire region are replete with many instances of just this form of inheritance. At the end of the eleventh century, for example, a set of two brothers made an extensive gift of property, which they had held together. The circumstances of their generosity were sad, however. The brothers had traveled to the monastery at Vendôme on the day that the monks buried their mother. Their gift of the land, and all that pertained to it, was intended to benefit her soul.[34]

The strategy of joint control and inheritance of property was practiced by other twelfth-century aristocratic families. Around 1130, Haimeric Baufredus and his brother Hugo, who was a monk, gave to the monks of Tiron all that pertained to their fief in land and woods, as well as additional nearby properties that they also held jointly.[35] Even though Hugo had joined a monastic order, he continued to possess family property, proof that placement of

---

32. Duby, *Medieval Marriage*, p. 102. Bouchard challenges this notion; "*Strong of Body, Brave and Noble*," pp. 149–51. Evidence from the lands of the Loire demonstrates that all types of property, including ecclesiastical holdings, were eligible for partition. For examples, see *Père*, vol. 1, no. 18, pp. 140–41; AD Eure-et-Loir, H 505; AD Eure-et-Loir, H 2514. See also *CMPD*, no. 25, pp. 26–27.

33. Evergates similarly challenges the use of terms describing birth order as anything other than place holders. *Aristocracy in the County of Champagne*, pp. 85, 125–26.

34. *MV*, no. 58, pp. 94–95.

35. *Tiron*, vol. 1, no. 157, pp. 179–80.

sons and daughters in the church did not sever their rights to or possession of property and therefore was not a way of reducing the number of children with rights to the patrimony. Although the property granted in these pious benefactions was shared by the brothers, it is not clear whether or not the brothers had inherited the land collectively. Two other twelfth-century charters tell us more about how this was handled in other families. Sometime in the first three decades of the century, five brothers sold "all of their fisc [or fief] among Villandon which they possess *jure hereditario* [by right or custom of inheritance]."[36] This family had chosen to pass this land down to the brothers collectively. Moreover, the wives, children, and grandchildren of these five brothers consented to the negotiated sale. In another case from around 1140, Herbert and his brother sold land to the reformed abbey of St. Jean-en-Vallée that they together possessed *jure hereditario*.[37] As in the preceding case, these brothers shared control over their inherited properties.

Dominion over property was particularly at issue for fiefs that had a myriad of lordly rights and obligations attached to them. Did brothers "holding" land together also mean they shared authority over the property? Several acts suggest that dominion over fiefs and honors was indeed shared by siblings. Recall that the sons of Lord Ivo of Courville shared control over their lands with their father. Other acts provide additional examples. Rotrou the knight and his brothers possessed land together that they held in fief from two brothers, Rodulf and Hildgod, the sons of Girald Brunellus.[38] Girald Brunellus's sons clearly exercised lordship over these properties together. Nor was this practice an artifact of the decentralized nature of politics of the eleventh century. Sometime around 1127, two brothers donated land to the abbey of St. Jean-en-Vallée. Their lords, the brothers Mener and Gui of Étampes, consented to the gift and were granted countergifts for their cooperation.[39] Fraternal sharing of fiefs and the rights of lordship continued well into the more politically stable twelfth century.

Collectives of kin, nuclear families, and groups of siblings controlled and alienated family holdings. The sharing of family resources attests to a family ethos that stressed inclusion rather than privileging one child and his descendants. This version of impartible inheritance has received little attention from scholars. The "either-or" dyad—either partible or impartible—has dominated the discourse on aristocratic family life. Yet the evidence from the lands of the Loire demonstrates that inheritance practices were multihued

---

36. *Tiron,* vol. 1, no. 128, pp. 152–53.
37. *Jean,* no. 52, p. 31.
38. *CMPD,* no. 141, pp. 131–32.
39. *Jean,* no. 40, pp. 24–25.

and did not conform to the black-and-white designation of impartible inheritance equaling primogeniture and patrilineage, and partible inheritance equaling broad and inclusive family structures.

Partible Inheritance

Aristocratic families had several arrows in their quiver of inheritance. One was a division of the patrimony among children. As the staggering frequency with which property was described as being a quarter, third, half, sixth, even sixteenths suggests, aristocratic families divided their patrimonies throughout the central Middle Ages. Like William of Ponthieu and Arnulf of Boulogne, who were mentioned at the outset of this chapter, Hamelin II of Montoire parceled out his holdings among his children (see appendix, chart 13). Hamelin and his son Peter seized certain properties from the monks. In the charter recording the end to hostilities, dating from the 1120s, Peter was designated as Hamelin's heir.[40] Looking at this through a patrilinear lens, one would conclude that Hamelin and his eldest son were acting together to protect the family patrimony. But Peter was in fact a younger son, for his brother Philip was clearly labeled as the *primogenitus* in another act.[41] There was also a third son, Odo Dubellus. How, then, were Hamelin's holdings distributed among his heirs? Philip, as the eldest, inherited the family possessions at Montoire, which Hamelin had inherited through his mother. Odo—who was deliberately named for his great-grandfather Odo Dubellus, the lord of Mondoubleau—was heir to the Mondoubleau holdings, which had also passed to Hamelin through his mother. Peter, the troublemaker, inherited properties that his father had acquired in fief from the abbot of St. Trinité of Vendôme.[42] This distribution of inheritance follows a fairly traditional division of family property: the eldest son received the patrimonial lands, while the other two were provided with other inheritances and acquired lands, a practice particularly common among the Anglo-Norman kings and nobility.[43] While not a hard and fast rule, many families distributed their

---

40. *CTV,* vol. 2, no. 438, pp. 215–17. This was not the first time Hamelin had been in trouble with St. Trinité. Around 1104, he was excommunicated for "the evils" he had done to this church. Indeed, Abbot Geoffrey of Vendôme was incensed when Hamelin was pardoned by the bishop of Le Mans for these actions. Geoffrey asserted that justice had not been done and that Hamelin had not provided proper restitution. Geoffrey of Vendôme, *Oeuvres,* letters 40 and 41, pp. 72–74.

41. *CTV,* vol. 2, no. 397, pp. 147–49.

42. *CTV,* vol. 2, no. 438, pp. 215–17.

43. Emily Z. Tabuteau, "The Role of Law in the Succession to Normandy and England, 1087"; Andrew Lewis, *Royal Succession in Capetian France.*

property in this way.[44] What makes it unusual here is that a family of middling rank was adhering to the same pattern. Moreover, they were doing so generations after they were *supposed*—by scholars—to be investing *all* family properties in the line of the eldest son.

The example of Hamelin II of Montoire highlights another vital feature of inheritance and family structure: the importance of women and the collateral nature of the family. The property which made up Hamelin's patrimony, and which his sons inherited, came to him through his mother's family. Helvisa-Adierna, Hamelin's mother, was the daughter of Odo of Mondoubleau and Placentia of Montoire. The honors of Montoire passed first from Placentia to her daughter Helvisa-Adierna and her husband, and then to their son Hamelin II. The lordship of Mondoubleau was Helvisa-Adierna's paternal-family patrimony and eventually came under her control. Her grandson Odo Dubellus would follow as lord of Mondoubleau.[45] Helvisa-Adierna's ties to her natal family provided her son and grandsons with lordships and titles. But Helvisa-Adierna was more than a conduit through which land passed to noble males. She also played an important role in determining how such properties were distributed. A charter from 1081 records that her second husband wished to grant property to the church. "This [benefaction], however, [Hamelin of Langeais's] wife Helvisa[-Adierna] kindly authorized, [she] the daughter of Odo of Dubellus [Mondoubleau], who was born from his wife namely the daughter of Nithard of Montoire, from whose patrimonial right all of the aforementioned, most important, casamentum [castle and its holdings] belonged. And the right [to] which Hamelin now bore through marriage with the same Helvisa [-Adierna]."[46] In order for Hamelin to make a gift from these holdings, Helvisa-Adierna's approval and consent were required.

Like their predecessors, the women of the eleventh and twelfth centuries inherited property. The cases of Domitilla and Helvisa-Adierna supply further proof that the Dives clan practiced partible inheritance for these two women shared a common ancestor: Fulcher Dives. At least two of Fulcher's

---

44. Robert of Moncontour followed just this pattern. See this chapter pp. 101–3. Laurent Macé finds a similar practice in the Guilhem family of Montpellier. While he characterizes this inheritance pattern as "primogeniture," it has little in common with the primogeniture Duby hypothesized. Indeed, Macé finds that instead of creating tension between brothers over the distribution of resources, primogeniture ensured family peace and eldest sons were charged with the care of their younger siblings. Laurent Macé, "Les frères au sien du lignage."

45. Before her marriage to Hamelin of Langeais, Helvisa-Adierna was married to Pagan of Fréteval. Her son with this man, Pagan, was lord of Mondoubleau before her grandson Odo Dubellus.

46. *CTV,* vol. 2, no. 302, pp. 7–9.

children inherited portions of the church at Lancôme, which they passed along to their heirs. Domitilla received her share from her father, Fulcher Turre.[47] Her kinswoman Helvisa-Adierna's holdings at the same church came from her grandmother, Fulcher's sister.

The last will and testament of Domitilla and Helvisa-Adierna's ancestor Robert of Moncontour similarly provides an additional example of division of the patrimony and maternal inheritance. As he neared the end of his life at the close of the eleventh century, Robert of Moncontour, the brother of Adela of Bezai, wife of Fulcher Dives, made the following provision (see appendix, chart 9):

> In the name of the Father, Son and Holy Spirit, the only one and all-knowing God, I Robert, *miles* [knight] who is called of Moncontour, contemplative of the fragility of men and with fear and concern for my soul, give to St. Trinité of Vendôme and the monks there that which [comes] legally from my jurisdiction, I transfer into their dominion and I concede that they shall hold this perpetually and by irrefutable custom of law all of the lordship that I hold among the villa of Coulommiers, namely land, and all serfs and servants and... vines, woods, mills and pastures, and ponds and universal fishing rights, and all revenues that pertain to this same land, and [the monks] shall be the just possessors of these properties. Moreover, I make this [gift] gratefully and solemnly for the redemption of my sins, for my soul, for those of my kin, and hoping for the mercy of God. So that this gift will remain firm and stable for perpetuity, I and my two sons, Gervase and Hameric, who [are] in our presence, [let] it be recorded that we placed a knife upon the altar of the lord God by our own hands, enacting the agreement, we ordered this charter to be written, so that we could have our *fideles* [vassals] corroborate it through their hands.[48]

Robert goes on to state that he would like to take the habit and live out his days as a monk. Clearly, this nobleman was retiring from secular life and putting his affairs in order. As he states:

> This seeming good and just to me, so that all of my good lands which... came to me from paternal and maternal authority, and I

---

47. *MB,* no. 88, p. 97.

48. *CTV,* vol. 1, no. 299, pp. 455–60. The charter uses *parentes,* which in its broadest sense means biological descent. It can also mean parents, but I have chosen the former definition. For discussion of the meaning of *parentes,* see Bauduin, "Désigner les parents," 74.

labored hard and long in this world, God helping me, I acquired these honors which were given to me and I justly retained from my lord, and for my soul... none of my sons will give contradiction to what I have done, if they recognize me as their father, if they love me, especially since I would do the same for them, they should do this for me.[49]

Like the patrimony of other lords, Robert's consisted of what he had inherited through "paternal and maternal authority," in other words, what he had inherited from *both* his mother's and father's families. Robert also shared with his peers and neighbors the concern that his heirs might later dispute his gift. To prevent this, he had his sons consent to the agreement and symbolize their approval, and he issued an admonitory statement at the end of the charter. Unlike other admonitions, however, Robert did not use fear to encourage his progeny to abide by the charter; rather, he counted on their love for him. Robert was every inch the medieval warrior, as is indicated in his description of having to conquer his lands, but he was not without emotion: he cared for his children. That he could depend on his children's affection for him suggests a loving relationship between father and sons.

Yet the story of Robert of Moncontour's retirement does not end here. For an important member of Robert's family was missing in this grant: his eldest son, Bertran. Why was Bertran absent from his father's last act? Because he and his father had already come to an agreement about what Bertran would have from the family patrimony:

> I, Robert, knight of Moncontour, wish it to be known to my posterity and all Christians, that when I gave and relinquished my honors to my son Bertran, under the condition that he would have from me all of my land from the patrimony of Vendôme, which I retained faithfully and without committing bad deeds, I [thus] kept custody of it. [But] truly the land of Coulommiers, which belongs to me peacefully and in all perpetual claims, I may do as I please with it during my life, and after my death, without contradiction or molestation.[50]

While Bertran inherited his father's honors at Moncontour, Robert retained control of those lands that he had acquired through service or conquest. Was it unusual for a father to arrange for his son to become lord and inherit his honors, titles, and lands before his death? Unfortunately it is difficult to

---

49. *CTV,* vol. 1, no. 299, pp. 455–60.
50. *CTV,* vol. 1, no. 298, pp. 454–55.

judge. Certainly there are very few other instances where sons inherited during their father's lifetime, but the perception that this is an extraordinary event may have to do with the evidence itself. How many sons who were confirming what they had recently inherited had a similar agreement with their fathers, but the record has not survived? Robert of Moncontour's testaments are full of suggestive details and certainly challenge the notion that fathers and sons were continually at odds over land. Like that of his Montoire kin, Robert's disposition of land among his sons conforms to a fairly typical pattern. His eldest son was invested with the traditional patrimonial lands, while the other sons received shares of property that had been added to the family coffers by Robert's sword. Robert's distribution of his properties harkens back to Lambert of Ardres's description of Count Arnulf and Lord William. These three noble-born fathers clearly took pains to see that all of their sons inherited a proper share of their holdings.

The seigneurial family of Montigny confirms the practice of patrimony division and also offers some interesting insights into family dynamics.[51] Sometime around 1115, Agnes, the *domina* of Montigny, married Odo of Vallières (see appendix, chart 6). The union of these two houses essentially saved the lordship of Montigny from financial ruin. Infusion of wealth from the Vallières line, combined with the established seat of Montigny, created a powerful and wealthy noble dynasty. The revitalization of the Montignys is apparent in the family's foundation of a priory at their family seat and their generous patronage of the abbey of Marmoutier in general.[52] Agnes and Odo had all of their seven sons and daughters participate in these donations and consent to the alienation of property. Yet only two of the sons, Raher and Odo, are traceable as adults.[53] The names of these two sons are significant and served as indicators of which lands each could expect to inherit.[54] Raher was named for Raher I, the founder of the house of Montigny, and Odo was

---

51. Hamelin of Fréteval, the son of Fulcher and brother to Nivelon II, married Adela, the widow of Ganelon of Montigny. No children resulted from this union, however. Agnes, Adela and Ganelon's daughter, became the lord of Montigny after the death of her mother.

52. For the priory foundation, see AD Eure-et-Loir, H 2358; see also *CMPD*, no. 184, pp. 174–76. This document is a chirograph, meaning that it is one copy of the transaction. The scribe made two identical copies of the transaction on one piece of parchment and wrote "CHIRO-GRAPH" in the middle. The parchment was then cut through "CHIROGRAPH" and each party got a copy of the transaction. Interestingly, although all children consented to the donation, only Odo and Raher signed this document with their parents. It is possible that the daughters signed the original document and that their brothers only signed the chirograph.

53. For further discussion of this family, see Livingstone, "Kith and Kin," pp. 419–58.

54. For a discussion of aristocratic naming practices and preferences, see Bouchard, *Sword, Miter, and Cloister*, pp. 82–84; *"Strong of Body, Brave and Noble,"* pp. 71–73.

named for his father. Not surprisingly, Raher inherited the Montigny holdings, and Odo followed his father as lord of Vallières. The birth order of these
two sons is not recoverable, unfortunately, but may not be relevant since both
inherited one of their family's primary lordships.

Of the two sons, Odo's life experiences are the more intriguing. Odo
first appears in the extant documents in the 1130s when he was in trouble
with the monks of Notre Dame de Josaphat near Chartres. His first act,
significantly, was an abandonment of unjust claims that he had made in his
first years as a knight.[55] He also admitted to stealing cows from the monks
at the same time! This was clearly a restless and rambunctious young man.
What may have motivated such behavior? Duby would interpret it as a sign
of primogeniture: younger sons could not expect to inherit land and had
to resort to violent means to gain support.[56] But we know that Odo *could*
expect a share, or could he? At the time of abandonment and admission of
this behavior, his father was still living. So perhaps the dispersal of family
holdings among the various heirs had not yet been decided. But this act has
additional information that might explain Odo II's actions. At the conclusion, the charter states that Odo was departing for a trip to Jerusalem. What
motivated this trip is not clear. It could have been done as penitence for his
behavior toward the monks. Yet many noblemen and women usurped property from the monks and did not feel compelled to go to the Holy Land.
Nor was Odo a youth in search of adventure and loot. He was married at
the time of the resolution of his dispute. So why did he go? Perhaps for the
adventure, perhaps for penitence. While Odo's behavior does not necessarily
jibe with the various theories concerning the actions of young sons waiting
either for their inheritance or for their father to die, personalities need to be
taken into account. Charters from the later years of Odo's life demonstrate
that he continued to have many disputes with the church over his personal
properties. Apparently his bovine larceny as a youth prefigured a tense relationship with his monastic neighbors throughout his life.

Unlike Odo II, his brother Raher seems to have caused little trouble for
the monks or his family. Raher became lord of Montigny sometime before
1150. In contrast to his brother, whose interactions with the monks consist
nearly entirely of disputes and their resolution, Raher made several modest benefactions to the abbey of Tiron and exchanged lands with both this
abbey and Marmoutier. The differences between these two brothers also
extend to the structure of their two families. Appearing with Odo II in his

55. *Josaphat,* vol. 1, no. 32, pp. 48–49.
56. Duby, "Youth in Aristocratic Society"; Baldwin, *Aristocratic Life,* pp. 70–71.

various contestations and their eventual resolution was his nuclear family: his wife and their five children. Raher's immediate family, in contrast, was virtually absent. The only relative appearing with Raher was his *primogenitus,* Odo. Moreover, Odo was designated as lord of Montigny with his father, and as such, his father's heir. In this family the firstborn son enjoyed some special status among Raher's children.[57] Odo participated with his father in making gifts, acting as lord, and in swearing to guarantee and defend their gifts.

While these brothers accorded different rights to their children, they were similar in their lack of recognition of each other's claim or right to their property. As adults, Odo II and Raher never appeared in the other's acts. Indeed, it would appear that the close relationship between brothers, uncles, and cousins evident in other families did not exist here. Instead, the families of Raher and Odo II assume a more linear form. Given what we know about the two, this apparent rift could be the result of a clash of personalities. Odo may simply have been difficult to get along with. Yet unlike Raher, Odo did include all of his children in his acts. Raher clearly invested his eldest son with special privileges and staked the survival of the family on the success of this one child.

Like seigneurial families, those of vicecomital rank also divided their patrimonies among their sons. The viscounts of Chartres exemplify this practice (see appendix, chart 3). The first viscount of Chartres was Gelduin I, who, at the time of his inheritance, already controlled Breteuil in the Beauvaisis (see map 1). A charter from Marmoutier indicates that Gelduin inherited his alods at Chamars from his relatives, Bishop Hugh, Gelduin, and Fulcher of Chartres.[58] Gelduin also provided for a wide spectrum of kin in his benefaction: the relatives from whom he inherited his property, his wife, his sons, but also his lord, Count Odo. While we know that Viscount Gelduin and his wife Emmeline had four sons, Harduin, Evrard, Hugh, and Galeran, it is not possible to reconstruct their birth order. Harduin and Evrard, however, appear to be the elder sons since their participation in their father's acts dates farthest back and both sons were associated early on with Gelduin as lord of vicecomital holdings. When their vassal Ivo of Courville made a donation, he secured the consent of his *lords,* Viscount Gelduin of Chartres and his

---

57. *CMPD,* no. 192, pp. 181–83. There were at least two other sons, whose souls were provided for by an 1184 reconfirmation of previous gifts. Odo would seem to be named for his grandfather rather than his uncle, given the lack of connection between Raher I and Odo II.

58. *CMPD,* no. 21, pp. 21–22. A. de Dion, in "Les seigneurs de Breteuil," suggests that Gelduin inherited the viscounty of Chartres from his wife's family (198–99). He believes that Emmeline was the daughter of Fulcher of Chartres, who is designated as one of those from whom Gelduin inherited the donated alods.

two sons, Harduin and Evrard.[59] As Ivo stated: "I also concede to the monks [the various properties are listed]...with the assent of my lord Viscount Gelduin and his sons Harduin and Evrard, from whom [plural] I hold all of the land of Courville." The lordship of Courville was under the dominion of a triad of lords: Gelduin and his two sons. At about the same time as Ivo of Courville's grant, Gelduin and Harduin acted together to make a donation to Marmoutier. While the gift itself is unremarkable, what is really interesting about this benefaction is that Harduin was designated as viscount of Chartres even though his father was still alive.[60] Significantly, Gelduin was called "Gelduin of Breteuil" and not viscount. Gelduin may have invested Harduin with lands in the Loire region so that he was free to attend to the family holdings to the north. His use of the geographic cognomen of Breteuil supports such a hypothesis for in other acts Gelduin was usually labeled viscount of Chartres or Gelduin of Chartres. Like Robert of Moncontour, Gelduin appears to have passed on power over the Chartrain territories to his son during his lifetime.

Although Harduin was designated as his successor, Viscount Gelduin divided the vicecomital patrimony to provide each son with a share.[61] Harduin succeeded his father as viscount sometime around 1060, but his tenure was cut short by an early death. His brother Evrard, "one of the most highly born nobles in France,"[62] assumed the title after Harduin died.[63] The two younger sons, Hugh and Galeran, were vested with other lordships. Hugh was lord of Le Puiset, a powerful seigneury located just outside Chartres, and Galeran received the lordship of Breteuil, which had been the family's original powerbase. This family practiced just the reverse of the custom of granting the patrimonial lands to the eldest son and acquired lands to the younger. The eldest son got the newly gained property in the Chartrain, and the youngest succeeded to the traditional family lands in the Beauvaisis. While there may have been informal traditions or customs that influenced how noble families dispersed property, personal preferences and circumstances prevailed.

---

59. *CMPD,* no. 109, p. 101.

60. AD Eure-et-Loir, H 2307. See also *CMPD,* no. 110, pp. 101–2.

61. *CMPD,* nos. 39 and 41, p. 36 and p. 39 respectively. In particular, vicecomital holdings at Nottonville were partitioned. Nottonville is located in the heart of the Chartrain among rich and fertile wheat fields. The monks of Marmoutier established a priory at Nottonville, likely to collect grain for distribution to the mother house and other sister foundations. These rich lands were divided among the viscount's sons. Parts of the fortified priory remain today. See Philippe Rachinet, *Archéologie et histoire d'un prieuré bénédictin en Beauce,* for a discussion of the historical and economic importance of the priory and community.

62. Orderic Vitalis, *Ecclesiastical History,* vol. 3, p. 139.

63. AD Eure-et-Loir, H 2307.

Although the vicecomital family lands and lordships were spread out all over northern France, these brothers actively participated in each other's transactions and maintained strong family ties.

In 1073, Viscount Evrard decided to abandon the secular world and become a monk at Marmoutier. The charter recording his entrance says that he had listened to the words of the Lord: "Unless you renounce all that you possess, you are not able to be my disciple."[64] Evrard subsequently turned his back on the world and left "his patrimony in the hands of his relatives [i.e., his brothers]."[65] Hugh gave his portion of the family holdings at Nottonville "out of love for his brother," and Galeran authorized Hugh's donations at the monastery, again at Blois, and once more when he traveled to Le Puiset to visit. Evrard's transition from the secular world to monastic life was not entirely smooth, however. His wife tried to prevent him from becoming a monk, preferring that he "remain a layman."[66] Evrard's brother Hugh may have been present at Evrard's entrance into the monastery to help ease matters between Evrard and his discontented spouse. Yet his efforts did not yield success for the discord between Evrard and his wife persisted for some time. The situation seems to have come to a head at Hugh's castle of Le Puiset, where his sister-in-law was staying. Abbot Bernard of Marmoutier had journeyed to the castle to try to seek a solution. Hugh and Galeran were also concerned with the situation and used their persuasion to convince their sister-in-law to let their brother join the monastery. These brothers had affection for each other. Both Hugh and Galeran supported Evrard in his decision to become a monk, made additional benefactions to Marmoutier out of love for him, and tried to smooth things over with their sister-in-law.

The inheritance arrangements in the next generation of viscounts were shaped by larger events, specifically the Crusades. Viscount Hugh I, Evrard's brother, had three sons: Evrard II, Hugh II of Le Puiset, and Gui. Two of the sons left on Crusade and the third entered the church. While the eldest son, Evrard, did succeed his father, he left on Crusade immediately after his father's death. After Evrard left for the Holy Land, his brother Hugh became viscount and lord of Le Puiset.[67] He also assumed guardianship of Evrard's minor son, Hugh III the Younger. The fact that Hugh II acted as guardian

---

64. AD Eure-et-Loir, H 2367. For discussion of Evrard's conversion and its broader implications, see Dominique Iogna-Prat, "Évrard de Breteuil et son double," pp. 537–38.

65. *CMPD*, no. 41, p. 39. Brothers in seigneurial families also inherited property from one another. See *Père*, vol. 2, no. 15, p. 273.

66. AD Eure-et-Loir, H 2307.

67. *CMPD*, no. 149, pp. 137–38. A later confirmation of the act recording the arrangement of the celebration of Hugh I's anniversary states that Viscount Evrard III "after the death of his father

of his nephew, combined with Evrard II's naming choice, may indicate that these brothers—just like their father and uncle in the previous generation—were particularly close. In 1105, once Hugh III the Younger came of age,[68] the elder Hugh followed his brother's example and departed for the Holy Land. Unlike Evrard II who met a rather hasty death in the East, Hugh II had considerable success. He became the lord of Jaffa and was able to establish a dynasty that controlled this territory for several decades.[69]

In contrast to his crusading brothers, Hugh I's third son, Gui, entered the church.[70] But at some point, Gui abandoned the clerical life, married the daughter of the viscount of Étampes, and adopted the title of Gui of Méréville. The motivations for Gui's abandonment of monastic life remain frustratingly obscure. Gui's actions do suggest he was not suited to the contemplative life, but it is not clear whether Gui was acting with the support of his family or on his own. But we should not conclude that Gui would have faced family disapproval since marriage with this woman expanded family holdings and their political clout. Ultimately, Gui married an heiress and became an important lord in the region. Étampes and Méréville were strategically placed between the vicecomital seat of Le Puiset and the royal demesne. Joined with the holdings of Gui's mother's family of Montlhéry and Rochefort, these lands created an arc of influence that could alternately present a threat to the French king *and* provide a line of defense from any attempt at royal expansion from the north or east.

Gui's nephew, Viscount Hugh III "the Younger" of Chartres and lord of Le Puiset, inherited a powerful and rich patrimony. Hugh used these properties to create a powerbase at Le Puiset, which came to the attention of King

---

became the lord of [Le Puiset]," an indication that the office of viscount of Chartres had become associated with this important seigneury.

68. It would seem that Hugh III's coming-of-age might have encouraged his uncle to go to the Holy Land. Hugh II's departure could also have been part of the second wave of Crusaders who left the West after a series of devastating defeats in the Holy Land. Hugh III Le Puiset was one of the strongest and most obstreperous lords of his time. His protracted battles with King Louis the Fat are well documented in Suger's deeds of the king. In order for Hugh III to have been such an accomplished warrior and such a threat to the king, he could not have been a mere boy. His contests with Louis occurred in the early 1110s, so he must have come of age about 1105, just at the time his uncle departed for the Holy Land.

69. Indeed, the Le Puisets were part of an important crusading house: the Montlhérys. Their mother, Adelaide, was the daughter of Gui Montlhéry. This family counted many crusaders among its ranks and controlled some of the most important lordships in the Latin kingdoms. See John La Monte, "The Lords of Le Puiset on Crusade"; Riley-Smith, *The First Crusaders, 1095–1131,* pp. 169–89.

70. "Gui" was a new name for the vicecomital family. Gui of Méréville was named after his maternal grandfather, Gui of Montlhéry.

Philip I and King Louis VI. Philip I imprisoned Hugh sometime before 1106, for just after his release—perhaps to give thanks for it—Hugh abandoned "unjust customs" that he had exacted from the monks of St. Père.[71] This initial imprisonment was the precursor of a long, violent, and contentious relationship between viscount and kings. While family connections with the Rocheforts and Montlhérys amplified the viscounts' difficulties with the crown, their own behavior contributed greatly to Louis VI's antipathy for this family. According to Suger, Viscount Hugh III was a violent lord who abused his power. Although he was not the first viscount of Chartres to use his power this way, Louis VI, in attempting to gain back royal lands, was far less tolerant of such behavior and may have been looking for any excuse to keep Hugh III in check.

The inheritance practices of the vicecomital family were affected by the hostilities between them and the king. During the several sieges of Le Puiset, the property of the viscounts was ravaged and destroyed—the coup de grâce coming when Louis VI razed the château in his third battle at Le Puiset. Hugh III had three sons. His eldest, Evrard III, became viscount and seems to have inherited the lion's share of his family's holdings. The two younger sons, Hugh and Bouchard, consented to their father's gifts but do not appear to have received a share of the patrimony.[72] Hugh entered the church and may have become the bishop of Durham. Bouchard disappears from the charters at a relatively early age. It is difficult to determine whether this transition in inheritance pattern was a result of the wars between viscount and king or if it was merely a continuation of an earlier practice dating back to the generation preceding Hugh III. Whatever the catalyst, by the decade of the 1130s, the vicecomital family of Chartres seems to have abandoned its practice of partible inheritance and close ties between lines. Indeed by 1130, several clear lines of descendants of the viscount of Chartres had emerged, specifically the lords of Breteuil, the viscounts of Chartres cum lords of Le Puiset, and the lords of Méréville. While these houses were separate, they did continue to interact with each other and with other extended kin, evidence that primogenitary inheritance did not always signal a lack of engagement with extended relatives.[73] Yet within each house itself, the family had

---

71. *Père,* vol. 2, no. 57, p. 452.

72. See *Tiron,* vol. 1, no. 108, pp. 127–28; *Josaphat,* vol. 1, no. 30, pp. 45–47; *Père,* vol. 2, no. 15, pp. 412–13.

73. For example, Hugh III's uncles Gui of Rochefort and Gui of Méréville participated with him in his acts concerning Aimery Chenard (*Jean,* nos. 33, 34, 35, pp. 19–22). Evrard III, Hugh III's son, had his cousin John of Méréville and his nephew Henry witness one of his acts (*CMPD,* no. 189, p. 179).

assumed a more lineal pattern. A sign of this change in inheritance and family ethos is apparent in the fact that instead of making benefactions to benefit
the souls of relatives and kin, the viscounts primarily sought to assure their
own place in the afterlife.

From mighty viscounts to simple knights, nobles with a broad range of
familial, social, political, and economic standing divided their holdings among
their children. Sometimes the practice of partitioning the patrimony coex-
isted with other kinds of inheritance. At the midpoint of the twelfth century,
Turpin of Faye's two sons gave part of "their patrimony" to the church. Here
we have a case of impartible inheritance: these brothers shared control of this
property.[74] Yet this was not always how inheritance had been determined
because in the same charter, Simon, their paternal uncle, gave *his half* of
the same holding for the redemption of his soul and so he could become a
monk.[75] In the preceding generation, the patrimony of this family had been
divided between Turpin of Faye and his brother. Turpin did provide for both
of his sons, although not by partitioning the patrimony but rather through
shared fraternal inheritance.

Partible and impartible inheritance were also used simultaneously. Remember Matthew Griponis who was excommunicated by the monks? In the
decade between 1073 and 1084, he tried to give his quarter of the church of
Rodon to the church. It turned out, however, that his brother, Adelard, who
had the unusual cognomen of Eel Biter, had placed this property in mortgage to the monks.[76] The dispersal of lands at Rodon suggests that Adelard
and Matthew each received a share of the property for Adelard would not
have been able to mortgage a quarter of the church if he had not held it
legitimately. The coexistence of partible and impartible inheritance is borne
out in another charter concerning this family. Recall that Matthew, his sister,
and their mother granted what they held *together* at Rodon to the monks of

---

74. For other examples, see AD Loir-et-Cher, 16 H 84. See also *MB,* no. 82, p. 90. When Hugh
the prevot of Blois and his wife, Praxedis, made a gift to Marmoutier of what they held, "the other
part" of the property, they stated, was held by Hugh's *cognatus,* who similarly donated his portion to
the monks. At some point in the past, likely the generation before, the property had been divided
between two kin. Given that Hugh's relative is called *cognatus* (the best translation being cousin),
Hugh's father and uncle probably each inherited a part of this property. Praxedis also signed a later
gift by her son; AD Loir-et-Cher, 16 H 119.

75. *CTV,* vol. 2, no. 538, pp. 383–84.

76. Matthew and his brother had different cognomens. Matthew used "Griponis," which was
a form of his father's cognomen "Grippe." Adelard had a more colorful sobriquet. The use of two
different cognomens could indicate the development of distinct lines in this family. Unfortunately, it
is not possible to determine which of the brothers was the elder. Interestingly, their sister was named
"Agrippa," which could have been a form of "Grippe," her father's cognomen.

St. Trinité of Vendôme. Although ecclesiastical holdings of the church were divided between Matthew and Adelard, other properties were controlled collectively by Matthew, his sister (Agrippa), and their mother. Still other holdings belonged solely to Matthew, and probably Adelard and Agrippa each had holdings belonging solely to them.[77]

The family of Aimery Chenard highlights the range of inheritance modes that noble families could employ at one time. Around 1123 Aimery gave *his part* of the family holdings at Mantarville to St. Jean-en-Vallée. In the same year, his nephews also gave their property in the same village, which "they held through their ancestors."[78] Aimery and his brother Isnard had both received a portion of this village. But in the next generation, Isnard's sons shared control of his part of Mantarville as their inheritance. In contrast to others, the family of Isnard and Aimery chose to change their dispersal of family resources from partible to collective inheritance from one generation to the next. While the mode of passing on property had changed, the underlying ethos had not: both strategies used family coffers to provide for all progeny. Yet there are signs of another mode of inheritance evident in these acts. When Isnard's sons swore to protect their gift against any who would claim it (a fairly common practice), the charter singled out family members, in particular *parentela,* or kin and their progeny, and "Hugh of St. Hilaire who had their father's sister as wife" as those who might disrupt the gift. This one clause seems to reflect two different inheritance and family forms: the recognition of the claim that a broad group of kin had to family holdings and the sense that paternal uncles could pose a threat. Perhaps unlike their uncle and father, their aunt had had her share of family resources diminished or restricted, thus making it likely her husband might make a claim. But this evidence needs to be balanced with the fact that these brothers had their sister and her family consent to this charter, an acknowledgment of their claim to the donated property. Reading further, the charter tells us that one brother held his portion of this property in fief from his older brother. Combined with the use of individual cognomens—Chenard, Lohold, Sine Nappe—to delineate separate lines of the family, it would seem this family was adhering to patrilineage and some form of primogeniture.

What are we to make of this conflicting evidence: divisible patrimony; collective inheritance; signs of a limiting of women's and children's rights to

---

77. Matthew's son Burchard disputed what he had given the monks of Marmoutier at Villeberfol. The claim was easily dealt with, however, for once the monks offered Burchard a cash countergift, he dismissed his claim. AD Loir-et-Cher, 16 H 120. See also *MB*, no. 73, p. 84.

78. *Jean,* nos. 33, 34, 35, pp. 19–21.

property in some cases, but the recognition of these same rights in others; an elder son acting as the feudal lord of a younger brother; and the use of individual cognomens? One explanation emerges: families of the noble born did not see aspects of collective inheritance, the rights of a large group of kin, and attributes of patrilineage as mutually exclusive. Rather, the family of Aimery Chenard demonstrates the vast complexity of aristocratic inheritance and the contemporaneous use of what scholars have described as competing models of inheritance and family organization.

Primogeniture and Patrilineage

Primogeniture and patrilineage were indeed options for inheritance modes and family organization available to the nobility in the lands of the Loire, but they were not the dominant hues. Forty-four percent of acts in the charter database were initiated by males alone. But when the consent and participation of family members are figured in, this drops to 22 percent. Thus about one in five or one in four aristocratic families assumed a more rigid linear form and invested heavily in the eldest male child. However, when considered alongside collective inheritance, which occurred at a rate of 15 percent, inheritance by an eldest son was only slightly more frequent than collective inheritance (approximately one in three families in comparison with between one in either four or five).

One of the features of twelfth-century charters is an increase in the use of the term *primogenitus* and like terms to designate firstborn sons and daughters. At first glance, this could be indicative of a revolution in family structure and definitive evidence of primogenitary inheritance. But does the increased interest in birth order necessarily mean that inheritance practices conformed to primogeniture? Specifically, did the designation of the firstborn mean that other siblings no longer exercised a right to family lands or had status as potential heirs? Furthermore, was the use of such designators or an interest in birth order a result of a change in family patterns or simply a device used to clarify which child was referenced? While the use of such terms did increase in the twelfth century, the frequency of birth-order designators still occurred in the vast minority of acts (2.4 percent). Analysis of the charters themselves cautions against rushing to the conclusion that interest in birth order was consonant with primogeniture or patrilineage, as the following examples demonstrate.

Early in the twelfth century, William of Castellaria made a gift to the monks of St. Père for the soul of his son Radulf. His *primogenitus*, Gaufred, consented to the gift and acted with his father in promising to defend the

gift against all claims. This would seem to be definitive evidence of primogenitary inheritance and the power of the firstborn son. Yet William's
other three sons also consented to the gift, so their rights and claims to
family land had not been superseded by their eldest brother.[79] This family was concerned with birth order, however, for in addition to identifying
the *primogenitus,* the charter designates William's son Hugh the "third son."
Interest in birth order also applied to daughters. Daniel of La Ferté's wife is
clearly designated as *primogenita* in their dispute with the monks, indicating
that birth order was important to daughters' place in the family as well as
sons'.[80] Did Daniel make his claim because he believed that his wife, as firstborn, had some particular or stronger right to the property? The chronicle
evidence contains examples of just such motivations for disputes. Lambert
of Ardres, for example, records a contestation over Guines in the twelfth
century based on the assertion that the rights of the eldest daughter were
stronger than those of her younger siblings.[81] In the case of Daniel La Ferté
and his wife, however, her younger siblings still had a right to the patrimony.
Her sister and her husband made a gift to the church and witnessed the
couple's quitclaim.[82]

Another case provides further evidence. When Otrann the knight was
approaching death, he made a gift of what properties he held at Gallardon.
His *filius major* approved the gift and was the only son to consent and witness
his father's placement of a symbol of his gift upon the altar.[83] The preference
shown to the eldest son would signal that his place in the family was different
from those of his younger siblings, supporting an interpretation of primogeniture with the accompanying patrilineage. However, the fact that Otrann
had his sister's husband and his *cognatus* also consent and witness his sym-
bolization of his gift challenges such a narrow reading. While Otrann and
others may have singled out their eldest children in some ways, they clearly
still valued their extended kin and even recognized their right (through their
consent and witnessing) to property.

---

79. *Père,* vol. 2, no. 108, pp. 599–600.

80. *Père,* vol. 2, no. 6, pp. 474–75. The same concern with birth order among daughters is evident in *Tiron,* vol. 1, no. 97, pp. 117–18.

81. The first cousin of the current lord of Guines made a claim to the lordship saying that because his mother was the elder of the two sisters, the lordship belonged to her—and subsequently to
him. Lambert of Ardres, *History of the Counts of Guines and Lords of Ardres,* pp. 103–4. Moreover, in
Champagne, it was customary for inheritance among daughters to be determined by birth order. See
Evergates, trans. and ed., *Feudal Society in Medieval France,* pp. 51–57.

82. *Père,* vol. 2, no. 6, pp. 474–75.

83. *Josaphat,* vol. 1, no. 36, pp. 52–53. Evergates also questions the primacy of the first son over
all other children; "Nobles and Knights in Twelfth-Century France," pp. 17–28.

In other cases, birth order clearly was important in establishing a special right to property. Adelaide, who was the sister to a monk of St. Trinité, claimed a church belonged to her "because she was the first born from her parents."[84] This is a revealing statement, for it suggests that as firstborn, she—like firstborn sons—could expect some preferential treatment. Adelaide had at least one younger brother,[85] but she asserted that her place as eldest child gave her rights that would trump his. While Adelaide based her claim to the property in question on her place as *primogenita,* like other firstborn children, she found her rights went only so far. Approving the gift, and giving their consent to the alienation of property, were Adelaide's son and daughter, her husband, her three sisters, and a nephew. Moreover, the dispute was resolved and the additional property given, in the presence of her brother, a monk.

The case of Adelaide raises some interesting points about aristocratic families. First, it is clear that some families held the right of firstborn kin—daughters as well as sons—in precedence over other progeny. The rights of such progeny were not absolute, however, as is exemplified in Adelaide securing the consent of her immediate family and her siblings and nephew. While Adelaide might expect some preference as the eldest child, other children also asserted a right to family property—particularly that inherited from *parentes.* Second, Adelaide's attestation reflects a broad concept of kinship. She was concerned for the souls of her ancestors who, out of ignorance, possessed ecclesiastical properties against God's law.

The signifiers of firstborn status (*primogenitus, primogenita*) thus do not seem to be reliable indicators of an overall change in family structure and inheritance. Perhaps a better way of evaluating the status of firstborn sons is to examine their roles in the management of the patrimony or within the family itself. In the act above, Otrann's eldest son was the only one to approve and witness his father's gift. Other firstborn sons also appeared solo with their fathers.[86] When Hugo Nepos abandoned his claim to lands

---

84. *CTV,* vol. 1, no. 282, pp. 438–40.

85. Some might argue that Odo could not be considered a "real" brother since he had entered the church and abandoned all interests in the secular world. Such removal from the secular world was purely an ideal. In reality, clerical sons and daughters continued to exercise a right to the patrimony, and in the charters from the lands of the Loire, they participate as donors, buyers, sellers, consenters, and witnesses, as well as disputing gifts. These elites were not dead to the world, but rather, very active and concerned members of their families. See Amy Livingstone, "Brother Monk." See also Johnson, *Equal in Monastic Profession,* pp. 13–33.

86. But it is also possible that his younger siblings were too young to leave home or to participate in the charter. When Hugo Berbellus made a donation to the church, his eldest son, Gaufred, swore upon the relics to defend his father's benefaction. This would seem to suggest that Gaufred's place as eldest son accorded him special status and privileges within the family. But the charter states

and actually returned the property to the abbey of St. Père, his *primogenitus,* Isnard, consented to the resolution of the conflict and the transferal of the lands.[87] Moreover, Isnard was the only one of Hugo Nepos's relatives to participate in the charter.

The eldest sons of two other noblemen, Pagan and Robert, seem to mirror Isnard's special role as firstborn son. Sometime between 1130 and 1145, Pagan and his brother Robert gave meadowland to the monks of Tiron and acted together to place a knife upon the altar to commemorate their benefaction. Consenting to this gift were their wives and their eldest sons.[88] In this case, where the fathers clearly shared possession of property and had likely inherited the property jointly, it appears they privileged their eldest sons over their other progeny. Yet they had not adopted a fully patrilinear form of inheritance since both Pagan and Robert also secured the consent of their wives. Furthermore, when Robert made an additional gift, he made sure that his brother and his eldest nephew consented to it and had his sister-in-law approve the donation. This family may have been transitioning from an inheritance mode of both shared and partible to one that would invest eldest sons with stronger or exclusive rights to family holdings.

Monks and their lay patrons used a variety of means to assure that gifts remained undisputed. To discourage any potential claimant, donors would sometimes swear to defend the gift against any who would dispute it. Sometimes donors would provide their personal oath, while at other times a constellation of kin would be invoked as the protectors of the gift. In the twelfth century, children often assumed responsibility for defending the gift, but firstborn sons sometimes were the only ones to swear on the relics. When Pagan of Fenis confirmed what his vassal had given to St. Père, he swore upon the relics that he would do everything in his power to defend the gift. His son Gislebert, who was *primogenitus,* likewise pledged to protect the donated lands by placing his hand on the relics. While Gislebert was associated with his father as lord of this territory, and hence was responsible for defending the gift and upholding the family's agreement with the monks, his place as firstborn son did not mean that other children were ignored. Pagan secured

---

that Gaufred was the only son who swore upon the relics because the others were too young—although they were old enough to consent. *Père,* vol. 2, no. 71, p. 319.

87. *Père,* vol. 2, no. 110, p. 601. Macé finds that the eldest sons of the Guilhem family were charged with being sure their younger siblings received their portion of the patrimony once they reached majority or, in the case of daughters, married. Instead of characterizing the eldest son as a tyrant, however, Macé suggests that care and affection motivated his oversight of his younger siblings; "Les frères au sien du lignage," pp. 127–36.

88. *Tiron,* vol. 1, no. 149, pp. 172–73.

the consent of "the rest of his sons" and his two daughters as well as his wife regarding the alienation of this fief from family possession.[89] A similar situation occurred in 1123 when Robert of Poncellis quitclaimed his right to certain properties to resolve an ongoing conflict with Notre Dame de Josaphat. A few days after the agreement had been arranged, Mainer, Robert's *primogenitus filius,* confirmed his father's gift and pact with the monks by placing a symbol of the accord in the hand of the bishop in front of the chapter.[90] Yet Mainer's younger brother Philip was present at the arrangement of the original pact, and Robert had the rest of his children and his wife travel to the abbey, where they consented to his gift and agreement with the monks. In some families, eldest sons were accorded special privileges and did inherit the lion's share of the patrimony. But they did not do so to the exclusion or disenfranchisement of other kin.

The experience of younger sons varied among families. A charter from Marmoutier raises further questions about established notions concerning the experience of younger sons, in particular their relationship with their fathers. In 1096, Hugh Guernonatus decided to go on Crusade, accompanied by his eldest son, Warin.[91] Before they departed, Hugo reconciled with the monks over a property dispute. Warin and his younger brother, Peter, both approved the agreement and joined with their father in granting the property to the church to benefit their souls and the soul of their mother.[92] Peter then pledged to protect the aforementioned gift from all disputants, since he would be in charge of his father's honors until Hugo or Warin returned from Crusade. Peter was given considerable responsibility as guardian of his father's land and possibly of his younger half-brother as well. Birth order may have been designated and eldest sons may appear in different roles from their younger siblings, but such behavior did not necessarily result in the strict patrilineal family structure that has so dominated how modern scholars view aristocratic family life.

---

89. *Père,* vol. 2, no. 12, p. 524.

90. *Josaphat,* vol. 1, no. 10, pp. 20–23.

91. William II Gouet was also accompanied by his eldest son when he went on Crusade. These examples are in direct contrast to Duby's assertion that younger sons were more likely to go on Crusade so that they could secure lands to make up for their lack of an inheritance. Indeed, in the lands of the Loire, it was more common for eldest sons to go on Crusade. The same was true in Maine. Lemesle, *La société aristocratique dans le Haut-Maine,* p. 123; Duby, "Youth in Aristocratic Society," pp. 112–23.

92. AD Loir-et-Cher, 16 H 118. See also *CMPD,* no. 152, p. 141. See chapter 2, p. 29 for discussion of this family and note 7. Hugh went on Crusade with his lord, Count Stephen of Blois-Chartres.

The powerlessness of women, an accepted corollary of the triumph of primogeniture and patrilineage, may prove a better predictor of the adoption of these practices than designation of birth order. As patrilineage and primogeniture vested control of family resources in men, women became subject to them, losing their right to property and positions of authority or leadership within the family.[93] So, for example, mothers could no longer act as guardians for their children or manage family properties. While most women of the Loire region were not familiar with such experiences, some were.

In the twelfth century, Robert Calvus entered the church, with his wife, Helvisa, and his children providing their consent. Robert's brothers-in-law acted as guarantors of their nieces' and nephews' approbation of the gift because the children were under their guardianship until they came of age.[94] Helvisa's brothers had taken control of her children and probably her lands. She was present in the charter but clearly not in a guardian capacity. For whatever reason, Helvisa was not allowed to act as guardian for her progeny.

The situation was similar in the family of Ursio Garembert. Between 1156 and 1159, Thomas, one of Ursio's sons, desired to take the habit. Accompanying Thomas when he petitioned the bishop to allow him to enter St. Jean-en-Vallée was his mother, Eufemia, and his brother Garembert. Mother and brother affirmed that they supported Thomas's desire to become a canon and they gave tithes, which they held jointly, for his soul.[95] Although her husband was dead, Eufemia did not assume guardianship of their property or progeny. Rather, her eldest son acted with her in controlling property and in determining the future of one of his siblings. Moreover, Eufemia's two brothers frequently appeared as consenters and guarantors to her various transactions. While it would be possible to read the participation of these men as supportive or as symbolic of family solidarity, this does not seem to be the case. Her son and her natal kin continually interfered in Eufemia's life and took over the responsibilities that other women at other times or in other families would have rightfully assumed. But before we rush to interpret these cases as proof of the ascendancy of patrilineage, it is important to consider personal circumstance as a potential factor.[96] For all we know, Eufemia or Helvisa were unable to take on these responsibilities. Perhaps they were unwell or ill-disposed to such duties. Regrettably, we will probably never know.

---

93. Erin Jordan suggests that the emphasis on linear descent in primogeniture and patrilineage worked to benefit some women. See *Women, Power and Religious Patronage,* pp. 19–21, 58.

94. AD Eure-et-Loir, H 3261. See also *Jean,* no. 32, pp. 18–19.

95. *Jean,* no. 73, pp. 41–42.

96. *Jean,* no. 74, p. 42.

Primogeniture and patrilineage were options chosen by some aristocratic families of the Loire region. In these cases, eldest sons did enjoy certain privileges and authority over their younger brothers and sisters. Some women, furthermore, found their claim to the patrimony restricted and themselves under the control of their male kin. But it appears that patrilineage and the investment of all family resources solely in the firstborn son made up a relatively small portion of the entirety of aristocratic family experience. Even when primogeniture and patrilineage appear among the families of this region, they were not the male-dominated, repressive, cold type postulated by historians. Instead, cousins participated in the disposition of family assets. Younger sons inherited property and took on important roles in their family. Daughters maintained a voice in their natal family as well as a right to land after they were married. And wives acted with their husbands in dispensing family resources.

Conclusion

The twelfth-century historian Lambert of Ardres described noblemen partitioning their lands among all of their sons. The nobles of the lands of the Loire approached inheritance in much the same way. These aristocratic families employed a variety of sometimes overlapping strategies to provide for their members. Many families followed the pattern described by Lambert of Ardres, while others used shared inheritance of family resources. Still others invested all property in the patriline. Although many families did keep the patrimony indivisible, the sensibility underlying this practice differs significantly from what has been previously postulated. Indivisible primogeniture's prime objective was to guarantee the well-being of only one child and his descendants. In contrast, the use of shared impartible inheritance was aimed at providing for all children and their descendants.

These inheritance patterns are the manifestation of the broad and inclusive nature of noble family life in the lands of the Loire. Members of elite families supported each other, acted together to manage and protect family resources, looked after minor children, and made gifts to provide for the eternal salvation of their kin. Taking into account the instabilities and violence of the time, we should not be surprised that aristocratic men and women remained tied affectively, and through land, to a network of family that could be depended upon to provide defense, support, aid, and advice in periods of trouble. Instead of cutting loose family members who would be deemed extraneous in a system rigidly determined by patrilineage and primogeniture, families valued their kin, many of whom played important roles in each other's lives. Cognatic kinship, breadth of kin, and collective rights were the foundations upon which the inheritance practices and family dynamics of the medieval aristocratic families of the lands of the Loire were built. Some families did make adjustments to their inheritance strategies, but there was not a profound rupture or wholesale adoption of primogeniture or patrilineage at any point in the eleventh or twelfth centuries. Rather, continuity and diversity are key features of inheritance patterns among the elite of the mid-Loire.

The introduction of new members into the family significantly affected family interactions and the disposition of property. Marriage was a pivotal moment not only in the life of an individual noble but also in the life of the aristocratic family. The next chapter will address the practicalities and realities of medieval marriage for the aristocrats living in the lands of the Loire.

❧ CHAPTER 5

Marriage and the Disposition of Property

A Sign of Status?

Arranging marriage portions was a serious matter that worried aristocratic fathers.[1] As life was slowly ebbing away from the once-indomitable lord of Montlhéry, for example, the future of his daughter occupied his thoughts. To provide her with security, he decided she should wed Philip, the son of King Philip and the countess of Anjou. The castle of Montlhéry was designated as this young woman's dowry, causing her in-laws to "rejoice as if they had plucked a mote from their eyes or had broken down the barriers that had enclosed them."[2] Castles were

---

· 1. Scholars have long attempted to trace the origins of marriage portions. André Lemaire argues that the old Germanic form of dower slowly developed into a third of acquired and inherited property and then, by the central Middle Ages, into the customary third of the husband's acquired property. "Les origines de la communauté de biens entre époux dans le droit coutumier français." More recently, however, Lemaire's model has been modified, and historians have sought the origin of dowry and dower in the combination of Roman and Germanic marital gifts. Dowry, in particular, had its roots in the gift made by the Roman father at his daughter's marriage. Among the Germanic tribes, a *premium nuptiale*, or bride price, was given by the father or guardian as a counterbalance to the morning gift, or *morgengabe*. See Régine Le Jan-Hennebicque, "Aux origines du douaire médiéval (VIe-Xe siècles)," pp. 109–11; Laurent Feller, "Morgengabe, dot, *tertia*," pp. 5–10; Christian Lauranson-Rosaz, "Douaire et sponsalicium"; Jean-Louis Thireau, "Les pratiques communautaires entre époux dans l'Anjou feudal (Xe-XIIe siècles)," pp. 208–10. Southern Italy's custom of giving gifts at marriage was essentially a conflation of Roman and Germanic legal practices with Norman influences. Drell, *Kinship and Conquest,* pp. 65–80.

2. Abbot Suger, *The Deeds of Louis the Fat,* p. 40.

important property in the twelfth century, and the royal family triumphed in finally bringing the seat of the lord of Montlhéry under their control. Dowry provided them the means to do so and gave the royal house a political advantage.

For better or worse, historians have used the disposition of property at the time of marriage as a way to evaluate the status of women and the nature of aristocratic marriage.[3] The change from a gift given by the groom to a dowry given by the bride's family has been represented as a decline in women's overall standing. The type of arrangement made at marriage has shaped how historians have characterized the experiences of noblewomen. The granting of dower, for example, is usually interpreted as indicating husbands valued their wives and recognized their right to property. Dowry, in contrast, has been portrayed as a kind of one-time-only buyout for daughters whose families were really not concerned with their future and actively sought to limit their rights to property.[4]

The aristocratic families of the lands of the Loire employed both dowry and dower.[5] If disposition of property at marriage reflects female status, then it would seem that the women of the mid-Loire were powerful indeed. Both their birth family and their husband's family provided them with material support. Examination of the property dispositions made for the support of

---

3. Replacing potential inheritance of a portion of the patrimony with one single grant at the time of marriage—i.e., a dowry—has been characterized as a symptom of patrilineage and thus a sign of a diminution in the rights and status of aristocratic women. See Diane Owen Hughes, "From Brideprice to Dowry in Mediterranean Europe"; Georges Duby, *Medieval Marriage*, pp. 1–18; Jack Goody, *The Development of the Family and Marriage*, pp. 206–7; Herlihy, *Medieval Households*, pp. 73–87.

4. In this regard, the Loire region conforms to what seems to have been the common practice throughout medieval Europe. Medieval women could expect to receive some sort of support from their natal family and their groom. Feller, "Morgengabe, dot, *tertia*"; Frantz Pellaton, "La veuve et ses droits de la Basse-Antiquité au haut Moyen Âge"; Lemesle, *La société aristocratique dans le Haut-Maine*, pp. 123–32; Evergates, *The Aristocracy in the County of Champagne*, pp. 103–14. Dowries and dowers were provided to the young couple to address two needs: the establishment of their household and support of the wife should she become widowed. Husbands and wives needed each other's consent, if not participation, to make gifts or otherwise alienate property. Because of the conditions and intent of the marriage grants, husbands and wives exercised somewhat different rights to different portions of their combined patrimony. See Emmanuelle Santinelli, "Ni 'morgengabe' ni *tertia* mais *dos* et dispositions en faveur du dernier vivant."

5. Determining whether the property was dowry or dower can sometimes be tricky since terms for dowry and dower were not fixed until the twelfth century. If the charter uses a form of *dotarium* or *maritagium*, I have translated it as "dowry." If the terms *dos, dote,* or *dotalicus* are employed, I take it to mean "dower." Because these terms were rather fluid, discussion of these grants needs to be evaluated on a case-by-case basis. Lauranson-Rosaz, "Douaire et sponsalicium durant le haut Moyen Âge"; Laurent Morelle, "Mariage et diplomatique"; Santinelli, "Ni 'morgengabe' ni *tertia* mais dos," pp. 245–59.

wives yields details about the powerful status of women, their pivotal place in their natal and affinal families, and the relationship between husbands and wives.

The Disposition of Property: Dowry

The Granting of Dowry

Around 1130, Galeran of Thionville made a gift to the monks of Notre Dame de Josaphat. There was one provision, however. All the other land in the village not designated in the gift was to be used as a dowry for his daughter, Columba. Marriage represented an important transition in the life of a medieval aristocrat. In contrast to what it meant for her brothers, however, scholars would argue that for Columba, marriage meant joining a new family and becoming a member of another noble house.[6] While brides did become part of a new family, ties to natal kin were not severed. This is quite clear in a transaction between the family of Landric and the monks of St. Père. Sometime late in the eleventh century, this family had placed their oven at Brou in mortgage to the monks in return for twenty-five *solidi*. Each member received countergifts, including Landric's daughter Adelina, who had been granted part of the oven as her dowry when she married.[7] Even though Adelina was married and had received a dowry, she was still involved in her natal family's disposition of property. Indeed, the dowry itself bound her to her family for her consent was needed for any transaction concerning its alienation. The grant reconnected Adelina with her kin through a benefaction for the souls of at least three generations of her family, indicating that the ties of blood, memory, and ancestry tied women to their natal family even after their marriage and entry into another noble house.[8]

---

6. The experience of brides in their affinal houses has been interpreted in various ways. See Duby, *Medieval Marriage,* pp. 25–83, and *William Marshal,* pp. 39–55; Bouchard, "Family Structure and Family Consciousness," "Patterns of Women's Names," "Genealogy and Politics," "Twelfth-Century Family Structures," and *"Strong of Body, Brave and Noble,"* p. 74, 86–98; Baldwin, *Aristocratic Life,* pp. 122–28, 135–60; Barthélemy, "Kinship."

7. *Père,* vol. 1, no. 27, p. 253.

8. See AD Loir-et-Cher, 16 H 105, for example. Women continued to inherit land from their natal family and exercised a right to it even after marriage. See Eliana Magnani Soares-Christen, "Alliances matrimoniales et circulation des biens à travers les chartes provençales (Xe–début du XIIe siècle)," pp. 136–38; Claudie Amado, "Donation maritale et dot parentale," pp. 153–70. Philadelphia Ricketts finds that aristocratic women in Yorkshire remained closely connected to their natal families after marriage; "Widows, Religious Patronage and Family Identity." For the Italian parallel, see Drell, *Kinship and Conquest,* pp. 76–78.

When families arranged a dowry for a daughter, it came out of the complex of properties that made up the patrimony. The *Gesta* of the Lords of Amboise, composed in the twelfth century, provides some examples. Hugh of Lavardin was married twice and had four children. He endowed Avelina, his daughter from his first marriage, with a dowry consisting of property at Lavardin. His son Lisois received what his mother had been granted as a dowry, which he possessed by right or custom of inheritance (*jure hereditario*). In this family, dowry was made up of different types of holdings and was used in various ways to provide futures for both brides and their children.[9] Sulpice, the treasurer of St. Martin of Tours, needed to furnish his niece with a dowry when she married Lisois of Amboise. He arranged a dowry consisting of the stone tower he had built just after he became the guardian of his young nephew and nieces, all that pertained to the tower, the same at Verneuil-sur-Indre with all pertaining fiefs, and a house at Loches that Sulpice himself held *jure hereditario*. His niece's dowry, hence, consisted of properties that came to her from her father, what her uncle had built, and even property that he had personally inherited.[10]

The experience of another noble couple, Gaufred Norman and Alburgis, also holds some interesting information about the "co-optation" of women into the patriline. Alburgis's father, Hubert Magonis, arranged a dowry for her when she married. Sometime after her marriage, Hubert decided to give his portion of these holdings to the monks. Alburgis and her husband consented to the gift. Similar to Adelina's, Alburgis's dowry acted as a filament binding her to her natal family through the arrangement of gifts made to benefit the souls of their nuclear kin. After Alburgis's death, however, her husband, Gaufred Norman, disputed what Hubert had given to the monks.[11] Intriguingly, the charter recording the dispute calls Gaufred "the son of Hubert," when in fact he was the *son-in-law* of Hubert.[12] Was this simply confusion on the part of the scribe? It seems unlikely. Rather, it appears that Gaufred Norman had "married up" into a family and wanted to

---

9. *Gesta Ambaziensium dominorum,* pp. 75–76.

10. *Gesta Ambaziensium dominorum,* pp. 83–84.

11. Given that Alburgis's dowry came from the same properties that Hubert had donated to the monks, such a dispute was probably inevitable. Moreover, the time of the dispute is interesting. Gaufred may have wanted to maintain control of Alburgis's dowry after her death. He clearly feared losing the land. While he did not get the land back, he was awarded a cash countergift. With the passing of Alburgis, Gaufred would lose her dowry and also association with her kin. His contestation was multivalent: he obviously wanted the property, but he also apparently wished to remind the community of his connection to both Alburgis's family and the monks. For further discussion of the timing of disputes, see chapter 8.

12. AD Loir-et-Cher, 16 H 105.

be associated with them.[13] It has been suggested that women were subsumed by their husband's line.[14] In this instance, a nobleman elected to be identified with his wife's kin, a preference exercised by many male aristocrats who married into socially or politically superior families.

Control of Dowry

Once daughters received their dowries, who had control of such properties?[15] The quote from Suger implies that the bride would have little control over her dowry. But was this the experience of women of the aristocracy in general? The charters suggest not. Dowry property was not absorbed completely into the patrimony for it remained under the purview of noble wives. Nithard, the great-grandson of Fulcher Dives, for example, charged that his uncle Guismand had no right to the mill at La Chappe because it was the dowry of Guismand's mother (and Nithard's grandmother).[16] Thus Nithard based his objection to his uncle's grant on a woman's right to her dowry.[17] Similarly, when the count and countess of Vendôme purchased land, they found that a knight named Adam of Avasiaco and his wife, Emma, held the land in question because the property came from her dowry.[18] Even though Emma remarried upon Adam's death, she retained control of the dowry from her

---

13. It is possible that both Gaufred and Alburgis had fathers named Hubert. But the disputed property was given to Alburgis by her father, Hubert, in dowry. So the "father" who made the pious donation of the property was in fact Hubert, who was Gaufred's father-in-law.

14. This is particularly apparent in a woman's adoption of a name or cognomen associated with her husband's family. See Régine Le Jan, "Personal Names and the Transformation of Kinship," p. 37. For a somewhat different interpretation, see Monique Bourin, "How Changes in Naming Reflect the Evolution of Familial Structures in Southern Europe, 950–1250." See also Bouchard, "The Migration of Women's Names in the Upper Nobility, Ninth–Twelfth Centuries," and "Patterns of Women's Names in Royal Lineages, Ninth–Eleventh Centuries"; Herlihy, "Land, Family and Women in Continental Europe, 701–1200."

15. In contrast to England, where women could not exercise a right to their property during their marriage, Germanic law ensured the right of widows to their dowers. Le Jan-Hennebicque, "Aux origines du douaire médiéval," pp. 116–20; Feller, "Morgengabe, dot, *tertia,*" pp. 8–19. Thireau argues that women controlled property given to them in both dowry and dower; "Les pratiques communautaires entre époux." See also Claire de Trafford, "Share and Share Alike? The Marriage Portion, Inheritance, and Family Politics." For the significance of dower to medieval Irish women, see Gillian Kenny, "The Power of Dower." For England, see Mitchell, *Portraits of Medieval Women,* pp. 7–10, and Michael M. Sheehan, "The Influence of Canon Law on the Property Rights of Married Women in England."

16. *MV,* no. 32, pp. 51–55.

17. Women in the south of France also enjoyed control over property and continued to have a right to their natal properties, at least up to the twelfth century. Soares-Christen, "Alliances matrimoniales et circulation des biens," pp. 131–47. For a somewhat different interpretation, see Amado, "Femmes entre elles," pp. 125–34.

18. *CTV,* vol. 1, no. 187, pp. 323–24.

first marriage. While Emma's second husband witnessed and agreed to her quitclaim, his right to the property was in no way recognized in the grant.

Lord Radulf of Beaugency found out in 1105 that his bride retained control of the property she had brought to their marriage. Radulf wished to grant privileges from a particular wood to the monks, but his wife held the rights over the collection of wood from the forest as part of her dowry. These appurtenances were *not* given because the lady herself did not want them to pass to the monks and she did not give way to her husband's desire to be generous to the church.[19] Noble husbands had to consult their wives when alienating property that came from their dowry, and if wives were not willing, their dowry properties were not alienated. Wives' consent was also needed when property was sold. Salomon of Lavardin provided his daughter Eva with a dowry when she married Haimeric of Alluyes. At a later point, this couple sold the land and church that made up Eva's dowry to the countess of Vendôme.[20] Similarly, when Teduin sold houses in Blois to the monks of Marmoutier, his wife, Humberga, and their daughter consented. "And because the houses themselves were from the dowry of Umberga [i.e., Humberga], she received twenty pounds and four *solidi*" in recognition of her rights to the property and its alienation.[21] Women's control of their dowries is further apparent in two particular types of actions: gifts made from dowry property and the settlement of disputes concerning dowry holdings.

Gifts from Dowry

Like other properties, dowry could be used to secure the spiritual salvation of the wife herself or other family members.[22] "I, Adela, daughter of Fulcher [Dives], wife of Hugh [of Mondoubleau], for the glory of Christ and supplication of eternal punishment, give to St. Trinité from my dowry one

---

19. *CTV*, vol. 2, no. 410, pp. 169–70. Mathilda is described as simply "holding" these rights, so it is difficult to determine if these properties came from her dowry or dower. Since the woods do not appear to be part of the Beaugency patrimony, I have assigned these rights as coming from her dowry rather than a dower. For another example of a husband securing his wife's consent to a gift from her dowry, see *Tiron*, vol. 1, no. 71, pp. 88–89.

20. *CTV*, vol. 1, no. 62, pp. 117–18.

21. *MB*, no. 67, pp. 77–78. See also Livingstone, "Noblewomen's Control of Property in Eleventh- and Early Twelfth-Century Blois-Chartres."

22. Women frequently acted as the memorializers of their family by ensuring that relatives—distant and immediate—were prayed for by the monks. Van Houts, *Memory and Gender*, pp. 63–120; Jordan, *Women, Power and Religious Patronage*, pp. 87–90; Carolyn Edwards, "Dynastic Sanctity in Two Early Medieval Women's *Lives*," pp. 10–11; Matthew Innes, "Keeping It in the Family." In contrast to these scholars, Patrick Geary argues that women's role as family memorializer was taken over by the monks in the eleventh century; *Phantoms of Remembrance*, pp. 48–80.

carrucate of land from the village which is called Marcilly, with the consent of my son Fulcher and also my daughter Agnete" (see appendix, chart 10).[23] Other women used their dowries to assist their husbands. At the end of the eleventh century, Halvis used her dowry so her husband could become a monk at St. Vincent of Le Mans. She, along with her sons, approved of the grant and her spouse's new status as a monk.[24] Wives also permitted use of their dowry property to secure spiritual benefits. In 1066, a noblewoman let her dowry be used to benefit her affinal kin, specifically her father-in-law, her mother-in-law and her brother-in-law. Coincidently, the couple from whom this woman held her property made similar arrangements. Around 1115, Eusebia and her husband, Odo Rufus, donated from her dowry to benefit their souls and to secure the prayers of the monks.[25] Clearly these women did not feel like outsiders in their affinal houses and raised no objection to using their property on behalf of their marital family. This act also provides a window into interactions between husbands and wives and how they managed their holdings for in addition to Eusebia's dowry, the couple also gave the fief of one of their castellans. Since both husband and wife were described as holding and giving the land, Eusebia exercised power as a lord of this property in much the same way her husband did.[26] Wives could, therefore, be intimately involved in the management of all family property—including that which entailed some sort of military obligation.

Hersend, the daughter of Fulcher Turre, used her dowry property to benefit her family in several ways (see appendix, chart 9). First, Hersend and her husband, Gradulf, made a pious gift to the monks of Marmoutier of the *manufirma* (life estate) that she had received from her father when she married, as well as granting other properties that she held in a different village.[27] The initial grant was typical of pious benefactions made for the redemption of their souls. Yet Hersend was not finished utilizing her dowry to secure spiritual rewards. When Gradulf left on pilgrimage sometime between 1060 and 1080, Hersend traveled with her household knights (*familiae milites*) to Marmoutier, which was a fair distance from her home in Châteaudun, to implore the grace of Saint Martin. There she asked the abbot to accept herself, her husband, and her children, as well as all those who had come with

---

23. *CTV,* vol. 1, no. 23, pp. 44–45.

24. *CSVM,* no. 645, p. 373.

25. *CTV,* vol. 1, no. 197, pp. 331–32.

26. Eusebia's experience resonates with that of Countess Ermessende of Barcelona. See Martin Aurell I Cardona, "Les avatars de la viduité princière."

27. *MV,* no. 126, pp. 215–17. The couple made the donation in their house in Châteaudun in the presence of Domina Hersend's brother and two monks.

her, into their prayers and pious endeavors. To guarantee the monks' cooperation, she regranted the *manufirma* and sacramentalized the transaction by
placing a symbol of the gift upon the altar of Marmoutier.[28] Hersend's dowry
was thus employed twice to secure the spiritual health of her family and to
establish an important bond with the monks. Gradulf's departure undoubtedly catalyzed the second benefaction. Hersend was likely concerned about
her spouse and used her property to help ensure the intercession of the saint
in any difficulties he might encounter while on his journey. If something
went awry, Gradulf could count on the monks' prayers for his soul and their
protection for his family. Hersend's benevolence also assured the association
between her family and the monks in another way. While the monks would
hold the *manufirma* free and clear, the rent that was due each year at the
feast of St. John the Baptist went to Hersend and her family. Every June,
when rent was collected, the community at large, Hersend's relatives, and the
monks themselves would be reminded of Hersend's family's generosity and
their perpetual association with the monks.

Disputes over Dowry

Dowries were used to advance or benefit the family or the individual in
many ways. Not surprisingly, rights to dowry property were guarded very
carefully. Among those protecting a wife's dowry were Hersend and Gradulf
Albus. Shortly after the birth of their third son, several men made a series
of claims to the *manufirma* they had granted to Marmoutier.[29] Sometime before 1044, Gradulf asked the counts of Chartres and Anjou to provide justice
over three claims that had been made to his wife's dowry. The third dispute
is most relevant for our purposes, however. A certain Rainald asserted that
Hersend had mortgaged the property to him in return for two measures of a
wheat field, which he had paid her. This was apparently a valid claim, for the
monk representing Marmoutier had the land returned to Rainald so that he
would quitclaim his right to the property. After settling these contestations,
Gradulf and Hersend gave the property to the monks of Marmoutier in the
presence of both counts, the lord from whom the couple held the land, and
Hersend's brother-in-law, Ingelbald Brito. Hersend had the ability to arrange

---

28. For an in-depth discussion of *manufirma*, see Barthélemy, *La société dans le comté de Vendôme*,
pp. 44–56.

29. AD Loir-et-Cher, 16 H 81. See also *CMPD*, no. 102, pp. 94–95. In footnote 2 on p. 94 of
CMPD, Mabille suggests that these events must have taken place before 1044 when Count Thibaut
of Chartres was captured by Geoffrey Martel of Anjou in the war that followed the peace conference
described in charter 102 of *CMPD*.

transactions pertaining to her dowry as she saw fit. Once married, wives did not cede complete control over their dowries to their husbands, but rather retained the right to decide what would happen to these holdings.

Noble patrimonies were divided and donated over the course of many generations, making it likely that the property next to or surrounding the dowry, as well as the revenues, were controlled by relatives or the church. Moreover, because of the rights that family members exercised to each other's property, dowries were subject to claims by kin, neighbors, or the monks themselves. A complex of transactions surrounding the gift of a mill to St. Père underscores the complications that could arise in donating property. The grant was initiated by a family who held it from a certain Hugo, who consented to the transfer of this property to the church along with his brothers and uncle. Hugo's paternal aunt, her husband, and their daughter were also required to approve the alienation of this mill because it had been given to this woman at the time of her marriage as part of her dowry.[30] This woman and her family's approbation was sought out precisely because she would have grounds to dispute the gift if she were not consulted.

Just such a situation occurred when Hugh of Sichervilla gave land to Marmoutier sometime in the last fifteen years of the eleventh century. He had already granted the same land in dowry when he arranged for his daughter Isemberg to marry Fulcald of Dangeau. When the monks tried to claim the land, Fulcald became enraged and threw their plow off the property.[31] Poor Fulcald and Isemberg! They had clearly counted upon the land to support their fledgling household, only to find out that dear old Dad had already given it to the monks. No wonder Fulcald was perturbed. Once he had a chance to cool down, and perhaps once Isemberg had a chance to soothe him, he recognized the error of his actions. A "truly remorseful" Fulcald and Isemberg traveled to the monks' chapter house where they both pleaded to be restored to the monks' good graces. The couple quitclaimed their right to the land and conceded the gift that Hugh had made to the monks. At the urging of Isemberg, Fulcald also symbolized the restoration of the land to the monks and their reconciliation with them by placing the abbot's crosier on the altar. Dowry property was an essential part of many noble family patrimonies. Consequently, families fought for their rights to such holdings.

Because of the claim of family members to each other's property, steps were taken to delineate what belonged to the dowry and what belonged

---

30. AD Eure-et-Loir, H 359. See also *Père*, vol. 2, no. 28, pp. 536–38.
31. *CMPD*, no. 55, p. 50.

to other relatives or local religious houses. During the course of his life, Archembald Occha granted extensive portions of his holdings to St. Trinité of Vendôme. When Ada, his daughter, married Fulco of Patay, he granted her a portion of these properties as a dowry.[32] Unfortunately, Archembald's nephews or grandsons contested this arrangement and seized the land so that neither the monks nor Fulco and Ada could cultivate it. The situation grew so bad that in 1146 the abbot of St. Trinité himself intervened to arrange an agreement among Archembald's unruly descendants, Fulco and Ada, and his monastery. After long and complicated negotiations that involved the lords who ultimately controlled this property and the cooperation of a myriad of kin, a resolution was reached.[33] Fulco and Ada would exchange certain of her dowry properties for other lands. In this case, Fulco and Ada were able to secure new properties in exchange for her dowry holdings. In addition, the couple also gained Ada's brother's recognition of their control of other dowry properties as well as his promise not to dispute the couple's arrangement with the monks and his oath to defend this agreement.

Our discussion of dowry began with Galeran of Thionville's arrangement of his daughter Columba's dowry.[34] Several years after the marriage,[35] a dispute developed over what Columba and her husband held versus what the monks possessed. The family was called to the monks to discuss the situation. It would appear the couple had been laying claim to more than what they should have and consequently their holdings were reduced. In recompense, Columba's husband asked for, and was granted, a palfrey. This couple, and their sons, confirmed what the monks held and were granted countergifts for their cooperation and perhaps as compensation.

Dowry was intended to provide brides with support, but it often ended up supplementing the patrimony. While husbands and nuclear families enjoyed the fruits of dowry property, women retained authority over it. Noble ladies could donate their dowry to aid their family and kin in a variety of ways. They could also alienate their property for their own motivations: to

---

32. *CTV,* vol. 2, no. 513, pp. 337–42.

33. What is interesting about the resolution is that the original disputants, the nephews/grandsons of Archembald, did not receive anything. Instead their dispute seems to have been a catalyst for the married couple and the monks to rearrange what they held at these places so that each party got what they wanted.

34. *Josaphat,* vol. 1, no. 82, pp. 104–5.

35. Some time had elapsed since the granting of the dowry and the arrangement of the gift because Fulcher Pagan and Columba had two sons who witnessed and consented to the pact between the monks and their parents.

establish relationships with the monks, as in the case of Hersend of Montigny; to provide for the well-being of their own eternal souls, as Hersend's aunt Adela did; or to benefit the souls of a wide range of kin and allies. This issue of dowry and its control has important implications for the status of women and noble family interactions. Fundamentally, the grant of a dowry did not sever a woman from her natal family. Nor was it a means of sloughing off extraneous daughters by granting them a minimal portion of the family patrimony. No, indeed. Marriage and dowry grants merely extended the family's influence and bound more people to the family through the threads of mutual claim or interest in property. Once married, women did not fall under the dominion of their spouses, nor did their dowries. Dowry property was certainly used to assist or promote family interests, but with the consent and approval of noblewomen. The evidence of dowry from the lands of the Loire draws a picture of strong women who were valued members of their families (natal, nuclear, and affinal), the helpmates of their husbands, and who had the resources to forge important relationships with local religious houses. The shift from the practice of grooms providing a bride price to one in which the bride's family granted a dowry did not mean a diminution in status or influence for the noble-born women of the region of the Loire.[36]

The Disposition of Property: Dower

In addition to dowries, husbands also provided their brides with property that was intended for their support throughout their lives, but especially when they were widowed. Like dowry, the granting of such provisions has been interpreted in a variety of ways. Although dowers have not been read as a symbol of women's marginality or a decline in their status, the question of whether or not women really enjoyed authority over their dowers has been raised consistently—in spite of the fact that Germanic legal practice assured women control of their dowers.[37] A more negative reading of women's relationship to their dowers would assert that although women were granted property for their use, they never really controlled it themselves. As long as

---

36. Nor were the women of the lands of the Loire unusual in their control of dowries. Women all over France exercised the same sorts of power, see: Theodore Evergates, "Aristocratic Women in the County of Champagne," pp. 91–93; Karen Nicholas, "Countesses as Rulers in Flanders," pp. 119–120, 129; Cheyette, *Ermengard of Narbonne,* pp. 28–29, 183; Morelle, "Mariage et diplomatique," pp. 225–284; Thireau, "Les pratiques communautaires entre époux," pp. 217, 221–222; Santinelli, "Ni 'morgengabe,' ni *tertia,*" pp. 255–257; Souares-Christen, "Alliance matrimoniales et circulation des biens," pp. 136–140.

37. Le Jan-Hennebicque, "Aux origines du douaire," pp. 110–18.

she was married, a woman's dower was under her husband's control, and once she became widowed, the dower would be subject to the authority of her son or sons.[38] Dower custom and experience differed throughout medieval France. In Champagne, for instance, it was "customary" for women to be granted a half of their husband's future and current possessions as their dower.[39] Other areas, like eleventh-century Normandy, used devised dowers consisting of a discretionary grant made by the husband for his wife's support.[40] Devised dower was the only form of dower extant in the eleventh- and twelfth-century lands of the Loire, with the development of a customary dower presumably postdating the twelfth century. Fortunately, many acts survive that discuss the creation and management of dowers.

The Granting of Dower

In the Loire region, the custom of providing wives with dowers dates back at least to the tenth century.[41] Countess Eldegard of Dreux was an extremely pious woman who chose to make the monks of St. Père of Chartres heir to some of her personal property. Specifically, she stipulated that the monks receive an alod that her husband, "following Salic law and the custom where a man dowers his wife with his property," had granted for her support.[42] Eldegard hoped that transferring the property in gift from her suzerainty as a feudal lord (*dominatio*[43]) would help atone for her many crimes

---

38. Duby, *Medieval Marriage*, p. 6; Herlihy, *Medieval Households*, pp. 100–101.

39. Evergates, "Aristocratic Women in the County of Champagne," p. 93.

40. Tabuteau, *Transfers of Property*, pp. 176–77. By the late Middle Ages, a woman could expect a third of her husband's property as her dower. See Lemaire, "Les origines de la communauté," pp. 634–37; Pellaton, "La veuve et ses droits de la Basse-Antiquité au haut Moyen Âge," pp. 51–98.

41. In addition to the practical matter of providing support for a widow, dowers also served an important symbolic purpose. The granting of a dower came to be considered as requisite for a legitimate marriage. In contrast to marriage by abduction or associations with concubines, legitimate wives were granted property by their spouses. Canonists picked up on this idea and used whether or not a dower was granted as an indication of a proper or legitimate union. However, Patrick Corbet argues that the dower as a signifier of a legitimate marriage became passé after Gratian, who did not see dower as necessary to formalizing a marriage. Consent rather than gift came to be deemed more significant. Patrick Corbet, "Le douaire dans le droit canonique jusqu'à Gratien." See also Brundage, *Law, Sex and Christian Society*, pp. 176–254.

42. *Père*, vol. 1, no. 5, pp. 87–88. This act indicates a conscious following of old Salic or Germanic practice. A charter from the eighth century similarly records adherence to Salic law in the granting of a wife's marriage portion. See *NDDC*, no. 2, pp. 68–70. Like dowry, the origin of the medieval dower practice was based on a conflation of Roman and Germanic practices. See Le Jan-Hennebicque, "Aux origines du douaire," 107–13; Lauranson-Rosaz, "Douaire et *sponsalicium*," pp. 99–102.

43. J. F. Niermeyer, *Mediae Latinitatis Lexicon Minus*, p. 349.

and sins as well as those of her husband. Husbands from all ranks within the landholding elite of the eleventh through the twelfth century would follow the count of Dreux's example and dower their wives from their own lands. About a century after Eldegard, in 1037, Adam, who held considerable property in the mid-Loire region, provided a dower for his "beloved" wife, Hildegard:

> Therefore I, Adam, in the name of God, give to my beloved wife named Hildegard a *donatum,* which are from my things or from my benefices, which are situated in the pagus of Anjou.... All obligations and all things that are due to me, I give you half. And in another *comitate,* which is called Dunois in a village which is called Valarias...half of the same things from the same village; and above the Lid river [property] which is worth four pounds and five *solidi,* and above the road to Chalceda, an arpent of vines; in the suburb of St. Valerian half of the houses and half an area for a house. If anyone tries to dispute this dower, they will be fined five pounds of cooked gold.[44]

Similar to the dowries granted by the lords of Amboise, Hildegard's dower was made up of a collection of different kinds of property, including attendant rights and revenues. It was a generous settlement and would provide well for her once she was widowed. Intriguingly, the grant implies that a wife had a right to half of her husband's estate. By granting Hildegard half of his estates, Adam recognized her as his equal. If dowers are any indication of husbandly affection, then Adam was certainly enamored with his wife.

The dower provisions for Hildegard's contemporary, Gila, the wife of Rodulf, adds to the picture. Rodulf, the nephew of Bishop Fulbert of Chartres, gave Gila vines from a benefice, which he held from the monks of St. Père. The monks were concerned with who would provide the service on the benefice and they agreed to follow "the customary practice." Rodulf would provide military service during his lifetime, and after his death this obligation would fall to his heirs.[45] Not only was Gila granted land for her support but she was also expected to provide the same service as her husband. Moreover, if, as Rodulf's heir, she failed to provide this service, she would forfeit the benefice. The control of warriors and fiefs were integral

---

44. *CTV,* vol. 1, no. 12, pp. 28–29. Santinelli analyzes this charter in her discussion of dower. See "Ni *'morgengabe'* ni *tertia,*" pp. 249–50.

45. *Père,* vol. 2, no. 12, pp. 271–72.

to the politics of the medieval world, and women clearly enjoyed this power. Nor was Gila's situation out of the ordinary. Recall the examples of Eusebia, who controlled fiefs and knights with her husband; Hersend, who traveled with her household knights; and Countess Eldegard, who held fiefs.[46]

A reference to *jus dotis* in a charter from Notre Dame de Josaphat demonstrates that the custom of dowers continued into the twelfth century. Sometime in the first three decades of this century, the monks of the abbey received a portion of property in gift. A woman named Bruneild held the other portion because her husband had granted it to her *jus dotis*.[47] The monks made it clear that Bruneild would hold the property only for her lifetime and warned that neither she nor her heirs should become accustomed to having the land nor should they expect to inherit it. Like dowry and other property, dowers were subject to claims made by a woman's heirs, a reality which the monks of Notre Dame de Josaphat were certainly familiar with and attempted to avoid.[48]

Control of Dower

As we know from the discussion above, women were successful in controlling their dowries. Was this true of dowers as well? Wives were likely familiar with the property in their dowry, which came from their natal family lands, and thus were better placed to manage it. Dower property, however, was different. It came from the groom's patrimony, which may have made it more difficult for brides to control.[49] At the bare minimum, women were required to consent to any transfer involving property from their dower.[50] In 1132, Salomon Dosnellus gave land to the abbey at Tiron. His wife, from whose

---

46. Other women also enjoyed control of fiefs and knights connected to their dowers. See Aurell I Cardona, "Les avatars de la viduité princière." Duby and others have argued that women could not control fiefs or wield public power. See Duby, "Women and Power."

47. *Josaphat*, vol. 1, no. 83, p. 106.

48. Both Germanic and Roman practice recognized the right of children to their mother's dower. See Lauranson-Rosaz, "Douaire et *sponsalicium*," pp. 102–4; Le Jan-Hennebicque, "Aux origines du douaire," pp. 108–9.

49. Ricketts, "Widows, Religious Patronage, and Family Identity"; Thompson, "Dowry and Inheritance Patterns."

50. Even in England, where women's control of property was more limited, husbands could not alienate their wives' dowers without their consent. Mitchell, *Portraits of Medieval Women*, pp. 8–9; Sue Sheridan Walker, "Litigation as Personal Quest." See also Janet Senderwitz Loengard, "'Of the Gift of her Husband.'" Italian wives were also able to get back their dowers if their husbands had granted them away. See Julius Kirshner, "Wives' Claims against Insolvent Husbands in Late Medieval Italy." Drell also finds that women's control of the *morgengabe* (which is sometimes equated with dower)

dower the land pertained, praised the gift and consented to it—along with her children.[51]

Other women exerted more direct control over their dowers. Around the mid-eleventh century, Pagan of Frouville arranged an exchange with the monks of Tiron. In return for land at one place, the monks gave Pagan a *carrucata* of land elsewhere, which they had received from Helgod of Memberolles.[52] But, "so that the monks would hold in perpetuity the three *carrucatae* of land which they had accepted from Pagan of Frouville," they had Blanche, Helgod's mother, give the *carrucata* to Pagan "because she holds it from her dower." The brothers of Tiron were rightly concerned that this pyramid of exchanges would crumble if Blanche did not approve of having her dower granted to Pagan of Frouville. The right of women to their dowers was clearly recognized here by the monks and the other participants in these exchanges. Perhaps to solidify the deal, Blanche specified that the quarter of the oven which she held at Châteaudun would pass to Pagan, with the provision that she would always be able to bake her bread in the oven.

A charter from St. Trinité of Vendôme demonstrates that if a woman did not want to have her dower property alienated or donated to the church, she had the power to prevent it. In 1150 Lord Simon of Beaugency wished to give the right to markets for the soul of "a certain knight who owed him service," who had recently died in the monks' hospital and was buried in the close. Simon's benefaction hit a snag, however, when his wife, Adenord, did not wish to concede the markets at that time. And since Simon had granted them to her as a dower, her cooperation was necessary for the benefaction to go through.[53] Sometime after her refusal, however, Adenord became gravely ill and, realizing her sins, gave her consent to the alienation of her dower. Once he had her approval, Simon acted promptly and donated the markets to the monks to aid Adenord's soul as well as those of his parents. While Simon's gift was eventually realized, the charter indicates that women controlled their dowers and had the power to determine the future of such property.

---

was undisputed and her interests in this property were protected during widowhood; *Kinship and Conquest,* pp. 73–74, 82–88.

51. *Tiron,* vol. 1, no. 162, pp. 186–87. Similarly, when Teduin Le Faye gave land in the mid-eleventh century, he stated that he had the consent of his wife because this property came from her dower. *CTV,* vol. 1, no. 185, pp. 320–21.

52. *Tiron,* vol. 1, no. 109, pp. 129–30.

53. *CTV,* vol. 2, no. 526, pp. 364–65. Thireau finds that women's consent was needed to alienate dower property in Anjou as well. See "Les pratiques communautaires entre époux," pp. 215–17.

Wives continued to exert their authority over their dowers after the death of their husbands and their own eventual remarriage.[54] In 1065, Odo the knight wished to sell certain family holdings to the church.[55] Yet he found that his elder half-brother had previously granted part of the land to his wife as her dower. Odo's sister-in-law had remarried after the death of his half-brother and stated that she wished to keep the land for the duration of her life. Her wishes were respected, and it was agreed that the property would pass to the monks of Marmoutier only after her death.

The experiences of two women named Roscelina further affirm that dowers remained in a woman's control even after her remarriage or when her children achieved their majority. Between 1084 and 1100, Roscelina made a gift of what she held in dower for the soul of her husband, Geoffrey Freslavena.[56] Sometime after this initial benefaction, Roscelina and her sons gave the other half of the property, which was the fee or fief (*fevum*) for three knights. Not only did this woman control land, she also served as a lord to three military dependents even though she had grown sons who could have assumed this role. Clearly the aristocracy of the Loire region was not as reluctant to allow women's control of knights as modern scholars have assumed.[57]

Another woman named Roscelina had a somewhat different experience. The monks of St. Père of Chartres recorded that this Roscelina relinquished property to the monks that she had received as a dower from her first husband more than twenty years earlier.[58] At the time of her gift, this woman had been married four times! Roscelina knew that she had earned the monks' censure, perhaps a result of her marrying so many times. In the presence of her fourth husband and her son, Roscelina "relinquished her perpetual possession [of the property], as well as giving it and quitclaiming [it]" to the monks. Roscelina controlled her dower through four marriages and over the course of several decades. While her marital exploits may have earned her

---

54. Women in other parts of France did not enjoy such autonomy. In Maine, for example, dowers reverted to the husband's family upon his death. Lemesle, *La société aristocratique dans le Haut-Maine,* pp. 125–26.

55. *MV,* no. 54, pp. 88–89.

56. AD Eure-et-Loir, H 2431. See also *CMPD,* no. 38, pp. 35–36.

57. Duby, "Communal Living," and "Women and Power"; Bloch, *Feudal Society,* vol. 1, pp. 200–201. Jane Martindale also sees women's power as curtailed. She does acknowledge that women could inherit, but in those rare cases, women did not exercise control over the inheritance. Jane Martindale, "Succession and Politics in the Romance-speaking World."

58. *Père,* vol. 1, no. 79, p. 205. Soares-Christen finds women controlling their dowers in the Provençale documents; "Alliances matrimoniales et circulation des biens," pp. 139–42. In Champagne, women also had authority over their dowers and frequently made grants from them; Evergates, "Aristocratic Women in the County of Champagne," pp. 93–96. For Countess Adele's use of her dower, see LoPrete, "Adela of Blois: Familial Alliances and Female Lordship," pp. 21–22.

the disapproval of the monks, she retained her property, and her generosity made up for her perceived indiscretions.

Gifts from Dower

Noblewomen used their dowers to benefit themselves and their family.[59] When he was preparing to depart for Jerusalem, Ansold of Beauvoir and his mother, Richeld, donated certain properties to the church to benefit Ansold's soul and those of his relatives.[60] As well as giving new properties in preparation for Ansold's perilous journey, Richeld also confirmed a previous transfer of property by herself and her husband. Part of the property had come from her dower; the other part she and her husband had purchased. Richeld's control of her dower is evident. She acted with her husband in granting it to the monks, and then later affirmed that it would pass, along with the property from her son's benefaction, in perpetuity to the monks if her son died without legitimate heirs—which was not improbable considering the dangers he would face on his voyage to the East.

Like Richeld, Habelina used her dower to benefit her family. Sometime between 1092 and 1120, Girard Brunellus made an extremely generous donation to the abbey of Cluny. At the very end of the charter, Girard says that half of his wife Habelina's dower of a vineyard would also pass to the monks, with her freest consent and praise, so that "on the day of judgment, God will be merciful to our souls as well as those of our children, and all of our relatives, both living and dead."[61] Habelina used her property to secure divine favor for herself, her children, and all of her relatives. Her concern for souls included several generations, as well as extended and affinal kin. Nobles made gifts for people who were important to them or for whom they felt some affection. That Habelina and other women willingly made donations for their affinal kin attests to their inclusion in their husband's family.

The experience of a noblewoman named Hildiard gives us another view into the lives of married aristocrats. Sometime before 1128, Robert of

---

59. Scholars have made much of widows' contributions to the church, basing their arguments on the assumption that women could only truly control property and make endowments when they were widowed. Goody, *The Development of the Family and Marriage,* pp. 63–68; Jean Verdon, "Les veuves des rois de France aux Xe et XIe siècles," pp. 187–201; Corbet, "*Pro anima senioris sui:* La pastoral ottonienne du veuvage," pp. 233–54; and Lemesle, *La société aristocratique dans le Haut-Maine,* pp. 131–32. In contrast, the noblewomen of the Loire region were generous patrons of the church while they were married.

60. *Père,* vol. 2, no. 69, pp. 317–18.

61. *Père,* vol. 2, no. 48, pp. 504–5. The gift consisted of half of the church of St. Lubin of Brou and half of the tithes of the same church.

Tachainville was severely wounded as a result of his knightly profession.[62] He asked the abbot of Notre Dame de Josaphat if he could abandon the life of a secular knight and "join the warriors of God." His entrance into religious life, however, required the consent of his wife. "The power of God was truly running through the soul of his wife, for she responded to the aforementioned request by saying that she wished to be made a nun and be released from marriage."[63] She also agreed to give back her dower of money, clothes, and books to her husband so that he could use the cash to aide his entrance into the monastery.[64] The abbot agreed to the arrangement but further requested that Robert's mother provide an additional ten pounds and that Robert himself give half of his holdings at Tachainville. With the consent of the appropriate parties, among them the bishop and Robert's mother, wife, and brothers, Robert began his life as a monk. The marriage of Robert and Hildiard provides insight into the more private dimensions of noble marriage. While it is possible that both Robert and Hildiard may have been more suited to the religious life, it is clear that they respected each other and acted to ensure a future that satisfied them both. Hildiard willingly used her dower to provide her wounded husband entrance into the church. She could have used this property to secure her own admission into a convent but chose, instead, to assist her husband in his pursuit of the contemplative life. Although canon law did state that spousal consent was required before a married person could enter the religious life, not all spouses agreed, nor did they all provide the fiscal means for them to do so. Viscount Evrard I of Chartres, for example, encountered trouble when his viscountess did not want him to become a monk. Considerable family pressure had to be brought to bear to finally bring her around.[65] The relationship between Robert and Hildiard provides a sharp contrast.

---

62. Robert did not seem terribly well suited to knighthood. He may have had some physical limitation that made it difficult for him to be a warrior.

63. *Josaphat,* vol. 1, no. 28, pp. 42–43. Throughout the charter Robert is called *juvenis,* which is unusual. The charter states that Robert was married and had had a career as a knight before sustaining his injuries. In this instance, *juvenis* does not denote a particular stage of life for medieval men (i.e., that between adolescence and marriage) but rather seems to be an indication that Robert was still a young man.

64. The fact that Hildiard's dower consisted partly of books suggests this woman was literate. Countess Jeanne of Flanders also gave her considerable library to a Dominican house in Lille. Jordan, *Women, Power and Religious Patronage,* p. 96. See also Susan Groag Bell, "Medieval Women Book Owners"; Joan Ferrante, "Women's Role in Latin Letters from the Fourth to the Early Twelfth Century" and *To the Glory of Her Sex;* Miriam Shadis, "Piety, Politics and Power."

65. For discussion of this situation, see chapter 4. Many saints' lives depict the spouses of saints as reluctant to have their spouse abandon the world and dedicate their lives to God. Such examples can

Disputes over Dower

Disputes concerning dowers demonstrate both noblewomen's control over these properties and what valuable assets dowers were. Early in the eleventh century, Gradulf the knight reached an agreement with St. Père over certain holdings. Gradulf was willing to give this land to the monks in precarial tenure if the monks agreed that he and his wife, Oda, would hold the land while they lived.[66] The property in question came from Oda's dower, and she was willing to use her dower to support both herself and her spouse throughout the rest of their lives. In spite of securing the consent of several concerned parties, Oda and Gradulf had to deal with disputes over their arrangements with the monks several times. On two occasions, *placita* were arranged by the monks to hear the disputes but found in the couple's favor each time. The relationship of the disputants to Oda and Gradulf is not clear, but the charter does state that the relatives of this couple "perpetrated many bad deeds against the monks."

Dower assets were desirable resources. As such, noble-born wives and their husbands vigorously asserted and defended a woman's right to dower properties. In the eleventh century, Isembard Peregrinus and his wife, Gundrada, challenged the monks' possession of lands. The property in question, they argued, came from Gundrada's dower that her first husband had granted her.[67] Isembard presented the case on behalf of his wife, stating that because she had not consented to its alienation, the land belonged to them. In order to placate Isembard and Gundrada, the monks provided them a cash countergift and gave them certain spiritual benefits. Although Gundrada had waited until her second marriage to dispute the loss of this property, we can conclude that her complaint had merit since the monks provided the couple with compensation.

The monks of St. Trinité of Vendôme found themselves in a similar situation with another couple, Florentia and Fulcher.[68] The count of Anjou had given land to the monks. Perhaps unbeknownst to him, the prefect of Ferrières had granted this property as a dower to his wife, Florentia. Yet the competing claims to the land went undisputed until the prefect died and Florentia remarried. Florentia and her new husband, Fulcher, not only brought a claim but they must have regained control of the property, for the scribe

---

be read as topoi of the struggles that the holy endured to pursue their dedication to God. In contrast, the husband of Mary of Oignes, like Hildiard, supported his spouse's desire to enter the church.

66. *Père,* vol. 1, no. 7, pp. 99–100.

67. *MV,* no. 44, pp. 71–72.

68. *CTV,* vol. 2, no. 481, pp. 294–96.

recording the dispute complained that they "grew sleek" from the reduction of the monks' fisc. As he neared the end of his life, Fulcher acknowledged the illegitimacy of the claim. He and his wife traveled to the monks' chapter house, where they abandoned their claim into the hands of the abbot, with their daughter, son-in-law, and grandchildren witnessing. While Fulcher and Florentia did eventually give up their right to this property, it was only after they had enjoyed control of the property for several years.

Like other parts of the patrimony, dowers were subject to claim by family members. The case of the wife of Robert Corneus is particularly instructive. After Robert had died, the monks tried to claim his lands. His wife, however, objected on the grounds that her husband had given these lands to her in dower. To prove her right to the property, she even underwent a judicial ordeal.[69] The story, however, does not end here. A generation later, the grandchildren of Robert Corneus tried to reclaim the disputed property. Two of his grandsons asserted that since their grandmother had undergone a judicial ordeal, her right to the property was established and, as her heirs, they had the right to hold the land in fisc or fief from the monastery. A *placitum* was called, with both the count and bishop presiding. The count declared the matter would be settled by trial by combat. A judicial duel was arranged, but the bishop was able to orchestrate a pact between the monks and Robert's grandsons. The abbot of St. Père agreed to pay the brothers forty *solidi* and return two acres of vines that their grandfather had given previously. In return, these men were to quitclaim their right to their grandmother's dower lands and provide oath-bearers so that if they tried to reclaim the land, they would lose all that the monks had given them. The example of Robert Corneus's family demonstrates the strength of a woman's right to her dower. When the monks tried to gain the property of Robert's wife, she underwent an ordeal to validate her right to it. Moreover, her grandsons used this precedent to make their own claim. While they did eventually settle with the monks, the agreement reached recognized the grandchildren's right to the land. They received both a cash payment and additional lands to make up for the loss of this important dower property.

In contrast to the grandsons of Robert Corneus, recall that Joscelin of Mongerville did not meet with much success in his attempt to claim his mother's dower lands. Two factors prevented Joscelin from attaining these lands. First, his mother had clearly wanted the property to become part of the

---

69. *Père,* vol. 1, no. 33, pp. 160–61. For a discussion of women's roles in judicial ordeals, see Belle Tuten, "Women and Ordeals."

patrimony of St. Père of Chartres. As she was dying, Hildegard gave what she held at Boisville in dower from her first husband, Radulf Bigotus, for her soul as well as that of her first husband, "who had given her" the property.[70] Secondly, the land in question "was not from Joscelin's patrimony," meaning that it belonged to his mother through a previous marriage, and as such, he did not have a claim to it. Yet Joscelin persisted in his claim for many years and committed so "many evil deeds" against the monks that he was excommunicated. Joscelin finally saw the error of his ways and appeared in front of the chapter in bare feet and "truly penitent" for his actions. He dismissed his claim, as did his son William. The case of Hildegard of Mongerville's dower is illustrative of the rights that women exercised over their marriage portions. Dowers could be used to enrich the family and seek redemption for the souls of loved ones, but they remained the property of women. Joscelin tried to usurp his mother's dower from her first marriage, but his attempt was unsuccessful. That he waited until she was dead suggests that even he recognized the strength of his mother's right to her dower lands.[71]

Conclusion

As the passage quoted above concerning the disposition of Elizabeth of Montlhéry's dowry indicates, the granting of a dowry was something to celebrate for it increased family coffers, leverage, and even status. Yet while these properties clearly benefited families, the control of such holdings remained the purview of the wife. Dower property, too, was used to benefit husbands and kin, but only with the wife's approval. If disposition of marriage portions is a reliable indicator of women's power, then the women of the lands of the Loire were powerful indeed. Not only were these women endowed with considerable properties, they enjoyed control over them. Women's rights to their dowry and dower, moreover, were both recognized and protected by their male relatives.

Now that we understand marriage from the point of view of the granting and control of property, it is time to turn to other practicalities of noble marriage, such as age at marriage, number of marriages, and additional relevant issues.

---

70. *Père,* vol. 2, no. 58, p. 453. For a quoted portion of this charter, see chapter 2, p. 45.

71. Only children "from the marriage bed" could exercise a right to their mother's dower. So children had no right to a dower granted to their mother by anyone other than their biological father. See Soares-Christen, "Alliances matrimoniales et circulation des biens," pp. 146–47; Feller, "Morgengabe, dot, *tertia,*" p. 13; Amado, "Donation maritale et dot parentale," p. 161.

CHAPTER 6

Marriage

Practicalities, Ideologies, and Affection

Two roughly contemporary twelfth-century writers, Chrétien de Troyes and Marie de France, each offered commentaries on the nature of aristocratic marriage. In her poem *Yonec,* Marie de France juxtaposed the power of the mature man against the powerlessness of his young bride.

> The man was very far along in years
> but because he possessed a large fortune
> he took a wife in order to have children,
> who would come after him and be his heirs.
> The girl who was given to the rich man
> came from a good family;
> she was wise and gracious and very beautiful—
> for her beauty he loved her very much.
> Because she was beautiful and noble
> he made every effort to guard her.
> He locked her inside his tower
> in a great paved chamber.
> A sister of his,
> who was old and a widow without her own lord,

> he stationed with his lady
> to guard her even more closely.[1]

Property provisions made at the time of marriage indicate that women in the lands of the Loire were endowed with considerable property and that they controlled these holdings throughout their lives. Such findings seem at odds with the passage above and more in keeping with Chrétien's view of marriage as expressed in his romance, *Erec et Enide:* "[Erec and Enide] were very well and evenly matched in courtliness, in beauty and in great nobility. They were so similar, of one character and of one essence, that no one wanting to speak truly could have chosen the better one or the more beautiful or the wiser. They were very equal in spirit and very well suited to one another."[2] The crux of the difference between Chrétien de Troyes and Marie de France would be that Chrétien saw marriage as occurring between contemporaries and equals, while Marie emphasizes the imbalance in age as symptomatic of an imbalance in power. Unlike literature or ecclesiastical prescriptions, both of which portray an idealized or imagined view of marriage, charters, as documents of actual practice, can provide insight into real marriages and the experiences of individual elites.

Aristocratic marriage has been largely read through the lens of patrilineage and the presumed corollary that women were completely dominated, indeed brutalized, by their husbands. These assumptions—often buttressed by examples culled from medieval literature or the exceptional case that drew the attention of a bishop or comment of a chronicler—have led to certain assertions about the age of marriage, the frequency of marriage, and the nature of the relationship between husband and wife. Using demographic studies of the early modern period as a benchmark, historians have argued that elite women married young and were separated in age by many years—if not decades—from their husbands. Since marriage was a political tool, aristocrats, especially aristocratic women, married many times. Wives were regarded as "disposable" and often were repudiated if a better match came along. Clerical ideals and reforms have also shaped the narrative of medieval marriage.[3]

---

1. Hanning and Ferrante, *The Lais of Marie de France,* p. 137. For an analysis of medieval marriage based on literature, see Christopher N. L. Brooke, *The Medieval Idea of Marriage* and R. Howard Bloch, *Medieval Misogyny and the Invention of Western Romantic Love.*

2. Chrétien de Troyes, *Arthurian Romances,* p. 56. Constance Bouchard interprets the relationship between Erec and Enide as tension between love and honor, which was part of what she calls "the discourse of opposites" of the twelfth century, in *Every Valley Shall Be Exalted,* pp. 66–69.

3. Duby, *Medieval Marriage,* pp. 1–24, and *The Knight, the Lady and the Priest,* pp. 189–284.

The evidence from the lands of the Loire is at odds with the general application of these assertions about noble marriage. While some elites experienced marriage in these ways, many others did not.[4] My aim in this chapter is to integrate the more positive marital experiences into the narrative of aristocratic marriage.

Practicalities

Betrothal

Before noblemen and women were married, a period of betrothal was observed. Oaths between the two parties were exchanged, promising marriage in the near or distant future. The promise to marry was given significant weight, and, in an attempt to prevent secret marriages, clerical reformers insisted that betrothals be public ceremonies.[5] While once a strictly secular, and sometimes rowdy, event, betrothals came to be considered an important step to what the church viewed as a legitimate marriage.[6] Bishop Fulbert of Chartres, for example, insisted that someone who had entered into a betrothal could not make another such promise without committing perjury.[7] Implicit in a promise to wed was the consent of the parties involved.[8] Canonists required that both bride and groom be willing participants in the match.

Betrothals, regrettably, do not figure prominently in the charters from the lands of the Loire. Yet a handful of acts provides insight into the betrotheds' standing in regard to each other's property and suggests that they enjoyed a right to it. Sometime around 1050, Ingelbald Brito made a gift of a serf to the abbey of St. Trinité at Vendôme. At the time of this gift, his intended wife, Domitilla, was still "in a state of girlhood." Since Domitilla was apparently not of an age to consent, she could not confirm what Ingelbald was giving. Ingelbald solved this problem by promising that Domitilla would confirm the gift when they were married, as well as after they had children.[9]

4. In other words, medieval aristocrats enjoyed the "companionate" marriage that anthropologists have argued was characteristic of early modern and modern European marriage. Goody, *The Development of the Family and Marriage*, p. 129; Peter Laslett, ed. *Family Life and Illicit Love in Earlier Generations*, p. 13, and *Household and Family in Past Time*.

5. Brundage, *Law, Sex, and Christian Society*, pp. 189–90.

6. Duby, *The Knight, the Lady and the Priest*, pp. 57–75, 161–88.

7. Fulbert of Chartres, *The Letters and Poems*, letter no. 84, pp. 150–52.

8. Jacqueline Murray, "Individualism and Consensual Marriage"; Charles Donahue, Jr., "The Policy of Alexander the Third's Consent Theory of Marriage," pp. 251–52; John T. Noonan, "The Power to Choose."

9. *CTV,* vol. 1, no. 219, pp. 352–53.

Although she was simply too young to be married, as Ingelbald's intended wife, Domitilla had a potential right to his property, which he recognized.

A similar situation occurred in another family. Around 1098, Oda made a donation to Marmoutier so she could be buried with the monks. Her sons and daughter consented to the transaction and were awarded countergifts. Her sons were of age, but Oda's daughter was still a minor. But this young woman was also designated as "the wife of Hervé Belonius" in the charter. Oda's daughter may have been the wife of Hervé in the sense that they had been betrothed, but she was not yet married for she was still underage.[10] Like Hervé and Ingelbald, Gallesius was also betrothed to a *"puella,"* or young girl. When Gallesius quitclaimed all "evil deeds" he had carried out against the brothers of St. Père, this girl, "who was to be the wife of Gallesius in the near future," also consented to the transaction and promised that the agreement would not be disputed by either herself or Gallesius's heirs.[11] Albeit slim, the evidence suggests that although they were betrothed quite young, women did not marry until they had reached maturity. As prospective wives, however, these young women needed to be consulted in actions regarding their future husband's property.

Age at Marriage

Some of the most basic aspects of noble life, such as the age at which aristocrats married, remain obscure. Establishing with any precision how old noblemen and women were when they married for the first time entails deductive guesswork. The charters discussed above indicate that girls were betrothed quite young. But at what age did they actually marry? Much debate and discussion have centered on this issue for the age of the noble born at their first marriage has implications for the nature of noble marriage and family life. What can be accepted with some confidence is that aristocratic girls did marry earlier than their peasant counterparts.[12] However, they did not marry as young as future queens, who were betrothed and married at a very early age.[13] Noble daughters first make their appearance in charters as

---

10. AD Loir-et-Cher, 16 H 88. See also *MB,* no. 75, pp. 86–87.

11. *Père,* vol. 2, no. 66, pp. 460–61.

12. Judith Bennett, *A Medieval Life,* pp. 82–85; Barbara Hanawalt, *The Ties That Bound,* pp. 171–84.

13. Isabelle of Hainaut, the first wife of Philip Augustus and daughter of Count Baldwin V of Hainaut, was betrothed at the age of one to the future count of Champagne. This match was abandoned when Isabelle was about nine in favor of an alliance with the royal house. She was ten when she married Philip. See Aline G. Hornaday, "A Capetian Queen as Street Demonstrator," pp. 79–81.

witnesses or consenters to family transactions around the age of eight, the age of canonical consent.[14] There are instances, however, of very young children appearing in the charters, for their young age is remarked on in the document and accommodations made.[15]

A survey of several elite women suggests that they married in their late teens, in keeping with canon law that stated that girls could give their "present consent" at the age of twelve (see table 1).[16] While it is not possible to be absolute about these estimations of ages, after piecing together the charter evidence, a pattern does emerge. It appears that women did not marry much before the age of fifteen for the first time and that most brides were closer to eighteen or twenty years of age when they first married.[17]

The age at marriage for noble grooms is equally difficult to determine with any surety (see table 2). Most men appear first in the charters as witnesses to their progenitors' transactions. Few are designated as *puer* or *infans,* which suggests that the majority of these men were of the age of consent—meaning over eight. In contrast to aristocratic women, *juvenis,* meaning a youth or adolescent, does seem to refer to a discrete period of development for aristocratic men, designating a young man who had not yet reached complete majority.[18] Odo II of Vallières, the son of Agnes of Montigny, saw his youth as a distinct stage in his life (see appendix, chart 6). In 1130, he made

---

In contrast to this example, John Carmi Parsons has found that while future queens were betrothed at an early age, most were not married until they were over fifteen and having reached—or passed—menarche; "Mothers, Daughters, Marriage, Power," pp. 66–67.

14. Evergates, "Aristocratic Women in the County of Champagne," p. 90; Brundage, *Law, Sex, and Christian Society,* p. 38; Charles Donahue, Jr., "The Canon Law of the Formation of Marriage and Social Practice in the Late Middle Ages."

15. For example, Hugh of Alluyes and Richeld's son Hugh, "who was still a boy," consented to their transactions. Young Hugh is called *infans* and is referred to by the diminutive *Hugonellus.* Their daughter, Adelaide, in contrast, was apparently of age. *CTV,* vol. 1, no. 242, pp. 382–84 and vol. 1, no. 260, pp. 409–10. When a child was not of age, the charters often make note. So it is relatively safe to assume that those children appearing in grants had reached at the very least the age of consent of eight or even their majority.

16. Evergates, "Aristocratic Women in the County of Champagne," p. 90.

17. These findings are consonant with what others have found for various areas of northern medieval Europe. See Herlihy, *Medieval Households,* pp. 74–78, 104–11; Karl Leyser, *Rule and Conflict in Early Medieval Society,* pp. 52–54. See also Evergates, "Aristocratic Women in the County of Champagne," pp. 86–87, 97.

18. But it was not used to refer simply to unmarried men. The young sons of Turpin le Faye, for instance, are clearly young men. The charter does label them *juvenes,* but also goes on to state "the young boys" came into the chapter house to make their gift. *CTV,* vol. 2, no. 538, pp. 383–84. *Juvenis* is used in the same context in *CTV,* vol. 2, no. 571, pp. 436–37. Youth, in this context, was clearly a stage of development in the life of the medieval male aristocrat. See Duby, "Youth in Aristocratic Society" and Bouchard, *"Strong of Body, Brave and Noble,"* pp. 80–81. Barthélemy establishes the age of majority for aristocrats at fifteen; *La société dans le comté de Vendôme,* p. 526.

Table 1 Women's Marital Experience

NAME	FIRST APPEARANCE IN THE CHARTERS	DATE OF MARRIAGE	AGE AT MARRIAGE	AGE AT WIDOWHOOD OR DEATH	LENGTH OF MARRIAGE (YEARS)
Comitissa of Fréteval[a]	1072/1084	c. 1080	c. 20	c. 45/50	c. 25/30
Vicedomina Elizabeth[b]	1103	1108	15–18	d. 1144	c. 20
Agnes of Montigny[c]					
1. Vicedominus Hugh	1087	1097/1100	15–20	c. 27	8–10
2. Odo of Vallières		c. 1110	25–30	c. 60	c. 30
Eustachia Gouet	1079	1065/1069	17–18	d.c. 70	c. 50
Mahild of Alluyes					
1. William I Gouet	1035	1035	14/15	c. 29	15
2. Geoffrey of Mayenne		1050s	30s	d.c. 70	c. 30

[a] Comitissa, the daughter of Fulcher I of Fréteval, first appeared in an act with her siblings in 1072 (see appendix, charts 2 and 5). Although she was born with the name Agnes, she came to be called or to call herself "Comitissa" after her betrothal to Viscount Hugh II of Châteaudun, which took place before 1072/1084. Perhaps she used this name in anticipation of her pending marriage, for she appears as early as 1072 as Comitissa in a charter with her father that does not mention her husband (CMPD, no. 86, p. 76). An act from St. Trinité of Vendôme of 1087 is the first time Comitissa appears as a married woman, but she was married sometime before this act since her son Geoffrey first appeared in 1095 as consenting to his parents' gifts (CMPD, no. 150, pp. 138–39), placing his birth around 1086 and their marriage likely in the previous year. Comitissa's life experience paralleled that of Domitilla and suggests that noblewomen were betrothed sometime around age ten, but that there was a considerable lapse of time before the actual marriage took place. While it is not possible to establish when Comitissa died, Hugh's death occurred around 1110. Their marriage lasted approximately thirty years, and Comitissa was anywhere from forty-five to fifty years old when it ended. There is no evidence that she remarried.

[b] The age at marriage for Vicedomina Elizabeth of Chartres is a bit more certain. She first appeared in a charter with her mother in 1103, when they arranged a gift to establish the anniversary of the death of her father (Père, vol. 2, no. 56, p. 563; see appendix, chart 4). Five years later, Elizabeth appears as a married woman (Jean, no. 7, p. 6). If she was between eight and ten at the time of the benefaction to secure the anniversary of her father's death, then she was anywhere from fifteen to eighteen when she married William of Ferrières.

[c] Elizabeth's sister-in-law, Agnes of Montigny, was also in her late teens when she married. Agnes was of age by 1087, when she witnessed Nivelon of Fréteval's resolution with the monks of Marmoutier at the time of her mother's second marriage to Hamelin of Fréteval (see appendix, chart 6). Agnes herself was married to Vidame Hugh by 1097/1100. Hugh died in 1107, and Agnes assumed control of the lordship of Montigny. See CMPD, no. 76b, p. 68, no. 89, pp. 77–78, no. 184, pp. 174–76; Tiron, vol. 1, no. 3, pp. 14–16, and vol. 1, no. 4, pp. 22–23; vol. 1, no. 10, pp. 22–23; Josaphat, vol. 1, no. 32, pp. 48–49. By 1110 she had remarried, and one of her sons from this union was married by 1130. Agnes bore at least seven children after her marriage in c. 1110. If she was eight in 1087, then Agnes was in her late teens when she married for the first time and nearing thirty when she married for the second. Marrying at thirty for the second time was not an experience unique to Agnes. See Karen Nicholas, "Countesses as Rulers in Flanders," pp. 117 and 122. In 1159, Agnes appeared in a charter reconfirming gifts to the abbey of Tiron in which she is referred to as the "former wife" of Odo of Vallières and domina of these lands, indicators that Agnes was a widow and had assumed control of property pertaining to the lordship (perhaps her dower). If Agnes was born around 1080, she lived to be over eighty years of age. AD Eure-et-Loir, H 1896.

Table 2   Men's Marital Experience

NAME	FIRST APPEARANCE IN THE CHARTERS	DATE OF MARRIAGE	AGE AT MARRIAGE	AGE WHEN WIDOWED OR AT DEATH	LENGTH OF MARRIAGE (YEARS)
Odo II of Vallières					
1. Marie	c. 1120	bf. 1130	teens–early 20s	late 20s	c. 10
2. Martha		c. 1140	30s	d.c. 60	c. 30
Fulcher I of Fréteval[a]	c. 1038	1040/1041	early 20s	c. 52–64	30–35
William I Gouet	c. 1030	c. 1035	30+	d.c. 50	c. 15
William II Gouet[b]	1059	1065/1070	c. 20	d.c. 70	50
Hamelin of Fréteval	c. 1050	1087	40s	c. 50	c. 15

[a] Appearing with Fulcher in one of his earliest acts was his wife, Hildeberg Gouet. The act refers to the dower that Fulcher had recently given his wife. CMPD, no. 9, pp. 10–11. But how old was Fulcher at the time of his marriage? Estimating his age is difficult, but Fulcher was clearly old enough to be invested with knighthood since he "became a secular knight" at his brother's death around 1038. Since children were placed in the church at a young age, Fulcher could easily have been in his teens when his brother died and he became lord. So when he and Hildeberg were married between 1040 and 1041, Fulcher was likely in his early twenties (see appendix, chart 8).

[b] The same pattern of early marriage for men is apparent in Fulcher's brother-in-law, William II Gouet. In 1059, William II first appears in the charters with his mother, Mahild. Père, vol. 1, no. 36, pp. 163–64. His father, William I Gouet, had died by 1050, and his mother assumed control of their combined patrimonies and guardianship of their infant son. By 1071 William was of age, for he was married to Eustachia (see appendix, chart 5). Eight years later, William II was the father of two mature sons (CMPD, no. 44, p. 41). If both sons were of the age to consent, or older than eight, in other words—which seems likely since neither is called a young boy—then William and his wife, Eustachia, were married sometime in the mid- to late 1060s. This would make William around twenty at his marriage. William and Eustachia, furthermore, enjoyed a long marriage. He died around 1120, and Eustachia either retired from public life or died about the same time. Tiron, vol. 1, no. 12, p. 27. If Eustachia had two sons in their early teens by 1079, and went on to have three more children over the course of the next decade, she was probably also in her late teens and not much younger than William at the time of their marriage. While Eustachia's age at marriage does conform to the presumed marriage pattern, the fact that she and William were contemporaries does not. William may have been a few years older than his bride, but no more than a few.

restitution to the monks of Notre Dame de Josaphat for actions that he had taken against them when he was a *juvenis*. At the time of the resolution, Odo was about twenty, married, and clearly no longer an adolescent.[19] Such a practice is at odds with the presumed pattern for premodern European marriage, where the typical age for marriage advanced for men has been their late twenties and for women, the midteens. This assumption that men married much later in life than women stems from literary evidence—such as the excerpt from Marie de France—and the data from Italy, where men do appear to have married much later and to considerably younger women.[20] But Odo was not an isolated example. Many men married in their early twenties to women who were their contemporaries—Fulcher I of Fréteval and William II Gouet, for example.[21]

Marriage patterns in the lands of the Loire were diverse and fluctuated from generation to generation depending on family circumstance and opportunity (see tables 1–3). While William II Gouet and Eustachia were contemporaries at the time of their union, William's parents were not. When their marriage took place, between 1030 and 1035, William I controlled an impressive array of lordships that he had worked his entire life to accumulate, placing him in his midthirties at marriage (see appendix, chart 5).[22] Mahild, in contrast, was a very young woman, probably in her early to middle teens. She had her first child with William sometime in the early to mid-1030s and bore their last child about 1050, either just before or shortly after William's death. Mahild eventually remarried to Geoffrey of Mayenne, a prominent and powerful lord from Maine, and three more children were born to them before 1073.[23] Over the period from the mid-1030s to the late

---

19. Odo's parents were married about 1110/12, and he was likely the firstborn, which would mean he was about twenty in the early 1130s when he and the monks reached this agreement. *Josaphat*, vol. 1, no. 32, pp. 48–49.

20. In contrast to the north, Italy is rich in sources that lend themselves to demographic analysis. See David Herlihy and Christiane Klapisch-Zuber, *The Tuscans and Their Families.*

21. Herlihy, *Medieval Households*, pp. 74–78, 104–11; Evergates, "Aristocratic Women," pp. 77, 86–87, 89; Nicholas, "Countesses as Rulers," p. 124.

22. Because there are no acts extant from William I Gouet, determining when he and Mahild were married is difficult. Based on the fact that their daughter, Hildeberg, was married to Fulcher of Fréteval by 1041 and no later than 1048 (*CMPD*, no. 9, p. 10), and considering that she must have been at least twelve at the time of her marriage, it would seem that William and Mahild's wedding took place between 1030 and 1035.

23. Given that these children consented to a grant by one of Mahild's vassals made between 1071 and 1080, they were likely born in the 1060s. *CMPD*, no. 37, pp. 34–35. Geoffrey ceases to participate in the politics of Maine in 1073, which, combined with the Chartrain evidence, suggests that he died sometime in the 1070s. Mahild made a grant to St. Père to benefit the souls of her husbands, a further suggestion that Geoffrey died before this date. Geoffrey himself appears in only two acts with Mahild, both datable from approximately 1070.

1050s, a span of about twenty-five years, Mahild bore six children. She must have borne her first child when she was in her midteens and her last in her mid- to late thirties. Mahild's two marriages reflect the diversity of marital experience. Her first husband was considerably older than she, but Geoffrey of Mayenne,[24] her second, was her contemporary, or may have been even younger than she.[25]

The marriage of Hamelin of Fréteval presents yet another scenario. In contrast to many of his contemporaries, Hamelin married quite late in life, to the widow of Ganelon II of Montigny (see appendix, charts 6 and 8).[26] The selection of his bride, a widow who was heiress to a powerful lordship, is significant. While Hamelin's elder brother and his three sisters married in their late teens and twenties, the younger son did not. Was Hamelin discouraged from marrying as a means to limit claims to the patrimony? This seems unlikely because we know that Hamelin exercised a right to the Fréteval patrimony and controlled his own lands.[27] Hamelin's marriage may have been delayed or discouraged, but it is also possible that he was waiting for the right match. His choice of spouse is suggestive. Adela of Montigny was approaching the end of her childbearing years, making it unlikely for the marriage to result in any children. Alliance with the widow of Montigny bore other fruit, however, by providing Hamelin and his family with access to additional resources and allying them with one of the prominent families of the region.

Frequency of Marriage

The example of Hamelin of Fréteval raises important questions about aristocratic marriage. An assumed strategy of noble families was to allow only the sons to marry—sometimes just the eldest—thus reducing the number of potential claims to the patrimony and the number of family members in need of support.[28] A survey of families from the Loire region between the

---

24. David Douglass, *William the Conqueror,* p. 57. See also Kathleen Thompson, "The Formation of the County of Perche," pp. 299–314.

25. Mahild's experience was shared by other medieval women. Evergates, "Aristocratic Women in the County of Champagne," p. 102.

26. By 1072, the earliest date for his father's retirement from the secular world, Hamelin was a mature man but did not marry for fifteen years after his father took the habit. If Fulcher and Hildeberg were married in the 1040s, Hamelin was probably born late in this decade or early in the next.

27. See chapter 3, pp. 66–69.

28. Duby, *Medieval Marriage,* pp. 12–15; "Youth in Aristocratic Society"; Bouchard, "Twelfth-Century Family Structures," pp. 167–68.

years 1050 and 1150, or roughly three generations, however, indicates that nearly all children married (see table 3). In some cases all children—sons and daughters—married, indicating that the alliances of daughters and younger sons were important to the well-being or expansion of the family's power and influence. Indeed, the average for the number of children marrying in these three generations is 77.5 percent. Marriage was a means of making connections with important families and individuals, as well as a way of adding to family resources.[29]

Did the twelfth century witness a change in the practice of a majority of children marrying? It would seem so, but because the later history of some families is not recoverable from the charters, it can be difficult to tell. For example, Fulcher Dives's grandson Jeremy of Lisle and his wife, Helvisa Sacracerra, had six children who survived to adulthood. Of the six, the marriages of only two are traceable (see appendix, chart 12).[30] Jeremy and Helvisa Sacracerra's other children may have died, married, entered the church, or remained single, but the extant evidence does not tell us which. It is tempting to argue from such examples that families were in fact limiting which children could marry. There are problems inherent with this argument, however. Such an interpretation rests on the proposition that marriage was in some way draining to family resources. While marriages and the creation of new branches did result in more people with potential claims to the patrimony, marriage could also be used to secure additional properties for the family.[31] Moreover, the majority of offspring did continue to marry. For example, all of Vicedomina Elizabeth's three children married (see appendix, chart 4), as did all of the children of the vicecomital family of Châteaudun of the two generations spanning the late eleventh and early twelfth centuries (see appendix, chart 2). One could surmise that marriage of most offspring was a luxury available to only the richest families of the region, but for the vast number of children of seigneurial, knightly, and lesser noble families who appear in the charters with their spouses and children. Moreover, the charters are replete with affinal kin, an indication that many noble children married

---

29. The same strategy was employed elsewhere in medieval France; Evergates, *The Aristocracy in the County of Champagne,* pp. 102–107; LoPrete, "Adela of Blois: Familial Alliances," pp. 31–39; Le Jan, "Continuity and Change," p. 59; Bouchard, "Genealogy and Politics," and "Twelfth-Century Family Structures."

30. Their daughter Berta married Ursio I of Fréteval, and their son Rainald also married.

31. When Odo of Vallières married Agnes of Montigny, their combined patrimonies created a rich lordship and provided each family with additional resources. The marriages by various members of the Fréteval-Dives kindred enriched and extended both the social status and financial resources of these families.

Table 3 Frequency of Marriage by Family, c. 1050–1150

FAMILY	FIRST GENERATION		SECOND GENERATION		THIRD GENERATION	
	CHILDREN (NO.)	MARRIAGES (NO.)	CHILDREN (NO.)	MARRIAGES (NO.)	CHILDREN (NO.)	MARRIAGES (NO.)
Vidames	3	1	4	2	3	3
Gallardon	3	1	4	4	unknown	unknown
Fréteval	4	4	5	5	1	1
Lèves	3	2	4	3	5	1
Montigny	2	2	5	4	2	1
Alluyes-Gouet	1	1	3	3	4	2
Dives	4	4	6	5	4	3
Langeais	3	1	3	2	4	3
Brito	3	1	4	3	unknown	unknown
Mondoubleau	6	4	3	2	3	2
Viscounts of Chartres	4	4	3	3	1	1
Viscounts of Châteaudun	3	2	2	2	5	5
Counts of Le Perche	unknown	5	5	unknown	4	5
Counts of Chartres	4	3	3	2	3	3
Total	43	35	54	40	39	30
Children married (%)	81.4		74.1		76.9	

151

and had offspring of their own. When viewed in its entirety, the evidence underscores that marriage was not a privilege enjoyed by a few.

Frequency of marriage also plays a formative role in how medieval marriage and family life have been characterized. Elites have been portrayed as marrying often and even viewing marriage as disposable—at least up to the twelfth century.[32] Once again the evidence from the lands of the Loire does not fit this model.[33] With few exceptions, most men and women married only once or twice. Analysis of 129 documented marriages demonstrates that only fifteen, or about 12 percent, involved remarriage. Moreover, the frequency of women marrying more than once is only slightly higher than the frequency of men remarrying: nine women married more than once versus six men, indicating that wives were not particularly "disposable." Of those who did remarry, eleven of the fifteen involved remarriages of members of either vicecomital or comital families. In the region of the Loire, serial monogamy would appear to have been a phenomenon restricted nearly entirely to the very upper reaches of the aristocracy. For the men of these families, five of the six instances of male aristocrats marrying more than once occurred among counts and viscounts. Similarly, two-thirds of women who remarried were of this elite aristocratic status, double the proportion of women who remarried from families of lords.

With few exceptions, marriage was experienced in the following way among the aristocrats of the lands of the Loire. Most married only once and were married for many years. William II Gouet and Eustachia, for example, were wed for nearly fifty years, and Fulcher of Fréteval and his wife for over thirty. Even those who married more than once tended to have long marriages. Agnes of Montigny, for example, was married to her first husband for about ten years, and to her second for about thirty. While the noble born surely did marry for political gain and social ascendancy, they did not use marriage as an easy way to make and break alliances. Once married, they stayed married. Divorce or repudiation was virtually unknown among these families.[34] Indeed, the only divorce among the aristocracy of this region occurred

---

32. Duby, *Medieval Marriage* and *The Knight, the Lady and the Priest;* Baldwin, *Aristocratic Life in Medieval France,* 122–160; Freed, *Noble Bondsmen,* pp. 89–103.

33. David d'Avray questions the viability of this "ecclesiastical" model. He asserts that nobles paid only "lip service" to its ideals and found loopholes to suit their own marital ambitions. David d'Avray, *Medieval Marriage,* pp. 91–99.

34. The perception that nobles married often and discarded their spouses seems to be based on a few examples in the chronicle evidence. Granted these are wonderfully colorful exploits, but they seem hardly representative of what most nobles experienced as marriage. The very genre of chronicles tends to focus on the extraordinary rather than the mundane, hence skewing our perception.

early in the eleventh century and involved Countess Bertha of Chartres and King Robert the Pious.[35] The marital gymnastics of the most powerful did not trickle down into the rest of the nobility. For better or for worse, marriage for these people usually meant the commitment of a lifetime.

Motivations for Marriage

Political advancement, social improvement, and economic gain all motivated aristocratic marriage. The families of the Loire region, like their peers in other places, used marriage to benefit the position of their family. A brief survey of the marriages of some elites illuminates the variety of factors that shaped the union of two individuals and, through them, their families.

Like the marriages of kings, queens, counts, and countesses, those of lesser elites were dictated by political circumstance and the need for allies. The changing political realities of the eleventh and early twelfth century shaped the marriages of the first three generations of the Fréteval family. Nivelon I, the founder of the house, married a prominent and well-established woman. Her name, "Ermengard," may also indicate that she came from a family with Carolingian roots or connections.[36] Marriage with her helped Nivelon I solidify his position as the new lord of a potentially powerful seigneury. The children of Nivelon and Ermengard were allied to two strategically important local families: the Alluyes-Gouet line and the seigneurial family of Mondoubleau (see map 1).

Alliance with a neighbor brought certain benefits during turbulent times, most particularly a handy military force that could help provide defense. A newly married couple setting up a household close by enabled both husband and wife to participate in family matters. Two of Nivelon I and Ermengard's sons, Pagan and Nivelon Pagan, married the daughters of Lord Odo of Mondoubleau, which is separated from Fréteval by only a handful of kilometers. Fulcher, who became lord of Fréteval, also married a woman from a local house; Hildeberg Gouet was the daughter of William I Gouet and Mahild of Alluyes. Union with Hildeberg, whose maternal kin were well-placed in the region, conferred further prestige upon the Fréteval house.

Moreover, some chroniclers' accounts may have been dramatized to demonstrate just how badly noble marriage practices were in need of reform.

35. Duby, *The Knight, The Lady and the Priest,* pp. 75–87.

36. Bouchard, "Origins of the French Nobility" and "Migration of Women's Names"; Martindale, "The French Aristocracy in the Early Middle Ages"; Bernard Bachrach, "Some Observations on the Origins of Countess Gerberga of the Angevins"; and *Fulk Nerra,* pp. 4–7.

The marriages of the three Fréteval sons shared a political motivation. Marriage with the lords of Alluyes forged a tie between two of the count of Chartres' most powerful supporters. Yet the Frétevals did not confine their interest to the territories of the Chartrain, for they were also tied to the counts of Vendôme and other powerful families to the southwest. Their neighbors and kin, the Mondoubleaus, were well connected to this political sphere. Alliance with this family allowed the Frétevals to hedge their bets. While allying themselves with the count of Chartres, they were also connected to families with interests and affiliations to the powers of the mid-Loire.

In the next generation, Fulcher and Hildeberg followed a similar strategy of marital alliances for their five children, four of whose marriages are recoverable from the charters. Ironically, the exact identity of the wife of their eldest son, and eventually the lord of Fréteval, remains uncertain.[37] Although the identity of Eustachia's natal family is unsure, she was apparently from either a comital or vicecomital family, demonstrating that by the second generation, the Fréteval family was of a status where its members could marry into such highly placed families. In addition to Nivelon II's marriage, his sister Agnes/Comitissa married Viscount Hugh II of Châteaudun.

The other children of Fulcher and Hildeberg married into well-placed seigneurial families. Hamelin, their other son, was eventually married to Adela, the widow of the lord of Montigny. Like Hildeberg's family, the Montignys were a very well-established family in the Chartrain and could trace their origins back to the late Carolingian service nobility. The other two daughters, Hildeberg and Pagana, married lords from the region, although the families were not as prestigious as the Montignys or the Alluyes-Gouet family. Hildeberg married Bernard of La Ferté, whose lordship was located to the east of Fréteval and bordered on the county of Le Perche (see appendix, chart 8). Her mother's natal family (the Alluyes-Gouet family) had a strong presence in the western lands of the Loire and may have encouraged this alliance, for marriage to Hildeberg Gouet's namesake would have served to remind the community of the Gouets' control of important lordships on the border with Le Perche.[38] Another daughter, Pagana, married a man whose holdings were

---

37. *CTV,* vol. 2, no. 330, pp. 45–46 states that Nivelon had the consent of his wife "Comitissa Eustachia, and another Comitissa, his sister [the viscountess of Châteaudun]." Eustachia was clearly of important status and related to a comital or vicecomital family, but which one is obscure. There are a couple of possibilities: she could be descended from the counts of Dammartin, located to the northeast of Fréteval near the Ile de France, or she might have been the daughter of Count Rotrou I of Perche and Adelina of Domfront.

38. As will be discussed later, names were more than names in the Middle Ages. They were important markers for family, political, and religious connections. For a discussion of women's names

closer to home: Pagan of Frouville (see appendix, chart 8). Like Bernard of La Ferté, Pagan seems to have been of more modest status and was perhaps a newly established seigneur. To sum up, the Frétevals sought spouses from two types of families: those who had a more prestigious lineage or who had been in the area for several generations, and those who, like the Frétevals themselves, owed their position to their military service, were more recently established, and were situated geographically to provide support.[39]

The descendants of Fulcher of Dives made many similar choices in arranging the marriages of their offspring. Fulcher Dives married a woman of considerable property and prestige: Adela, the *domina* of Bezai (see appendix, chart 9).[40] Adela used her own property to support and patronize the monasteries of the region, specifically that of St. Trinité in Vendôme and Marmoutier. Adela and Fulcher had four children: two sons and two daughters.

In the first two generations of the Dives family, sons and daughters married people of a similar status and who controlled lands near Vendôme. Fulcher Turre succeeded to his parents' lordships and became one of the most powerful men of the region. He married Hildiard, a daughter of the seigneurial family of Lisle (see maps 1 and 2). One of Fulcher Turre's sisters married Hugh of Mondoubleau, the other a member of an up-and-coming family of the region and one similar in status. The family, at this point, did seem to favor alliances with families holding land north of Vendôme. Given the political turbulence between the counts of Chartres and Anjou, which was centered in the southern Loire valley, Fulcher and Hildiard chose to ally their children with those who held lordships away from the focus of battle. These alliances may also have been motivated by their loyalty to the counts of Vendôme, who might have encouraged their trusted supporters to make alliances to the north as a buffer or line of defense from the general direction of Chartres.[41]

---

in particular, see Patricia Skinner, "'And Her Name Was...?'"; Bouchard, "Patterns of Women's Names" and "The Migration of Women's Names."

39. Because many elites made hypergamous marriages—in other words, marrying up the social ladder—scholars question the "equality" of marriage between husbands and wives. Duby, *Famille et parenté dans l'Occident médiévale,* p. 251. Aurell, "Stratégies matrimoniales de l'aristocratie (IXe–XIIIe siècle)." Nassiet, in turn, questions this "inequality" in his analysis of families in the late Middle Ages; "La monographie familiale à la fin du Moyen Âge," pp. 70–73.

40. *MV,* no. 30, pp. 46–48. Adela also appears as Hildiard in the charters. Yet it is clear that it is the same woman controlling the same property. It seems, therefore, that she was known by two different names. Her brother was Robert of Moncontour. *CTV,* vol. 1, no. 55, pp. 403–4.

41. The counts of Vendôme were allied with the Angevin house and eventually would become part of this dynasty through the marriage of Fulk Nerra's daughter Adela to the count of Vendôme. Dunbabin, *France in the Making,* p. 389. K. S. B. Keats-Rohan argues that the Capetians also allied with Vendôme as a check to the power of the comital house of Blois-Chartres. See "'Un vassal sans histoire'?" p. 199.

Fulcher Turre and Hildiard followed the same general principles as their predecessors in securing mates for their progeny. Their son Jeremy, the lord of Lisle, married Helvisa, who had the unusual cognomen of Sacracerra. Unfortunately, information about her family is not recoverable.[42] Interestingly, the charters are more forthcoming about the men that Jeremy's sisters married. Domitilla and her family seem to have been particularly close to her father since they appear frequently in charters with him. But her marriage was somewhat out of character for the alliances of the Dives family. Recall that she married Ingelbald Brito. Ingelbald's status in Brittany, the region of his birth, is not clear. That he was seeking his fortune far afield may suggest that his family was not that well off. If the selection of names for Domitilla's children is any indication, connection to his family was not high priority for the couple since three of their four sons were named for Domitilla's ancestors, specifically her father and uncles (see appendix, chart 11).

While Domitilla settled around Vendôme, the experience of her sister, Hersend, was somewhat different. This daughter of Fulcher and Hildiard married Gradulf Albus, who held lands near the lordship of Montigny (see appendix, chart 9).[43] While a man of some property, Gradulf Albus was not among the higher ranks of the region. The alliance between him and Hersend, a daughter of a very powerful family, may have been motivated by desire to secure allies in the north. Montigny is located on the Loir River in the heart of the Chartrain. Thus Hersend and Gradulf Albus's marriage should be read as a continuation of the Dives family desire to secure allies and lands at a distance from the mid-Loire region.

Both the seigneurial family of Fréteval and the descendants of Fulcher Dives were related by marriage to the lords of Mondoubleau.[44] Like Fulcher

---

42. The choice of names for Jeremy and Helvisa Sacracerra's children implies that her family may not have been as prestigious as the Dives clan since five of seven offspring were named for members of Jeremy's family—specifically for his mother, Hildiard; his father, Fulcher; his uncle Rainald; his uncle Hugh of Mondoubleau; and his great-uncle on his mother's side, Robert of Moncontour. "Helvisa" was a meaningful name within the Mondoubleau-Dives families. Helvisa Sacracerra kept her cognomen, which could be a reference to her natal family. It is possible that "Sacracerra" (which is confused by some with "Saracenna") was this woman's given name and she adopted "Helvisa" when she joined the Dives kindred. But "Helvisa" and its derivatives were popular names in the lands of the Loire, making it possible that it was the name this woman bore from birth.

43. *CTV*, vol. 1, no. 69, pp. 127–29. Although Gradulf held land near Montigny, he was not related to the seigneurial family of Montigny. Gradulf and Hersend had three sons, one of whom was named for Hersend's father, Fulcher.

44. Two Fréteval sons married two Mondoubleau daughters, and the Dives clan was connected to the lords of Mondoubleau and Fréteval through Adela, Fulcher Dives and Adela of Bezai's daughter (and namesake), who married Hugh of Mondoubleau and from whom all later lords of Mondoubleau were descended.

Dives and his son Fulcher Turre, Hugh and his son Odo of Mondoubleau were supporters of the counts of Anjou and Vendôme. Marriage between these two families would seem a natural way for both to extend their power, gain allies, and express their shared connection to the comital family. While the Dives family may have been motivated by politics to make alliances with families placed to the north of Vendôme, the Mondoubleaus in turn sought inclusion in the power and politics of the Vendômois. Odo Dubellus, the son of Hugh of Mondoubleau and Adela Dives,[45] married Placentia of Montoire (see appendix, chart 10).[46] Odo's sister Emmeline also married into a family with interests in the Vendômois. Guismand of Vendôme held part of the mill of La Chappe, which Adela of Bezai had given to the monks.[47] His family was also well established in the region and of a similar status as the Mondoubleau and Dives kin.

A shift occurred in the geographical orientation of Mondoubleau marriages in the following generation, however. Odo and Placentia had two daughters and a son. Their daughters, Helvisa-Adierna and Fredescind, both married sons of Nivelon I of Fréteval. Previously the Mondoubleaus had sought spouses from families to the south in the mid-Loire, but marriage with the Fréteval family had certain benefits: close-by allies and family members, and connection to the counts of Chartres. The counts of Chartres had an interest in defending the western flank of their territories, which could aid the lords of Mondoubleau. Moreover, such an alliance reaffirmed the Mondoubleaus' loyalty to these counts.

Yet this preference for alliance with families north of Vendôme and the Loire changed by the 1060s. Helvisa-Adierna and Fredescind were both widowed, and each remarried a man with interests and property further west along the Loire River. Fredescind married the lord of Semblançay, located to the northwest of Tours and distant from Mondoubleau (see maps 1 and 2).[48] After her first husband was killed during an Angevin attack sometime around 1038, Helvisa-Adierna married Hamelin of Langeais. This time her spouse, like that of her sister, came from a family far down the Loire River, past Tours (see appendix, chart 13).[49]

---

45. Adela is never called "Dives" in the charters. I use it here simply to highlight her descent.

46. Placentia may also have been distantly related to the lords of Montigny. Her father, Nithard, is listed as the nephew of Ganelon I of Montigny in an act from Marmoutier, but no other connections are recoverable from the source. *CMPD*, no. 22, pp. 22–23.

47. *MV,* nos. 23–33, pp. 35–57.

48. *CSVM*, no. 197, p. 124; no. 198, pp. 124–25.

49. While Hamelin carries the geographic cognomen "of Langeais," the property that he is associated with in the charters lay in the Vendômois. The *Gesta Ambaziensium dominorum* says that

The marriage alliances of the families of the lords of Fréteval and Mondoubleau and of the descendants of Fulcher Dives reflect the general patterns and choices that the aristocrats in the lands of the Loire made in arranging their marriages. The eleventh and twelfth centuries were often uncertain times. Aristocratic families needed allies and comrades-in-arms to help defend their holdings. Association with men and women more powerful than they was also important. Marrying an ally or the vassal of a count or king was a way of demonstrating support for him and creating a bond that could later prove useful. As well as association in the mundane world of politics, such families were also connected through their patronage of ecclesiastical foundations. All of the families discussed here gave generously to Marmoutier and St. Trinité of Vendôme, and, to a lesser extent, St. Père of Chartres. Indeed these nobles arranged gifts together, cementing through spiritual donations the ties of politics, affinity, and blood.[50]

What's in a Name? Family Structure, Family Life

Names were more than just names for the medieval aristocracy. They were important signifiers of alliances and family connections. Elites consciously chose names that would link their children to specific kin and even specific honors. For example, the Frétevals customarily named the son who was to inherit the title and lordship either Nivelon or Ursio, and the vicecomital family of Châteaudun used the names Hugh and Geoffrey in alternate generations to designate who would inherit the title of viscount. The selection of names thus provides insight into what kin were particularly significant to nobles and can indicate the nature and structure of aristocratic families.[51]

Count Fulk Nerra of Anjou seized Langeais when he heard that Count Odo II of Chartres had died while fighting in Germany (*Gesta Ambaziensium dominorum,* p. 83). Hamelin was likely displaced as a result of Angevin expansion up the Loire. If Hamelin was a vassal of the counts of Chartres, or hostile to the Angevins in any way, he would have lost this property. Or his dispossession could have been the result of the killing of one of the Count of Anjou's kinsmen. *CTV,* no. 16, pp. 34–35. Alliance with Helvisa-Adierna could have been motivated by Hamelin's need to gain property and reestablish himself. While his sons also carry the Langeais signifier, the properties they inherited came through their mother. For discussion of the strategic importance of Langeais, see Bachrach, "The Cost of Castle Building."

50. Lemesle argues that shared connections to ecclesiastical houses were an important way that the Manceau aristocracy created bonds and celebrated family ties. Lemesle, *La société aristocratique dans le Haut-Maine,* pp. 49–82.

51. The contributions of the German school of prosopography first analyzed the meaning of names: Karl Ferdinand Werner, "Die Nachkommen Karls des Großen bis um das Jahr 1000 (1–8. Generation)" and "L'apport de la prosopographie à l'histoire social des élites"; Gerd Tellenbach, "From the Carolingian Imperial Nobility to the German Estate of Imperial Princes." Other scholars

If the families of the lands of the Loire were truly patrilineal, one would expect agnatic names (those associated with the male line) to dominate. But was this the case?

In the third generation of the Fréteval lords, Nivelon II and Eustachia had only one child, a son named Ursio. Interestingly, the name Ursio had never been used by the Fréteval family before, suggesting the name came from Eustachia's natal family. Given the fact that she was descended from a comital or vicecomital family, Fréteval adoption of her family's names would not be surprising. Moreover, the use of matronymics was not unusual for the Frétevals. For example, three of Nivelon II's four siblings were named for their mother's kin (see appendix, chart 8). The prominence of names from the maternal line continued in this family throughout the twelfth century, in some cases eclipsing the names derived from the paternal line. Nivelon Fulcher III and his second wife, Adelicia, named four of their five children after her kin. The only child bearing a distinctly Fréteval name was Lord Ursio III, who followed this same pattern by naming only two of his five children for his ancestors. The dominance of names from the maternal line demonstrates the importance that this family vested in the women their sons married.[52] Noblewomen's use of natal cognomens—Helvisa Sacracerra and Hildeberg Gouet, for example—proves that women were not completely subsumed into the paternal line. Rather, they maintained their own identity.

The use of matronymics further reinforces the collateral structure of aristocratic families. Siblings, aunts, uncles, and cousins were also valued kin as noble couples named their children after them as well.[53] In spite of scholars' use of the term "lineage" and their insistence that medieval people privileged the patriline, the charters of the lands of the Loire never use the term *linea* to refer to their family. Indeed, Anita Guerreau-Jalabert has pointed out that the concept of "lineage," as modern historians understand and apply it, did not

---

adopted and critiqued this methodology: George T. Beech, "Les noms de personne poitevins du 9e au 12e siècle" and Bachrach, "Some Observations on the Origins of Countess Gerberga of the Angevins." For more recent applications of this approach, see the essays in George T. Beech, Monique Bourin, and Pascal Chareille, eds., *Personal Names and Studies of Medieval Europe* and Dunbabin, "What's in a Name?"

52. Pascual Martinez Sopena, "Personal Naming and Kinship in the Spanish Aristocracy"; Robert Durand, "Family Memory and the Durability of the *Nomen Paternum.*" For the importance of maternal kin, see Bouchard, "The Origins of the French Nobility," "Family Structure and Family Consciousness," and "Twelfth-Century Family Structures"; Johns, *Noblewomen, Aristocracy and Power,* pp. 53–164; Leyser, "Maternal Kin in Early Medieval Germany"; Herlihy, "Land, Family and Women in Continental Europe."

53. For example, Berta of Lisle and Ursio of Fréteval named five of their eight children for siblings, aunts, and uncles.

exist in the Middle Ages. She argues that families were cognatic, thus recognizing their descent from both maternal and paternal kin. The aristocracy from this region supports her assertion that the noble born did not conceive of their families as lineages.[54]

Unlike other families, men of the Dives family frequently used cognomens. For example, Fulcher Dives's son was called Fulcher Turre.[55] While it would be tempting to assume that these were indicators of patrilineage, this was not the case since these names were not passed along to either their sons or their daughters.[56] Moreover, women and children of these families used descriptors associated with maternal kin. Ingelbald Brito's children did not adopt his cognomen; instead, his sons were frequently called "the sons of Domitilla."[57] Association with their mother and, through her, with the Dives family, was what these sons chose to emphasize. Domitilla and Ingelbald's firstborn son, Vulgrin, linked his daughters to his maternal kin through his selection of their names. One was named Domitilla for his mother, the other Agnes for their distant relative Agnes of Vendôme (see appendix, chart 11). Even Vulgrin's granddaughter was called Richeld after her great-aunt.[58] Connection to Domitilla was so important to her sons that they named their children after her and made donations to commemorate her.[59] Significantly, the children of this couple did not make a gift to provide for their father's soul—at least none that is recorded in the charters. Combined with the onomastic evidence, it is apparent that women and maternal kin were important members of this family.

Onomastically, the Mondoubleau family made quite different selections. Hugh, the first lord of Mondoubleau, and his wife, Adela, used some family names for their seven children. One son was named Hugh after his father, but

---

54. Guerreau-Jalabert, "La désignation des relations et des groupes de parenté en Latin médiéval" and "La parenté dans l'Europe médiévale et moderne." Evergates finds the same in Champagne; *Aristocracy in the County of Champagne,* pp. 86–87.

55. Fulcher Turre's son, Jeremy of Lisle, also used the "Turre" cognomen occasionally, but not consistently. He was most frequently referred to in the documents as "Jeremy of Lisle."

56. Indeed, cognomens are abundant in the charters. Many men, in particular, carried a cognomen separate from their first name, such as Bodellus, Chotard, Brunellus, Sine Barbe, Brito, Boguerullus, Briderius, and many others. Yet these cognomens do not generally pass on to the next generation. One exception was the Gouet family, which used the cognomen of Gouet for at least four generations—men and women. However, while Hildeberg Gouet maintained her natal cognomen after her marriage with Fulcher I, she did not pass this cognomen along to her children.

57. See *CTV,* vol. 2, nos. 355, 361, and 392, pp. 95–97, 105–107, and 142–43, respectively, and *MV,* no. 187, pp. 266–68.

58. *CTV,* vol. 2, no. 576, pp. 442–43. Nor did the children of Gradulf Albus, who was married to Ingelbald's sister-in-law, take their father's cognomen.

59. *MV,* no. 187, pp. 266–68.

he went on to become a cleric instead of inheriting the lordship.[60] Another son was named Fulcher after Adela's father. The other four children carry names that have no connection to either maternal or paternal kin. Unlike the Dives family and the Frétevals, the Mondoubleau line tended to generate new names for their children (see appendix, chart 10). This pattern continued into the next generation. Of their three children, Odo of Mondoubleau and Placentia named only one for a relative: their son carried his grandfather's name, Hugh. Their daughters, however, had names unique to them. Indeed, there seems to be no strong naming pattern in this family, which is apparent in both Fredescind's and Helvisa-Adierna's selections of patronymics for their sons.[61] Yet this was not always the case.

In the twelfth century, perhaps in the hope that his daughter, too, would one day control Mondoubleau family lordships, Helvisa-Adierna's son Pagan named his daughter after his mother. Given the history of the family, Pagan could realistically expect that his daughter might be heir to a lordship, for both his mother and grandmother had inherited powerful seigneuries. Pagan's wish came to pass as his daughter Helvisa and her husband, Viscount Geoffrey III of Châteaudun, assumed control of Mondoubleau. When time came to name their own children, Helvisa and Geoffrey named one son Pagan.[62] This name held important associations for both Helvisa's and Geoffrey's families. The person from whom Helvisa and Geoffrey inherited Mondoubleau was her father, *Pagan* of Mondoubleau. Moreover, recall that Viscount Geoffrey's mother was Comitissa of Fréteval. Her uncles had both married daughters of Odo of Mondoubleau and had both carried the name Pagan in some form. By calling their son Pagan, Helvisa and Geoffrey demonstrated their knowledge of family history and sought to recall a time when the Fréteval and Mondoubleau families had been united, as the families would be under the lordship of their son (see appendix, charts 2 and 13).[63]

---

60. His brother Odo, who may have been named after the count of Chartres as an expression of Mondoubleau comital affiliation, became lord, but Hugh the cleric became interim lord in his role as guardian for Odo's young son after his death.

61. Fredescind's son was named Nivelon Pagan after his Fréteval progenitors, and her other children carried names associated with the Semblançay family. Helvisa-Adierna's sons were called Walter and Hamelin, the names of their father and paternal grandfather.

62. The other son was named Hugh, after Geoffrey III's father. But the name Hugh was also prominent in Helvisa's family: her maternal uncle, maternal great-uncle, and maternal great-grandfather had all been named Hugh.

63. Similarly Hamelin II, lord of Langeais and Montoire, named his son "Odo Dubellus" after his grandfather who had been the lord of Mondoubleau. Hamelin likely hoped his son would eventually inherit this lordship. The cognomen of "Dubellus" was not used by any of Odo Dubellus of Mondoubleau's children. It was only employed by his great grandson.

Relationships between Husband and Wife: Married Life

The practicalities of marriage, such as the age at which nobles married, the length of marriages, and the fact that most only married once and did not divorce, shaped relationships between husband and wife. While one can argue and debate whether noble men loved their wives, and vice versa, the charters demonstrate that they respected them, trusted them, and valued their assistance in overseeing and protecting family holdings.[64] Charters record that some husbands and wives used terms of endearment in referring to their spouses. We also know that spouses demonstrated concern for each other by arranging gifts to benefit their souls. Moreover, it seems that many noble couples spent a good deal of time in each other's company. When considered in toto, a picture of companionate marriage emerges, which is complemented and supported by examples from literary sources.

Chrétien de Troyes depicts the marriage of Erec and Enide as one based on parity, mutual attraction, and love.[65] Indeed, this romance can be read as a cautionary tale of the dangers that could come from loving your wife *too much*. John Gillingham believes that "love became a more important element in aristocratic marriage" in the twelfth century than it had ever been before.[66] He attributes this in part to the emphasis canonistic reformers placed on the indissolubility of marriage, arguing that because men and women could no longer divorce, compatibility, commitment, and love were weighed more heavily when seeking a spouse.[67] The relationship of Erec and Enide would certainly support this interpretation. So, too, do the chronicle accounts of Roger of Howden, William of Tyre, and others. When combined with what we already know about marriage in the lands of the Loire—that husbands and wives were not separated in age by many years, that most married only once, and that these marriages lasted for decades—it is perhaps not surprising that affection developed between spouses, perhaps in some cases out of necessity.

Chronicles and saints' lives provide additional clues to the emotional interactions of couples. Lambert of Ardres described one wife's particularly

---

64. The marital lives of the women of the Loire region closely parallel those of thirteenth-century England. Mitchell, *Portraits of Medieval Women,* pp. 43–56 and "The Lady Is a Lord."

65. Scholars since the 1990s examining literature from both England and Germany suggest that family life was more supportive and marriage more affectionate than previously thought. Kimberly Keller, "For Better and Worse"; Albrecht Classen, "Family Life in the High and Late Middle Ages."

66. John Gillingham, "Love, Marriage and Politics in the Twelfth Century," p. 292.

67. D'Avray suggests that Queen Esther served as a model to noble couples for staying married and not parting with their spouses even under difficult circumstances. *Medieval Marriage,* p. 61. Esther was a powerful figure for medieval aristocratic women, as will be discussed in the next chapter.

vivid response to the death of her spouse. When Humphrey of Ordres was murdered, his wife "planted within her female sex a manly spirit and manfully stripped the bloody and scarlet undershirt or singlet from her murdered husband. Not without tumult in her heart, she put it aside for the time being (Oh, virtuous woman!). She showed it often to her sons, not without sobs from her embittered throat, as an instigation to avenge their father."[68] This woman was devastated by the death of her husband and sought revenge for his murder. Her response was deeply visceral, sparked by the loss of her partner, the father of her children. Other women demonstrated their affection in gentler ways. Out of the love she felt for her "pious husband, the companion of her bed and devotion," Countess Emma followed through on his plan to build a church. The women described by Lambert adhere to the description of marriage outlined in the Gospel of Matthew: "It is not good for man to be alone. I will make him a helpmate. Therefore Man should relinquish his mother and father and cleave to his wife, and they will be two in one flesh as well as two in one body. And what God has joined, man cannot separate" (Matthew 19:5–19:7). These women "cleaved" to their husbands. They were loyal, devoted, supportive, and affectionate spouses.

Husbands felt similarly about their wives. A noblewoman lay dying, with her distraught husband in attendance. When she did finally pass away, he prayed fervently to St. Foy to have his wife come back to life.[69] Clearly the emotional bond between this husband and wife was strong. The "two in one flesh" was not easily severed. It could be similarly traumatic when one spouse wanted to leave the world and enter the church. The viscount of Chartres's wife was reluctant to lose her husband to God. Family resistance, even brutality, is a common topos in saints' lives when the married future saint decides to devote his or her life to God. Instead of being read as examples of domestic violence, perhaps they should be interpreted as evidence of how important each spouse was to the well-being of the family. Such dramatic reactions confirm the marital bond.

There are also examples of husbands and wives being supportive of the other's choice to dedicate themselves to piety. The husband of Marie of Oignes was one. He did not oppose her desire to end their marriage to devote herself to God, but rather "patiently supported her in her good works

---

68. Lambert of Ardres, pp. 69–70. The topos of wife as vengeance seeker is common in the romances as well. See Baldwin, *Aristocratic Life,* pp. 138–39, and Penny Schine Gold, *The Lady and the Virgin,* p. 18.

69. Bernard of Angers, *The Book of St. Foy,* p. 144. For a discussion of the use of saints' lives in reconstructing family life, see Kathleen Quirk, "Men, Women and Miracles in Normandy, 1050–1150."

and had compassion for her."[70] While their physical marriage ended, this husband did not abandon his responsibilities to his wife. Instead he continued to support her religious vocation. The departure of one spouse for the spiritual life disrupted family life, particularly when there were minor children. When one saint confided in his wife his desire to become a monk, "as she was of a noble family and noble in mind, she willingly annulled the sacred vows of her husband."[71] This woman, however, did express concern for the future of her children. In response, her husband, the future saint, made arrangements for their support. Although motivated by a desire to serve God, this nobleman recognized and cared for the needs of his wife and family. His actions underscore how much of a partnership marriage, and parenthood, were. Husband and wife relied on each other and counseled each other—for the saint had discussed with his wife his wish to enter the monastery.[72] Such behavior is brought home to the lands of the Loire by Hildiard of Tachainville, who granted her dower property to the church so her husband could become a monk.[73]

Certainly there were marriages that were not based on mutual support and affection, but the charters and the literary evidence are replete with as many examples of affectionate partnership marriages as they are of the other, more repressive, unions. In his analysis of marriage in the thirteenth century, John Baldwin states that "with the possible exception of Perceval's peculiar solution, all the male heroes are apparently satisfied both with their brides and with the institution of matrimony."[74] The evidence suggests that many of their eleventh- and twelfth-century predecessors felt much the same.

What were the realities, then, of marriage for the aristocrats living in the lands of the Loire? Undoubtedly some experienced marriage as Marie de France characterized it—vast age differences between husband and wife, with the wife destined to lead a sheltered, overprotected existence. Yet the evidence from this region indicates that another pattern or strand needs to be woven into the tapestry of aristocratic marriage. Many nobles married their contemporaries, married only once, enjoyed long marriages, and were not

---

70. Head, *Medieval Hagiography,* p. 714.

71. Head, *Medieval Hagiography,* p. 500.

72. The concept of a "partnership marriage" is not unique to the aristocracy of this region or to the aristocracy in general. LoPrete, *Adela of Blois,* pp. 71–94; 101–116; Evergates, *Aristocracy of the County of Champagne,* pp. 88–101. Barbara Hanawalt characterizes peasant marriages in medieval England as partnerships. Hanawalt, *The Ties that Bound,* pp. 141–155; 205–220.

73. *Josaphat,* I: 42–43, no. 28. See Chapter 5, pp. 136–37 for discussion of this couple.

74. Baldwin, *Aristocratic Life in Medieval France,* p. 160.

personally familiar with divorce. Onomastic evidence proves that families valued a woman's kin, further reinforcing an interpretation of aristocratic private life that was indeed collateral, meaning that both husband and wife were viewed as contributing something of value to the marriage. Marriage as a relationship of disparity also seems out of step with the evidence from this region. Husbands and wives seemed more to be companions than oppressed and oppressor. Now that some of the "realities" of marriage have been fleshed out, what ideas did the clergy have about aristocratic marriage?

Ideologies

The eleventh and twelfth centuries have been portrayed as a watershed in aristocratic life. Contemporaneous with transformations in family ethos were alterations in the clerical view of marriage.[75] The secular model of marriage, which made marriage virtually disposable and did not set any real restrictions on who individuals married, was to have been replaced by the "ecclesiastical" model of marriage. Crafted by reformers such as Bishop Ivo of Chartres, this model insisted on the indissolubility of marriage and prohibited marriage within seven degrees of kinship.[76] While these two models of marriage seem mutually exclusive, common to both was the fact that women, in particular those marrying into the family, were viewed with suspicion, if not outright hostility. Such women were strangers, never to be fully accepted or integrated into their new family. Indeed, this interpretation seems to have been based in part on language used by Lambert of Ardres to recount that Count Manassas of Guines referred to his sister's children as being of "an alien seed" and feared that they might inherit his county.[77]

The life experiences of the elite of the lands of the Loire once again allow for the testing of such theories. The widow of Thibaut Remendesac would have found the attitude described by Lambert of Ardres unfamiliar. Sometime early in the twelfth century, she made a gift to St. Père for the souls of

---

75. The twelfth century witnessed a revitalization in canon law, and with it discussions of what constituted marriage. While most scholars acknowledge a lively period in marriage legislation in the twelfth century (see Brundage, *Law, Sex, and Christian Society*), the construction of two competing models of marriage, secular and sacred, was developed by Duby in *The Knight, the Lady and the Priest* and *Medieval Marriage*.

76. Scholars suggest the motive for these kinship restrictions was the wish to prevent noble families from keeping land in the control of the extended family and to make it more likely that such properties would come under church control. Goody, *The Development of the Family and Marriage*, pp. 134–46; Herlihy, "Church Property on the European Continent, 701–1200" and *Medieval Households*, pp. 83–88.

77. Lambert of Ardres, pp. 86–87.

her husband and sons from "her own possessions." However, she stipulated that part of her property would not pass to the monks until after the death of her daughter-in-law.[78] Providing for the support of her daughter-in-law certainly departs from the expected behavior of a mother-in-law toward this "stranger" that her son had introduced into the family—not to mention the modern views about "monster-in-laws." Moreover, the property granted was not the daughter-in-law's dower, for the charter clearly describes the property as belonging entirely to Thibaut's widow. In other words, this provision went above and beyond what daughters-in-law could necessarily expect from their affinal family. Such behavior and concern for the well-being of a daughter-in-law reveal that they were not viewed as outsiders. Rather, elites made provisions to ensure the continued well-being of this "alien seed."

Twelfth-century marriage reform came to the lands of the Loire via Bishop Ivo of Chartres, who sought to enforce these abstractions by writing letters to local nobles who he thought were violating the laws of consanguinity.[79] His correspondence demonstrates that he thought some of the marriages of the aristocracy of the region were incestuous.[80] But what did the subjects of his letters themselves think? While we will likely never know completely, the charters do provide some insight.[81]

Overwhelmingly the charter evidence indicates that the pronouncements of the clergy on consanguinity and what made a suitable marriage partner did not inform how most aristocratic families selected spouses. In spite of clerical pronouncements, the Fréteval-Mondoubleau-Dives kindred continued to make what the clergy would have considered incestuous marriages through the twelfth century. Moreover, they had a long history of doing so

---

78. *Père,* vol. 1, no. 146, p. 361.

79. Burchard of Worms addressed many issues concerning marriage in the eleventh century, followed by Ivo of Chartres, Gratian, Peter Lombard, and Huggucio, canonists of the twelfth century interested in marriage. Pope Alexander III and Pope Innocent III wrote many decretals dealing with marriage. See Brundage, *Law, Sex, and Christian Society,* pp. 229–43, 256–97, 325–41, and 343–46. See also Constance Rousseau, "Kinship Ties, Behavioral Norms and Family Counseling in the Pontificate of Innocent III." For information on Ivo of Chartres, see Lynn Barker, "Ivo of Chartres and the Anglo-Norman Cultural Tradition" and "Ivo of Chartres and Anselm of Canterbury"; Bruce C. Brasington, "New Perspectives on the Letters of Ivo of Chartres" and "Lessons of Love."

80. For analysis of the impact of ecclesiastical reform on the nobility, see Fanning, *A Bishop and His World before the Gregorian Reform;* Constance B. Bouchard, "Noble Piety and Reformed Monasticism" and "Laymen and Church Reform around the Year 1000"; Giles Constable, *The Reformation of the Twelfth Century;* Foulon, "Stratégies lignagères et réforme ecclésiastique."

81. Historians have found that charters reflect penetration of the ideas of reform. Hubert Guillotel, "Combour: Protohistoire d'une seigneur et mis en œuvre de la réforme grégorienne"; Guillaume Mollat, "La restitution des églises privées au patrimoine ecclésiastique en France du IXe au XIe siècle"; Chédeville, "Les restitutions d'églises en faveur de l'abbaye de Saint-Vincent"; Ziezulewicz, "'Restored' Churches in the Fisc of St. Florent de Saumur."

starting in the eleventh century when two Fréteval brothers married two Mondoubleau sisters, a clear violation of the prescription against marrying affinal kin.[82] In the twelfth century, Helvisa, the granddaughter of Helvisa-Adierna of Mondoubleau, married Viscount Geoffrey III of Châteaudun (see appendix, charts 7 and 13). Each was descended from Fulcher of Fréteval, who was Helvisa's paternal uncle and Geoffrey's maternal grandfather. Berta of Lisle, Jeremy of Lisle's daughter, married Ursio of Fréteval in spite of the fact that two of Berta's cousins had been married to Ursio's great-uncles. In the second half of the twelfth century, long after the "ecclesiastical" model of marriage was put in place, Guitberg married Bartholomew of Vendôme. This couple shared descent from Fulcher Dives, making the match within the prohibited degrees of kinship (see appendix, charts 7 and 13).

Could these nobles have made these marriages unwittingly with prohibited kin? This is unlikely since family members were not mere abstractions. These men and women knew their kin. They participated in each other's transactions and they arranged gifts to memorialize their common ancestors, so they knew their shared ancestry. Moreover, their choice of names for their children demonstrates a familiarity with ancestors stretching back several generations. These "incestuous" marriages rather suggest unwillingness on the part of the aristocracy to conform to the ideals espoused by medieval clerics. Indeed, the match between Mathilda of Châteaudun,[83] the widow of Viscount Robert of Blois, and Count Geoffrey Grisegonnelle of Vendôme was expressly forbidden by Bishop Ivo of Chartres. Even though Ivo wrote to both Geoffrey and Mathilda explaining that their marriage would violate the laws of consanguinity, the couple and their families ignored his censure.[84] In his letter to Geoffrey, Ivo implies that the relationship preventing the marriage was unknown to the couple. He says he writes Geoffrey as "the shepherd of his flock" to warn him of the fate of being exposed to the "bites of invisible wolves"—a reference to Geoffrey's ignorance of the consanguineous impediment to his upcoming marriage. Ivo warns Geoffrey that if he

---

82. In the twelfth century, Bishop Ivo wrote to the bishop of Soissons concerning a man who wished to marry his deceased wife's sister. The women in question were the daughters of Galeran of Breteuil, kinsman to the viscounts of Chartres. The same prohibitions would have been applied to two brothers marrying two sisters, i.e., once married a husband would share the same relationship with kin as his wife. So if one brother married a sister, he became brother to his wife's siblings, thus making a marriage with them incestuous. Ivo of Chartres, *Lettres de Saint Ives,* letter 247, pp. 444–46.

83. Mathilda was the daughter of Comitissa of Fréteval and Viscount Hugh II of Châteaudun.

84. Ivo of Chartres, *Lettres de Saint Ives,* letters 132 and 133, pp. 241–43. For discussion of how genealogies may have been used, see Ryan Crisp, "Consanguinity and the Saint-Aubin Genealogies."

proceeds with the match, he will incur the sentence of excommunication. Why exactly did the bishop see the marriage as incestuous?

At the heart of the problem was that Ivo believed that Mathilda's first husband, Viscount Robert of Blois, and her fiancé, Geoffrey, were related to each other. Ivo's stance was based upon the supposition that once married, the bride or groom enjoyed the same degree of relationship as their spouse to all affinal kin. So after marriage, a wife or husband became the daughter, sister, brother, niece, nephew, or cousin to his or her spouse's parents, brothers, sisters, uncles, or cousins. Thus Mathilda and Geoffrey were themselves not related in the prohibited degrees; rather, Geoffrey was related to Mathilda's first husband. Perhaps this was why the couple ignored Ivo's warning. It did not seem like incest to them. They may have also gone ahead with the marriage because they knew that the bishop's reconstruction of Geoffrey's parentage was inaccurate and the two men were not as closely related as he thought.[85] In spite of Ivo's warnings and attempts to meet with Geoffrey and Mathilda, the couple was married in 1105.[86]

The evidence from the Loire region, while not abundant, does suggest that the medieval aristocracy ignored much of the church's attempt to legislate their marriages and to craft a new model of marriage. Perhaps they ignored it because the clerics' view of marriage—with the exception of consanguinity—was not that far from their own experiences. In regard to indissolubility, the aristocracy of the lands of the Loire followed the church's teachings, for virtually none of them divorced. Moreover, preambles to the charters demonstrate that the aristocracy was familiar with church teachings and reform. But the evidence also shows that families continued to make alliances within the prohibited degrees, even when threatened by the bishop with the dire consequences such alliances would bring. Why did they do this? Perhaps they resented church interference in determining family alliances and the future of their family. Perhaps they felt these reforms were aimed at undercutting their control of property, the same conclusion many modern scholars have reached about the reforms. The letter from Bishop Ivo

---

85. Merlet argues that Ivo made a mistake when determining Geoffrey's maternal kin beyond his grandfather. Ivo says that Fulk L'Oison was the son of Bouchard le Chauve. But he was the grandson of Bouchard Le Vieu of Nevers, adding one degree to the genealogical reconstruction, which made Robert of Blois, Mathilda's first husband, and her fiancé, Geoffrey, third cousins two times removed, or related within six degrees. Nor was this the only genealogy that Ivo got wrong. See Ivo of Chartres, *Yves de Chartres,* letter 45, pp. 185–89.

86. This was not the only couple to go through with what was considered an incestuous marriage. Nassiet finds that nobles at the end of the Middle Ages also ignored canonical prescriptions about consanguineous marriages. "La monographie familiale à la fin du Moyen Âge," pp. 67–70. See also Shadis, "Berenguela of Castile's Political Motherhood," pp. 334–40.

suggests that the clergy did not know the genealogies as well as the nobles themselves. Noble families might have subsequently felt they were better able to judge whether a marriage was incestuous or not.

Conclusion

The marital experiences of the aristocracy of the lands of the Loire paint a rather different picture of noble marriage than that offered by Marie de France. In most cases, the noble born did not find themselves bound to spouses much older or younger. On the contrary, many married men and women of their approximate age. Most noble-born men and women could expect to marry since in this region marriage was not a privilege conferred only upon the patriline of each generation. Rather, families depended on the alliances of all children to expand family influence and enrich family coffers. Once married, most men and women stayed married, many for decades. Some did remarry upon the death of a spouse, but these marriages too could last many years. The selection of names provides additional proof of marriage based on the importance of both man and wife, both maternal and paternal descent. Once married, women were not subsumed into the patriline. They remained distinct individuals and their ancestors and descent were recognized—indeed celebrated—by the use of names from their bloodline. As a consequence, many aristocrats experienced marriage much as Chrétien de Troyes described the relationship between Erec and Enide: a match between contemporaries who each brought something of value to the marriage.

Now that the practicalities of noble marriage have been examined in general, the more personal and individual aspects of the relationships between noble wives and husbands call out for consideration. Were these interpersonal relationships as brutal and barbaric as some have implied? Or do new voices herald a different experience that needs to be added to the narrative?

❧ CHAPTER 7

For Better, Not Worse

Wives and Husbands as Partners in Family and Lordship

Marriage, both as a transitional moment in their lives and as a lived reality, shaped the life experience of noble-born women. Much ink has been put to page recounting the more sensational marriages of the central Middle Ages. But within the tapestry that was medieval aristocratic life, there are lighter and brighter hues as well. It is these experiences that this chapter seeks to highlight. Chronicles are full of references to women acting with and in place of their husbands, indicating that in terms of authority and power, "the two were one." The charter evidence also offers a more moderate view of aristocratic marriage. Instead of repression, violence, and absence of affection, marriage for many was, as Eileen Power suggested over eighty years ago, a "rough and ready equality" between husband and wife.[1] As most nobles of the lands of the Loire could expect to be married to the same person for many years, partnership developed between spouses as they raised their children, managed their lands, addressed various challenges to their authority, and cultivated ties with the church.

---

1. Eileen Power, "The Position of Women," p. 410. Power's assertion of parity was largely over-shadowed by the view put forth by Jo Ann McNamara and Suzanne Wemple in their seminal article, "The Power of Women through the Family," which cast the central Middle Ages as the beginning of the end of women's power.

"Two in One Body": Husbands, Wives, and Lordship

The inclusion of scripture from the Gospel of Matthew in a dower grant made around 1040 indicates much about aristocratic marriage. "As the omnipotent and highest God was putting together man in his own image and likeness, he said: 'It is not good for man to be alone. I will make him a helpmate. Therefore Man should relinquish his mother and father and cleave to his wife, and they will be two in one flesh as well as two in one body. And what God has joined, man cannot separate'" (Matthew 19: 5–7).[2] The relationship between husband and wife portrayed in this passage is one of partnership. The wife is to assist her husband and their two separate identities are merged into one. Emotional connections are evident as well. Husbands are to "cleave" to their wives, a sentiment that extends beyond holding on to one's spouse, but rather encompasses loyalty, support, and commitment. Many noble-born husbands and wives in the lands of the Loire experienced marriage in just this way.[3]

War, whether defensive or offensive, was the primary function and obligation of male elites. While some military engagements might last only a matter of weeks, others could last months and, with the advent of the Crusades, even years. Such absences posed a challenge to aristocratic families: Who was to mind the castle, fiefs, vassals, children, and other dependents while the lord was away?[4]

In the lands of the Loire, wives and mothers were the likely—if not preferred—candidates (see map 2). The reality that the warrior lifestyle could take men from their homes for long stretches of time compelled wives to be familiar with family holdings and the details and procedures of how to run the lordship while their husband was away. To prepare their wives, daughters, and sisters, aristocratic husbands, fathers, and brothers had them join in making donations, securing allies, and providing justice. Significantly, wives appeared with their husbands in one in four transactions recorded in the database constructed from charters from the region.

---

2. *CTV,* vol. 1, no. 12, p. 2. Significantly, this same portion of scripture was included in the earliest extant charter recording a dower arrangement in Champagne. Evergates, *The Aristocracy in the County of Champagne,* pp. 107–8.

3. Most European scholars have been hesitant to recognize noblewomen as more than mere conduits through which property and titles passed. American historians have rigorously asserted that noblewomen were far more than place-markers in their family as they exercised direct power over both people and property. European scholars are critical of this approach and the American crafting of a "countermodel" to Duby. Hedwig Röckelien, for example, finds American characterizations of medieval women "anachronistic" and "clichéd." "Entre société et religion," p. 583. See also Jacques Dalarun, Danielle Bohler, and Christiane Klapisch-Zuber, "Pour une histoire des femmes," p. 560.

4. Brundage, "The Crusader's Wife" and "The Crusader's Wife Revisited."

When Count Geoffrey II of Le Perche fell ill while his son Rotrou was on Crusade, he instructed his wife and vassals "to keep the peace and maintain order honorably and to protect his land and castles."[5] The count clearly trusted his wife to maintain the patrimony and to act in the best interest of the family. When Rotrou returned several years later, the county was intact and thriving. Similarly, the crusader Count Stephen of Blois-Chartres left his county and progeny in the capable hands of his countess, Adela. A rare surviving letter between husband and wife provides illustration of Adela's partnership with her husband. Stephen wrote: "These things which I am writing to you, dearest, are indeed few of the many [that have happened]. And since I cannot express to you all that my heart holds, dearest, I [only] bid you well and make excellent arrangement for your land, and treat your children and your vassals with honor, as befits you, for you will surely see me as soon as I can possibly come."[6] This letter provides evidence of affection between the spouses and of Adela's command of the family holdings, military dependents, and her children while Stephen was away.

Imprisonment was a by-product of military campaigning with which families had to cope. In 1090, Geoffrey of Preuilly, the count of Vendôme, was captured and imprisoned. While incarcerated, Geoffrey grew increasingly worried because he had not followed through on donating property to St. Trinité of Vendôme. To redress this oversight, he sent three of his men to his wife, Countess Euphronia, and requested that she make the gift in his stead. She traveled to the monks' chapter house and gave "all that he wanted to give."[7] Moreover, Euphronia made the gift "not only for the redemption of [Geoffrey and Euphronia's] souls but also those of their mothers, their fathers, and all of their sons and daughters, as well as for the liberation of their bodies." Geoffrey did not ask his son or one of his men or another male relative to secure this vitally important donation. He turned instead to the person he felt he could best trust, his wife, who he knew had the ability to achieve this goal.

All seems to have proceeded smoothly with this gift until Geoffrey's death in 1101. At that point, there was some disagreement about the donated property, for Abbot Geoffrey of Vendôme wrote to the bishop of Le Mans complaining about Euphronia.[8] In a wonderfully descriptive letter, Geoffrey

---

5. Orderic Vitalis, *Ecclesiastical History,* vol. 6, p. 395.

6. August C. Krey, *The First Crusade,* p. 106. See also LoPrete, *Adela of Blois,* pp. 94–101.

7. *CTV,* vol. 2, no. 334, pp. 52–54. The circumstances of his capture are frustratingly absent from the charter. The count was imprisoned by the lord of Beaugency, but why is not clear. For further information on the comital couple and their patronage of St. Trinité, see Johnson, *Prayer, Patronage and Power,* pp. 59, 79–82, 123–24, and 187.

8. Geoffrey of Vendôme, *Oeuvres,* letter 32, pp. 58–60. Hereafter, Geoffrey of Vendôme, *Oeuvres.*

recounts Euphronia's actions. The countess disputed the monastery's control of the church of Savigny, as well as the movable and immovable goods pertaining to it, and resorted to violence to assert these rights. Just after the gathering of tithes, Euphronia and her retinue arrived at the church, beat down the doors, broke open the monks' coffers, and started distributing the tithes among "the impious who were with her."[9] Abbot Geoffrey was outraged at her presumption and demanded justice from his bishop. Like any male lord, Countess Euphronia was not afraid of using violence to assert what she believed were her rights. Moreover, the letter clearly casts her in a leadership role as commander of the men in her retinue. Indeed, the abbot seems to have been somewhat cowed by her power for he demanded safe escort from his bishop to the hearing being held to settle this matter. As a wife, Euphronia was the trusted confidante and emissary of her husband. As a lord, she was a power to be reckoned with.

Euphronia was far from the only noble wife dealing with the capture of a spouse. We have encountered Richeld, a woman who held land near Vendôme, before. She experienced the imprisonment of her spouse during the hostilities between the comital houses of Anjou and Chartres in the early 1040s.[10] About two decades later, in 1063, the lord of Château-Renault and Château-Gontier was captured while campaigning in Brittany. His wife, Lisebell, was left in charge of their properties during his imprisonment. But before he was taken prisoner, this lord had been involved in a dispute with Marmoutier. To atone for his actions, or perhaps to gain the support or intercession of the monks in arranging her husband's release, Lisebell traveled with her two sons to the monastery where she quitclaimed their right to the property.[11] Unfortunately the charter does not finish the story and tell us whether the lord was eventually released. Like other noblemen, the lord of Château-Renault relied on his wife to carry out this important business.

Wives did not assume positions of authority only in difficult times. Husbands counted on their wives in more mundane circumstances as well. The marriage of Domitilla and Ingelbald Brito provides illustration of typical

---

9. Abbot Geoffrey does not identify any of these men. In a later letter Geoffrey refers to a Vulgrin and Hilgot, whom the editor and translator of the letters, Geneviève Giordanengo, suggests might have been part of Euphronia's retinue. Geoffrey of Vendôme, *Oeuvres,* letter 33, pp. 60–62. Geoffrey continued to demand justice from Bishop Hildebert over this matter. In letter 33, he implies that Hildebert clearly favors the countess. Geoffrey warned Hildebert in a later letter not to be tricked by the duplicity of women, indicating he fears that the bishop was being taken advantage of by this countess. The issue seems to have been finally resolved around 1106. Geoffrey de Vendôme, *Oeuvres,* letters 71–72, pp. 128–31.

10. See chapter 2, pp. 57–58.

11. *MB,* no. 42, p. 55. Her sons later consented to this act, as did her daughter even though she was still a child.

interactions of an aristocratic couple (see appendix, chart 11).[12] Early in their marriage, Domitilla and Ingelbald witnessed a gift in the hospital of the monastery of Marmoutier.[13] This transaction would set the tone for their relationship for Domitilla appeared with her husband in alienating property to St. Trinité of Vendôme and in managing land held from the couple by other men who owed them service in a series of gifts spanning the years 1067 to 1079.[14]

"Let it be known by all men that Ingelbald Brito of Vendôme and his wife [Domitilla] gave a certain part of the land that they hold...to the monastery of Vendôme for the health of their souls and those of their relatives."[15] This charter from 1067 clearly states that this couple held the land together. Significantly, the other portion of this property was held from Domitilla and Ingelbald Brito by Teduin of Faye and his wife—providing yet another example of husbands and wives controlling property jointly. Nine years later, in 1076, Domitilla and her husband approved the sale of their half of a church, which is referred to as coming from "their lordship" and being "their property."[16] Further proof of Domitilla's authority over lordships and vassals is apparent when Ingelbald agreed to let one of their vassals give and sell land to the monks. Domitilla was given a countergift in recognition that the fief, with its attendant rights and obligations, belonged to her too.[17] As well as being lords in their own right, husband and wife were also vassals to several lords.[18] In 1066, Domitilla and Ingelbald were at the court of Count Fulk of Vendôme, where they witnessed a gift by the count and his wife.[19] This couple also appeared at Domitilla's father's court in 1079 to confirm what one of their men had granted to the monks.[20] Domitilla and Ingelbald jointly held and managed not only their property but also their retainers.

12. Aristocratic couples all over medieval Europe experienced marriage in much the same way as Ingelbald and Domitilla. Evergates, "Aristocratic Women in the County of Champagne," pp. 97–104; LoPrete, "Adela of Blois: Familial Alliances and Female Lordship," pp. 16–25; Cheyette, *Ermengard of Narbonne*, pp. 20–34; Livingstone, "Noblewomen's Control of Property in Eleventh- and Early Twelfth-Century Blois-Chartres"; Drell, *Kinship and Conquest*, pp. 55–57; Johns, *Noblewomen, Aristocracy and Power*, pp. 53–79.

13. *CMPD*, no. 115, pp. 108–9.

14. In all of the acts concerning the disposition of property, Domitilla acted as co-lord in all but two. In these two, however, she consented to the arrangement. *MB*, no. 24, pp. 28–30 and no. 92, p. 100. See also AD Loir-et-Cher, 16 H 49.

15. *CTV*, vol. 1, no. 185, pp. 320–21.

16. *CTV*, vol. 1, no. 255, pp. 403–4.

17. *MV*, no. 177, pp. 251–54.

18. Specifically, the lords of Beaugency and the count of Vendôme.

19. *CTV*, vol. 1, no. 179, pp. 309–10.

20. *CTV*, vol. 1, no. 272, pp. 423–24.

Domitilla was associated with her husband in virtually every aspect of overseeing their benefices, fiefs, and vassals. Moreover, on at least one occasion Domitilla acted independently to resolve a conflict concerning family possessions.[21] By 1090 Ingelbald was dead, and Domitilla continued to oversee the lordship. Just after his death, she made a gift of what she held at Lancé, and her interests in the church there were later recognized in an accord reached between the monks of Marmoutier and a local lord.[22] Domitilla's final act, a benefaction to provide for the souls of those she loved who had predeceased her, is dated 1096. The gift consisted of things that the "residents of Vendôme owe[d] to her."[23]

Domitilla and Ingelbald Brito were married for several decades. During their marriage the couple was "two in one body" in managing their considerable wealth and property. As such, Domitilla was associated with her husband as lord of men.[24] A contestation of Domitilla's grant of the church at Lancôme demonstrates this status. Radulf of Montfolet claimed the church from the monks because he held this property in fief and had not consented to its alienation. A resolution was quickly reached through monks' willingness to grant Radulf a countergift. When he confirmed that these properties could indeed pass to the church, it was made clear that Domitilla and Radulf shared the fiefs pertaining to the church.[25] Not only did Domitilla control property, she also controlled fiefs and assumed the seigneurial responsibilities associated with them. Noblewomen were not prevented from exercising authority over fiefs. Like Domitilla, Lady Roscelina enjoyed control over at least three knights, and Domitilla's sister, Hersend of Montigny, traveled to Marmoutier with her band of knights. Similarly, Agnes possessed a knight's fee at Rodon and maintained control of it during her subsequent marriages.[26] The use of the title *domina* also indicates that noblewomen wielded the same powers and

---

21. *CTV,* vol. 1, no. 288, p. 444. In 1079 she brokered a reconciliation with the monks over two manses. Her sons appeared with her, but Ingelbald was absent.

22. *MB,* no. 89, p. 98.

23. *CTV,* vol. 2, no. 354, p. 93.

24. *CTV,* vol. 1, no. 272, pp. 423–24, and *MV,* no. 177, pp. 251–54.

25. *MB,* no. 88, p. 97, and no. 89, p. 98. Scholars have argued that women lost these rights by the end of the eleventh century. Duby, "Women and Power"; McNamara and Wemple, "The Power of Women through the Family, 500–1100"; Amado, "Femmes entre elles," pp. 125–34; Aurell I Cardona, "Les avatars de la viduité princière." For a counterargument, see LoPrete, "The Gender of Lordly Women."

26. AD Loir-et-Cher, 16 H 120. See also *CMPD,* no. 132, pp. 122–23. Between 1070 and 1084, Agnes made a donation of property at Rodon for the soul of her dead son, with the exception of her knights' fee. When her second husband wished to make a journey to Rome, she asked the monks if they would buy the fee from her, "which she held." The monks agreed. Throughout the transactions, the fee is referred to as Agnes's and not her husband's.

authority exercised by men. Other feminized versions of titles were employed by women, such as *vicedomina* and *legedocta,* lending further proof that women exercised the powers incumbent with the particular office.

Marriage also gave Domitilla an opportunity to forge her own identity. "Domitilla" had actually begun life as Hildiard.[27] About ten years after her marriage—that is, sometime in the 1060s—she began to be referred to in the charters as "Domitilla" or "Dometa."[28] Which raises the question: What motivated Hildiard to adopt this new name? "Domitilla" and "Dometa" are names clearly associated with lordship, a fact supported by a manuscript dating from around 1060 where Domitilla's name is simply recorded as the abbreviation for female lord, *Domina.*[29] Later charters refer to her as "Domitilla," suggesting that her title was so closely associated with her that it became her name.[30] Did this woman come to be known as "Little Lord" as a result of her partnership with Ingelbald in managing their fiefs and lands? Possibly. If so, her use of this name is further evidence of the partnership that she enjoyed with her husband over their holdings.

The adoption of "Domitilla" may also have been influenced by events in her natal family. Domitilla's mother, Hildiard, died in 1066, just about the time the younger Hildiard became known as Domitilla. Domitilla and her family resided in Vendôme close to her father's castle. Fulcher, her father, did not remarry, and Domitilla likely took over as lady of the castle. So she may have become "Little Lord" in relation to her father. The use of Domitilla would also serve as a way of reminding the world of her place in one of the most prominent families of the region: the Dives clan. Domitilla's father and grandparents had carved out an impressive lordship and were allied to several of the most powerful families in the Vendômois. Her husband, Ingelbald, in contrast, was a newcomer to the region. The adoption of "Domitilla" could have been a way for Domitilla and her immediate family to maintain, and continually celebrate, their connection to this illustrious family.[31] Whatever

---

27. See, for example, *CTV,* vol. 1, no. 185, pp. 320–21; vol. 1, no. 273, pp. 424–25; *MV,* no. 128, pp. 219–21. For a discussion of the options open to women to forge their identity, see Ricketts, "Widows, Religious Patronage and Family Identity."

28. *CMPD,* no. 115, pp. 108–9; *MV,* no. 359, pp. 372–73; *MB,* nos. 88 and 89, pp. 97–98.

29. AD Loir-et-Cher, 16 H 118.

30. *CTV,* vol. 1, no. 179, pp. 309–10; no. 218, pp. 350–52; no. 219, pp. 352–53; no. 255, pp. 403–4; no. 272, pp. 423–24; no. 273, pp. 424–25; vol. 2, no. 354, p. 93; *MV,* no. 59, pp. 95–96; no. 60, pp. 97–98; no. 187, pp. 266–68; *MB,* no. 88, p. 97; no. 89, p. 98; no. 92, pp. 100–101. Yet she is also called by her birth name, Hildiard/Hildegard, in two charters after 1070: *CTV,* vol. 1, no. 185, pp. 320–21, and vol. 1, no. 273, pp. 424–25; AD Loir-et-Cher, 21 H 40 and 16 H 118 and AD Maine-et-Loire, H 3245. Why she switched back to Hildiard/Hildegard is a puzzle.

31. AD Loir-et-Cher, 16 H 83; *CTV,* vol. 1, no. 272, pp. 423–24. This is further reinforced by Domitilla's use of the geographic descriptor "of the castle of Vendôme." Moreover, her sons sought association with her and the Dives family by being called the "sons of Domitilla" rather than after

the cause, Domitilla's involvement in politics and property led her to be known by a name that forever associated her with the obligations and privileges of lordship.[32] Marriage clearly did not stifle this woman's ability for self identity. Indeed, marriage arguably gave Domitilla the ability to forge her own self-constructed identity.

Nor was Domitilla of Vendôme the only Domitilla. The case of another noblewoman who adopted the name of Domitilla corroborates that women assumed this name as a way of emphasizing their position as lord.[33] Craon was a strategically important Angevin lordship, and Ennoguena of Craon was the granddaughter of its lord, Warin of Craon. The lordship was lost by this family when the count of Anjou conquered it and then granted it to his trusted vassal, Robert the Burgundian. The Burgundian's hold on the honor was tenuous, however, since Ennoguena was the legitimate heir. To secure his, and his family's, possession of Craon, Robert's son Rainald married this heiress.[34] The extant charters concerning part of the honor of Craon reveal some important information about the intersections among women, property, and lordship.

In 1070 Rainald and Ennoguena confirmed the count of Anjou's transfer of the church of St. Clement to the monastery in Vendôme. The charter recording the transaction made Ennoguena's status as legitimate heir to the honor of Craon explicit: "I Rainald, son of Robert the Burgundian, and my wife Ennoguena, daughter of Robert of Vitré, born from the same man by a legitimate wife, namely the daughter of Warin, natural heir and lord of

---

their father. Another possible explanation for Domitilla's name comes from early Christian Rome. Domitilla was a wealthy Roman matron who was a generous supporter of the Christian church. She, in fact, gave property to house a catacomb outside the walls of Rome, which bears her name to this day. Perhaps our Domitilla had heard of this exemplar of Christian piety and changed her name to reflect her own patronage of the church. Given the geographical and chronological distance between the Loire and Rome, this seems improbable. But considering the frequency with which medieval people made pilgrimage to Rome, it cannot be ruled out as impossible.

32. Nor was Domitilla the only woman to trade in her birth name for one that reflected her status. Agnes, who was born to Fulcher of Fréteval and Ermengard, changed her name to "Comitissa" after her alliance with Viscount Hugh II of Châteaudun. Domitilla's cousin Helvisa-Adierna similarly changed her name at a key point in her and her family's history. Before 1081, when she and her husband inherited the lordship of Montoire from her mother, she stopped being called Adierna and became Helvisa. Why she changed her name is unclear. "Helvisa" does not seem to carry any particular significance for the lordship of Montoire. However, since the matronyms of the Montoire line remain obscure—outside that of Lady Placentia—it is possible the adoption of "Helvisa" was a reference to these kin. *CTV*, vol. 1, no. 250, pp. 394–96; vol. 2, no. 302, pp. 7–9; vol. 2, no. 326, pp. 37–38. Evergates finds instances of men changing their names when they married into a more prestigious family; *The Aristocracy in the County of Champagne*, pp. 107–8. See also Joseph Morsel, "Personal Naming and Representations of Feminine Identity in Franconia in the Later Middle Ages" and Jennifer C. Ward, "Noblewomen, Family and Identity in Later Medieval Europe."

33. Noblewomen in Champagne also adopted forms of "Domitilla" and "Comitissa." Evergates, *The Aristocracy in the County of Champagne*, pp. 108, 114, and 256.

34. Jessee, *Robert the Burgundian*, pp. 31–48, 73.

the honor of Craon... [confirm this gift]."[35] Later in the charter, the couple affirmed the monks as the "legitimate heirs" to the property. Clearly, the legitimacy of this couple's lordship was being emphasized: Ennoguena had it by virtue of descent, as did Rainald by virtue of his marriage with her. Eight years later, Ennoguena and Rainald gave St. Trinité the right of scutage. But the charter records an interesting development: "I Rainald, lord of the castle of Craon, and with me equally my wife Ennoguena, [who bears the] cognomen Domitilla, we grant and concede to St. Trinité and his monastery the scutage and the *denarii* which are collected in my castle from the blessing on the relics of the saints."[36] How are we to read "Domitilla" in this context? Ennoguena's adoption of this cognomen underscored her place as heir and lord to the honor of Craon. "Domitilla" served as a reminder of her status as lord through inheritance, and it harkened back to her descent from the original line of the lords of Craon. Significantly, the charter employs *Domitilla* as a parallel construction to Rainald's designation as *dominus,* and follows after Rainald stated that she "equally" made this grant. Much as Domitilla of Vendôme adopted her name as a reflection of her co-rule with her husband and her connection to her powerful natal family, Ennoguena used "Domitilla" to emphasize her place as the legitimate lord and co-ruler of Craon.

Like the two Domitillas, Placentia of Montoire also enjoyed authority over warriors and lordships with her husband (see appendix, chart 10).[37] Placentia was the only surviving child of Lord Nithard of Montoire, and she inherited the lordship of Montoire upon his death. As Nithard's heir, she was associated with her father as lord.[38] Placentia's inheritance of the lordship is recorded in a charter from St. Trinité:

> Abbot Oderic and the monks of Saint Trinité wish to make it known that they bought the following things in the pagus of Vendôme... with the approval of Nithard of Montoire, in whose *casamentum* [lordship]

---

35. *CTV,* vol. 1, no. 217, pp. 348–50.

36. *CTV,* vol. 1, no. 266, pp. 416–18. Bertran of Moncontour's wife was also named Domitilla, but the lack of extant information makes it impossible to determine whether she was born with this name or adopted it, like Ennoguena and Domitilla of Vendôme, as a way of highlighting her family background and/or as a sign of her status as lord or heir. *CTV,* vol. 2, nos. 360 and 361, pp. 104–7.

37. "Placentia" was an unusual name. In Lewis and Short, *A Latin Dictionary,* it is defined as suavity or courteousness (p. 1382). It could also refer to people of the city of Piacenza, but this seems an unlikely choice for the name of a daughter of a noble house situated in the Loire. Placentia was probably given her name in the hope that she would embody the courteousness and pleasing nature her name implied.

38. Around 1062, Placentia appeared with Nithard in witnessing an agreement between the monks of Marmoutier and St. Trinité. *CTV,* vol. 1, no. 230, pp. 360–61.

these things pertained. After the death of this same man, these things will be relinquished to his only daughter, who is called Placentia. And after the death of her father, she approved and authorized this sale to the monks of Saint Trinité, just as her father had.[39]

The wording of the charter makes it clear that Placentia exercised the same sort of authority as her paternal predecessor for she confirmed the gift "just as her father had." Placentia's life experience was somewhat different from other women in the lands of the Loire, however. She was married sometime in the 1030s to Lord Odo of Mondoubleau, with whom she had three children who survived to adulthood. Odo, it seems, died or was incapacitated sometime around 1058, for his brother Hugh acted as the children's guardian in an act dated from that year. Placentia survived her husband, which raises the question of why she was not with her children at the time they made this gift. The years surrounding 1058 were eventful ones for this noblewoman, as both her father and husband died within a short span of time. As heir to Montoire, she needed to secure her position as the next lord. Moreover, since Odo was dead, Placentia had to do this without the support of a spouse. Consequently, she left her children under the care of her brother-in-law and went to Montoire to assume her position as lord. Shortly after, Placentia married Alberic, who, after their marriage, came to be known as "Alberic of Montoire."[40]

Several factors likely necessitated Placentia placing her children with her first husband's family.[41] Since her children were slated to inherit their father's lands in Mondoubleau, it made sense for them to remain with their uncle. It is possible that Placentia knew it would be especially difficult or dangerous to secure control of the lordship of Montoire and wanted her children safely out of the way. Or perhaps her new husband did not want the children from his wife's previous marriage underfoot. Whatever the motivation, Placentia was free to devote her time and attention to Montoire.[42] Placentia was an active lord and participated in every extant act concerning the disposition of property. When Alberic, for instance, reconfirmed what one of the vassals of

---

39. *CTV,* vol. 1, no. 154, pp. 267–68.

40. For additional discussion of this family see Barthélemy, *La société dans le comté de Vendôme,* pp. 566–71.

41. By the time of Odo's death, their two eldest daughters had married. A charter recording Placentia's brother-in-law as guardian of her children refers to "the children of Odo of Mondoubleau." Placentia and Odo's son Hugh was still a minor, but the plural "children" suggests there were other minor children. These children must have died since there is no trace of them in later charters.

42. *CTV,* vol. 1, no. 128, pp. 229–30.

Montoire had granted to the monks, the confirmation would not stand until Placentia granted her consent. Placentia traveled to the "new monastery in Anjou" where she "made legitimate" the concession that her father and then Alberic had favored.[43] In spite of the fact that Alberic became lord through his marriage to Placentia, she was not a pawn for a man to gain power. She became, and remained, his partner in ruling the lordship of Montoire. Sadly for Placentia, the cost of being lord of Montoire was the loss of her children. But her daughter and granddaughter would thank Placentia for being such a good caretaker of these holdings for they would eventually inherit them from her.

Aristocratic women continued to act in partnership with their husbands in stewarding family resources into the twelfth century. Eustachia, the wife of William II Gouet, acted in authority over family honors with her husband in much the same way that Domitilla and Placentia had a generation earlier. The Gouet family commanded significant powers and resources (see appendix, chart 5). As a demonstration of their status, but also their piety, the family sponsored a priory of the abbey of Tiron at Châteigniers around the year 1117. Eustachia and her husband alienated significant properties, land, revenue, and tithes from the patrimony to benefit not only the monks but also the souls of their dead relatives, themselves, and their vassals.[44] The provision in the gift for the souls of vassals is particularly significant. As lords, Eustachia and William sought to garner the goodwill of those who held fiefs from them. Including them in their benefaction was one way to foster such allegiance. Eustachia's participation reinforces her position as lord and her shared concern or responsibility for maintaining favorable relationships with their vassals.

Eustachia was not a passive participant in the administration of their lordship. Indeed, her powers as lord, and her partnership with her husband, are evident in her frequent denomination as *domina,* as a charter from the Cluniac house of St. Denis of Nogent-le-Rotrou makes explicit. When a vassal made this pious donation, he secured the consent of dominus William and domina Eustachia. The use of this parallel construction makes clear the parallel powers that William and Eustachia exercised over the property. They were both lords, and as such, their vassals required their approval before alienating property from the fief that they held from them.[45] Lords were obligated to provide their vassals with justice. To respond to this need, they held courts

43. *CTV,* vol. 1, no. 155, pp. 268–69.
44. *Tiron,* vol. 1, no. 12, pp. 24–27.
45. *Saint-Denis de Nogent-le-Rotrou, 1031–1789,* no. 33, pp. 95–96 (hereafter, *SD*).

to hear cases and resolve disputes. Eustachia frequently acted as a witness in such courts, but she also took a direct part in dispensing lordly justice.[46] When Hilduin of Alluyes resolved his dispute with the monks of St. Père, he did so at the court of his lords, William and Eustachia, who had convened all of "their best men" to hear the case. Hilduin also sought to ensure his quitclaim by having his lords sign the document, which both William and Eustachia did. Arnulf Malesherbes also held land indirectly from this couple. Either terminally ill or at the end of his life, Arnulf gave *everything* that he held to the monks for his own spiritual well-being, but also out of love for another of his lords who had become a monk at Chartres. He affirmed and acknowledged his gift at the court of William and Eustachia.[47]

Eustachia was well prepared to assume sole control of the Gouet patrimony when her husband departed for Crusade in the early twelfth century. William II seems to have left at some point in the first decade of the twelfth century and was gone for several years—perhaps as long as ten.[48] While he was absent, Eustachia continued to perform individually the lordly functions that the couple had previously fulfilled together. Inevitably disputes arose among Gouet vassals, so Eustachia held courts to settle them. When, "after many vexations and invasions," Daniel of La Ferté, now penitent, quitclaimed his *calumnia* to what his brother-in-law had donated to St. Roman of Brou, he did so "at the court in front of many witnesses, in the presence of lord Eustachia."[49] Moreover, to symbolize and reinforce that he and his family had abandoned all claim to the property, Daniel placed an object in the hand of Prior Hubert at Eustachia's court. If Daniel violated his pact, he would incur the displeasure of God, but also that of the secular lord, in this case Eustachia, under whose authority he had sworn to abandon all claims. That Prior Hubert would permit such a ceremony to take place at a woman's court underscores two points. First, all clerics clearly did not mistrust women and cast them all as conniving Eves. And second, he recognized Eustachia as exercising the same powers as a male lord.[50]

---

46. *Tiron,* vol. 1, no. 57, pp. 78–79; AD Eure-et-Loir, H 2389; *Père,* vol. 2, no. 48, pp. 504–5; *SD,* no. 30, pp. 91–92; *SD,* no. 71, pp. 152–53.

47. *Père,* vol. 2, no. 12, p. 479.

48. William is absent from the charters from about 1105 to 1115, which suggests a lengthy stay in the Holy Land. This estimate could be flawed, however, since it is based upon the charters, which are sometimes difficult to date and which may not reflect William's absence but simply a lack or loss of charters from this time period.

49. *Père,* vol. 2, no. 6, pp. 474–75.

50. Nor was Eustachia the only woman in the lands of the Loire to participate in justice. In 1144, Juliana appeared at both her father's and her husband's court to concede to the resolution her father had made with the church concerning certain disputed properties. *CTV,* vol. 1, no. 521,

The resolutions of other Gouet vassals' *calumniae* provide further proof. When the tithes of Montrichard were falsely claimed and then returned to the monks, the guilty parties abandoned their rights in the presence of Lord Eustachia.[51] Yet the story does not end there. A husband and wife later made a claim to the tithes and other church property, even seizing other of the monks' property. Their actions were so egregious that they were called by the church to justice and threatened with excommunication. With such a threat hanging over them, the couple recognized the error of their ways and reached an agreement with the monks at the court of Lord Eustachia.[52] Once again Eustachia's authority was used to secure an agreement between unruly vassals and the monks. Her power as lord was clearly recognized by the monks. They trusted that Eustachia could ensure that her vassals abided by their oath and agreement.[53]

Not surprisingly, Eustachia did not fade from power after her husband's death. Questions concerning Gouet lordship over churches at Brou and Unverre, as well as vines at Montmirail and Brou, led to a dispute between the Gouets and the monks of St. Denis of Nogent. Eustachia's son William III came to recognize the right of the monks to these properties and quitclaimed them in return for the monks' prayers at Nogent and Cluny on the anniversary of the deaths of his mother and father.[54] Eustachia had not been quite so ready to give up, however. While celebrating the divine service, Prior Bernard conceded that the monks had no right to the parish rights associated with the church of St. Lubin of Brou. Eustachia was present at the service, and his concession was made in front of her. Here the unusual setting of a church service served as a ceremony for the lord of Gouet—in this case Eustachia—to have certain jurisdictions delineated. Like a judicial court, a church service was ideal for such a concession. It was made in public, in front of both the secular and monastic community, and was imbued with the power of the divine. Clearly no person, most particularly a cleric,

---

pp. 356–57. Countess Ermengard of Chartres also held law courts; *CMPD,* no. 97, pp. 90–91 and *Recueil des actes de Philippe Ier,* no. 74, pp. 186–87. A generation later another countess, Adela, the wife of Count Stephen, would also provide justice; LoPrete, "Adela of Blois: Familial Alliances and Female Lordship," pp. 15–25; *Adela of Blois,* pp. 74–94, 149–56. Noblewomen were also called to court to facilitate justice in other ways. Viscountess Melisend of Blois testified in a dispute to a grant made by her husband; *CMPD,* no. 14, pp. 14–16. Women were also frequent participants in transactions in Anjou; Gold, *The Lady and the Virgin,* pp. 116–45.

51. *Père,* vol. 2, no. 27, pp. 486–88.

52. *Père,* vol. 2, no. 27, pp. 486–88.

53. Eustachia also participated in a peace assembly in conjunction with Countess Adela. See LoPrete, *Adela of Blois,* pp. 240–41.

54. *SD,* no. 39, pp. 103–4.

would dispute what had been made public during a religious service and in a church. Since this is the sole incidence of this sort of action, it may have been done at Eustachia's insistence. If so, it certainly was a strategic use of the powers that were employed to sacramentalize and stabilize gifts. Young William may have been willing to concede these properties to the church, but Eustachia jealously guarded their lordly rights by securing the concession of the prior. It was such behavior that would later earn her the ire of these monks.[55]

The power of women to act as lords was recognized by both secular society and the clergy. No provisions or exceptions were made in dealing with Eustachia as a lord for she—like other women of her class—was invested with the same powers, abilities, and authorities as any other lord. Eustachia was sought out by the monks to help them resolve conflicts over the possession of property, thus raising some fundamental questions about the presumed hostility with which clerics were thought to view women and the attempts by secular society to repress women.[56] Nor were her powers curtailed by the fact that she had at least three grown sons who could have assumed control of the lordship and provide justice. While Eustachia's adult sons did frequently appear at her court as witnesses, it was very clearly *her* court. She resolved conflicts and meted out justice. Eustachia was her husband's full partner in governing their lordship and, in his absence, she ruled independently.

As well as sharing the title and powers of "lord," aristocratic wives controlled other titles and honors. The position of *vicedominus* was created in the eleventh century to assist the bishop in administering and protecting his lands. By the end of the century, one family had assumed control of the office and for the first half of the twelfth century, women acted as the *vicedominae* of Chartres (see appendix, chart 4).

Vidame Guerric died sometime around 1100,[57] and his wife, Helisend, assumed control of the vicedominal holdings, title, and heirs. Her son Hugh, who was already of age and married, shared the title of *vicedominus* with his mother upon his father's death. Vicedominus Hugh was dead by 1108 and Helisend was left to rule on her own.[58] The relationship between Hugh and Helisend had been generally one of cooperation, with the exception of

---

55. This incident will be discussed later in this chapter, pp. 220–221.

56. Farmer, "Persuasive Voices"; Lois L. Huneycutt, "Female Succession and the Language of Power in the Writings of Twelfth-Century Churchmen"; Murray, "Thinking about Gender."

57. His death was memorialized by his wife and children in 1103. *Père,* vol. 2, no. 56, p. 563.

58. Like his parents, Hugh and his wife, Agnes, ruled their holdings jointly. See AD Loir-et-Cher, 16 H 118.

tensions over property at Tréon. Helisend had made a gift, but Hugh disputed it and took part of the property. It was only after his death, and with the assistance of Bishop Ivo of Chartres and Helisend's other son, Abbot Stephen of St. Jean-en-Vallée, that the property was returned to the monks.[59] Helisend gave it for her own soul and the souls of her deceased husband, son, and all of their ancestors—a benefaction that commemorated a range of kin, including her obstreperous son.

Throughout her life, Helisend was called *vicedomina* and exercised authority over the properties, responsibilities, and obligations of the vicedominal honors. She made several donations to the church and was one of the advocates of the church of St. Maurice near the abbey of Notre Dame de Josaphat at Lèves.[60] Her status as a vassal of the bishop was also made clear,[61] as well as her allegiance to the counts of Chartres. Helisend remarried sometime around 1108 to Bartholomew Bodellus. She had a son with him named Girard. Although Bartholomew did style himself *vicedominus* in charters pertaining to his holdings, Helisend acted autonomously over the properties she was entrusted to protect by her first husband.[62] *Vicedominus* was thus an empty title for Bartholomew: he might have "styled" himself *vicedominus,* but he never exercised the powers. They rested in the firm grasp of his wife.

Like many a male lord, Vicedomina Helisend trained her successor in the art of managing the family domain. Elizabeth, Helisend and Guerric's daughter, was the only relative to appear with the *vicedomina* in transactions concerning family holdings.[63] Although she had a half-brother, he did not enjoy a claim to vicedominal authority.[64] Nor did Elizabeth's husband, William of Ferrières, ever use or claim this title. While he did appear in acts, it was only as Elizabeth's consort. The apple did not fall far from the tree in Elizabeth's case. Like her mother, she was an effective lord who managed

---

59. *Père, vol. 2,* no. 55, p. 562. Helisend made a similar gift to St. Jean-en-Vallée: AD Eure-et-Loir H 3114 r and l.

60. *Josaphat,* vol. 1, no. 2, pp. 2–4.

61. *Jean,* no. 7, p. 6; *Père* vol. 2, no. 10, pp. 408–9.

62. *Père,* vol. 2, no. 43, p. 297; vol. 2, no. 73, p. 320.

63. *Père,* vol. 2, no. 55, p. 562; vol. 2, no. 56, p. 563; *Jean,* no. 7, p. 6.

64. He did, however, bring claims against what his mother had given, but in both instances he was unsuccessful; *Jean,* no. 83, p. 46; no. 76, p. 43; no. 39, p. 34. Girard used his father's cognomen of Bodellus and seems to have inherited his property entirely from him. His attempts to claim a maternal inheritance went unrealized. One might be tempted to assume some favoritism on the part of Helisend toward the children from her first marriage. Certainly, other medieval women favored one child over others (see Gilsdorf, *Queenship and Sanctity,* pp. 96–97, 100, and 115 for examples). However, Helisend did share advocacy of St. Martin with Girard and used her influence with the monks of St. Jean-en-Vallée to have him made a standard-bearer of this monastery.

her properties and retainers and made generous gifts to the church.[65] She also had her young sons appear with her in these transactions, undoubtedly to prepare and train them as her successors. Henry, the eldest, succeeded his mother as *vicedominus* and appeared frequently with her in overseeing their vassals and making gifts to the church.[66] Although Elizabeth and William had grown sons, she continued to control the honors until her death in 1144. Shortly before she died, she granted lands to Notre Dame de Josaphat to ensure that her name would be written in their martyrology and that they would celebrate the anniversary of her death.[67] But while Elizabeth ruled alone, we should not jump to the conclusion that William was not important to her for in several charters she is called "Elizabeth of Ferrières, *vicedomina* of Chartres."[68] Elizabeth saw herself not only as *vicedomina* but also as William's wife.

The feminization of titles reflects wives' control and participation in the power politics of the region. In addition to *domina* and *vicedomina,* the office of *legedoctus* was controlled by a noble wife: Helvisa Legedocta. Regrettably, the origins of this office are obscure, but the duties associated with the honorific seem to be about on par with that of a sheriff.[69] Around 1116, two members of the *Legedoctus* family appear in the charters: Helvisa Legedocta and her son, Robert Legedoctus. Although Robert consented to transactions initiated by his mother, Helvisa was clearly the one in control. For example, when Helvisa gave property to St. Martin, the transaction took place at her home, in the presence of her lord, Viscount Geoffrey III of Châteaudun, who approved the gift "because it was his fief."[70] Helvisa held fiefs, alienated property, and acted as *legedocta*. Like the *vicedomina* and *domina* of the Chartrain, Helvisa's exercise of power was recognized and not diminished or supplanted by her husband or other male kin.

In matters of lordship, noble wives and husbands were "two in one body." Both enjoyed the power and authority that accompanied lordship as evident in their authority over vassals, control of property, and participation in justice. This "formal" partnership was also mirrored in the care for children.

---

65. *Josaphat,* vol. 1, no. 31, pp. 47–48; vol. 1, no. 36, pp. 53–54; vol. 1, no. 110, pp. 141–42; *Père,* vol. 2, no. 129, p. 616; vol. 2, no. 130, p. 616.

66. Henry seems to have been succeeded by his brother, William, around 1160.

67. *Josaphat,* vol. 1, no. 110, pp. 141–42. Her choice of Notre Dame de Josaphat is interesting considering her brother was abbot of St. Jean-en-Vallée. Perhaps she was aware that her brother had already ascertained that her name was inscribed in that abbey's necrology.

68. *Josaphat,* vol. 1, no. 37, pp. 53–54.

69. It is not possible to tell whether Helvisa became *legedocta* through marriage or inheritance.

70. AD Eure-et-Loir, H 2268. An episcopal confirmation followed. See also *CMPD,* no. 168, pp. 158–59. Helvisa's other children also consented. For discussion of this family, see chapter 2.

Heads of the Family

With marriage came children, and one of the challenges facing aristocratic households was who would assume responsibility for minor children during a warrior's temporary or permanent absence. Guardianship has also been interpreted as a marker of family structure, women's autonomy, and the character of medieval marriage. What does the evidence from the Anglo-Norman world, of which the lands of the Loire were a part, suggest? Orderic Vitalis records that Agnes, the wife of the earl of Buckingham, "bore her husband a son, Walter, whom she brought up carefully after his father's death until he attained manhood, and successfully administered his father's honor on his behalf for many years."[71] In contrast, Orderic also penned that the Countess Adelasia felt overwhelmed at the prospect of acting as guardian for her son and lands, so she consulted her counselors and quickly remarried.[72] The experience of women in the lands of the Loire reflects this spectrum of experience. While some wives, like Placentia of Montoire, clearly did not or could not assume responsibility for their children, many others did.

In 1067, Mathilda acted with her lord, Robert the Burgundian, to give their respective halves of a church to the monks of St. Trinité of Vendôme. Appearing as a witness to the gift was Mathilda's son Conan, the boy (*puer*).[73] Unfortunately the monks did not get to enjoy Mathilda's generosity for long, because a certain knight who held the rest of the church "in fief... from that venerable matron" disputed the gift. The original donation and the dispute attest to the fact that as a widow, Mathilda assumed command of family fiefs and was entrusted with the guardianship of her minor son. Such a role was supported and reaffirmed by Mathilda's lord, Robert the Burgundian, who recognized Mathilda as the co-holder of this fief.

The right of wives to act as guardians for minor children and their authority over family property are apparent in a confirmation by Lord Nivelon I of Fréteval.[74] In 1094, Philippa of Courville and her son Ivo gave the monks

---

71. Orderic Vitalis, *Ecclesiastical History,* vol. 6, p. 39.

72. Orderic Vitalis, *Ecclesiastical History,* vol. 6, pp. 429–31. See also Mitchell, *Portraits of Medieval Women,* pp. 29–43; LoPrete, "Adela of Blois as Mother and Countess"; Cheyette, *Ermengard of Narbonne,* pp. 25–35; and Shadis, "Berenguela of Castile's Political Motherhood," pp. 335–58, for other examples of noblewomen acting as guardians for their children.

73. *CTV,* vol. 1, no. 184, pp. 316–19. For a translation of this charter, and further discussion of Mathilda, see this chapter, p. 195.

74. For another example of women acting as guardian with Lord Nivelon's approval, see *CMPD,* no. 147, p. 135.

of St. Père jurisdiction over five fiefs that they held by right of the *ban* over a village, just as their predecessors Lord Ivo and Lord Girogius had:

> I, Philippa of Courville and Ivo, my son, for the memory of those in the future but also the present, to which this charter is testimony, we assign that which we hold from the *ban* just as our predecessors Ivo and Girogius [did], from the village of La Pomerae, for their souls as well as ours, with the consent of our lord and patron Nivelon, we give from our tenure all and absolutely to lord Eustace abbot of Chartres and the cenobitic monks of the place in honor of the most holy apostles Peter and Paul, the knights of the lord. And we decree from our faithful vassals, Warin of Friesia, Harduin Caput Ferri, Tetbald son of Suger, Frodo son of Themer, and Ivo his son, [in] the aforementioned pagus that *vicaria* which they hold in the aforementioned Pomerae…to the same abbot and monks, they concede it perpetually and quietly.[75]

Philippa was thus acting in authority over these fiefs and men in exactly the same way her husband and father-in-law had done before her. This *domina* also stated that she had the consent of her "lord and patron" Nivelon of Fréteval. Noblemen recognized that women had the right, if not the obligation, to care for minor children and family patrimonies. Male lords did not object to this practice. Instead, men like Nivelon of Fréteval and Robert the Burgundian supported these female vassals—just as they would their male dependents.

Patriarchal abstractions did not compel male relatives or lords to try to prevent women from assuming such control or from shaping the future of the family and their children. Indeed, a charter from the abbey of Tiron suggests that male relatives supported women in their role as guardians. In 1138, Oda and her son Raginald approved a gift made by their vassals, who were a married couple: "I, Froger of Mareuil, and my wife Osanna give to God and the monks of Tiron all of our land of Mareuil, with consent of my lord Oda and Raginald, her son, from whom the fief was [held]."[76] Witnessing this alienation of property were Oda's brothers and her brother-in-law. While there were many male kin who could have usurped Oda's role as guardian of

---

75. AD Eure-et-Loir, H 201. See also *Père,* vol. 2, no. 43, p. 499. Philippa also acted with her husband in giving the church of St. Nicholas to the monks of Marmoutier; AD Eure-et-Loir, H 2237.

76. *Tiron,* vol. 1, no. 220, p. 248.

her lands and children, they did not. Instead they acted with Oda, who alone is designated in the charter as the *domina* of these properties, in securing the gift of her vassals.

Like modern parents, medieval mothers and fathers worried about the effect that their death might have on the lives of their children. A charter from the priory of St. Gondon provides a glimpse into their preoccupation. At the very end of the eleventh century, a widow named Elizabeth was gravely ill. She was so concerned for her health that she made a gift to the monks in an attempt to aid her soul and perhaps also restore her to good health. As a result of Elizabeth's constitution, good nursing, or divine intervention, she recovered and made another donation to express her thanks and undoubtedly her relief. Her son Robert, "who was not yet a knight," witnessed both of these benefactions. He, like his mother, must have been put at ease by her recovery. What would have happened to Robert if Elizabeth had died? The charter provides possible insight into this question as well. Radulf, the brother of Elizabeth, witnessed both acts.[77] Although Radulf played a supporting role in these grants, his presence must have been reassuring to Elizabeth and her son. Radulf would likely have stepped in as the boy's guardian if Elizabeth had died.[78] Again we see here the cooperation of family in aiding or supporting women's guardianship of lands and children. The fact of their sex did not cause wives to be automatically disqualified as guardians or cause their family—natal or affinal—to try to restrict their ability to raise their children. While Elizabeth could not ensure she would survive to see her son come of age, she did guarantee that his spiritual life was secured, for her two grants "added the mother and son to the *beneficium* of the monks' prayers."

The cruel realities of life and death are apparent in another guardianship case. Recall Juliana of Pray who had assumed control of her minor children and the pertaining lordships. She and her son Peter became embroiled in controversy with St. Trinité in Vendôme. In spite of arbitration, Juliana vigorously asserted her claim to the property and was excommunicated by the monks as a result. Tragedy intervened, however. Juliana's young daughter (*puella*) died, which Juliana—no doubt encouraged to do so by the monks—attributed to her own improper behavior. Bereaved by the tragic loss of her child, Juliana came with her entourage to the monks' court, where she abandoned her claim and promised never to make a claim to the property

---

77. Given how common it was for uncles to foster their nephews, Radulf may have been present at this act as the foster parent of his sister's child. Unfortunately, it is not possible to determine from the charter where young Robert was currently residing.

78. *Gondon,* no. 16, pp. 37–38.

again.[79] Although Peter, her son, was of age, he accompanied his mother on her journey to make restitution to the monks only in a supportive role. Like other aristocratic males, Peter did not feel compelled to challenge his mother as guardian of his minor siblings or lord of the family holdings.

Husbands, Wives, and the Church

Patronage

Patronage was an expression of aristocratic piety, but it was also a reflection of social status and political connections.[80] Deciding which ecclesiastical communities would benefit from family largesse was central to the spiritual and temporal well-being of the family, for souls were—they believed—literally at stake, as well as the family's reputation and standing.[81] Wives played a pivotal role in directing patronage. The necrologies of the houses of the Chartrain prove useful in reconstructing noble patronage patterns for they record the names of patrons who were of special significance to their house and thus shed light on aristocratic patronage choices. The *vicedominae* of Chartres were instrumental in shaping this family's donation practices. Vicedomina Helisend, in particular, set in place patronage patterns that would affect generations to come.

In the early twelfth century, the abbey of St. Jean-en-Vallée was reformed, and the vicedominal family of Chartres began making gifts to this foundation. Helisend was the force that secured vicedominal family support for this newly reformed institution. Before Helisend's marriage, the vidames of Chartres had not made gifts to this institution. Helisend's family, on the other hand, had been patrons, for her father's death was commemorated by the brothers of St. Jean-en-Vallée late in the eleventh century.[82] Perhaps not surprisingly, Helisend's husband, Guerric, was the first *vicedominus* to be included in the necrology of this house, a precedent that would last for at least another

---

79. *CTV,* vol. 2, no. 532, pp. 375–77.

80. For a discussion of aristocratic piety, see Baldwin, *Aristocratic Life in Medieval France,* pp. 194–247; Marcus Bull, *Knightly Piety and the Lay Response to the First Crusade,* pp. 155–203; McLaughlin, *Consorting with Saints,* pp. 132–78.

81. Historians have argued that for much of the Middle Ages, the medieval economy was a "gift" economy. In such a system, donors did not necessarily expect anything from the gift. Rather, it was making the gift itself that was important. Little, *Religious Poverty and the Profit Economy in Medieval Europe,* pp. 3–18; Rosenwein, *To Be the Neighbor of St. Peter,* pp. 44–45, 125–42.

82. BNF MS Latin 991, p. 5 recto. See also *Obituaires de la province de Sens,* vol. 2, *Diocèse de Chartres,* p. 229 (hereafter, *Obituaires*). See also René Merlet and Abbot Clerval, eds., *Un manuscrit Chartrain du XI siècle,* pp. 97–186, for an analysis of the necrology of Notre Dame de Chartres.

century as his children, grandchildren, and great-grandchildren would similarly secure the monks' prayers on the anniversaries of their deaths.[83] The dedication to supporting reformed houses would also continue under later *vicedominae* as the women of this family patronized Notre Dame de Josaphat, which had been created when Bishop Geoffrey of Chartres and his brother replaced a community of canons with a reformed monastery.[84] Margaret, the wife of Helisend's grandson William, had her death recorded by this house, as did Margaret's daughter Mabel.[85] But seeking ties to reformed houses did not mean that the vicedominal family severed their ties to the Benedictine houses. At the same time the members of the family were memorialized by reformed monks, their names were also included in the prayers of the brothers of St. Père.[86]

Noblewomen were generous in patronizing the convent of St. Avit of Châteaudun. A striking feature of the handful of extant documents from this female house is the prominent role of wives and mothers in arranging gifts to the nuns.[87] Additionally, mothers, wives, and other female relatives were instrumental in securing the support of their male kin for this community. The vicecomital family of Châteaudun, for example, did not figure among the patrons of St. Avit until the late twelfth century when the viscount conceded property given by his kinswoman.[88] Such acts raise the intriguing prospect that women were more disposed toward patronage of nuns than their male peers.[89] What might motivate women and their sons and husbands to patronize this convent? Piety, certainly, as both Peter Abelard and Robert Arbrissel emphasized the unique spiritual opportunities that women's

---

83. The following members of the vidames of Chartres had their deaths recorded in the necrology of St. Jean-en-Vallée extant from the late twelfth century as recorded in BNF MS Latin 991: Vidame Guerric, p. 1 recto; Henry of Ferrières, son of the vidame, p. 1 verso; Vicedomina Elizabeth, p. 4 verso; Vidame Hugh, p. 5 recto; Ansculf, father of Vicedomina Helisend, p. 5 recto; William of Ferrières, husband of Vicedomina Elizabeth, p. 5 recto; Hersend, daughter of Vidame Guerric and sister to Abbot Stephen, p. 5 verso; Abbot Stephen, p. 6 verso; Vicedomina Helisend, p. 8 recto. See also *Obituaires,* pp. 226, 227, 228, 229, and 230.

84. See *Josaphat* vol. 1, nos. 1–3, pp. 1–6. Additional construction did take place for the charters indicate that by 1123 a refectory was completed, along with the church and other claustral buildings. *Josaphat,* p. xix.

85. *Obituaires,* pp. 252, 254.

86. *Obituaires,* pp. 180, 187, 189, 190, 191, 192, and 196.

87. AD Eure-et-Loir, H 4491, H 4408, and H 4385.

88. AD Eure-et-Loir, H 4545 and H 4332. For discussion of this woman's identity, see chapter 3, note 76.

89. Johnson, *Equal in Monastic Profession,* pp. 34–61. Erin Jordan has also determined that the countesses of Flanders played an important role in the support of female Cistercian houses; *Women, Power and Religious Patronage,* pp. 92–94. Philadelphia Ricketts finds the same for women in twelfth-century Yorkshire; "Widows, Religious Patronage and Family Identity."

intercession could provide for men.[90] Acts from St. Avit suggest other, more pragmatic, reasons as well. Around the year 1200, a man and wife gave property to St. Avit with the understanding that she would end her life there.[91] Other donors also made gifts to ensure the entrance of their female relatives into the convent.[92] Noblewomen may have encouraged their male relatives to support this convent to guarantee they could find a place among the nuns if they so desired.

As well as encouraging male kin to make donations, noblewomen were in a position to secure their vassals' support of ecclesiastical communities. Patronizing parish churches was a demonstration of both aristocratic piety and lordly influence. Many families of the Chartrain founded churches next to the seats of their secular power at a key moment in their family's history: just after they had gained the lordship and established their presence in the community. These "new men" (and women), like the recently established Capetian dynasty, sought to legitimate their rule and control of public power.[93] Patronage of the church provided a means for these families to gain approval and recognition. Mahild of Alluyes was certainly aware of the link between lordship and patronage, as a collection of charters from 1085 to 1130 from the abbey of Bonneval demonstrates.[94] Mahild was a generous patron of many local monasteries and gave Bonneval the church of Notre Dame sometime around 1085. This church was situated near the castle of Alluyes, her natal home and the seat of her family's power. In addition to her original gift, Mahild also gave the monks a mill and, on the day that they buried her

---

90. Fiona Griffiths, "The Cross and the *Cura monialium.*"

91. AD Eure-et-Loir, H 4275.

92. AD Eure-et-Loir, H 4455 and H 4333.

93. Jean-François Lemarignier, "Political and Monastic Structures in France at the End of the Tenth and Beginning of the Eleventh Century." Reformers struggled with the question of the legitimacy of the new political order, represented by the new lords who gained power in the eleventh and twelfth centuries. John van Engen argues that violent warriors were eventually transformed into keepers of the peace and maintainers of order; "Sacred Sanctions for Lordship," pp. 203–31, esp. p. 220. Philippe Buc agrees that the church was important in the legitimization of power but suggests it was a contentious process in *"Principes gentium dominantur eorum."* Lemesle also recognizes the important role that patronage of the church played in the developing power of the aristocracy of Maine. *La société aristocratique dans le Haut-Maine,* pp. 49–82.

94. *Cartulaire de l'abbaye Saint-Florentin de Bonneval,* no. 3, pp. 25–31. Editor Albert Sidoisne died before his edition of the cartulary could be published. The original manuscript of his edition is housed at the Bibliothèque Albert Sidoisne in Bonneval. Several microfilm copies are also available at the Bibliothèque nationale in Paris, the Archives départementales d'Eure-et-Loir, the Archives diocésaines de Chartres, and at the Bibliothèque Albert Sidoisne at Bonneval. I would like to thank M. René Robin, former president of the Fondation Albert Sidoisne, for his help in securing a copy of this document. For the foundation of this monastery, see René Merlet, ed., "Petite Chronique de l'abbaye de Bonneval de 857 à 1050 environ."

husband, "the venerable William," she conceded fishing rights as well. The vassals of this seigneurial family were encouraged by their lord's example, in this case domina Mahild, to sponsor and patronize this parish church. Adam of Brou, for example, gave eight pounds of coin to this church, and Albert gave what he held *jure hereditario* from this same church. Material support for the church of Notre Dame of Alluyes continued among members of the Alluyes family for generations. Their patronage ensured its continued survival but also served to reinforce ties of lordship and vassalage between the family and other powerful individuals in the area.

Esthers among Them

The story of Esther was one that resonated strongly among the elite of the lands of the Loire.[95] Esther, a young Jewish woman, was chosen by the king of Persia as his queen. Subsequently, it was through her intercession that her people were saved and even gained influence in the kingdom:

> So the king and Haman went to dine with Queen Esther, and as they were drinking wine on that second day, the king again asked, "Queen Esther, what is your petition? It will be given to you. What is your request? Even up to half the kingdom, it will be granted." Then Queen Esther answered: "If I have found favor with you, O king, and if it pleases your majesty, grant me my life—this is my petition. And spare my people—this is my request." (Esther 7:1–2)

Like Esther, the women of the Loire frequently acted as intermediaries for their families in two key ways: as securers of salvation through their many pious gifts on behalf of their kin and as intercessors and peacemakers when their families fell out with the church.[96] In these ways, noble wives were the

---

95. Huneycutt, "Intercession and the High-Medieval Queen." The example of Esther was used as a point of comparison for medieval women and was particularly resonant among medieval women writers. See Ferrante, *To the Glory of Her Sex,* pp. 51–52, 210–12. D'Avray argues that in sermons Esther was held up as an example for medieval married couples to encourage the indissolubility of their marriage bonds. *Medieval Marriage,* p. 61.

96. The topos of a woman, particularly a mother, as intercessor on behalf of loved ones appears in the literature of the thirteenth century. See Baldwin, *Aristocratic Life,* p. 136. For additional examples of women as intercessors beyond the Loire region, see Bernard of Angers, *Book of St. Foy,* pp. 45, 44, and 62–63; Gilsdorf, *Queenship and Sanctity,* pp. 76, 78, 83; Chibnall, "The Empress Matilda and Her Sons," pp. 288–90; Shadis, "Blanche of Castile and Facinger's 'Medieval Queenship,'" pp. 137–62.

helpmates of their husbands as described in the gospel of Matthew quoted at the outset of this chapter.

Women had long been spiritual caretakers of their family.[97] Scholars disagree as to whether or not women continued in this role into the central Middle Ages.[98] The evidence from the lands of the Loire does not reveal a distinct break or abrupt halt to the custom of aristocratic women arranging prayers and commemoration for their kin. Instead of women and monks competing for the honor of commemorating and praying for the dead, with one group supplanting the other, the evidence suggests that noble-born women and monks acted in complementary ways to make sure that souls were remembered and prayers secured. Such a division of labor is evident in the correspondence of Abbot Geoffrey of Vendôme, in a letter dated around 1110 to Countess Ermengard of Brittany.[99]

Geoffrey started his missive by effusively complimenting Countess Ermengard's abilities as a lord: "In exercising your terrestrial power . . . you have done much, you nourish the hungry poor, you give drink to those who have thirst, you clothe the nude and, surpassing the nobility of your race by the nobility of your character, you seem rather to militate for God than embracing the affairs of the world. These holy works of justice and piety, I am able and must praise them in you with joy."[100] The attributes that Geoffrey lauds are precisely those which Abbot Suger singled out in King Louis VI, proof that churchmen recognized female rulers as embodying the same qualities of leadership as their male counterparts.[101] But this praise also serves as prelude to Geoffrey's later rebuke of the countess's failure to act as a proper keeper of her father's memory. Specifically, he complains that she has shirked her filial duty to support the church where her father had chosen to be entombed. Geoffrey acknowledges she has been a generous patron of other churches, but insists that as her father's heir, she is obligated to honor this church before all others. Although Ermengard had two brothers, Geoffrey singles her out as the one responsible for memorializing their father. To this abbot's mind, responsibility for memorialization of the dead fell to daughters rather than sons. Geoffrey encourages Ermengard to remember her father by

---

97. Farmer, *Communities of Saint Martin*, pp. 96–117 and "Persuasive Voices"; Innes, "Keeping It in the Family."

98. See chapter 5, note 22.

99. While Ermengard ended her life as the countess of Brittany, she began life as a daughter of the house of Beaugency, one of the important seigneurial families of the lands of the Loire.

100. Geoffrey of Vendôme, letter 110, pp. 212–14.

101. Abbot Suger, *Deeds of Louis the Fat*, pp. 64, 86–87, and 106. Baudri of Bourgueil wrote a poem in which he praised Countess Adela's skills as a lord. See LoPrete, *Adela of Blois*, pp. 191–204.

providing additional support to the church. He also informs her that he has increased the number of monks singing prayers to redeem her father's soul. This noblewoman's role as memorializer was not perceived as a threat to the authority of the monks. Rather, Abbot Geoffrey believed that ensuring that the dead were remembered, and thus their souls redeemed, was the joint responsibility of noblewomen and the monks.

Clerics even saw women's prayers as uniquely effective in helping tormented souls. Peter Abelard indicated that women's entreaties in particular were efficacious in gaining God's ear, so to speak, and attaining his mercy for the object of their prayers. One of his letters to Heloise paid particular attention to the role that women had always played as intercessors between their unbelieving or reluctant spouses and the church: "We have indeed many examples as evidence of the high position in the eyes of God and his saints which has been won by the prayers of the faithful, especially those of women on behalf of their dear ones and of wives for their husbands."[102] About a generation before Abelard, Guibert of Nogent also recognized the intercessory power of women. "Thou knowest, O Lord, how much loyalty, how much love [my mother] rendered to her dead husband, how with almost daily masses, prayers and tears and much almsgiving, she strove without ceasing to release his soul, which she knew was fettered by his sins."[103] His mother, Guibert records, even experienced a vision concerning his dead father. She relayed that she had traveled to purgatory where she found her husband tormented by the cries of his bastard child, who had died as a result of his neglect. When asked if her prayers and good works were helpful to him, Guibert's father replied that they were. "Since she knew that these troubles were to purge away those of her husband, which she had seen in her vision, she bore them gladly, because she thought that by sharing his suffering herself, she was lessening the pains of the other sufferer."[104] Churchmen also counted on wives to have influence with their husbands. Indeed, Archbishop Anselm of Canterbury wrote to aristocratic women asking for their help in guiding their husbands' behavior toward the church.[105] Aristocratic husbands could count on their wives having the ear of not only the clergy but also God and the saints.

---

102. Peter Abelard, *The Letters of Abelard and Heloise*, p. 120.

103. Benton, *Self and Society in Medieval France*, p. 92. For a new interpretation of Guibert and his memoirs, see Jay Rubenstein, *Guibert of Nogent*.

104. Benton, *Self and Society in Medieval France*, p. 96.

105. Livingstone, "Aristocratic Women in the Chartrain," p. 60, and "Powerful Allies and Dangerous Adversaries."

Throughout the Middle Ages, aristocratic women acted as intermediaries between their kin and the monks. Women acted in concert with the monks—to the benefit of their family—in making sure that their relatives were commemorated and enjoyed the prayers of God's servants:

> We wish it to be known for the present and the future that Mathilda, a certain noble woman, daughter of William of Colentiaco, wife of Hato, who was called by the cognomen Otovedus, gave to mighty God, namely St. Clement of St. Trinité, half of her church, which is situated in the pagus of Craon... with half of all of the revenue from the same church she gives that pertains to it in tithes, burial dues, offerings and all other ecclesiastical customs or dues. And also it is given to the priory of St. Clement, all that pertains to the *vicaria*. Truly half of the *vicaria* of this same church lord Robert the Burgundian gave, for the soul of his lord Count Geoffrey, and the other half the venerable Mathilda gave for the soul of her dear husband Hato, and for herself, and for all of their *parentela,* so they will become free of venal sin, and will have eternal holiness.[106]

Mathilda's benefaction furnishes a general example of how a noblewoman acted to secure the salvation and freedom from sin for herself, her spouse, and her relatives. In this case the use of the term *parentela* is particularly significant. *Parentela* was a term coined in the Middle Ages to refer to all people who were related by blood and marriage.[107] Thus Mathilda's grant was made on behalf of a very wide range of kin, which provides further evidence of aristocrats configuring their kin and family as broadly as possible. Recall also Mahild of Alluyes, Countess Euphronia of Vendôme, and Vicedomina Helisend all granted property to commemorate the deaths and to benefit the souls of generations of their immediate, extended, and affinal kin.[108] This role of chief commemorator, moreover, was reinforced by the demographic differences that defined the life course of elite men and women. Women tended to outlive their husbands, thus they usually assumed responsibility for arranging pious benefactions on behalf of their husbands, children, and other kin. Ledgard, the widow of Ansold, certainly did: "The monks of St. Père wish it to be known by posterity that Ledgard, the wife of Ansold son

---

106. *CTV,* vol. 1, no. 184, pp. 316–19. This gift was later disputed after Hato had died. See p. 186 of this chapter.

107. Guerreau-Jalabert, "La désignation des relations et des groupes de parenté," pp. 81–85.

108. See chapter 2, pp. 47 and 55. For Euphronia's gift, see p. 172 of this chapter.

of Roger, after the death of her husband, for her own soul as well as for his, gave our church a pious gift."[109] As daughters, wives, and mothers, women were charged with caring for souls and remembering the dead. This was a role that gave them a great deal of influence with their family and the church. Indeed, the monks of St. Denis of Nogent-le-Rotrou were reticent to excommunicate Eustachia of Gouet because "of the good works she had done," referring to her patronage of the church, commemoration of her kin, and the encouragement she had provided to her male kin and vassals to restore ecclesiastical property to the church.[110] One wonders whether they would have extended the same courtesy to Eustachia's husband or sons.

The relationships that aristocratic women cultivated with local ecclesiastical houses frequently resulted in mutual respect and even affection.[111] The chronicle of Orderic Vitalis contains many examples. Adelaide of Le Puiset, the daughter of the viscount of Chartres, was praised for being "remarkable in her gentleness and piety" and for "encourag[ing] her husband to befriend the monks and protect the poor."[112] Women were also lauded for persuading their husbands to make gifts to the church. Walter, for instance, made gifts to the church "at her [his wife's] suggestion."[113] Her persuasiveness and intercession were also recognized: "By her advice and wise influence, Walter was restrained from his earlier folly [harassing the monks]. She was prudent and golden-tongued, devoted to God from her earliest years and utterly given over to good works."[114] Fittingly, when she died, Walter's wife was buried "in the cloister of the monks she so truly loved." Early in the twelfth century, Countess Helwise of Evreux advised her husband, who was advanced in years, to build a monastery on his patrimony. Unfortunately, the count did not live to see its completion, trusting Helwise to finish the project and to oversee the county.[115] Noblewomen did indeed prove to be

---

109. *Père,* vol. 2, no. 158, p. 370. See also *MB,* no. 42, pp. 83–84.

110. *SD,* no. 40, pp. 104–6.

111. Farmer, "Persuasive Voices." Johns finds that women in England played a similar role; *Noblewomen, Aristocracy and Power,* pp. 30–52. The respect that clergy had for aristocratic and royal women is apparent in their dedication of works to noble women as well as in how they portrayed women in essays and treatises. Ferrante, "Women's Role in Latin Letters"; Madeline H. Caviness, "Anchoress, Abbess and Queen"; Shadis, "Piety, Politics and Power"; Kathleen Schowalter, "The Ingeborg Psalter."

112. Orderic Vitalis, *Ecclesiastical History,* vol. 3, p. 139.

113. Avice, his wife, added to her husband's benefaction by providing money for the monks to purchase wax and oil to light the church. Orderic Vitalis, *Ecclesiastical History,* vol. 3, p. 251.

114. Orderic Vitalis, *Ecclesiastical History,* vol. 3, p. 257.

115. Orderic Vitalis, *Ecclesiastical History,* vol. 6, pp. 147–49. Orderic criticized Helwise for placing "more reliance than she should have done on her own judgment.... But ignoring the counsel of her husband's barons, she relied on her own judgment, often rushed into difficulties in secular

"persuasive voices" in advising their husbands to support the church and to mend their ways.

The charters of the Loire region also bring to life many examples of noblewomen interceding with the church on behalf of their male relatives. Noblemen often earned the wrath of the church through their acts of violence toward the clergy and the powerless, as well as their prosecution of what the monks considered "false claims" to monastic property. Bernard made just such a claim to what his mother-in-law had donated to the monks of Marmoutier. Unfortunately, Bernard realized the consequences of his actions too late, and it was up to his wife to restore him to the monks' good graces. As Bernard was dying, he abandoned his claim to the property, but perished before this could be formalized. Shortly after his death, his wife traveled to the priory of Vieuvique, donated the gift to the monks for the souls of her husband, herself, and her mother, and placed a symbol of the property upon the altar.[116] Bernard's actions had had profound consequences. His claim jeopardized the soul that was to receive the spiritual benefits derived from the gift, and put his own soul in peril.[117] As his wife traveled to the priory, she was undoubtedly aware of the importance of expediency: her husband had died before he could resolve his dispute with the monks, a circumstance that she believed could have eternal and damning consequences for both her loved ones. It was up to her to rectify the situation.

As a result of his attempts to claim certain customs that the monks of the abbey of Tiron claimed as their own, Viscount Geoffrey III of Châteaudun, his sons, and his "castle" were excommunicated by the bishop of Chartres in 1145. Like Adelaide of Le Puiset and Bernard's wife, Viscountess Helvisa tried to make amends for her husband's and sons' bad behavior and to restore her family's relationship with the local monastery. As Geoffrey was dying, Helvisa and their son Hugh appealed to the monks for peace. They promised to restore all that had been usurped by Geoffrey, with the proviso that if any later claims were made, the sentence of excommunication would be reinstated.[118] The situation was somewhat urgent for the viscount was near death and excommunication meant that neither baptism nor Christian

---

affairs.... So she was heartily disliked for her women's presumption by Robert, count of Meulan, and other Normans, who venomously abused her in the king's presence and incited him to hate her by their bitter recriminations" (p. 149). In other words, this woman earned the ire of her male peers because she was too powerful and self-reliant.

116. *CMPD*, no. 105, pp. 97–98.

117. Since Bernard's wife specified the gift was to benefit her mother, the soul in peril would seem to be that of Bernard's mother-in-law.

118. AD Eure-et-Loir, H 2272. See also *Tiron*, vol. 2, no. 269, pp. 38–40.

burial could take place. Geoffrey's soul was essentially in immortal peril, and his wife acted to ensure that her obstreperous husband would be able to pass from this life to the next.

Helvisa and Geoffrey appear to have been a devoted couple. Viscount Geoffrey's affection for Helvisa is evident in several charters where he refers to her as his "venerable wife."[119] In addition, this couple appeared in many acts together, suggesting that they spent a great deal of time in each other's company. Helvisa frequently acted with Geoffrey in making and confirming gifts. Indeed, this couple gave significant properties to the church, particularly the monks of Tiron. The support of this reformed house represented a departure in vicecomital patronage practices. Helvisa may have been the catalyst for this change.

Geoffrey's father, Viscount Hugh II, had been a generous patron of Marmoutier and eventually retired from life and became a monk there.[120] His decision to join this community was based on a long-standing relationship, for nearly all of his gifts were to this traditional Benedictine monastery. Yet his son Geoffrey chose to patronize the newly founded monasteries of Tiron and Notre Dame de Josaphat.[121] Given the affection between Geoffrey and Helvisa, and the fact that she appeared with him in most of his acts, could the change in family patronage have been Helvisa's doing? It seems probable. Consider the fact that it was Helvisa who acted to reach a resolution with the monks. Could another emissary have been as successful? Doubtful. Helvisa was the person to reach out to the monks because of her relationship with them. She had been a generous patron of this monastery and may have been the force behind vicecomital support for this community. Geoffrey's support only extended so far, however, since he was willing to claim customs and dues from the monks as his own. Helvisa was ideally placed to act as intercessor because of her good relationship with the monks on the one hand, and her husband's trust and affection on the other.

Like the viscountess of Châteaudun, Hilduisa, the wife of Rotho the knight, was troubled by unruly male kin. Rotho earned the displeasure of the church through his claim to property given to the monks by the Angevin count and countess. In 1078, he realized the error of his ways: "When this

---

119. *Tiron,* vol. 1, no. 215, pp. 242–43, and vol. 1, no. 185, pp. 207–8.

120. *CMPD,* no. 165, pp. 155–56.

121. Viscount Geoffrey also patronized the relatively new military orders, specifically the Templars. For examples, see *CV,* no. 137, pp. 169–70; no. 161, pp. 195–96; no. 165, pp. 200–201. His kinsman, Bartholomew of Bouchet also supported the Templars. *CV,* no. 132, pp. 164–65, for example.

knight was nearing death, he called his wife, and asked her to rectify the wrong he had done to the monks over this church."[122] Rotho was also concerned that his son, who would soon succeed him, should follow through and return the property to the monks. His concern was well founded for Rotho's son, "incessantly entreat[ed] his mother to intervene for him" with the monks. Owing to her patronage or piety, Hilduisa's relationship with local churchmen allowed her to negotiate the restoration of her husband and son to the monks' good graces.

As a consequence of the respect they enjoyed in their family and community, noble-born women also assumed the role of emissary in making peace between feuding parties. Berta of Lisle was chosen to resolve a conflict between two ecclesiastical houses that were at odds over the right to various properties. "I, Geoffrey, bishop of Chartres, wish all to know that the disagreement between our venerable brothers of Vendôme and Odo, abbot of St. Georges of the Woods, [who] have had a longstanding quarrel over certain possessions, have reconciled. It was through the intercession of that devoted woman, lord Berta of Lisle, from whose dominion these possessions were, that these servants of God were able to put an end to their quarrel."[123] As a lord, and because of her status as respected friend and patron of the church, Berta was able to secure an understanding between the two houses. Her actions at once resolved the matter and earned her the admiration of one of the leading ecclesiastics of the time, Bishop Geoffrey of Chartres. Countess Agnes of Vendôme also interceded when two of her vassals attempted to disrupt a gift of a family of serfs to the abbey of St. Trinité. "Therefore when the venerable countess Agnes, who had founded this monastery, heard of this contestation, [she] spoke with Odo Dubellus and with Lord Lancelin of Beaugency, from whose fief the servants were said to be, asking them that for the love of God and her, to make a gift of servants to the monastery and to concede this."[124] Lancelin and Odo did abandon their claim, and the threat to the monks passed. Agnes was at once a generous benefactress of this monastic community and a vigilant protector.

---

122. *CTV*, vol. 1, no. 268, pp. 419–20.

123. *CTV*, vol. 2, no. 512, pp. 335–37. Empress Mathilda and Countess Adela, like many elite women, acted as peacemakers; Chibnall, "Empress Matilda and Her Sons," pp. 286–87; LoPrete, *Adela of Blois*, pp. 290–91.

124. *CTV*, vol. 1, no. 74, pp. 135–37. Significantly, this charter assumed that any party interested in this transfer of people and property would be able to read the document, for it begins, "If anyone wishes to know how Hubert of Villethibauld, with his wife and children, came into our dominion, he/she is able to read this." This is an unusual preface in the charters and provides evidence of some level of functional literacy among the elite; Richard Britnell, "Pragmatic Literacy in Latin Christendom."

Wives also acted as a conduit through which the ideas of ecclesiastical reform passed to their families and dependents.[125] One of the key reforms set out by the Gregorians was the insistence that lay control of ecclesiastical property, such as tithes, churches, and other appurtenances, was improper. The Gouet family had a tradition of supporting church reform dating back to the time of Mahild of Alluyes. Mahild herself restored ecclesiastical holdings to the monks and encouraged her vassals to do the same. In 1059, a vassal gave a church, with the consent of "his most noble lord, Mahild."[126] Ten years later, another granted a priest's portion of the church of St. Mary with the permission of Mahild, his lord.[127] Her son William II and daughter-in-law Eustachia followed Mahild's example and demonstrated their piety by restoring the church of St. Roman at Brou. Quotations from scripture were included in this restoration, an indication of this couple's familiarity with the teachings of the church that also hold suggestive details concerning the process of reform:

> In the name of the Lord, our savior Jesus Christ. To hear the words of those who have gone before us and to know their example. No one surrendering to perverse acts or other rapines will be worthy of merit, unless like the vine he is made straight and zealous in good soil. Just as one's crude rapines emerge, so too are one's own generosity and compassion made evident, and he is filled up with [the words of] Scripture. Blessed are the merciful for they follow mercy.[128]

"Rapines" references the rapines of nobles who "usurped" property from the church or who held ecclesiastical property. Inclusion of this particular passage from scripture in Eustachia and William's grant also signals their comprehension of the ideals of reform and their attempt to conform to those ideals. Given the context of the grant, a restoration, these words would have been especially resonant with the donors.

Eustachia and William's support of reform is further apparent in their patronage choices. While the couple continued to be generous to communities

---

125. Siblings could also play an influential role in introducing each other to new religious ideas. For an example, see William Chester Jordan, "Isabelle of France and Religious Devotion at the Court of Louis IX."

126. *Père,* vol. 1, no. 36, pp. 163–64.

127. *Père,* vol. 1, no. 87, p. 211.

128. *Père,* vol. 2, no. 4, pp. 471–72. This passage appears to be a conflation of the passage in Matthew 5:7 and other bits of scripture from the New Testament. It would seem that these verses were not copied accurately but were added from the scribe's memory.

of Benedictine monks, they also sponsored a priory of the reformed abbey of Tiron at Châteigniers. The family gave extensively from their own holdings and also encouraged their vassals to restore churches and tithes. Eustachia herself promoted and fiercely protected the interests of certain ecclesiastical foundations. Indeed, she continued the work started by her mother-in-law by supporting and encouraging her vassals to restore property to the church.[129] She also arranged a very generous gift and restoration herself. Eustachia asked the monks of St. Père if she could give the properties that she held from the church of St. Roman in Brou to their abbey to establish a new community of monks there. The monks consented, with the stipulation that her family agree to this benefaction. William II and her sons did affirm Eustachia's desire to use these estates to create such a community, and they all traveled together to Chartres where Eustachia granted many properties, including land, a mill, tithes from a mill, fishing and marketing rights, and pannage, to furnish support for the brothers.[130] These were extensive holdings designed to help this fledgling house. While Eustachia and William II clearly shared a zeal to reform and support the church, Eustachia herself was able to express her individual piety by this benefaction and she clearly had the resources to do so.

While Eustachia's patronage may have made her a favorite of the monks, she remained a strong and formidable lord. Her relationship with the Cluniac foundation of St. Denis of Nogent-le-Rotrou provides illustration. Recall that when William III had renounced their right to the church of St. Lubin of Brou, Eustachia insisted that the monks concede that they did not have any parochial rights. Her real falling out with this abbey, however, came over the church of St. Martin of Unverre:

> Let it be known by all that Eustachia, the wife of [William II] Gouet, did a great injury to the monks of Cluny who serve God in the church of St. Denis of Nogent-le-Rotrou, over the church of St. Martin of Unverre, which Lord Gastho of Brou gave completely to them, without retaining a single thing, and they held it for a year and more. But the aforementioned Eustachia seized their priest, and imprisoned the priest, but they [the monks] did not want to excommunicate her because of the good works she had done and at least hopeful that they would discover her mercy. After her death truly, William the younger,

---

129. Between 1115 and 1125, Waldin, for example, gave the church and tithes of Estellieux to the monks of St. Père in Eustachia's presence. *Père,* vol. 2, no. 30, p. 489.

130. *Père,* vol. 2, no. 5, pp. 472–74.

her son, willingly persevered in the evil, as well as the unjust and ne-
farious, ways of his mother.[131]

While Eustachia had generally supported her vassals' alienation of ecclesiastical property, it seems that she took exception to Gastho of Brou's grant
at Unverre. Eustachia's relationship with the monks of St. Denis had been
uneasy. William II and Eustachia did grant land to St. Denis of Nogent-le-
Rotrou and allowed some of their vassals to do so, but they clearly favored
the monks of St. Père of Chartres and the abbey of Tiron.[132] Moreover, she
had previously used a religious service to reinforce her lordly powers—an
action that would have hardly endeared her to the community of St. Denis.
At a later point, Eustachia actually held the priest from this church prisoner
perhaps in protest or as leverage. This act clearly outraged the monks and
was certainly grounds for excommunication. Yet the monks hesitated. Why?
They stated that they were mindful of Eustachia's previous "good acts" and
were hopeful she would realize the error of her ways. This did not happen.
After her death, it was left to her son William to negotiate the resolution
that would restore Eustachia to the good graces of the church. Eustachia
certainly had been a good daughter of the church. She promoted reform and
had been a generous benefactor, facts that the aggrieved monks themselves
recognized. But she was also a powerful lord. The monks of St. Denis were
clearly hesitant to excommunicate a lord who commanded such power and
respect, and who had otherwise been in good standing with the church.
Eustachia's example demonstrates what powerful allies, but also dangerous
adversaries, noble-born wives could be.

Conclusion

"Dionisia, pious daughter, agreeable wife, clement lord and beneficial mother
died on the fourth kalends of May; where at Pontlevoy she rests in peace buried next to her parents."[133] This obituary encapsulates the roles that women
played throughout the course of their lives. As pious daughters of the church
and their family, noblewomen acted as "clement lords" in co-ruling family property, in establishing peace between the monks and their male kin

---

131. *SD,* no. 40, pp. 104–6.
132. Their son William III's attempt to dispossess the monks of Nogent-le-Rotrou and give the
property to the monks of Chartres also reflects this family's preference for the ecclesiastical foundations at Chartres, as well as those at Tiron and Marmoutier.
133. *Gesta Ambaziensium dominorum,* p. 98.

or vassals, and in memorializing their predecessors. As "agreeable wives," they encouraged their husbands to patronize reform and certain ecclesiastical communities. As "beneficial mothers," they acted to restore their male relatives—particularly sons and husbands—to the good graces of the church.

The last clause of Dionisia's obituary illustrates why women assumed such powers. Dionisia was buried next to her kin. As a respected member of this kin group, Dionisia was entitled to a place of burial in her family's necropolis, where the anniversary of her death—along with her relatives'—would be recalled in the monks' prayers. Noblewomen in the lands of the Loire were the partners (often affectionate partners) of their husbands. The Gospel of Matthew instructed husbands and wives to "cleave" to each other. The "two" became "one" in their exercise of lordship, as stewards of their property and dependents, and as parents raising their children. When all facets of noblewomen's lives are viewed as a whole, it is perhaps not surprising that such "agreeable" women were worthy of praise and remembrance. What the scribe penned in remembrance of Dionisia could serve as a general encomium for aristocratic women in the lands of the Loire.

As this discussion of patronage and intercession indicates, building relationships with the monks and saints was of vital importance to noble houses. Yet these donations did not always remain uncontested. What insight can such disputes provide into the inner workings of the medieval aristocratic family?

❧ CHAPTER 8

Contestations

Asserting and Reasserting a Place in the Family

Medieval monks and modern scholars alike have grappled with making sense of property contestations. Guibert of Nogent laid the blame on "the growing laxity of modern times," and lamented that "for now, alas, those gifts which their parents, moved with love of such things, made to the holy places, their sons now withdraw entirely or continually demand payment for their renewal, having utterly degenerated from the good will of their sires."[1] Bernard of Angers offered a stronger condemnation: "But it should thoroughly frighten those who violently steal goods from God's holy Church, or those who appropriate, as if it were legally their own, property that the saints have inherited, and unjustly claim the rents and services due its owners.... Blinded by their greed, they dare to seize what rightfully belongs to the Church."[2] Modern scholars have offered different insights and interpretations, but Jeffrey Bowman perhaps sums up the situation best: "Property disputes reflect tensions ranging from intimate conflicts between brothers and sisters to sweeping political struggles affecting the very shape of Latin Europe in a period of territorial, demographic, and economic

---

1. Benton, *Self and Society in Medieval France,* p. 63.
2. Bernard of Angers, *The Book of St. Foy,* pp. 71–72.

growth."[3] Contestations are a fascinating feature of the medieval cultural landscape for no two seems to be alike. Different circumstances, motivations, and resolutions triggered disputes over property. Scholarship since the mid-1980s recognizes this diversity and makes clear that disputes were complex, numerous, and multivalent; thus no one interpretation can adequately explain every contestation.[4]

Guibert's and Bernard's comments would have resonated with the aristocracy of the lands of the Loire. Contestations gave these nobles the opportunity to seek justice and have their complaints heard. But disputing a gift also provided them with a unique opportunity for reminding their kin, lords, vassals, neighbors, and the monks of their place in a complex web of family relationships and rights to property. In short, contestations allowed a noble to reinforce his/her claim to property that came with being a member of an aristocratic family. Contestations and their resolution were also a place where all of the strands of aristocratic life came together: family, friends, foes, patrons, and the clergy. Examination of such actions is thus a fitting way to complete our examination of aristocratic life.

I will begin this chapter by examining the process through which disputes were made. I will then proceed to a discussion of who thought they had a claim and why. Finally, I will argue that contestations served as a means through which elites could assert and reassert their place within the aristocratic family.

---

3. Bowman, *Shifting Landmarks*, p. viii.

4. Historians interested in the development of law and systems of governance have examined contestations as a way of understanding the way that medieval people resolved disputes. See Tabuteau, *Transfers of Property;* Stephen D. White, "'*Pactum...Legem Vincit et Amor Judicium*'"; Bowman, *Shifting Landmarks;* Paul Fouracre, "'*Placita*' and the Settlement of Disputes in Later Merovingian Francia"; Janet T. Nelson, "Dispute Settlement in Carolingian West Francia"; Timothy Reuter, "Property Transactions and Social Relations between Rulers, Bishops and Nobles in Early Eleventh-Century Saxony." Claims made by nobles have also been used to evaluate or determine who had a legal claim to property as indicators of inheritance practices and family structure; White, *Custom, Kinship and Gifts to Saints,* pp. 51–53, 63–69, and "Inheritances and Legal Arguments in Western France, 1050–1150"; Bouchard, *Holy Entrepreneurs,* pp. 148–50; Livingstone, "Kith and Kin," and "Diversity and Continuity"; Lemesle, *La société aristocratique dans le Haut-Maine,* pp. 203–11. Anthropological insights have also influenced how medieval historians have interpreted contestations. Rosenwein has suggested that disputes and their resolutions provided monks and nobles with a way of revisiting the bonds that connected them; Rosenwein, *To Be the Neighbor of St. Peter,* pp. 49–78. See also White, "Feuding and Peace-Making in the Touraine around the Year 1100"; Patrick Geary, "Extra-Judicial Means of Conflict Resolution" and "Moral Obligations and Peer Pressure"; Geoffrey Koziol, "Baldwin VII of Flanders and the Toll of St. Vaast (1111)." Bouchard sees the resolution of conflicts as part of the "discourse of opposites"; *Every Valley Shall be Exalted,* pp. 94–112. Cheyette has suggested that contestations were part of a larger dialogue of love and honor; *Ermengard of Narbonne,* pp. 199–219, esp. p. 205.

Disputes: Process and Consequences

Bernard of Angers provides a colorful eyewitness account of a *placitum,* or court convened to settle a dispute:

> On the appointed day Abbot Airad and the senior monks, escorted by a noble band of armed riders supplied by their benefactors, set out honorably to that place [where the dispute was to be heard]. Bernard the Hairy and the false accuser, his wife, presented a pompous appearance with their strong band of vassals. A place was prepared for hearing the case, the seats were arranged, and the speakers for both parties took their places. The proceedings began as one would expect when the arbitrary judgments of humankind are considered to be equivalent to laws: the speakers each argued for their own point of view; there was a confused racket as shouting voices mixed together; it was difficult to judge what was true and what was false. Finally [another man named] Bernard, who held firmly to what was right and just, gave a verdict for the monks' party and rebuked the offensive opposition party with threatening authority. But they became more vehemently insistent and raved like madmen. Finally the lord's opinion prevailed; he calmed the mad raving and forced them to return to the matter at hand. He didn't dismiss the stepson's case until he was satisfied that he had found the truth, which he then proclaimed openly. The two sides began to reach something of an agreement because the woman was willing to give up her wicked and malicious charge in return for a payment in money.[5]

While not as lively in its retelling of events, the charter below mirrors Bernard's account:

> Let it be known for the present and the future that a disagreement over certain land between the monks of Vendôme and Hervé of Echelles which had lasted a long time, through the will of God, in this way was reconciled. The aforementioned Hervé, inspired through divine grace, with his two sons Hervé, his first born, and Walter and many other men,

---

5. Bernard of Angers, *Book of St. Foy, pp.* 73–74. The letters of Abbot Geoffrey of Vendôme provide another perspective on the issue of settling disputes. Geoffrey had to write to the bishop of Chartres several times to have his complaint against Nivelon II, Ursio, and Pagan of Fréteval heard. His letters convey his growing frustration with bringing these men to justice and setting a date so the matter could be resolved. Geoffrey of Vendôme, *Oeuvres,* letters no. 94, p. 177–78; no. 106, p. 203; no. 159, p. 353; no. 182, pp. 417–23; no. 184, pp. 425–27.

came to the chapter house of St. Trinité, and there in the presence of abbot Robert and all of the monks, his son Hervé and Walter agreeing, all of the quarrels which Hervé had with the monks, were dismissed and he freely and quietly conceded the contested land to the monks. In return, abbot Robert acquitted Hervé of all of the quarrels, with the assent of the whole chapter. These people saw and heard this: on the part of the monks: Lord Abbot Robert. . . . On the part of Hervé: Hervé himself, his sons Hervé and Walter. . . . These [people] all [witnessed] the same Hervé as he conceded at Plessis, Ascelina his wife, Rainald his son, Hildegard and Sicilia his daughters, and Henry his son. Witnesses: Hervé of Echelles, Walter his son. . . . Even Juliana, daughter of Hervé, conceded [to this] at the court of her father and at the court of her husband.[6]

Like Bernard's disputants, Hervé and his sons traveled to meet with the monks to resolve their quarrel. They then made their quitclaim in front of the whole chapter and many local laymen. To ensure that his family knew, but also approved, of his abandonment of his claim, Hervé confirmed the quitclaim at his home of Plessis, with the participation of his natal family and in front of many of his relatives. In an attempt to prevent Hervé's kin or descendants from making a later claim, the monks had Hervé's married daughter recognize the quitclaim twice: at her father's court and at her husband's court. Hervé's dispute lasted a long time and required considerable planning to make sure that as many potential claimants as possible agreed to the abandonment of rights.

Like Hervé's, "which lasted a long time," other contestations persisted for decades, sometimes spanning several generations.[7] Others were easily resolved and short-lived.[8] Some required the intercession of an outside party or were settled by more violent means such as a judicial ordeal.[9] Still others resulted in violence,[10] for the charters are full of references to nobles "invading,"

---

6. *CTV,* vol. 2, no. 521, pp. 356–57. Although the charter does not reference it, Hervé's claim to the property had been aired at some earlier point.

7. For another example of a protracted dispute, in this case a claim brought by a grandson, see *Père,* vol. 1, no. 7, pp. 118–19.

8. AD Loir-et-Cher, 16 H 119. See also *MB,* no. 39, pp. 50–51.

9. At the same court described by Bernard of Angers, the son of the disputant volunteered to fight a judicial duel to prove their claim to the property. Bernard of Angers, *Book of St. Foy,* p. 74. The provost of Blois arranged for a judicial ordeal between two disputants to settle their claims; *MB,* no. 21, pp. 25–26. Yet the church did not support judicial ordeals as a means of justice. See Ivo of Chartres, *Lettres de Saint Ives,* no. 248, pp. 446–47.

10. In 1150 when Hildiard made a gift to Notre Dame de Josaphat, her son Hugo initially consented, but "after his concession, he became angry" and violently seized the goods given in tithes

"seizing," and "capturing" property or "perpetrating evil deeds" against the monastery to lay claim to property they believed was theirs.[11] A scribe of Marmoutier narrates Martin Tirollus's violent actions:

> Let it be known for the present, but also the future, that Martin Tirollus did many and evil injuries to the estates of Holy Marmoutier and its monks, the worst of which he perpetrated against the priory and monks of Villeberfol. For in the time when Haton the monk was prior [of Villeberfol], at the time he said vespers, when he was at the end of the service, suddenly and furtively Martin and his horsemen invaded the monks, and chased Haton so that he was forced to flee to a house. Ultimately, however, all of Martin's malice, as well as his rage and fury, culminated when he burned and pillaged the dwellings of the saint, which the monks of Villeberfol held, and he did other evil deeds as well.[12]

Martin's actions were grievous. The monks were no strangers to violence on the part of noble donors.[13] Yet even in this context, the monastic scribe dramatically recounts Martin's infamous acts against the brothers of Villeberfol priory. More astounding is that Martin's violence seems to have been justified. He had cause to be very angry indeed, for the monks' men had killed one of Martin's sons.

---

to the monks, which earned him the sentence of excommunication. Hugo eventually repented and restored the property to the church; *Josaphat*, vol. 1, no. 171, pp. 214–15. Anger clearly played a role in the process of dispute and resolution. See the following essays in *Anger's Past*, edited by Barbara Rosenwein: Little, "Anger in Monastic Curses"; White, "The Politics of Anger"; and Barton, "'Zealous Anger' and the Renegotiation of Aristocratic Relationships in Eleventh- and Twelfth-Century France."

11. A charter from St. Trinité in Vendôme recites a litany of violent acts carried out by nobles against the monks: "After many injuries done to the lord God and to the place of St. Trinité unjustly done by these two, after many fires and evil deeds, after the capture of men and the innocent, and after the perpetration of innumerable other evil deeds [these men came to an agreement with the monks]." *CTV,* vol. 1, no. 224, pp. 357–58. The question of the nature and intensity of violence has informed the debate on the "feudal revolution." Bloch saw the first feudal age as a time of unrestrained violence. A key feature of Bloch's second feudal age was the end to violence and the establishment of law as a means to provide order. Marc Bloch, *Feudal Society,* vol. 2, pp. 359–74, 408–20. In their contributions to the debate on the "feudal revolution," Bisson, White, and Barthélemy examine the intent and frequency of violence. Bisson, "The Feudal Revolution"; Barthélemy and White, "Debate: The 'Feudal Revolution.'" For a response to this debate in regard to the issues of violence and resolution, see Cheyette, "Some Reflections on Violence, Reconciliation and the 'Feudal Revolution.'" And most recently, in 2008 Bisson asserts that violence was a characteristic of twelfth-century politics; *The Crisis of the Twelfth Century.*

12. AD Loir-et-Cher, 16 H 118. See also *CMPD,* no. 57, p. 51.

13. Rosenwein, Head, and Farmer, "Monks and Their Enemies"; Stephen Weinberger, "Les conflits entre clercs et laïcs dans la Provence au XIe siècle."

What is perhaps most astonishing is that such violent episodes did not completely rend the relationship between the aristocratic aggressor and the monks.[14] On the contrary, these occasions frequently provided the monks and the nobles with an opportunity to come together and reinforce their ties and relationships. After weaving his tale of Martin's violence and treachery, the monk of Marmoutier goes on to report: "Wishing to do penance, Martin came to Marmoutier, nude, barefoot and bearing rods in his hands, which he carried into the presence of the lord abbot Bernard and the other brothers, begging them for mercy." Martin sought restitution with the monks and promised to forfeit his rights to the property in question if he could become "the man" of the abbot and monks, whom he promises he will serve faithfully. The monastic community agreed and accepted Martin into the benefit of their prayers. Furthermore, the monks extended the same status to Martin's wife and sons if they foreswore any claim to the land and promised not to retract their oath. Thus "affection, strong friendship, and fidelity" were restored between St. Martin and his monks and Martin Tirollus.

There were also undercurrents of supplication and domination at play in this resolution. Martin's posture as a barefoot, nude penitent dramatically demonstrated regret for his unjust actions. His bearing of the rods and their transfer to the abbot is significant for rods were also used to symbolize guardianship and tutelage,[15] an indication that Martin now recognized the power and authority that the abbot had over him as "his man." Furthermore, the public drama of the event would live on in community memory. Out of the ashes of Martin's violence, a new relationship with the monks (and through them, St. Martin) was created. What began as a tale of vengeance and outlawry ends with reconciliation, friendship, and even love between the monks and Martin Tirollus.[16]

Motives for Disputes: Consent, Great Expectations, and Economic Privation

Claims to property in the Middle Ages consisted of many layers. A sure impediment to a donation was a charge that the property in question did not belong to the donor and hence was not his or hers to give. This was a

---

14. Rosenwein, *To Be the Neighbor of St. Peter* and "Feudal War and Monastic Peace"; Bowman, *Shifting Landmarks,* pp. 185–210.

15. Niermayer, *Mediae Latinitatis Lexicon Minus,* p. 1110.

16. Paul R. Hyams, "Nastiness and Wrong, Rancor and Reconciliation" and Cheyette, "Some Reflections on Violence."

fairly common complaint.[17] Because families recognized the rights of a wide spectrum of kin and practiced an array of inheritance strategies, inheritance claims or expectations could be used as grounds to contest a gift. Historians have puzzled over the participation of a range of kin in transfers of property. Stephen White has discerned no clear pattern. In other words, there does not seem to have been a requirement or legal prescription that insisted that certain kin be present or consent to the alienation of property. Instead, what he finds is that nobles had different groups of kin consent to their various gifts. The inclusion of such kin could be the result of a certain claim or something as pragmatic as the relative's presence at court or close geographical proximity.[18] Dominique Barthélemy characterizes those who appeared in transactions as "practical kin." Like White, Barthélemy does not find any one pattern of kin participating in acts, although he does find that certain kin—like siblings and children—did participate more frequently.[19] Scholars agree that consent indicated that the consenter was believed to have some claim or right to the property.

Medieval aristocrats based their disputes on a lack of consent. In 1135, a son of the Beaugency line contested what had been given to the church:

> Let all in the present and future know that Boellus of Beaugency gave to God, and we the monks of Vendôme, land among Rocé, which we used to bury his wife. And to which his son Boellus consented. But after this, Boellus junior challenged the gift, asserting that he had not consented to it. But afterward, having made use of wise counsel, he came to Vendôme and recognized his previous bad behavior, [he] made the gift again, and placed a knife upon the altar of the Lord. Act of Vendôme in the 1135 year of the incarnation.[20]

While the charter relays that Boellus junior had had a change of heart concerning this grant, it remains stubbornly silent as to why he changed his mind. Now it is possible that the monks embellished young Boellus's consent in light of his later actions. Whatever the case, Boellus clearly knew

---

17. Odo Bevinus, for example, brought a *calumnia* stating the property belonged to his patrimony and someone other than Odo had given these holdings to the church. *CMPD*, no. 133, p. 123. Similarly, Ingelbald Brito asserted that the person who donated vines to the church was a serf and thus unable to give the property. Apparently Ingelbald was right since the agreement was declared null by the monks. *MV*, no. 128, pp. 219–21. For another example, see *MP*, no. 151, pp. 155–56.

18. White, *Custom, Kinship and Gifts to Saints*, pp. 44–85.

19. Barthélemy, *La société dans le comté de Vendôme*, pp. 519–23.

20. *CTV*, vol. 2, no. 476, p. 279. For a similar example, see *MB*, no. 73, p. 84.

that claiming he had not consented to the gift would lend legitimacy to his action.[21]

The dense web of ties of clientage gave others the grounds to contest donations. When Mathilda Otovedus and her lord, Robert the Burgundian, gave their respective halves of a church, the monks "did not get to enjoy this [gift] for long, because a certain knight named Caloius, who held in fief the remaining half of the church from that venerable matron, instantly disputed this gift."[22] Not surprising, lords also based contestations on the assertion that fiefs that belonged to them had been alienated without their consent. William II Gouet disputed a sale made to Marmoutier by one of his men "saying we [the monks] made this [agreement] without his assent or authorization."[23] Moreover, who held what from whom was not always clear and resulted in disputes. Hamelin of Langeais, for example, contested a gift based on the assertion that the fiefs in question belonged to him. The other party countered by saying the property belonged to his fief and thus he had the right to make the grant.[24]

A failure to meet one of the terms agreed upon in the initial grant similarly motivated disputes. Countergifts served an important purpose in the dialogue of gift-dispute-reconciliation. These grants reinforced the act of consent in the donor's and community's memory and served as a symbol of the recipients' right to the property in question.[25] When those involved in the alienation of property did not receive their countergifts, they reacted. Archdeacon Hugh of Mondoubleau contested Marmoutier's possession of a church because he had not received what had been pledged to him.[26] At the

---

21. Around the same time, Gastho of Remalast contested two alienations based on the fact he had not provided his consent. *Jean*, no. 22, p. 14.

22. *CTV,* vol. 1, no. 184, pp. 316–19. Although Caloius asserted he had a right to the land as the vassal of Mathilda Otovedus, the men who were assembled to judge the dispute did not find his claim valid. As a result, Caloius abandoned his claim at the court and conceded the monks' possession of the property. In return, the monks granted him a countergift of thirty *solidi*. For the full text of the charter, see chapter 7, p. 195.

23. *MM*, no. 5, pp. 117–19. William II Gouet's right to the property was recognized, and the sale by one of his vassals was voided. William, however, made gifts from the property in question to make up for what the monks would lose from the nullification of the sale. The issue was not so much about the actual property but demonstrating rights to it.

24. *MV,* no. 4, pp. 6–7.

25. In a gift economy, gifts are made simply for the importance of making a gift. Remuneration thus was not the motivation behind countergifts. Rather, it was the recognition of rights and authority over property as well as the recipient's place in a hierarchy (familial or political) that such gifts symbolized. Tabuteau, *Transfers of Property*, pp. 115–19; Bouchard, *Holy Entrepreneurs*, pp. 87–93; Barthélemy, *La société dans le comté de Vendôme*, pp. 681–92.

26. *MV,* no. 2, pp. 3–4. This charge was serious enough that a *placitum* was convened. Although the assembled body found that Hugh's claim did not vitiate the gift, the monks did give him forty *solidi*.

end of the eleventh century, Pagan disputed a sale made by his family because "he did not have all that the monks promised him."[27] At the time of the original grant, the whole family had been granted cash countergifts. Pagan, who was not listed with his siblings, challenged the transaction because he had not received a countergift. Was Pagan motivated by petty sibling rivalry? Yes, of a sort. Pagan contested his lack of a countergift because it was symbolic of his legitimate claim to family property and his place as a son of this family. Pagan wanted to be absolutely sure that his family and the community recognized his right to the patrimony. To placate Pagan and resolve the conflict, the monks of St. Trinité gave him a countergift of over a third more coin than his siblings had received, including the eldest son. Pagan was not petty; he was savvy.

While procedural irregularities provided elites with the means to contest what had been given to the church, more pragmatic concerns also underlay *calumnia*. In a handful of cases, donors justified their contestations by saying they *needed* property previously donated. For instance, even though their father's gift to St. Père was "small and unfruitful," the sons of Hugo of Dreux contested his gift.[28] Some elites had cause to regret their predecessors' ecclesiastical generosity. Poverty-stricken or resource-strapped individual nobles and families saw taking property previously granted to the church as one means, albeit desperate and infrequent, of continued survival. Girbert the knight claimed he was compelled by need when he tried to reclaim estates. The monks were persuaded by his case for they granted Girbert half of the property as a life estate, but warned that "neither his blood kin nor kin by marriage" would be able to inherit the land after his death.[29] The same monks demonstrated their care for the less fortunate in their resolution of the claim brought by Drogo Freslavena. In response to Drogo's claim against properties his ancestors had given, a monk seized his horse. To bring to a close what had essentially become a standoff between the abbey of Marmoutier and Drogo, Brother Ivo, knowing of Drogo's poverty, restored his horse to him and gave him twenty *solidi*. In turn, Drogo quitclaimed his right.[30] The loss of a horse could be a fatal blow to a man who made his living as a mounted combatant. But if the short-term loss of his horse pushed Drogo to such desperation, he was clearly in severe economic straits.

---

27. *CTV,* vol. 2, no. 383, pp. 130–31.

28. *Père,* vol. 1, no. 94, pp. 218–19. The dispute was settled after the death of one of these sons, who wanted to be buried with the brothers of St. Père.

29. *CMPD,* no. 98, p. 91.

30. *CMPD,* no. 143, pp. 132–33.

Aristocrats were motivated by diverse forces and circumstances to contest gifts. Although some brought disputes or usurped property out of desperation or when there was either lack of consent or procedural irregularity, demonstrating or acting upon a right to family land was also a common motivation. Prominent among disputes were those made by relatives contesting each other's gifts. Who made these claims, and what motivated such actions?

Who Had a Claim? (Or Thought They Did)

Approximately 32.3 percent of the charters from the lands of the Loire recorded contestations.[31] Of these, 55 percent were made by family members. Perhaps not surprisingly, children were the most frequent disputants of gifts, with 45 percent of contestations by family members being brought by sons and daughters. More surprising is that siblings, spouses, and affinal kin contested gifts less frequently. Significantly, extended kin appear as disputants at over double the rate (25 percent) of any one group of closer kin, such as spouses (9 percent) or siblings (9 percent).[32] What do these numbers reveal? If one assumes that disputants only brought claims to property to which they actually did have some sort of legitimate claim, then the nobles of the lands of the Loire recognized the rights of cousins, aunts, uncles, nephews, and nieces to a family's or individual's holdings.[33] These data support what the charters themselves record about inheritance practices and aristocratic family structure: families did not seek to *exclude,* but rather sought to include a broad range of kin.

Rights and Claims: Children

While these numbers indicate which kin were those most likely to contest gifts, what were the stories and circumstances behind these disputes? Nivelon Pagan of Fréteval contested "what his father and ancestors had given to

---

31. This is derived from analysis of the database of acts from the Loire region. For further description, see chapter 4, note 15.

32. These percentages are based on the total number of contestations being brought by relatives. In addition to family members, lords and vassals also disputed transactions. In some cases, contestations were brought by neither family nor lords or vassals. Such outliers have not been figured into these percentages.

33. White and Barthélemy have also analyzed the role of kin in property transactions. Both conclude that family organization and rights to property were far more complex than that described by patrilineage or primogeniture. White, *Custom, Kinship and Gifts to Saints,* pp. 86–129; Barthélemy, *La société dans le comté de Vendôme,* pp. 519–37.

this church."[34] He eventually saw the error of his ways, perhaps because the monks called him to the count's court, and allowed the property to pass to the church. The fact that his father held the property *jure hereditario* may have provided the grounds for Nivelon Pagan's claim: his father had inherited the property, and Nivelon Pagan likely expected it would have been part of his inheritance.

Walter, "the boy," went beyond contesting what his father had given and actually invaded the property. When the monks heard of this outrage, they called Walter to court, where they asked him why he had taken land that he himself had given, with his parents, to the monks. Walter replied that he was a young child when he assented to the gift and did not remember giving his consent.[35] Walter was willing to compromise, however, if the monks gave him something in return. The brothers responded by granting him seventy *solidi,* and he confirmed the monks' possession of the property "in court in front of many people."

The bastard son of Rodulf Rufus claimed his father's holdings had unjustly passed to his father's brother. This arrangement was not what this bastard son had expected, and he contested the monks' possession of what his father's brother had held and subsequently given to the church. Once again a *placitum* was called. Rodulf's bastard's right to the property was recognized by the monks in their award of thirty *solidi* as a countergift.[36] About a century later—that is, in the mid-1100s—Rainald Cannaillardus disputed St. Trinité's possession of certain holdings at Lisle, stating that the property in question belonged to him by right through inheritance from his ancestors.[37]

Contestations by sons have been cast as rapacious acts carried out by violently desperate men. While these examples indicate that sons did use violence to seize property, they did so because they believed they had a legitimate right to it. They were not, in most cases, young ruffians grabbing what they could from their elders. These contestations indicate that sons— legitimate and illegitimate—made claims because they thought—or at least stated they thought—the property was legitimately theirs.[38] Moreover, these

---

34. *CTV,* vol. 2, no. 325, pp. 36–37.

35. *CSVM,* no. 790, p. 448. See chapter 2, p. 30 for another example.

36. *MV,* no. 60, pp. 97–98.

37. *CTV,* vol. 2, no. 536, pp. 381–82. Unlike other claimants, however, Rainald Cannaillardus opted not to have his claim heard in front of a court. Instead, he settled with the monks by coming into the convened chapter at the monks' chapter house and placing the charter that recorded this reconciliation into the hand of the abbot and then on the altar. Since Rainald Cannaillardus was not compensated in any way by the monks, his claim to the property may have been spurious.

38. For another example, see *MP,* no. 151, pp. 155–56.

sons disputed their fathers' gifts after their fathers had died. Duby believed that such contestations revealed intragenerational tension between fathers and sons.[39] These acts suggest another interpretation: sons made claim to what they thought they should inherit from their father.

Aristocratic daughters also disputed what their parents or relatives had granted. In 1063, Fredescind, the daughter of Odo Dubellus, lord of Mondoubleau, claimed property her father had given to St. Trinité. Her husband, Nivelon Pagan, at her request, invaded the property (see appendix, chart 10). Since Fredescind and the monks could not reach an agreement, a *placitum* was assembled. "Many of [the monks'] friends and officials met," and found, unsurprisingly, that the property should belong to the monastery.[40] Helvisa-Adierna, Fredescind's sister, behaved in a similar way. She "did not wish to accede the tithes" to the church.[41] Eventually both sisters were persuaded to grant the respective properties to the monks, and their quitclaims were confirmed at the comital court. The claims brought by these two sisters demonstrate the strength of a daughter's claim to noble family holdings. If they "did not wish" for property to be alienated or transferred to the monks, noble-born daughters had the ability and right to dispute the transfer and even take possession of the property itself. In this regard, daughters of the house assumed a degree of parity with their male siblings.

Rights and Claims: Siblings

Brothers and sisters believed they had a right, or at least an interest, in each other's holdings. Two brothers, Robert Michael and Almaric, sold and gave part of the property they held jointly to the monks of Marmoutier.[42] Five years later, their brother, Salomon of Fréteval, claimed "all of the fief of Almaric and Michael, his brothers" as his own. At the intervention of the monks, who promised to receive him, his wife, and sons into their *societas,*

---

39. Duby, "Youth in Aristocratic Society," pp. 116–19; Bouchard, *"Strong of Body, Brave and Noble,"* pp. 73–81. In contrast to what Duby argued in "Youth in Aristocratic Society," the charters of the lands of the Loire record only instances of violence done to the church. I am not aware of any charters recording acts of sons usurping property from their fathers or acting violently toward their fathers.

40. *CTV,* vol. 1, no. 166, pp. 292–93. Fredescind and Nivelon Pagan traveled to Vendôme and placed a symbol of their agreement with the monks on the altar.

41. *CTV,* vol. 1, no. 46, pp. 99–100.

42. AD Loir-et-Cher, 16 H 77. There are two documents in this dossier, one recording the brothers' initial grant (see also *CMPD,* no. 151, pp. 139–40), and the other their brother's contestation (see also *CMPD,* no. 106, pp. 59–60). Only Robert went on Crusade. Almaric ended up staying behind.

Salomon was persuaded to give up his claim. Why did Salomon dispute this gift? The charter recording his contestation remains mute on this question, but the earlier grant made by his brothers may provide some clues.

Although Almaric and Robert Michael had been scrupulous about having their lord and their lord's lord consent to their sale and gift, Salomon did not participate in the charter, thus leaving him grounds for disputing the gift. Sisters had the same right. Two other brothers, Herlebald and Odo of Dangeau, shared control of properties, part of which they gave to the church. After their deaths, their sister Osilid and her husband disputed what her brothers had granted Marmoutier. The claim was made "because she was the sister of the aforementioned brothers," and, as such, had a claim to their property.[43] Siblings exercised a right to each other's property, which made securing their consent to gifts in the best interest of the benefactor and the monks. If a sibling did not approve a gift, the door was left open for possible contestations.

Because some aristocratic families practiced shared inheritance and control of property, siblings joined as a group to put forward their right to property. The children of Erchembald—William, Guido, Radulf the cleric, Adelard, and their sister—claimed land that their father had given to the church, although they eventually abandoned their claim and swore to defend the land against anyone trying to claim it, either through the law or through arms.[44] This group of siblings acted collectively first to contest the abbey's possession of the property, then to abandon their claim, and finally to agree to act as the defenders of the gift. Such action conveys a sense of solidarity and connection among these three brothers and their sister through affinity and a shared right to property.[45] The disputes brought by siblings—either individually or collectively—illustrate that aristocratic patrimonies were not the sole possession of eldest brothers. Indeed, the lack of a sibling's consent provided legitimate grounds for a contestation. Donors were aware of this and sought to secure the approval of their brothers and sisters. Provisions demonstrate that the church also recognized the rights of children and siblings and had to accommodate the rights, and potential rights, of immediate family to aristocratic holdings.

---

43. AD Eure-et-Loir, H 4861; *CMPD,* no. 26, pp. 27–28.

44. *Père,* vol. 2, no. 22, pp. 415–16.

45. Sometimes siblings joined with their parents to bring claims. In the decades between 1130 and 1150, the grant of vines made by Odo Belerrut was disputed by Radulf of Humblières and his sons and daughter. The charter describes the *calumnia* as being made by the family as a group. The monks of St. Père convened a *placitum,* and it was found that none of these people had claim to the property. Interestingly, the response of Radulf and his children to this finding is not recorded in the act. *Père,* vol. 2, no. 170, p. 386.

Rights and Claims: Extended Kin

Second only to children in disputations of gifts were extended kin.[46] A series of contestations by the kindred of Hildiard of Vendôme illustrates the multitude of claims made by kin. When Hildiard gave a mill at La Chappe to the monks, her grandson and his wife and children (from whom she had originally purchased the gift), her own sons, and another grandson all consented. In spite of taking this precaution, about twenty-five years later her daughter and son-in-law and grandson disputed the transaction and seized the property. Hildiard's great-grandson also challenged the grant and attempted to claim the mill for himself. Even Ingelbald Brito asserted a claim by stating that his father-in-law, Hildiard's son, had not consented to the original transaction. The litigation concerning the Dives kindred and the mill at La Chappe throws into relief the multiplicity of potential claims to property.[47] Distant kin, even those who were not involved in or alive at the time of the initial transaction, believed they had some right to property simply because they were related to the original donor. Asserting a claim to this property gave these kin a chance to underscore their descent from this prominent kinswoman.

The rights of extended kin were acknowledged by their relatives and the monks—many of whom were members of aristocratic families themselves. In the year 1067, Hugh of Rocé allowed a church to pass into the hands of Marmoutier so that he could become a monk. But shortly afterwards, his relative, Hervé of Breviard, disputed what Hugh had given. To compensate him for giving up this property, Hervé was given four pounds in countergift and granted ten *solidi* annually. In return, he recognized Marmoutier's control of the property and promised that none of his heirs would claim it.[48] Significantly, Hervé's association with the land, and his family, would be recalled each year as he was granted his ten *solidi*.

A dispute made by Stephan of Bordenido also underscores that extended kin believed they had the right to a family member's property. Sometime early in the twelfth century Hubert Pagan desired to go to Jerusalem on pilgrimage as penance for his many crimes.[49] He put his affairs in order,

---

46. I am defining extended kin as those family members outside the immediate kin group and/ or those who are related in the second degree, i.e., cousins, aunts, uncles, grandparents, nephews, and nieces.

47. *MV,* nos. 30, 31, 32, pp. 46–54; no. 34, p. 57.

48. *MP,* no. 6, pp. 16–17. The consent and participation of Hugh's illegitimate son in the charter suggests that bastards also could stake a claim to their progenitor's holdings.

49. *Josaphat,* vol. 1, no. 29, pp. 44–45. These crimes would seem to be keeping his father's donations from transferring to the church.

which included confirming the church's possession of what his father had previously given and mortgaging some of his property. Sadly, Hubert died while on pilgrimage, and his *consanguineus* Stephen of Bordenido contested what Hubert had arranged with Notre Dame de Josaphat. He was summoned to the church to account for his actions and appeared before the abbot and bishop of Chartres. The convened court arranged a compromise: Stephen was to retain part of the property that his kinsman had given to the church. The story does not end there, for Stephen granted the monks the *census,* or dues owed, which "had fallen to him through inheritance after the death of Hubert." In this case, Stephen, who was Hubert's relative, had actually inherited rights to this revenue from him. This casts Stephen's dispute and reconciliation not as a nuisance claim made by a rapacious relative but as one brought by a legitimate heir. Contestations by extended kin were not empty claims since elites could expect to inherit from their relatives.[50]

Given the role of surrogate parent that uncles often played, it is not surprising that, like parents and children, nephews and uncles sometimes became embroiled in disputes. Sometime in the mid-eleventh century, the boy Matthew was under the tutelage of his uncle, Odo of Montoire. In his role as guardian, Odo arranged to sell part of Matthew's land. But when Matthew came of age, he contested the sale of his property and stated that he had not consented to its alienation. His right to it was recognized, and Matthew recuperated the property. The plot thickens, however, for Matthew wished to make a pilgrimage to Rome. "Of his own free will [Matthew] came to the monastery of St. Trinité, and made a gift of the same [property], and for it to remain firm, the monks gave him five *solidi,* which he would use for his pilgrimage."[51] This act provides a window into the relationship between uncle and nephew. Matthew was raised by Odo, yet he came to challenge how his guardian had supervised his lands. Tension between the two men undoubtedly developed over this issue. Given that Matthew subsequently

---

50. About the same time, another Stephen also desired to go to Jerusalem, and before departing, he gave property to St. Père. The benefaction was made for his soul and the souls of his relatives, just in case they died before he returned from Crusade. Yet several of Stephen's relatives (*parentes*) were not happy with his generosity and joined together in seizing the property granted by their kinsman. After much time and many *placita,* this group of kin and the church reached an agreement. They appeared first before the court of the canons of Chartres, followed by another appearance in the chapter of St. Père, and they finally dismissed their claim "for love of peace and concord" with the church. Even though Stephen had provided for these kin in his original donation—perhaps in an attempt to discourage them from claiming what he had given—his relatives disputed the alienation of this property from family possession. Only after negotiation and compromise were they persuaded to let the gift pass to the church. *Père,* vol. 2, no. 149, pp. 363–64.

51. *CTV,* vol. 2, no. 210, p. 342.

gave the property to the church, the issue was not the property itself but who had the right to give it. Disputing what predecessors had given seems to have been a coming-of-age ritual for many noblemen. Their objective in airing the claim was to establish themselves as the one now in control of both property and lordship.

Uncles and nephews also acted in solidarity to dispute gifts.[52] Hugo and his brother Achard joined with their uncle Hugo Cadebertus to challenge what their *consanguineus* had sold to the monks of St. Trinité of Vendôme.[53] Tragedy intervened, however, and Achard was murdered. Regrettably, the charter merely states that Achard was killed and provides no motive or explanation for the murder. Was the murder connected to the disposition of the property? Was the murderer a jealous husband? As tantalizing as these speculations are, the record gives us no clues. It does, however, indicate the affection with which brother and uncle held Achard. After his violent death, the two Hugos joined together to abandon their claim to the property and specified that this action was to benefit the soul of their fallen kinsman.[54]

Nieces likewise caused trouble by disputing pious donations. In the middle of the eleventh century a certain *matrona* named Gertrude gave the abbey of St. Père her considerable holdings. Gertrude was a special friend to the monks, and she ultimately received the honor of burial in front of the atrium of one of their houses. The text of her donation was peppered with quotes from scripture, suggesting a deep devotion and familiarity with holy teachings that would have endeared her to the monks. The monks' possession of her property went uncontested for quite some time. Eventually, though, Gertrude's niece Hildeberg, "at the instigation of the devil," acted with her husband to invade the lands that her aunt had given. But Hildeberg was

---

52. In the first three decades of the twelfth century, Simon of Montepinceon conceded that his *calumnia* to what his uncle had given to the church was unjust. His three sons assented to the quitclaim, and the family accepted sixty *solidi* as a countergift. See *Père,* vol. 2, no. 21, pp. 531–32. Like Simon, the knight Walter also claimed land that his uncle had given to the monks. He, too, recognized the injustice of his claim and confirmed Notre Dame de Josaphat's possession of the land. See *Josaphat,* vol. 1, no. 212, pp. 257–58.

53. *MV,* no. 46, pp. 73–74.

54. In addition to disputing arrangements made by their uncles, nephews also sometimes made claims to their aunts' property. Around 1124, Robert of Coudray-au-Perche and his wife, Elizabeth, gave part of her dowry to the abbey of Tiron to benefit their souls and those of their relatives. Although the couple secured the consent of Elizabeth's sister and her three sons, one of her nephews brought a claim to the gift. He and his family eventually abandoned their claim at the court of William II Gouet and Eustachia, but they did retain two *solidi* of *cens,* which would be due to them at Pentecost. This revenue was too small to be anything other than symbolic. It served to remind the community, monks, and relatives alike of this nobleman's and his family's continued connection to maternal properties and kin. *Tiron,* vol. 1, no. 57, pp. 77–79.

acting on more than diabolical encouragement. The charter states that Gertrude and her husband preferred to make humble men (i.e., the monks) their heirs, thus disinheriting Hildeberg. Hildeberg must have felt cheated by her aunt's generosity to St. Père and acted, with her husband, to attempt to secure what she believed was rightfully hers.[55]

Rights and Claims: Affinal Kin

Like blood kin, daughters-in-law asserted rights to their affinal kin's holdings. In the decade of the 1040s, Adela of Mantes's parents-in-law desired that the monks of St. Père should become the heirs to their property. But "without doubt to the detriment of their souls," their daughter-in-law Adela, who "suffered the chains of anathema for more than twenty years after the death of her husband," seized these lands.[56] To make amends, Adela swore in front of her lords that the monks would have the original lands, as well as her own, if they gave her property sufficient for her support for the duration of her life. Witnessing the quitclaim were Adela's brother-in-law and his several daughters. Indeed the monks were quite diligent in securing the consent of all of Adela's nieces, for they sent their agents to no fewer than four places to ensure they consented to the quitclaim.[57] Their experience with Adela, and others like her, encouraged the monks to gain the consent of nieces, daughters, and other female relatives. As the example of Adela makes clear, women were capable of not only contesting gifts but seizing property from the monks, thus making them formidable adversaries.

Interactions with brothers-in-law also underscore the collateral structure of the aristocracy of the lands of the Loire. When Gilo Mansellus left to go to Jerusalem, he confirmed gifts of property that his father and uncle had made to the church. Daniel of La Ferté, who had married Gilo's eldest sister, seized property and invaded the monks' lands several times. After "many vexations and invasions," Daniel finally repented his actions and appeared penitent in the court of Lord Eustachia Gouet, where he and his wife and children abandoned their claim to the property. The right of daughters to holdings was strong in this family, for Daniel's sister-in-law (his wife's sister) and her husband were also asked to confirm the monks' possession of this

---

55. *Père*, vol. 1, no. 58, pp. 183–84. The charter is frustratingly vague about the outcome of this dispute. The monks merely say that they will leave it up to divine judgment.

56. It seems likely that Adela and her husband acted together to seize the land. However, while she may have acted with her husband to usurp the land, Adela was able to keep it in her possession for more than twenty years after his death.

57. *Père*, vol. 1, no. 59, pp. 184–86.

property.[58] Other brothers-by-marriage banded together to act in their mutual best interest. In the mid-twelfth century, the monks of St. Trinité were involved in a dispute over the dowry of the daughter of Archembald Occha. The couple wanted to give property to the monks, but the wife's kinsmen made a *calumnia*.[59] They were successful, for the land remained uncultivated by either the monks or the couple. After much persuasion, the abbot of St. Trinité was able to arrange a resolution that allowed the property to transfer into their possession. The community of St. Père ran into a similar difficulty when the brothers-in-law of Radulf Minter, a descendant of Adelina and Walter, acted collectively to contest his grant.[60]

Kin by marriage, like blood relatives, believed they exercised a right to each other's property. They took action to dispute gifts, but also to usurp holdings they saw as rightfully theirs. Property was bound by a dense web of claim and potential rights. Aristocrats were not reticent about asserting these rights—no matter how distantly they might have been related to the donor.

Contestations as Assertions of Family Identity

So what are we to make of these contestations? Looking at them as a whole, the suggestion that nobles were using contestations as some sort of extortion racket seems improbable for when disputes were settled, the parties involved generally got no more than token compensation. Nor were these "hidden sales." Influenced by anthropological models, scholars now interpret these actions as part of the symbolic importance of giving. The economic ethos underpinning medieval aristocratic society of these centuries has come to be known as "the gift economy."[61] In such a system, people were not motivated by gain or a quest for capital. The act of giving was invested with symbolic and cultural resonance rather than economic meaning, and nobles gave gifts in order to create relationships or draw attention to their position in the community. Contestation and reconciliation served much the same function. Making and settling claims provided the noble with a public

---

58. *Père*, vol. 2, no. 6, pp. 474–75. In return, their son was to be buried with the monks. It may have been the death of this child that compelled Daniel to settle his claim. Like Juliana of Pray (see chapter 2, pp. 32–33), he may have believed that his actions against the monks—and thus against God—were responsible for his son's death.

59. *CTV*, vol. 2, no. 531, pp. 337–42. One kinsman was either this woman's cousin or nephew. The other was related through marriage.

60. *Père*, vol. 2, no. 53, pp. 306–7. Radulf was related to Adelina and Walter Minter, but it is not clear how. He may have been Walter's nephew or grandson.

61. Little, *Religious Poverty and the Profit Economy*, pp. 3–18.

opportunity to remind monks, friends, neighbors, lords, clients, and family of his or her connection with a saint or a particular monastery or relationship with other elites. Ceremony and ritual were vitally important in the Middle Ages for they served to reflect or recall powerful hierarchies and an individual's place in them.[62] When we consider the whole spectrum of contestations in this light, another possible explanation emerges.

As previous discussion has demonstrated, aristocrats were part of large, extended, and tangled kinship groups. Intimately connected to the family and the individual was property. Most noble families gained their name, identity, and authority from their association with a particular collection of properties and privileges. When an individual noble felt the need to express his or her place in his or her family, asserting one's right to family property was a way to remind family, friends, and foes of the disputant's family connections. The entire process of claim and resolution provided a public hearing for revisiting the contester's lineage and place in several kinship groups.[63] Such affiliations would then be immortalized in the monks' record of the gift/claim/quitclaim. The timing of these contestations provides further support for the view that property contestations were an assertion of family identity.

Contestations frequently occurred at transitional points in a family's history. Many disputes were lodged shortly after the death of a parent (usually the father). As the family shifted from one generation to the next, some family members, in an attempt to reinforce their place in this broad and dense network of kin, asserted their rights to family property—even though they may have earlier approved a particular grant. Another occasion that triggered an affirmation of rights was the coming-of-age of children. When sons succeeded to their fathers, they frequently contested what their predecessor had granted to the church to demonstrate their newly won authority and to differentiate themselves from their elders. As daughters married, moved away from their natal home, and created new households, they too sought to be sure that their right to their natal family's holdings, as well as their position in their natal lineage, were not forgotten. Contestations thus furnished nobles with a means to establish or reestablish their place in the family.

A Life Cycle of Contestations: Reaching Maturity

Long before he became a monk, Viscount Evrard I of Chartres was embroiled in a property conflict with the monks when he succeeded as viscount. He

---

62. Koziol, *Begging Pardon and Favor,* pp. 128–30, 178–79.
63. Macé believes that litigation of disputes was a way of creating peace and cohesion in the family; "Les frères au sien du lignage," p. 133.

seized estates that had been given by the previous viscounts, his father and brother. When the monks heard of his claim, they rallied their allies and made the case that the current viscount's possession of these properties was unfounded. Equal parts of reason, persuasion, and the monks' show of will compelled Evrard to recognize his claim as unjust and quitclaim all of the holdings, which were extensive, to Marmoutier.[64] The timing of this dispute is revealing. Evrard's brother had just died, and Evrard had succeeded him as viscount. Evrard used seizure of property previously given to the monks as a way of communicating his power and his new status as viscount to the community at large.

About the same time—that is, the mid-eleventh century—Herbert Barba disputed what his kinsmen had sold to the church. This contestation came just as Herbert was on the brink of manhood.[65] Herbert abandoned his objection to the sale once he was reminded that he had received a countergift in return for his approval of the transaction. Had Herbert really forgotten? Or was he using this opportunity to highlight his arrival into adulthood and to remind his kin and community of his place in his family and his right to the patrimony? When considered alongside similar contestations made by young noblemen, the latter explanation accounts for what appear to be nuisance claims.

The marriage of daughters also acted as a catalyst for contestations. Some scholars read this as evidence of a daughter's diminished rights to family property once she married, or suggest that daughters became lost to their natal house as they were co-opted into the patriarchy.[66] We need not view these actions in such a light, however. They can also be interpreted as supporting a daughter's (and her descendants') continued claim to her natal patrimony and as evidence that daughters (and their husbands) actively sought association with the bride's birth family. Noblemen and their families desired brides whose social standing, connections, or wealth would benefit them. Once married, it would make little sense for noble families to ignore the connection they had orchestrated for their social, political, or economic gain. Because both bride and groom were part of dense and extended kinship networks, each exercised a variety of claims and potential rights to family holdings. Indeed, being sure one's right to property was recognized and respected must have taken some effort. A grant to Marmoutier provides illustration.

---

64. *CMPD*, no. 117, p. 112.

65. The charter labels him *infans*, or a child, but the sobriquet *Barba*, or bearded, indicates he was likely a young man who had just come of age. *CTV*, vol. 1, no. 125, pp. 225–26.

66. Duby, *Medieval Marriage*, pp. 1–18; Goody, *The Development of the Family and Marriage*, pp. 206–7; Owen Hughes, "From Brideprice to Dowry in Mediterranean Europe," pp. 262–96.

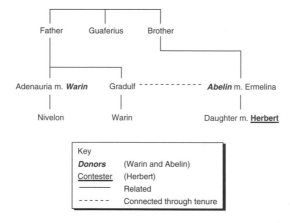

FIGURE 1. Diagram of a contestation

Sometime in the first four decades of the eleventh century, Warin, the vicarius of Blois, and the knight Abelin wished to sell their half of a salt marsh (see figure 1). Abelin, however, held his portion of the marsh from Gradulf, Warin's brother. Gradulf traveled to the court where the sale was made in order to approve it, and his son Warin accompanied him. In return for the sale, the elder Warin and his nephew of the same name were granted a countergift.[67] To ensure that Warin senior's immediate family approved of the transaction, his wife and son affirmed the sale at their home.[68]

This arrangement did not remain undisputed, however, for Abelin's son-in-law Herbert made a claim to the property. He asserted that he held part of the marsh because it had been granted to him by the younger Warin. Gradulf took exception to this claim and called an uncle to testify to the "rectitude" of the sale to the monks. In spite of the fact that Gradulf's uncle refuted his claim, Herbert persisted. Abelin, in frustration over his son-in-law's continued *calumnia,* gave the monks additional properties that they could use until the dispute was settled, to make up for the loss of the marsh. Abelin's wife, Ermelina, approved of her husband's generosity and was relieved that the family could make recompense since the disputed marsh came from her *"jus,"* providing yet another clue: Abelin's claim to the salt marsh came to him through his marriage to Ermelina, who was related to Gradulf and Warin—their cousin most likely.[69]

---

67. Evidently the salt marsh had been divided among members of Warin and Gradulf's family at some point in the family's history. *MB,* no. 25, pp. 30–32.

68. Both were also granted the same amount of cash in countergift.

69. *MB,* no. 25, pp. 30–32.

Herbert's dispute illustrates the many layers of property claims. This action also demonstrates the array of noble kin connected by both blood and property. We begin with the two brothers, Warin and Gradulf, who each held a half of the property. Then add Abelin, who held the marsh in tenure from Gradulf. Next come the claims that Warin's and Gradulf's children exercise to the property. Add an uncle, who provides testimony about the disposition of family property, but who also has some right to it. Let's not forget Abelin's family, specifically his daughter, who holds a right to the property through her parents. Herbert, Abelin's troublemaker son-in-law, asserted his wife's right by making a claim to the gift. Finally, we find out at the end that the marsh property comes through Abelin's wife, thus it likely was part of her natal family patrimony. And if it was her dowry, it may have been granted to her daughter for the same purpose. Any children that Herbert and his wife may have also had a right to all of the property addressed in the charter. What a tangled mess. Yet by contesting his father-in-law's sale, Herbert sliced through the knots of family ties and property claims, clarifying his and his wife's right to property, but also their place in this family. While daughters may be absent—and significantly, Herbert's wife does not appear in this transaction—contestations brought for and by them served as reminder of the connection to their natal family. They might be living elsewhere and part of another family, but they and their husbands used contestations to make sure they were not forgotten or overlooked in the thick and tangled threads of their family tapestry.

Marriages triggered contestations in other families as well. Remember the dispute that Archembald Occha's kinsman made to his property after his daughter married.[70] Her cousin contested this couple's possession of the property. This marriage represented the creation of a new household that would have a claim to the family patrimony. To establish his own claims to these resources, this nobleman contested his cousin's gift. While the dispute was settled—through the intervention of another cousin—the contestation had served to remind the couple and other members of the family, as well as the wider community, of this man's relationship to Archembald and his connection to the land. In this same year, that is, 1146, the marriage of Rainald of Geneste's sister Orguellosa prompted a similar dispute which would take years to resolve.[71] Earlier in the twelfth century, Rainald's father had donated

---

70. *CTV,* vol. 2, no. 513, pp. 337–42.

71. Orguellosa is an intriguing and unusual name—at least within in the lands of the Loire. It may derive from the French *orgueilleuse,* meaning a haughty, prideful, or arrogant person. If so, it presents this woman in an interesting light. Her generosity toward her family, however, belies such an appellation.

land to the monks. "A long time after" this benefaction, Rainald's brother-in-law Mainard contested the donation based on the fact that his wife had not consented to the gift.[72] A resolution was sought: it was agreed that the monks would accept Rainald and Orguellosa's younger brother as a monk. Mainard's contestation reminded family and community that his spouse was an important and recognized member of her natal family—a fact that was reenacted in the process of dispute and resolution. Orguellosa's concern for her family is also apparent in the agreement that the monks would allow one of her brothers to join their community. Customarily, disputants were awarded cash countergifts. Orguellosa eschewed such compensation in favor of making sure her brother had a secure future, a testament to Orguellosa's piety and care for her sibling.

Adelaide of Espiers also disputed her brother's gift shortly after her marriage. Her brother, Raher, had made an exceedingly generous gift to the monks of Marmoutier, "with the assent of my sisters, namely Milisend, Raionsoind and Adelaide, with the agreement that after I leave this world, unless I have a son with a legitimate wife, dominion over these properties will go to St. Martin." Not only did Adelaide consent to the gift, she also signed the charter. Some time later, Adelaide contested the gift stating that she had not consented. What could account for Adelaide's apparent amnesia? This "younger but more cunning" sister of Raher had married.[73] A need to assert her place in her natal family motivated Adelaide's contestation. But Adelaide went beyond claiming the properties, as she and her husband "committed violent injuries against the monks." This couple was eventually brought to heel and dismissed their claim—although the monks insisted that they confirm the quitclaim "in a clear voice, again and again" and through "palpable touch" when they placed a copy of the charter upon the altar with their own hands. The drama of this contestation fixed in public memory Adelaide's place as a daughter of her natal house, with incumbent rights.

A competing claim to his wife's family's property caused Hamelin of Langeais to contest a gift. The church of Naveil was one of Marmoutier's oldest possessions in the Vendômois and built on property that was controlled by the Mondoubleau and Langeais families (see appendix, charts 10 and 13).[74] When Hamelin of Langeais married into the Mondoubleau family, a dowry at Naveil complemented what the Langeais family already held there (see map 1). So when Thibaut of Vendôme asserted this property belonged

---

72. *CTV,* vol. 2, no. 531, pp. 374–75.
73. AD Eure-et-Loir, H 2430. See also *CMPD,* no. 116, p. 110.
74. *MV,* nos. 1–5, pp. 1–10. See also no. 7, pp. 10–11, and no. 12, pp. 19–22.

to him, Hamelin challenged Thibaut's claim, and the monks assured him that no charters recorded either Thibaut's or his ancestors' claim to the land. Hamelin's contestation thus reminded the community of not only his marriage to Helvisa-Adierna but also the long association between their two families and the monks. The social hierarchy was also reinforced for Thibaut of Vendôme was clearly a man on the make. He frequently challenged gifts by families who were better established and more prestigious than his own in order to climb his way up the social ladder. Hamelin's counterclaim derailed this attempt, causing Thibaut's plan to backfire.

Aristocratic families were thus familiar with daughters and sons-in-law asserting their rights to family property. In some cases, nobles made more than one claim. Shortly after their marriage, Arnulf Ceotard and his wife asserted their right to property that her parents had granted to Marmoutier. This noble daughter's claim was strong, for when a *placitum* was called, the monks recognized this couple's right to the property by granting them part of the property as a life estate and providing them with countergifts.[75] The dispute worked well for this couple: they received property and community recognition of their connection to the bride's natal family and patrimony. About twenty years later, Arnulf, acting alone, made another claim to his wife's patrimony. This time he contested his father-in-law and mother-in-law's gift of an oven to the abbey of St. Trinité. Once again Arnulf's rights were recognized, for he was granted the right to bake bread in the oven free of charge.[76] The lack of any wifely participation in this act is significant and suggests that another family milestone had come to pass: Arnulf's wife's death. His claim, coming on the heels of her death, would remind his affinal kin, as well as the community, that his children still had a right to family holdings. Given that this contestation occurred about twenty years after his marriage, Arnulf's children were coming of age, and he sought to reaffirm their place in their mother's family.

A Life Cycle of Contestations: Death

As the example of Arnulf Ceotard indicates, death represented a transition point in the life cycle of aristocratic families that could trigger contestations. Bernard La Ferté was motivated both by death and the maturing of his children to claim and then quitclaim land from his wife's natal patrimony. The property that Bernard claimed pertained to what his father-in-law, Fulcher

---

75. *MV*, no. 157, pp. 251–54.
76. *CTV*, vol. 2, no. 303, p. 9.

of Fréteval, had given to the monks at Chamars (see appendix, chart 8). When he abandoned his claim, he was given a horse "from the charity of St. Martin."[77] Appearing with Bernard were his five sons and sole daughter. His wife, Hildeberg, was conspicuously absent and probably dead. The countergift of a horse would have been particularly useful to a man who had several sons coming of age or being trained as knights. Like Arnulf Ceotard, Bernard faced simultaneously two key moments in his family's life cycle: the death of his spouse and the maturation of his children. His direct blood tie to the house of Fréteval may have been severed, but his contestation reminded his affinal kin and fellow elites of his children's right to their mother's natal patrimony.

The death of fathers, in particular, represented the changing of the guard. As a new generation rose to prominence, positions within the family and control of family resources were negotiated and renegotiated. As part of this dynamic process, gifts made by parents were challenged. Recall that the daughters of Odo Dubellus both brought contestations to property their father had previously alienated from family coffers shortly after his death.[78] These sisters' disputes illustrate the complex motivations behind contestations. Since Helvisa-Adierna and her husband succeeded to the family honors, their contestation should be read as an attempt to assert their own independent identities as lords. Fredescind's dispute and eventual invasion of the property, however, was motivated by different concerns. She was seeking to remind kith and kin of her place in her family and her right to her natal patrimony. Although Fredescind's husband took the additional trouble of invading the land—beyond just contesting what had been given—they resolved their dispute easily, suggesting they had accomplished what they had set out to do.[79]

Given the density of the kinship ties that made up the Fréteval-Mondoubleau-Dives kindred, it is not surprising that some of its members felt they had to rigorously assert their rights to remind the community (and each other) of their place in this tangled network of kin and property. Adela of Bezai, the wife of Fulcher Dives, was a generous benefactor of the newly founded abbey of St. Trinité of Vendôme. She made extensive gifts and encouraged her family and vassals to do the same. As we know from previous contestations, not all of her benefactions remained undisputed. Her son Fulcher Turre needed to reconcile himself with the monks over the control of properties that his mother had earlier given to the church but that Fulcher

---

77. AD Eure-et-Loir, H 2271.
78. *CTV,* vol. 1, no. 46, pp. 99–100. See p. 215 of this chapter for further discussion.
79. *CTV,* vol. 1, no. 166, pp. 292–93.

had claimed as his own.[80] In return for conceding the property, the monks recorded in the charter that they extended Fulcher their *societas*. In this case, Fulcher's dispute and resolution resulted in the affirmation of his relationship with the monks, as well as calling attention to his descent from his mother and his place in a powerful aristocratic family.

Following the adage "like father, like son," Fulcher's son disputed a grant his father had made. In 1098, the monks noted that "Fulcher Turre had given to us the chapel at Lisle, for his soul. After his death, his son Jeremy took it away from us, but he then returned it."[81] The perfunctory tone of the record suggests that the dispute was nearly pro forma. Moreover, the description of the event suggests that Jeremy really did not intend to keep the property. Like other noble sons, he seized the opportunity to demonstrate that he was now lord. His actions were part of a dialogue of give-then-take-then-give-again.[82]

Bertran of Moncontour, Fulcher and Jeremy's cousin, also contested his father's gifts after his father died. In 1092 Bertran, who the monks described as "liking injustice," falsely claimed his father's gift and rampaged the monks' property with his men. The count of Vendôme called both parties to his court, where he found on behalf of Bertran.[83] Intriguingly, although he won his suit, Bertran remained concerned about his dispute and his relationship with the monks. For "eventually Bertran listened to the advise of his friends and an agreement was made. Bertran would get one third of the property in question to use for his lifetime, but it would revert to the monks once he died and none of his heirs would have a claim to it."[84] While Bertran won this dispute, six years later he was back in court. His father had made a gift to the monks, which many Turre kin witnessed. "But truly Bertran the *primogenitus* son of Robert was not there when the gift was made, and as a result of this, what his father had justly given he afterward unjustly claimed."[85]

---

80. *CTV,* vol. 1, no. 206, pp. 338–39.

81. *CTV,* vol. 2, no. 363, p. 109. Events seven years later caused the monks to have Jeremy reconfirm his quitclaim. In 1105, Count Geoffrey Martel died. The death of such a powerful political figure could potentially cause considerable disarray in the region, and amid the general upheaval nobles might try to take properties previously given to the church. Perhaps in an attempt to avoid such trouble, the monks called Jeremy to them to reassert their pact and had him ceremonialize their agreement by placing a sprig of fennel on the altar of their church and then place the same symbol in the hand of the abbot. *CTV,* vol. 1, no. 413, pp. 176–77.

82. Rosenwein, *To Be the Neighbor of St. Peter,* pp. 49–77.

83. *CTV,* vol. 2, no. 340, pp. 63–66.

84. Bertran's case is unusual, since most charters record only the monks' victories over those who brought claims.

85. *CTV,* vol. 2, no. 361, pp. 105–7.

Because Bertran wanted to go on Crusade, he quitclaimed his right to the property. The charter records that Bertran took the initiative in sending for the abbot of St. Trinité, who arranged for Bertran to publicly recognize his transgression against the monastery and renounce his claim.

A variety of motivations compelled Bertran to try to establish a right to his family lands. In the later act, he seems to have grounds for the dispute (a lack of consent), but for the 1092 dispute he did not. Bertran's right to property and his place in the lineage was revisited each time he disputed a gift. Indeed, just before departing for the Holy Land, Bertran himself sought public reconciliation with the monks over his contestation of one of his father's gift. Undoubtedly, he was motivated by concern for his immortal soul as he left on what promised to be a perilous venture. But Bertran may have had other issues weighing on his mind for his quitclaim also established his right and the rights of his children to Moncontour lands, rights which were further reinforced by the monks' grant of countergifts. Such recognition would have been important in an uncertain time. Would the crusaders' lands be protected from rapacious neighbors or kin? Would Bertran ever return?[86] Settling his dispute with the monks gave Bertran and his family spiritual and practical assurance at a key moment in their history.

Given the frequency with which crusaders' gifts were challenged, Bertran was perhaps wise to be concerned.[87] Bardolus, for example, contested a gift his crusader brother-in-law had made just before he left for the East, claiming that the land in question pertained to his (Bardolus's) wife's dowry. To settle the dispute, the monks offered him sixty *solidi,* and Bardolus, his wife Gervisa, and their children quitclaimed their right to the property in front of the chapter.[88] Bardolus used this claim to remind his affinal kin, but also the community at large, that Gervisa and their children had a right to her family's holdings. Although Gervisa was married and part of another kin group, she did not eschew her right (and through her, her children's right) to family property or abandon her place as a daughter of this house. Like Bertran of Moncontour, Bardolus's family was facing uncertainty: the departure of Bardolus's brother-in-law put into question who would have a claim to family property if he died on Crusade. While the disputant inevitably

---

86. For those going on the First Crusade, these questions must have been paramount. Riley-Smith, *The First Crusaders,* pp. 109–23; Bull, *Knightly Piety,* pp. 274–81; Brundage, "The Crusader's Wife," and "The Crusader's Wife Revisited."

87. For other examples, see this chapter, notes 49 and 50.

88. *Père,* vol. 2, no. 2, p. 516.

had to give up claim to the property, such actions were far from futile. The process of dispute and reconciliation served as a tool of remembrance that crystallized an individual's place in a complicated web of family ties and competing rights.

The noblewoman Hermensend also used a contestation as a means to reestablish her connection to property, and through it, her place in an extensive family network. After the death of her father in 1065, Hermensend disputed what her father had sold (along with his brothers) to the abbey of Marmoutier. Interestingly, she insisted that she be given a measure of tapestry in return for her consent to the gift. Perhaps she intended to use this tapestry as a visual reminder of her right. Apparently fresh out of the requested tapestry, the monks gave Hermensend and her husband ten *solidi* instead, and the dispute was resolved.[89] While she was not successful in gaining back the land, this does not seem to have been her intention. She demanded, and was granted, recognition of her connection to the property. Given that one of her uncle's kin had already made a claim, Hermensend was motivated by a need to reinsert herself into the family tree. Contestations of this sort were apparently so common that the monks of Marmoutier tried to circumvent such claims when arranging gifts. For example, when Ascelin sold part of his mill to the monks, his children and kin were granted a countergift with the agreement that "if after the death of their father, a claim is brought, they will testify that the monks had acquired the mill free from claims."[90] In spite of this precaution, the sale was disputed after Ascelin's death—although *not* by one of his children, who presumably lived up to their agreement with the monks and testified on their behalf.

Even when the monks could prove (or claimed they could prove) that a parent had given property to the church, aristocratic sons and daughters were known to ignore them and made claims anyway. In 1100, Hugh and Pagan contested Marmoutier's possession of a mill and continued their dispute even after the monks produced a charter that recorded their father "conceded the mill at court in front of many people."[91] The monks, however, were interested in making peace. So they sent one of their own to broker a deal with the brothers: the monks agreed to pay the pair thirty-one *solidi,* for which the brothers, their mother, and other siblings would concede that the monks possessed the mill. About two generations earlier, sometime between 1032 and 1064, Maurice challenged what his father had given to the church. He

---

89. *MV,* no. 54, pp. 88–89.
90. *MB,* no. 58, pp. 67–68.
91. *MB,* no. 77, pp. 87–88.

"brought a claim against the gift and violently took the property from the monks." Peace was eventually restored between Maurice and Marmoutier, however, when he relinquished his claim in exchange for ten *solidi* and was granted the *societas* of the monks. In return, Maurice quitclaimed his right and swore that his progenitor had made the gift.[92] In addition to calling attention to Maurice's place as his father's heir and his right to the property, the settlement of this claim also ensured his continued association with the monks through the extension of their *societas*. Maurice and his connection to this property would thus be recalled every time the monks included him in their prayers.

Even when nobles received no compensation for their claim, contestations served a useful purpose. When his case was heard, Robert of Marcilly was forced to admit that he had no legitimate claim. His mother and sister also abandoned any right they had to the property. In this case, the recognition of a *lack* of rights served to reinforce that the parties were part of a kin group who once had rights to and were identified with this property. The descendants of Archbishop Arnulf of Tours were also unsuccessful in contesting a grant by their prominent relative. While their claim was proven to be void, they did get their claim heard in the count's court, affirming their relationship with their illustrious ancestor.[93] After the death of Fulco, his son Hugo contested a gift because he had been a child when he had consented. "Now an adult, motivated by greed, Hugo invaded the *vicaria* that his father had given; but after he accepted thirty *solidi* from us, the *vicaria*, which he had unjustly invaded, he relinquished and quitclaimed, with his brother Warin, and publicly placed [a symbol] upon the altar of holy Peter."[94] Given that most elites did not win their case, why did they actively assert their rights to property? Did they actually think they could win? Perhaps they did, since in some cases at least they seized the property or were granted something in return. But such actions came at a high price. While some nobles seem unfazed by threats of excommunication, this was clearly not true of all elites. So what did they hope to gain? Recognition of their place in a vast and tangled skein of relationships and rights to property. For many, such recognition was worth the cost.

---

92. *MB,* no. 18, pp. 22–23. Linda Seidel argues that the community of St. Lazare of Autun used a sculptural program as a way of discouraging any claims donors might be tempted to bring to gifts made to the abbey. Linda Seidel, *Legends in Limestone,* pp. 145–61.

93. *MB,* no. 59, pp. 68–69.

94. *Père,* vol. 1, no. 85, pp. 209–10.

Conclusion

Property disputes are thus far more nuanced than they first appear. Most were not due to "greed," as Bernard of Angers and Guibert so passionately declaimed. In a society where the granting of property had so many facets, disputes over property were also complicated. A gift was a useful, indeed powerful, political tool that could bind individuals together and create networks of power and alliance. The giving of gifts was also charged with religious meaning as elites sought to associate themselves with the divine and God's servants. Property grants, therefore, were an essential part of the fabric of noble political, religious, economic, cultural, and family life. Is it any surprise, then, that contestations were imbued with rich cultural resonance?

Contestations were a natural by-product of the broad and inclusive family structures in place in the lands of the Loire. Like the donation process, contesting a gift provided the noble born with a stage on which they could enact their family relationships. The fact that many contestations were made at key points of transition (marriage and death mostly) suggests that disputants were unsure or anxious about the changes looming on the horizon.

As one generation yielded to another, as new families were formed and new bonds forged, noblemen and women asserted their right to property and their place in a large and complex family by contesting what their relatives had given to the church. These actions resulted in a review of the individual's right to the property and connection to the family that had donated it. As the monks refuted the claimant's suit, kinship ties were heralded. Scholars have long puzzled over how little nobles seemed to gain materially from such actions—a few *solidi* here and there. Yet the rewards of establishing one's position in the family tree were invaluable, for it conveyed prestige, identity, and belonging, as well as rights to property. Family was the life force for medieval aristocrats, for family determined one's place in the social and power hierarchies of the time. Is it any wonder, then, that aristocrats would seize any opportunity to remind their neighbors, friends, family, and confessors of their place in their kindred? Contestations were merely one more strand in the tapestry of aristocratic life that could be employed to showcase family ties and connections. As a monk and then abbot whose monastery was the target of contestations, Guibert of Nogent would naturally criticize such actions. But as a member of the medieval aristocracy, he would likely have understood them.

Conclusion

Out of Love for My Kin

To end this discussion of aristocratic family life, it is appropriate to come full circle to where we began in the introduction: the Minter family. The charters recorded that Adelina and Walter Minter chose to divide their holdings among all of their children, and that the couple acted in tandem in deciding the future of their progeny and property. Furthermore, although Adelina had two adult sons at the time of Walter's death, she remained in control of family holdings and acted as head of the family. These experiences are clearly at odds with modern assumptions of patrilineage, patriarchy, and primogeniture for the aristocratic family of the central Middle Ages. Indeed, the lives examined here have shown that the Minters were not exceptional and the fallibility of these assumptions.

The aristocrats living in the lands of the Loire in the years between 1000 and 1200 witnessed significant social, political, and economic transformations. These changes were so profound that scholars expected a family revolution to accompany the "feudal revolution." But the Duby-Schmid model of family life does not dovetail with the lived experience of medieval aristocrats. A tectonic shift in family structure from a collateral, inclusive pattern to patrilineage, primogeniture, and exclusion did not occur in this region in these centuries. The twelfth-century lords and ladies of Montigny, for example, would have experienced family life in much the same way as their late Carolingian predecessors. This is not to say that adjustments were not made. Evidence of changes in inheritance is apparent, often generation by generation. Nor is this to suggest that there were not disputes or tensions within families. There certainly were. Children disputed what their parents had given. Siblings objected when lands were alienated. Sons-in-law took back movable property their in-laws had donated. But this was not the totality of an aristocrat's interactions with his or her family. There were also times of mutual support, intercession, and affection.

So we are left with a dilemma. If patriarchy, patrilineage, and primogeniture do not encapsulate the family life of medieval aristocrats, what does? What new lexicon can we use to be true to the family experiences of medieval elites? The evidence from the lands of the Loire suggests qualities such as cooperation, affection, and parity, and descriptors such as supportive and collateral. But these traits rest firmly on one underlying ethos: inclusion.

Inclusion best describes the configuration of aristocratic kinship. The noble born of the Loire region did not adhere to lineages. Not one charter describes a noble family in linear terms. Rather, words that emphasized the breadth of kin, such as *parentes* and *parentela,* were employed. Going beyond semantics, the experiences recorded in the documents testify to the various and important roles that relatives assumed in each other's lives. Extended, affinal, and immediate family participated in charters as witnesses, guarantors, and consenters. Relatives intervened with the monks on behalf of their kin. They acted as guardians for minor children. Affection, too, was a feature of aristocratic families. Parents loved their children and each other. Siblings provided care and attended to one another. Uncles protected their young charges. Cousins were even willing to lay down their lives for their kin.

The strategies that aristocratic families employed to distribute resources also rest upon inclusion. Most families adopted inheritance practices that were aimed at providing support for the many rather than the one. Patrimonies were divided among children. Collectives of kin ranging from groups of siblings to cousins inherited property together. Claims made to donations further underscore the rights that a range of kin exercised to family property. Cousins, siblings, and in-laws as well as children contested gifts based on the assertion that their right to the property had been violated or overlooked. The granting of countergifts and the compromises arranged to resolve disputes reinforce the claims that aristocrats—even those born on the wrong side of the blanket—had to property.

Inclusion also characterizes marriage among the nobles of the lands of the Loire. These noble families did not deem marriage the sole privilege of the eldest son. Instead, marriage was an important tool for expanding family power and garnering influential allies. Consequently, with few exceptions, all sons and daughters could expect to marry. As wives, noblewomen were included in the control of family property, with all of its responsibilities and powers. They acted as co-lords with their husbands and, in most cases, were able to assume sole control of patrimonies and children in the absence of their spouse. The provisions made at marriage and aristocratic women's control of these properties provide testimony to their important place in the family. Inclusion also describes noble wives' place in their natal and affinal families. Once married, women did not lose their identity as members of their natal family, and many took action in the form of contestations to revisit their place in their natal kindred. Wives also became important and recognized members of their new affinal family. These women were not subsumed into the patriarchy or viewed as hostile outsiders. On the contrary, they were respected members of both families and used their influence—both material and spiritual—to the betterment of each.

Threads of patrilineage, primogeniture, and patriarchy were interwoven into the tapestry of the lives of medieval elites. They were not the dominant hues, however, but merely part of the warp and woof of aristocratic society. The recovered lives of Viscount Evrard I of Chartres, Domitilla of Vendôme, Lord Ivo of Courville, Bertran of Moncontour, Vicedomina Helisend of Chartres, Matthew Griponis, Eufemia Garembert, and the many others examined here, all add something new to our understanding of aristocratic family life and demonstrate the considerable diversity of aristocratic experience. In analyzing their lives, it becomes obvious that our perception of aristocratic families needs to be readjusted. Medieval elites living in the lands of the Loire in these centuries, on balance, experienced family life in positive and inclusive ways. Their experiences, in combination with evidence from other parts of medieval Europe, call out for a new way of conceptualizing family life. It is time to abandon the old model of patrilineage, primogeniture, and repressive patriarchy and replace it with an understanding that aristocratic families were inherently inclusive. The scene that the eighteenth-century poet Oliver Goldsmith described of families gamboling on the banks of the Loire River in his own time could easily describe those living in medieval centuries. It is not difficult to imagine that Helvisa-Adierna of Langeais "led [her] children through the mirthful maze," or that William Gouet, "the gay grandsire, skill'd in gestic lore," regaled his grandchildren with tales of his time on Crusades.[1]

---

1. Oliver Goldsmith, "The Traveller," in *The Traveller and the Deserted Village,* ed. Horatio Nelson Drury (New York: D. Appleton, 1910), lines 239 and 269.

Genealogical Charts

Chart 1. The Counts of Chartres

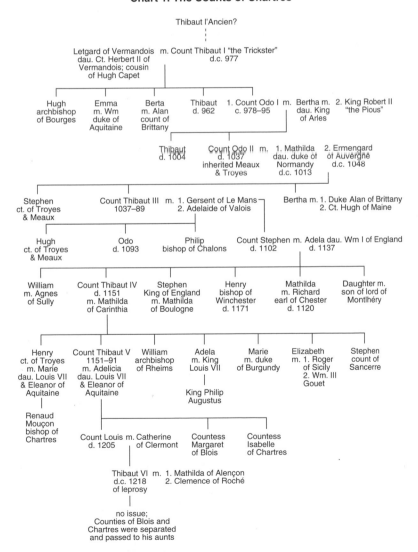

Chart 2. The Viscounts of Châteaudun to c. 1200

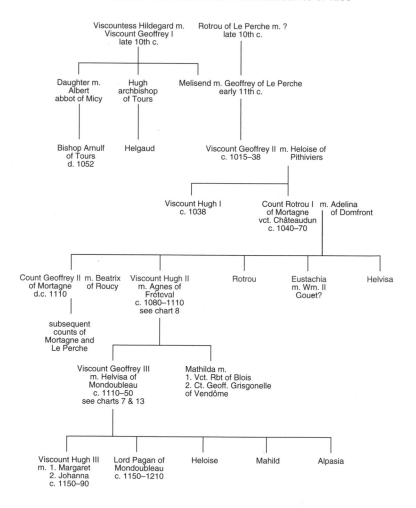

Chart 3. The Viscounts of Chartres

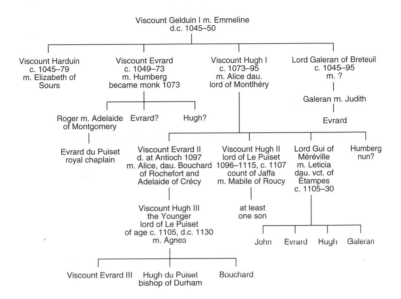

Viscount Gelduin I m. Emmeline
d.c. 1045–50

- Viscount Harduin
c. 1045–79
m. Elizabeth of
Sours
- Viscount Evrard
c. 1049–73
m. Humberg
became monk 1073
- Viscount Hugh I
c. 1073–95
m. Alice dau.
lord of Montlhéry
- Lord Galeran of Breteuil
c. 1045–95
m. ?

Galeran m. Judith

Evrard

Roger m. Adelaide   Evrard?   Hugh?
of Montgomery

Evrard du Puiset
royal chaplain

Viscount Evrard II
d. at Antioch 1097
m. Alice, dau. Bouchard
of Rochefort and
Adelaide of Crécy

Viscount Hugh II
lord of Le Puiset
1096–1115, c. 1107
count of Jaffa
m. Mabile of Roucy

Lord Gui of
Méréville
m. Leticia
dau. vct. of
Étampes
c. 1105–30

Humberg
nun?

Viscount Hugh III
the Younger
lord of Le Puiset
of age c. 1105, d.c. 1130
m. Agnes

at least
one son

John   Evrard   Hugh   Galeran

Viscount Evrard III   Hugh du Puiset   Bouchard
bishop of Durham

Chart 4. The Vidames of Chartres

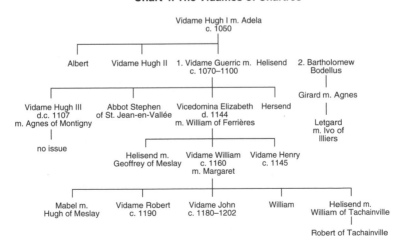

Vidame Hugh I m. Adela
c. 1050

- Albert
- Vidame Hugh II
- 1. Vidame Guerric m. Helisend
c. 1070–1100
- 2. Bartholomew
Bodellus

Girard m. Agnes

Vidame Hugh III
d.c. 1107
m. Agnes of Montigny

Abbot Stephen
of St. Jean-en-Vallée

Vicedomina Elizabeth   Hersend
d. 1144
m. William of Ferrières

Letgard
m. Ivo of
Illiers

no issue

Helisend m.
Geoffrey of Meslay

Vidame William
c. 1160
m. Margaret

Vidame Henry
c. 1145

Mabel m.
Hugh of Meslay

Vidame Robert
c. 1190

Vidame John
c. 1180–1202

William

Helisend m.
William of Tachainville

Robert of Tachainville

Chart 5. The Lords of Alluyes-Gouet

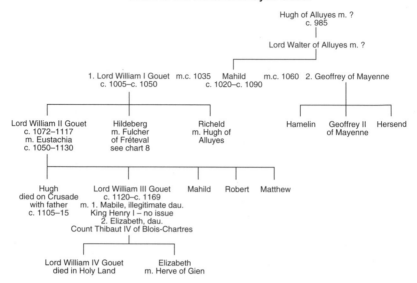

Chart 6. The Lords of Montigny

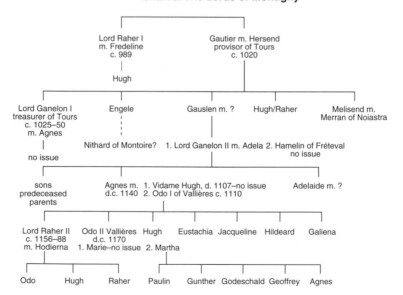

Chart 7. The Fréteval-Mondoubleau-Dives Kindred

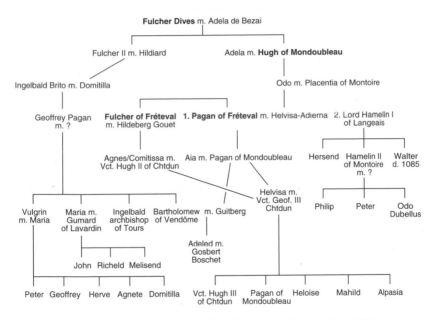

Names in **bold face** indicate the founders of the Fréteval, Mondoubleau, and Dives families.

Chart 8. The Lords of Fréteval

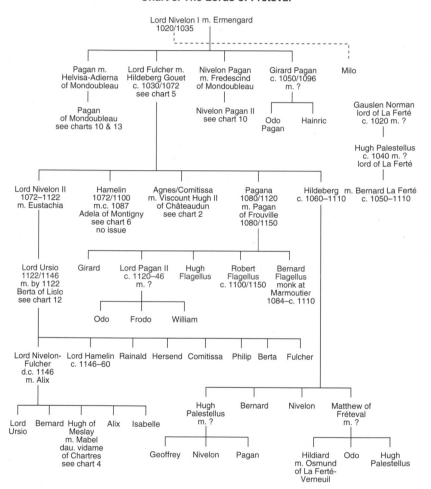

Chart 9. The Dives Family

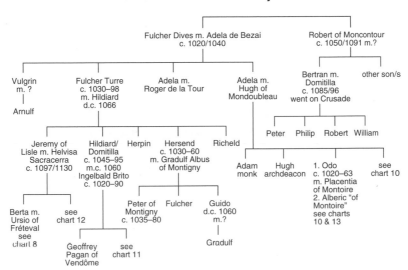

Fulcher Dives m. Adela de Bezai
c. 1020/1040

Robert of Moncontour
c. 1050/1091 m.?

Vulgrin
m. ?

Arnulf

Fulcher Turre
c. 1030–98
m. Hildiard
d.c. 1066

Adela m.
Roger de la Tour

Adela m.
Hugh of
Mondoubleau

Bertran m.
Domitilla
c. 1085/96
went on Crusade

other son/s

Peter   Philip   Robert   William

Jeremy of
Lisle m. Helvisa
Sacracerra
c. 1097/1130

Hildiard/
Domitilla
c. 1045–95
m.c. 1060
Ingelbald Brito
c. 1020–90

Herpin

Hersend
c. 1030–60
m. Gradulf Albus
of Montigny

Richeld

Adam
monk

Hugh
archdeacon

1. Odo
c. 1020–63
m. Placentia
of Montoire
2. Alberic "of
Montoire"
see charts
10 & 13

see
chart 10

Berta m.
Ursio of
Fréteval
see
chart 8

see
chart 12

Peter of
Montigny
c. 1035–80

Fulcher

Guido
d.c. 1060
m.?

Gradulf

Geoffrey
Pagan of
Vendôme

see
chart 11

Chart 10. The Lords of Mondoubleau

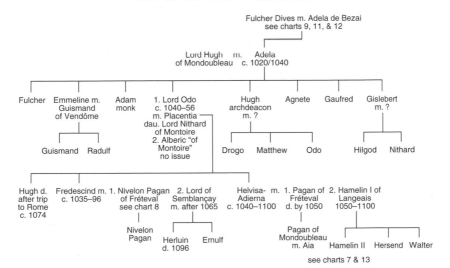

Fulcher Dives m. Adela de Bezai
see charts 9, 11, & 12

Lord Hugh   m.   Adela
of Mondoubleau   c. 1020/1040

Fulcher

Emmeline m.
Guismand
of Vendôme

Adam
monk

1. Lord Odo
c. 1040–56
m. Placentia
dau. Lord Nithard
of Montoire
2. Alberic "of
Montoire"
no issue

Hugh
archdeacon
m. ?

Agnete

Gaufred

Gislebert
m. ?

Guismand   Radulf

Drogo   Matthew   Odo

Hilgod   Nithard

Hugh d.
after trip
to Rome
c. 1074

Fredescind m.
c. 1035–96

1. Nivelon Pagan
of Fréteval
see chart 8

2. Lord of
Semblançay
m. after 1065

Helvisa- m.
Adierna
c. 1040–1100

1. Pagan of
Fréteval
d. by 1050

2. Hamelin I of
Langeais
1050–1100

Nivelon
Pagan

Herluin
d. 1096

Ernulf

Pagan of
Mondoubleau
m. Aia

Hamelin II   Hersend   Walter

see charts 7 & 13

Chart 11. The Descendants of Ingelbald Brito and Domitilla of Vendôme

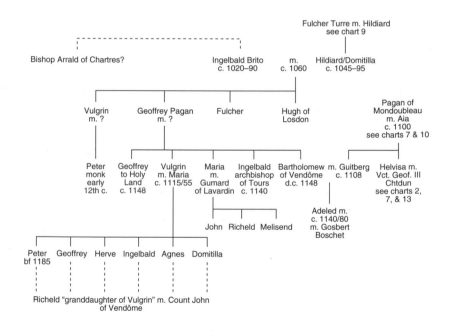

Chart 12. The Lords of Lisle

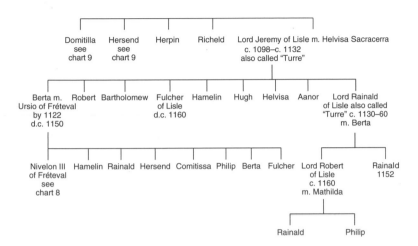

Chart 13. The Lords of Langeais

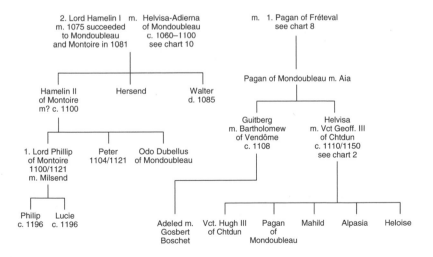

✒ WORKS CITED

Archival Sources

Archives départementales d'Eure-et-Loir (Chartres)

H 201	H 2271	H 2389	H 4332
H 359	H 2272	H 2429	H 4333
H 500	H 2275	H 2430	H 4385
H 505	H 2280	H 2431	H 4408
H 570	H 2302	H 2514	H 4455
H 1417	H 2305	H 3114	H 4491
H 1422	H 2307	H 3260	H 4545
H 1896	H 2308	H 3261	H 4557
H 2237	H 2350	H 3451	H 4861
H 2268	H 2358	H 4275	
H 2270	H 2367	H 4288	

Archives départementales de Loir-et-Cher (Blois)

16 H 49	16 H 83	16 H 105	21 H 40
16 H 77	16 H 84	16 H 118	21 H 69
16 H 80	16 H 87	16 H 119	
16 H 81	16 H 88	16 H 120	

Archives départementales de Maine-et-Loire (Angers)

39 H 2
H 3107
H 3245
H 3497

Bibliothèque nationale de France (Paris)

MS Latin 991

Published Primary Sources

Abbot Suger. *The Deeds of Louis the Fat.* Translated by Richard Cusimano and John
    Moorhead. Washington, DC: Catholic University of America Press, 1992.

———. *Vie de Louis VI.* Translated and edited by Henri Waquet. Paris: Société d'édition les Belles-Lettres, 1964.

Abelard, Peter. *Historia calamitatum.* In *The Letters of Abelard and Heloise.* Translated by Betty Radice. London: Penguin Classics, 1974.

Benton, John F., trans. and ed. *Self and Society in Medieval France: The Memoirs of Abbot Guibert of Nogent.* Toronto: University of Toronto Press, 1985.

Bernard of Angers. *The Book of St. Foy.* Translated and edited by Pamela Sheingorn. Philadelphia: University of Pennsylvania Press, 1995.

Cartulaire de l'abbaye cardinale de la Trinité de Vendôme. 5 vols. Edited by Charles Métais. Paris: Picard, 1893–1904.

Cartulaire de l'abbaye de la Sainte-Trinité de Tiron. 2 vols. Edited by Lucien Merlet. Chartres: Garnier, 1883.

Cartulaire de l'abbaye de Saint Vincent du Mans (ordre de Saint-Benoît). Edited by Robert Charles and Vicomte Menjot d'Elbenne. Le Mans: Fleury, 1886–1913.

Cartulaire de l'abbaye Saint-Florentin de Bonneval. Edited by Albert Sidoisne. Bibliothèque Albert Sidoisne, Bonneval, Microfilm, n.d.

Cartulaire de Marmoutier pour le Dunois. Edited by Emile Mabille. Châteaudun: Lecesne, 1874.

Cartulaire de Marmoutier pour le Vendômois. Edited by Charles Auguste de Trémault. Paris: Picard, 1893.

Cartulaire de Notre Dame de Chartres d'après les cartulaires et les titres originaux. 3 vols. Edited by Eugène de Lépinois and Lucien Merlet. Chartres: Garnier, 1862–65.

Cartulaire de Notre-Dame de Josaphat. 2 vols. Edited by Charles Métais. Chartres: Garnier, 1911–12.

Cartulaire de Saint-Jean-en-Vallée de Chartres. Edited by René Merlet. Chartres: Garnier, 1906.

Cartulaire de Saint-Père de Chartres. 2 vols. Edited by Benjamin Guérard. Paris: Crapelet, 1840.

Cartulaire du prieuré bénédictin de Saint-Gondon-sur-Loire (866–1172) tire des archives de l'abbaye de Saint-Florent près Saumur. Edited by Paul Marchegay. Les Roche—Baritaude: Forrest et Grimaud, 1879.

Cartulaire manceau de Marmoutier. 2 vols. Edited by Ernest Laurain. Laval: Imprimerie-Librairie Vicomte A. Goupil, 1911–45.

Catalogue des actes de Henri Ier, roi de France (1031–1060). Edited by Frédéric Soehnée. Paris: Champion, 1907.

Catalogue des actes de Robert II. Edited by William F. Newman. Paris: Librairie du Recueil Sirey, 1937.

Chartes Vendômoises. Edited by Charles Métais. Vendôme: Société Archéologique, Scientifique et Littéraire du Vendômois, 1905.

Chronica de gestis consulum Andegavorum. In *Chroniques des comtes d'Anjou et des seigneurs d'Amboise,* edited by Louis Halphen and René Poupardin. Paris: Picard, 1913.

Chroniques des comtes d'Anjou et des seigneurs d'Amboise. Edited by Louis Halphen and René Poupardin. Paris: Picard, 1913.

de Troyes, Chrétien. *Arthurian Romances.* Translated by William Kibler and Carelton W. Carroll. London: Penguin Classics, 1991.

Evergates, Theodore, trans. and ed. *Feudal Society in Medieval France: Documents from the County of Champagne.* Philadelphia: University of Pennsylvania Press, 1993.

Fulbert of Chartres. *The Letters and Poems of Fulbert of Chartres.* Translated and edited by Frederick Behrends. Oxford: Oxford University Press, 1976.

Geoffrey of Vendôme. *Oeuvres.* Translated and edited by Geneviève Giordanengo. Turnhout, Belgium: Brepols and éditions CNRS, 1996.

Gesta Ambaziensium dominorum. In *Chroniques des comtes d'Anjou et des seigneurs d'Amboise,* edited by Louis Halphen and René Poupardin. Paris: Picard, 1913.

Gilsdorf, Sean, trans. *Queenship and Sanctity: The Lives of Mathilda and the Epitaph of Adelheid.* Washington, DC: Catholic University of America Press, 2004.

Glaber, Raoul. *Opera.* Edited by John France, Neithard Bulst, and Paul Reynolds. Oxford: Oxford University Press, 1989.

Head, Thomas, trans. and ed. *Medieval Hagiography: An Anthology.* New York: Routledge, 2001.

Ivo of Chartres. *Lettres de Saint Yves.* Translated and edited by Lucien Merlet. Chartres: Garnier, 1885.

Ivo of Chartres. *Yves de Chartres: Correspondence.* Translated and edited by Jean Leclercq. Paris: Les Belles-Lettres, 1949.

Krey, August C., trans. and ed. *The First Crusade: The Account of Eye-Witnesses and Participants.* Princeton, NJ: Princeton University Press, 1921.

Lambert of Ardres. *The History of the Counts of Guines and Lords of Ardres.* Translated by Leah Shopkow. Philadelphia: University of Pennsylvania Press, 2001.

Luchaire, Achille. *Louis VI le Gros: Annales de sa vie et de son règne (1081–1137).* Paris: Picard, 1890.

Marie de France. *The Lais of Marie de France.* Translated and edited by Robert Hanning and Joan Ferrante. Durham, NC: Labyrinth Press, 1978.

Marmoutier-cartulaire Blésois. Edited by Charles Métais. Blois: Moreau, 1889–91.

Merlet, René, ed. "Petite chronique de l'abbaye de Bonneval de 857 à 1050 environ." *MSAEL* 10 (1896): 14–38.

———, and Abbott Clerval, eds. *Un manuscrit Chartrain du XI siècle.* Chartres: Garnier, 1893.

Obituaires de la province de Sens. Edited by Auguste Molinier and August Longnon. Vol. 2, *Diocèse de Chartres.* Paris: Klincksieck, 1906.

Orderic Vitalis. *The Ecclesiastical History.* 6 vols. Translated and edited by Marjorie Chibnall. Oxford: Oxford University Press, 1969–81.

Recueil des actes de Philippe Ier, roi de France (1059–1108). Edited by Maurice Prou. Paris: Académie des Inscriptions et Belles-Lettres, 1908.

Regesta pontificum Romanorum ab condita ecclesia ad annum post Christum natum 1198. Edited by Philipp Jaffé. 2 vols. 2nd rev. ed. Leipzig: Veit, 1885–88.

Sacrorum Conciliorum nova et amplissima collectio. Edited by Giovanni Domenico Mansi et al. 35 vols. Venice: Graz, Akademische Drucken Verlagsanstalt, 1774–75.

Saint-Denis de Nogent-le-Rotrou, 1031–1789, histoire et cartulaire. Edited by Vicomte de Souance and Charles Métais. Vannes: Lafolye, 1894.

Secondary Sources

Amado, Claudie Duhamel. "Donation maritale et dot parentale: Pratiques aristocratiques languedociennes aux Xe-XIe siècles." In *Dots et douaires dans le haut*

Moyen Âge, edited by François Bougard, Laurent Feller, and Régine Le Jan, pp. 153–70. Rome: École Française de Rome, 2002.

——. "Femmes entre elles: Filles et épouses languedociennes (XIe-XIIe siècles)." In *Femmes-mariages-lignages, XIIe-XIVe siècles: Mélanges offerts à Georges Duby,* edited by Jean Dufournet, Michel Jezierski, André Joris, and Pierre Toubert, pp. 125–56. Brussels: De Boek Université, 1992.

Atkinson, Clarissa. *The Oldest Vocation: Christian Motherhood in the Middle Ages.* Ithaca, NY: Cornell University Press, 1991.

Aurell, Martin, ed. *Le médiéviste et la monographie familiale: Sources, méthodes et problématiques.* Turnhout, Belgium: Brepols, 2004.

——. "Stratégies matrimoniales de l'aristocratie (IXe-XIIIe siècle)." In *Mariage et sexualité au Moyen Âge. Accord ou crise?* edited by Michel Rouche, pp. 185–202. Paris: Sorbonne, 2000.

Aurell I Cardona, Martin. "Les avatars de la viduité princière: Ermessende (ca. 975–1058), comtesse de Barcelone." In *Veuves et veuvage dans le haut Moyen Âge,* edited by Michel Parisse, pp. 201–33. Paris: Picard, 1993.

Bachrach, Bernard S. "The Cost of Castle Building: The Case of the Tower at Langeais, 992–994." In *The Medieval Castle: Romance and Reality,* edited by Kathryn Reyerson, pp. 46–62. Dubuque, IA: Center for Medieval Studies, 1984.

——. *Fulk Nerra: The Neo-Roman Consul, 987–1040.* Berkeley: University of California Press, 1993.

——. "Robert of Blois: Abbot of St. Florent de Saumur and St. Mesmin de Micy (985–1011): A Study in Small Power Politics." *Revue bénédictine* 90 (1980): 249–62.

——. "Some Observations on the Origins of Countess Gerberga of the Angevins: An Essay in the Application of the Tellenbach-Werner Prosopographical Method." *Medieval Prosopography* 7 (1986): 1–23.

Baldwin, John W. *Aristocratic Life in Medieval France: The Romances of Jean Renart and Gerbert de Montreuil, 1190–1230.* Baltimore: Johns Hopkins University Press, 2000.

Barker, Lynn. "Ivo of Chartres and the Anglo-Norman Cultural Tradition." *Anglo-Norman Studies* 13 (1990): 15–33.

——. "Ivo of Chartres and the Anselm of Canterbury." *Anselm Studies* 2 (1988): 13–33.

Barthélemy, Dominique. "Castles, Barons, and Vavassors in the Vendômois and Neighboring Regions in the Eleventh and Twelfth Centuries." In *Cultures of Power,* edited by Thomas N. Bisson, pp. 56–68. Philadelphia: University of Pennsylvania Press, 1995.

——. "Debate: The 'Feudal Revolution' I." *Past and Present* 152 (1996): 196–205.

——. "Kinship." In *A History of Private Life,* vol. 2, *Revelations of the Medieval Worlds,* edited by Georges Duby, translated by Arthur Goldhammer, pp. 88–105. Cambridge, MA: Harvard University Press, 1988.

——. "La mutation féodale a-t-elle eu lieu?" *AESC* 47 (1992): 767–77.

——. "Note sur les cartulaires de Marmoutier (Touraine) au XIe siècle." In *Les Cartulaires,* edited by Oliver Guyotjeannin, Laurent Morelle, and Michel Parisse, pp. 247–59. Paris: École des Chartes, 1993.

———. *La société dans le comté de Vendôme de l'an mil au XIVe siècle.* Paris: Fayard, 1993.

Barton, Richard. *Lordship in the County of Maine, c. 890–1160.* Woodbridge, UK: Boydell Press, 2004.

———. "'Zealous Anger' and the Renegotiation of Aristocratic Relationships in Eleventh- and Twelfth-Century France." In *Anger's Past: The Social Uses of an Emotion in the Middle Ages,* edited by Barbara Rosenwein, pp. 153–70. Ithaca, NY: Cornell University Press, 1998.

Bauduin, Pierre. "Désigner les parents: Le champs de la parenté dans l'œuvre des premiers chroniques normands." *Anglo-Norman Studies* 25 (2001): 71–84.

Beck, Bernard. *Saint Bernard de Tiron, l'ermite, le moine et le monde.* Paris: Mandragore, 1998.

Beech, George T. "Les noms de personne poitevins du 9e au 12e siècle." *Revue internationale d'onomastique* 26 (1974): 81–100.

———. *A Rural Society in Medieval France: The Gâtine of Poitou in the Eleventh and Twelfth Centuries.* Baltimore: Johns Hopkins University Press, 1964.

Beech, George T., Monique Bourin, and Pascal Chareille, eds. *Personal Names and Studies of Medieval Europe: Social Identity and Familial Structures.* Kalamazoo, MI: Medieval Institute Publications, 2002.

Bell, Susan Groag. "Medieval Women Book Owners: Arbiters of Lay Piety and Ambassadors of Culture." In *Women and Power in the Middle Ages,* edited by Mary Erler and Maryanne Kowaleski, pp. 149–87. Athens: University of Georgia Press, 1988.

Bennett, Judith. *A Medieval Life: Cecilia Penifader of Brigstock, c. 1295–1344.* New York: McGraw Hill, 2000.

Berkhofer, Robert F., III. *Day of Reckoning: Power and Accountability in Medieval France.* Philadelphia: University of Pennsylvania Press, 2004.

Bisson, Thomas N. *The Crisis of the Twelfth Century: Power, Lordship, and the Origins of European Government.* Princeton, NJ: Princeton University Press, 2008.

———. "The 'Feudal Revolution.'" *Past and Present* 142 (1994): 6–42.

———. "Nobility and Family in Medieval France." *French Historical Studies* 16 (1990): 597–613.

———. "Princely Nobility in an Age of Ambition (1050–1150)." In *Nobles and Nobility in Medieval Europe: Concepts, Origins and Transformations,* edited by Anne E. Dugan, pp. 101–13. Woodbridge, UK: Boydell Press, 2000.

Bloch, Marc. *Feudal Society.* Translated by Louis Manyon. 2 vols. Chicago: University of Chicago Press, 1961.

Bloch, R. Howard. *Etymologies and Genealogies: A Literary Anthropology of the French Middle Ages.* Chicago: University of Chicago Press, 1986.

———. *Medieval Misogyny and the Invention of Western Romantic Love.* Chicago: University of Chicago Press, 1992.

Bouchard, Constance Brittain. "The Bosonids: Or Rising to Power in the Late Carolingian Age." *French Historical Studies* 15 (1988): 407–31. Reprinted in Bouchard, *Those of My Blood,* pp. 74–97.

———. "The Carolingian Creation of a Model of Patrilineage." In *Paradigms and Methods in Early Medieval Studies,* edited by Celia Chazelle and Felice Lifshitz, pp. 135–51. New York: Palgrave MacMillan, 2007.

——. "Consanguinity and Noble Marriages in the Tenth and Eleventh Centuries." *Speculum* 56 (1981): 268–87. Reprinted in Bouchard, *Those of My Blood,* pp. 39–58.

——. *Every Valley Shall Be Exalted: The Discourse of Opposites in Twelfth-Century Thought.* Ithaca, NY: Cornell University Press, 2003.

——. "Family Structure and Family Consciousness among the Aristocracy in the Ninth to the Eleventh Centuries." *Francia* 14 (1986): 639–58. Reprinted in Bouchard, *Those of My Blood,* pp. 59–73.

——. "Genealogy and Politics: The Counts of Autun and Countess Adelaide of Chalon." In *Those of My Blood,* pp. 135–54. Philadelphia: University of Pennsylvania Press, 2000.

——. "The Geographical, Social and Ecclesiastical Origins of the Bishops of Auxerre and Sens in the Central Middle Ages." *Church History* 46 (1977): 277–95.

——. *Holy Entrepreneurs: Cistercians, Knights, and Economic Exchange in Twelfth-Century Burgundy.* Ithaca, NY: Cornell University Press, 1991.

——. "Laymen and Church Reform around the Year 1000: The Case of Otto-William, the Count of Burgundy." *Journal of Medieval History* 5 (1979): 1–10.

——. "The Migration of Women's Names in the Upper Nobility, Ninth–Twelfth Centuries." *Medieval Prosopography* 9/2 (1988): 1–19. Reprinted in Bouchard, *Those of My Blood,* pp. 120–34.

——. "Noble Piety and Reformed Monasticism: The Dukes of Burgundy in the Twelfth Century." In *Noble Piety and Reformed Monasticism: Studies in Medieval Cistercian History VII,* edited by E. Rozanne Elder, pp. 1–9. Kalamazoo, MI: Cistercian Publications, 1981.

——. "The Origins of the French Nobility: A Reassessment." *AHR* 86 (1981): 501–32. Reprinted in Bouchard, *Those of My Blood,* pp. 13–38.

——. "Patterns of Women's Names in Royal Lineages, Ninth–Eleventh Centuries." *Medieval Prosopography* 9/1 (1988): 1–32. Reprinted in Bouchard, *Those of My Blood,* pp. 98–119.

——. *Spirituality and Administration: The Role of the Bishop in Twelfth-Century Auxerre.* Cambridge, MA: Harvard University Press, 1979.

——. *"Strong of Body, Brave and Noble": Chivalry and Society in Medieval France.* Ithaca, NY: Cornell University Press, 1998.

——. "The Structure of a Twelfth-Century French Family: The Lords of Seignelay." *Viator* 10 (1979): 39–56. Revised as "Twelfth-Century Family Structures" in Bouchard, *Those of My Blood,* pp. 155–74.

——. *Sword, Miter, and Cloister: Nobility and the Church in Burgundy, 980–1198.* Ithaca, NY: Cornell University Press, 1987.

——. *"Those of My Blood": Constructing Noble Families in Medieval Francia.* Philadelphia: University of Pennsylvania Press, 2001.

——. "Twelfth-Century Family Structures." Revision of "The Structure of a Twelfth-Century French Family: The Lords of Seignelay," in Bouchard, *Those of My Blood,* pp. 155–74.

Bougard, François, Laurent Feller, and Régine Le Jan, eds. *Dots et douaires dans le haut Moyen Âge.* Rome: École Française de Rome, 2002.

Bourin, Monique. "How Changes in Naming Reflect the Evolution of Familial Structures in Southern Europe, 950–1250." In *Personal Names Studies of Medieval Europe: Social Identity and Familial Structures,* edited by George T. Beech,

Monique Bourin, and Pascal Chareille, pp. 3–13. Kalamazoo, MI: Medieval Institute Publications, 2002.

Boussard, Jacques. "Les évêques en Neustrie avant la réforme grégorienne (950–1050 environ)." *Journal des savants* (1970): 161–96.

——. "L'origine des familles seigneuriales dans la région de la Loire moyenne." *Cahiers de civilisation médiévale* 5 (1962): 303–22.

——. "Le trésorier de Saint-Martin de Tours." *Revue d'histoire de l'église de France* 47 (1961): 66–88.

Bowman, Jeffrey A. *Shifting Landmarks: Property, Proof, and Dispute in Catalonia around 1000.* Ithaca, NY: Cornell University Press, 2004.

Brasington, Bruce C. "Lessons of Love: Bishop Ivo of Chartres as Teacher." In *Teaching and Learning in Northern Europe, 1000–1200,* edited by Sally N. Vaughn and Jay Rubenstein, pp. 129–48. Turnhout, Belgium: Brepols, 2006.

——. "New Perspectives on the Letters of Ivo of Chartres." *Manuscripta* 37.2 (1993): 168–78.

Britnell, Richard. "Pragmatic Literacy in Latin Christendom." In *Pragmatic Literacy East and West, 1200–1300,* edited by Richard Britnell, pp. 3–24. Woodbridge, UK: Boydell Press, 1997.

Brooke, Christopher N. L. "Gregorian Reform in Action: Clerical Marriage in England, 1050–1200." *Cambridge Historical Journal* 13 (1956): 1–21.

——. *The Medieval Idea of Marriage.* Oxford: Oxford University Press, 1989.

Brown, Warren C. *Unjust Seizure: Conflict, Interest, and Authority in an Early Medieval Society.* Ithaca, NY: Cornell University Press, 2001.

Brown, Warren C., and Piotr Górecki. *Conflict in Medieval Europe: Changing Perspectives on Society and Culture.* Aldershot, UK: Ashgate, 2003.

Brundage, James. "The Crusader's Wife: A Canonistic Quandary." *Studia Gratiana* 12 (1967): 425–41.

——. "The Crusader's Wife Revisited." *Studia Gratiana* 14 (1967): 241–51.

——. *Law, Sex, and Christian Society in Medieval Europe.* Chicago: University of Chicago Press, 1987.

Buc, Philippe. "*Principes gentium dominantur eorum:* Princely Power between Legitimacy and Illegitimacy in Twelfth-Century Exegesis." In *Cultures of Power,* edited by Thomas N. Bisson, pp. 310–28. Philadelphia: University of Pennsylvania Press, 1995.

Bull, Marcus. *Knightly Piety and the Lay Response to the First Crusade: The Limousin and Gascony c.970–c.1130.* Oxford: Oxford University Press, 1993.

Bur, Michel. *La formation du comté Champagne, v. 950–1150.* Nancy: Publications de l'Université de Nancy, 1977.

Carpentier, Elisabeth. "La place des femmes dans le plus anciennes chartes poitevins." In *Femmes-Mariages-Lignages, XIIe-XIVe siècles: Mélanges offerts á Georges Duby,* edited by Jean Dufournet, André Joris, Michel Jezierski, and Pierre Toubert, pp. 69–78. Brussels: De Boek Université, 1992.

Cassagnes-Brouquet, Sophie, and Martine Yvernault, eds. *Frères et sœurs: Les liens adelphiques dans l'Occident antique et médiéval.* Turnhout, Belgium: Brepols, 2007.

Caviness, Madeline H. "Anchoress, Abbess and Queen: Donors and Patrons or Intercessors and Matrons?" In *The Cultural Patronage of Medieval Women,* edited by June Hall McCash, pp. 105–54. Athens: University of Georgia Press, 1995.

Chédeville, André. *Chartres et ses campagnes.* Rennes: Publications de l'Université de Haute-Bretagne, 1972.

——. "Les restitutions d'églises en faveur de l'abbaye de Saint-Vincent." *Cahiers de civilisation médiévale* 3 (1960): 209–17.

Cheyette, Fredric L. *Ermengard of Narbonne and the World of the Troubadours.* Ithaca, NY: Cornell University Press, 2001.

——. "Georges Duby's *La société dans la région Mâconnaise* after Fifty Years: Reading It Then and Now." *Journal of Medieval History* 28 (2002): 291–317.

——. "Some Reflections on Violence, Reconciliation and the 'Feudal Revolution.'" In *Conflict in Medieval Europe: Changing Perspectives on Society and Culture,* edited by Warren C. Brown and Piotr Górecki, pp. 243–64. Aldershot, UK: Ashgate, 2003.

——. "Women, Poets, and Politics in Occitania." In *Aristocratic Women in Medieval France,* edited by Theodore Evergates, pp. 138–77. Philadelphia: University of Pennsylvania Press, 1999.

Chibnall, Marjorie. "The Empress Matilda and Her Sons." In *Medieval Mothering,* edited by John Carmi Parsons and Bonnie Wheeler, pp. 279–94. New York: Garland, 1999.

Choux, Jacques. *L'épiscopat de Pibon (1064–1107): Recherches sur le diocèse de Toul au temps de la réforme grégorienne.* Nancy: Recueil de document sur l'histoire de Lorraine 33, 1952.

Christelow, Stephanie Mooers. "The Division of Inheritance and the Provision of Non-Inheriting Offspring among the Anglo-Norman Elite." *Medieval Prosopography* 17 (1996): 3–44.

Classen, Albrecht. "Family Life in the High and Late Middle Ages: The Testimony of German Literary Sources." In *Medieval Family Roles: A Book of Essays,* edited by Cathy Jorgensen Itnyre, pp. 39–66. New York: Garland, 1996.

Clerval, Jules Alexander. *Les écoles de Chartres au Moyen-Âge: De Ve au XVIe siècle.* Paris: Minerva, 1895.

Cline, Ruth H. "The Congregation of Tiron in the Twelfth Century: Foundation and Expansion." PhD diss., Georgetown University, 2000.

Constable, Giles. *The Reformation of the Twelfth Century.* Cambridge: Cambridge University Press, 1998.

Corbet, Patrick. "Le douaire dans le droit canonique jusqu'à Gratien." In *Dots et douaires dans le haut Moyen Âge,* edited by François Bougard, Laurent Feller, and Régine Le Jan, pp. 43–55. Rome: Ecole Française de Rome, 2002.

——. "*Pro anima senioris sui:* La pastoral ottonienne du veuvage." In *Veuves et veuvage,* edited by Michel Parisse, pp. 233–53. Paris: Picard, 1993.

Crisp, Ryan. "Consanguinity and the Saint-Aubin Genealogies," *The Haskins Society Journal* 14 (2005): 105–15.

Crouch, David. *The Image of Aristocracy in Britain, 1100–1300.* London: Routledge, 1992.

Cuissard, Charles. "Les seigneurs du Puiset (980–1789)." *Bulletin de la société Dunoise* 3 (1875–1880): 313–98.

Dalarun, Jacques, Danielle Bohler, and Christiane Klapisch-Zuber. "Pour une histoire des femmes," in *Les tendances actuelles de l'histoire du Moyen Âge en France et en Allemagne,* edited by Otto Gerhard Oexle and Jean-Claude Schmitt, pp. 561–82. Paris: Publications de la Sorbonne, 2002.

Davies, Wendy, and Paul Fouracre, eds. *Property and Power in the Early Middle Ages.* Cambridge: Cambridge University Press, 1995.

———, eds. *The Settlement of Disputes in Early Medieval Europe.* Cambridge: Cambridge University Press, 1986.

d'Avray, David. *Medieval Marriage: Symbolism and Society.* Oxford: Oxford University Press, 2005.

DeAragon, RaGena C. "Dowager Countesses, 1069–1230," *Anglo-Norman Studies* 17 (1995): 87–100.

Depoin, Jacques. "Etudes préparatoires à l'histoire des grandes familles palatines III: Thibaut le Tricheur; Fut-il un bâtard et mourut-il presque centenaire?" *Revue des études historiques* 74 (1908): 557.

de Trafford, Claire. "Share and Share Alike? The Marriage Portion, Inheritance, and Family Politics." In *Pawns or Players? Studies on Medieval and Early Modern Women,* edited by Christine Meeks and Catherine Lawless, pp. 36–48. Dublin: Four Courts Press, 2003.

Devailly, Guy. *Le Berry du Xe siècle au milieu de XIIIe siècle: Étude politique, religieuse, sociale et économique.* Paris: Mouton, 1973.

———. "Les grandes familles et l'épiscopat dans l'ouest de France et les pays de la Loire." *Cahiers de civilisation médiévale* 27 (1966): 49–55.

Dhondt, Jan. "Sept femmes et un trio de rois (Robert le pieux, Henri Ier, Philippe Ier)." *Contributions à l'histoire économique et sociale* 3 (1964–65): 35–70.

Dillay, Madeleine. "Le régime de l'église privée du XIe au XIIe siècle dans l'Anjou, le Maine et la Touraine." *RHDF* 4th series, 4 (1925): 253–94.

Dion, Adolphe de. "Le Puiset aux XIe et XIIe siècles." *MSAEL* 9 (1889): 1–34, 71–85.

———. "Les seigneurs de Breteuil-en-Beauvaisis." *Mémoires de la société de l'histoire de Paris et de l'Ile de France,* 10 (1883): 191–242.

Donahue, Charles, Jr. "The Canon Law of the Formation of Marriage and Social Practice in the Late Middle Ages." *Journal of Family History* 8 (1983): 144–58.

———. "The Policy of Alexander the Third's Consent Theory of Marriage." In *Proceedings of the Fourth International Congress of Medieval Canon Law,* edited by Stephen Kuttner, pp. 251–81. Vatican City: Biblioteca Apostolica Vaticana, 1976.

Douglass, David. *William the Conqueror: The Norman Impact upon England.* Berkeley: University of California Press, 1964.

Drell, Joanna. *Kinship and Conquest: Family Strategies in the Principality of Salerno during the Norman Period, 1077–1194.* Ithaca, NY: Cornell University Press, 2002.

Duby, Georges. *The Chivalrous Society.* Translated by Cynthia Postan. Berkeley: University of California Press, 1978.

———. "Communal Living." In Duby, *A History of Private Life.* Vol. 2, *Revelations of the Medieval World,* pp. 35–85.

———. *Famille et parenté dans l'Occident médiévale.* Rome: Actes du colloque de Paris, 1977.

———, ed. *A History of Private Life.* Vol. 2, *Revelations of the Medieval World.* Translated by Arthur Goldhammer. Cambridge, MA: Harvard University Press, 1988.

——. *The Knight, the Lady and the Priest: The Making of Modern Marriage in Medieval France.* Translated by Barbara Bray. New York: Pantheon Press, 1983.

——. "Lineage, Nobility and Knighthood." In Duby, *Chivalrous Society,* pp. 59–80.

——. *Love and Marriage in the Middle Ages.* Translated by Janet Dunnett. Chicago: University of Chicago Press, 1996.

——. *Medieval Marriage: Two Models from Twelfth-Century France.* Translated by Elbourg Forster. Baltimore: Johns Hopkins University Press, 1978.

——. "The Structure of Kinship and Nobility." In Duby, *Chivalrous Society,* pp. 134–48.

——. *William Marshal: The Flower of Chivalry.* Translated by Richard Howard. New York: Pantheon, 1987.

——. "Women and Power." In *Cultures of Power: Lordship, Status and Process in Twelfth-Century Europe,* edited by Thomas N. Bisson, pp. 69–85. Philadelphia: University of Pennsylvania Press, 1995.

——. *Women of the Twelfth Century.* Vol. 1, *Eleanor of Aquitaine and Six Others.* Chicago: University of Chicago Press, 1997.

——. "Youth in Aristocratic Society." In Duby, *Chivalrous Society,* pp. 112–22.

Duby, Georges, and Philippe Braunstein. "Solitude: Eleventh to Thirteenth Century." In Duby, *A History of Private Life,* pp. 509–34.

Duggan, Anne J., ed. *Nobles and Nobility in Medieval Europe: Concepts, Origins, Transformations.* Woodbridge, UK: Boydell Press, 2000.

——, ed. *Queens and Queenship in Medieval Europe.* Woodbridge, UK: Boydell Press, 1997.

Dunbabin, Jean. *France in the Making, 843–1180.* Oxford: Oxford University Press, 1985.

——. "What's in a Name? Philip, King of France." *Speculum* 68 (1993): 949–68.

Durand, Robert. "Family Memory and the Durability of the *Nomen Paternum.*" In *Personal Names and Studies of Medieval Europe: Social Identity and Familial Structures,* edited by George T. Beech, Monique Bourin, and Pascal Chareille, pp. 77–86. Kalamazoo, MI: Medieval Institute Publications, 2002.

Durand, Rogier. "Chronologie des premiers seigneurs de Courville: Courville et Vieuxpont, notice généalogique." *MSAEL* 12 (1899–1900): 243–93.

Edwards, Carolyn. "Dynastic Sanctity in Two Early Medieval Women's *Lives.*" In *Medieval Family Roles,* edited by Cathy Jorgensen Itnyre, pp. 3–19. New York: Garland, 1996.

Evergates, Theodore. *The Aristocracy in the County of Champagne, 1100–1300.* Philadelphia: University of Pennsylvania Press, 2007.

——, ed. *Aristocratic Women in Medieval France.* Philadelphia: University of Pennsylvania Press, 1999.

——. "Aristocratic Women in the County of Champagne." In Evergates, *Aristocratic Women in Medieval France,* pp. 74–110.

——. "The Feudal Imaginary of Georges Duby." *Journal of Medieval and Early Modern Studies* 27 (1997): 641–60.

——. *Feudal Society in the Baillage of Troyes under the Counts of Champagne, 1152–1284.* Baltimore: Johns Hopkins University Press, 1975.

——. "Nobles and Knights in Twelfth-Century France." In *Cultures of Power,* edited by Thomas N. Bisson, pp. 11–35. Philadelphia: University of Pennsylvania Press, 1995.

Fanning, Steven. *A Bishop and His World before the Gregorian Reform: Hubert of Angers 1006–1047. Transactions of the American Philosophical Society* 78, no. 1 (1988): i–193.

———. "Family and Episcopal Election 900–1050 and the Case of Hubert of Angers (1006–1047)." *Medieval Prosopography* 7 (1986): 39–56.

———. "La lutte entre Hubert de Vendôme, évêque d'Angers et l'archevêque de Tours en 1016." *Bulletin de la société archéologique, scientifique et littéraire du Vendômois* (1980): 31–33.

———. "From *Miles* to *Episcopus:* The Influence of Family on the Career of Vulgrinus of Vendôme (ca. 1000–1065)." *Medieval Prosopography* 4 (1983): 9–30.

———. "Les origines familiales de Vulgrin: Abbé de Saint-Serge d'Angers (1046–1056) et évêque du Mans (1065+), petit-fils de vicomte Fulcrade de Vendôme." *La province du Maine* 82 (1980): 243–55.

Farmer, Sharon. *Communities of Saint Martin: Legend and Ritual in Medieval Tours.* Ithaca, NY: Cornell University Press, 1991.

———. "Persuasive Voices: Clerical Images of Medieval Wives." *Speculum* 61 (1986): 517–43.

———. "La voix des femmes. Une réception américaine." *Clio: Georges Duby et l'histoire des femmes* 8 (1998): 155–66.

Faulk, Josephine M. "Bishop Fulbert of Chartres (1006–1028): A Political Biography." PhD diss., University of Illinois at Chicago, 2006.

Fein, Susanna Greer. "Maternity in Aelred of Rievaulx's Letter to His Sister." In *Medieval Mothering,* edited by John Carmi Parsons and Bonnie Wheeler, pp. 139–56. New York: Routledge, 1999.

Feller, Laurent. "Morgengabe, dot, *tertia:* Rapport introductif." In *Dots et douaires dans le haut Moyen Âge,* edited by François Bougard, Laurent Feller, and Régine Le Jan, pp. 1–25. Rome: École Française de Rome, 2002.

Ferrante, Joan. *To the Glory of Her Sex: Women's Roles in the Composition of Medieval Texts.* Bloomington: Indiana University Press, 1997.

———. "Women's Role in Latin Letters from the Fourth to the Early Twelfth Century." In *The Cultural Patronage of Medieval Women,* edited by June Hall Mc-Cash, pp. 73–102. Athens: University of Georgia Press, 1995.

Fliché, Augustin. "Premiers résultats d'un enquête sur la réforme grégorienne dans le diocèse français de Narbonne." *Académie des inscriptions et de belles-lettres. Comptes Rendues* (1944): 162–80.

———. *La réforme grégorienne et la reconquête chrétienne (1057–1123).* 2 vols. Paris: Bloud and Gay, 1950.

Fossier, Robert, ed., *La petite enfance dans l'Europe médiévale et moderne.* Toulouse: Presse Universitaires de Mirail, 1997.

Foulon, Jean-Hervé. *Église et réforme au Moyen Âge: Papauté, milieux réformateurs et ecclésiologie dans les Pays de la Loire au tournant des XIe-XIIe siècles.* Brussels: De Boeck, 2008.

———. "Stratégies lignagères et réforme ecclésiastique: La question du lignage de Geoffrey de Vendôme (av. 1070–1132)." *Journal des Savants* (2001): 3–41.

Fouracre, Paul. "The Origins of the Nobility in Francia." In *Nobles and Nobility,* edited by Anne J. Duggan, pp. 17–24. Woodbridge, UK: Boydell Press, 2000.

———. "*'Placita'* and the Settlement of Disputes in Later Merovingian Francia." In *The Settlement of Disputes in Early Medieval Europe,* edited by Paul Fouracre and Wendy Davies, pp. 7–22. Cambridge: Cambridge University Press, 1986.

Freed, John. *Noble Bondsmen: Ministerial Marriages in the Archdiocese of Salzburg, 1100–1343.* Ithaca, NY: Cornell University Press, 1995.

———. "Reflections on the Medieval German Nobility." *AHR* 91 (1986): 553–75.

Gaudemet, Jean. "Recherches sur l'épiscopat médiévale en France." In *Proceedings of the Second International Congress on Medieval Canon Law,* edited by Stephen Kuttner and J. Joseph Ryan, pp. 139–54. Vatican City: S. Congregatium de Seminaris et Studiorum Universitatibus, 1965.

Gay, Jean. "Remarques sur l'évolution de la pratique contractuelle en Champagne méridionale (XIIe-XIXe siècle)." *Mémoires de la société pour l'histoire du droit et des institutions des anciens pays bourguignons, comtois et romands,* 54 (1997): 7–58.

Geary, Patrick. "Extra-Judicial Means of Conflict Resolution." In *La giustizia nell'alto medioevo (secoli V–VIII),* vol. 1, edited by Geniève Giordanengo, pp. 570–601. Spoleto: Settimane di studio del Centro Italiano di studi sull'alto medioevo 42, 1995.

———. *Furta Sacra: Thefts of Relics in the Central Middle Ages.* Princeton, NJ: Princeton University Press, 1991.

———. "Living with Conflicts in a Stateless France: A Typology of Conflict Management Mechanisms, 1050–1200." In Geary, *Living with the Dead in the Middle Ages,* pp. 125–60.

———. *Living with the Dead in the Middle Ages.* Ithaca: Cornell University Press, 1994.

———. "Moral Obligations and Peer Pressure: Conflict Resolution in the Medieval Aristocracy." In *Georges Duby: L'écriture de l'histoire,* edited by Claudie Duhamel Amado and Guy Lobrichon, pp. 217–222. Brussels: De Boeck Université, 1996.

———. *Phantoms of Remembrance: Memory and Oblivion at the End of the First Millennium.* Princeton, NJ: Princeton University Press, 1994.

Génicot, Léopold. *La noblesse dans l'Occident médiévale.* London: Variorum Reprints, 1982.

———. "La noblesse du Moyen Age dans l'ancienne 'Francie': Continuité, rupture ou évolution?" *Comparative Studies of Society and History* 5 (1962): 52–59.

Gillingham, John. "Love, Marriage and Politics in the Twelfth Century." *Forum for Modern Language Studies* 25 (1989): 292–302. Reprinted in John Gillingham, *Richard Coeur de Lion: Kingship, Chivalry and War in Twelfth Century.* London: Hambledon, 1994.

Gold, Penny Schine. *The Lady and the Virgin: Image, Attitude, and Experience in Twelfth-Century France.* Chicago: University of Chicago Press, 1985.

Goody, Jack. *The Development of the Family and Marriage in Europe.* London: Cambridge University Press, 1983.

Griffiths, Fiona. "The Cross and the *Cura monialium:* Robert of Arbrissel, John the Evangelist, and the Pastoral Care of Women in the Age of Reform." *Speculum* 83 (2008): 303–30.

Griffiths, Quentin. "The Capetian Kings and St. Martin of Tours." *Studies in Medieval and Renaissance History* 9 (1987): 83–134.

Guerreau-Jalabert, Anita. "La désignation des relations et des groupes de parenté en Latin médiévale." *Bulletin du Cange* 46 (1988): 65–108.

———. "La parenté dans l'Europe médiévale et moderne: À propos d'une synthèse récente." *L'Homme* 29 (1989): 69–93.

Guerreau-Jalabert, Anita, Régine Le Jan, and Joseph Morsel. "De l'histoire de la famille à l'anthropologie de la parenté." In *Les tendances actuelles de l'histoire du Moyen Âge en France et en Allemagne,* edited by Otto Gerhard Oexle and Jean-Claude Schmitt, pp. 433–46. Paris: Publications de la Sorbonne, 2002.

Guillot, Oliver. *Le comté d'Anjou et son entourage au XIe siècle.* 2 vols. Paris: Picard, 1972.

Guillotel, Hubert. "Combour: Protohistoire d'une seigneur et mis en œuvre de la réforme grégorienne." In *Family Trees and the Roots of Politics: The Prosopography of Britain and France from the Tenth to the Twelfth Century,* edited by K. S. B. Rohan, pp. 268–98. Woodbridge: Boydell Press, 1997.

Haas, Louis. "Social Connections between Parents and Godparents in Late Medieval Yorkshire." *Medieval Prosopography* 10 (1989): 1–21.

Hajnal, J. "European Marriage Patterns in Perspective." In *Population in History: Essays in Historical Demography,* edited by D. V. Glass and D. E. C. Eversley, pp. 101–43. London: Arnold, 1965.

Halphen, Louis. "La lettre d'Odo II de Blois de roi Robert." *Revue historique* 97 (1908): 294.

Hamilton, Tracy Chapman. "Queenship and Kinship in the French *Bible moralisée:* The Example of Blanche of Castile and Vienna ÖNB 2554." In *Capetian Women,* edited by Kathleen Nolan, pp. 177–208. New York: Palgrave MacMillan, 2003.

Hanawalt, Barbara A. "Female Networks for Fostering Lady Lisle's Daughters." In *Medieval Mothering,* edited by John Carmi Parsons and Bonnie Wheeler, pp. 239–58. New York: Garland, 1999.

———. *Growing Up in Medieval London.* Oxford: Oxford University Press, 1993.

———. "Medievalists and the Study of Childhood." *Speculum* 22 (2002): 440–60.

———. *The Ties That Bound: Peasant Families in Medieval England.* Oxford: Oxford University Press, 1986.

Harrison, Dick. *The Age of Abbesses and Queens.* Lund: Nordic Academic Press, 1998.

Head, Thomas. *Hagiography and the Cult of the Saints in the Diocese of Orléans, 800–1200.* Cambridge: Cambridge University Press, 1990.

———, trans. and ed. *Medieval Hagiography: An Anthology.* New York: Routledge, 2001.

Herlihy, David. "Church Property on the European Continent, 701–1200." *Speculum* 36 (1961): 81–105.

———. "Land, Family and Women in Continental Europe, 701–1200." In *Women in Medieval Society,* edited by Susan Mosher Stuard, pp. 13–46. Philadelphia: University of Pennsylvania Press, 1983.

———. "The Making of the Medieval Family: Symmetry, Structure and Sentiment." *Journal of Family History* 8 (1983): 116–30.

———. *Medieval Households.* Cambridge, MA: Harvard University Press, 1985.

Herlihy, David, and Christiane Klapisch-Zuber. *The Tuscans and Their Families: A Study of the Florentine Catasto of 1427.* New Haven, CT: Yale University Press, 1985.

Hoareau, Jacqueline. "Meu d'amour naturelle... Défendre l'honneur de sa sœur à la fin du Moyen Âge." In *Frères et sœurs: Les liens adelphiques dans l'Occident antique et médiévale,* edited by Sophie Cassagnes-Brouquet and Martine Yvernault, pp. 191–98. Turnhout, Belgium: Brepols, 2007.

Hornaday, Aline G. "A Capetian Queen as Street Demonstrator: Isabelle of Hainaut." In *Capetian Women,* edited by Kathleen Nolan, pp. 77–97. New York: Palgrave MacMillan, 2003.

———. "Early Medieval Kinship Structures as Social and Political Controls." In *Medieval Family Roles,* edited by Cathy Jorgensen Itnyre, pp. 21–38. New York: Garland, 1996.

Hughes, Diane Owen. "From Brideprice to Dowry in Mediterranean Europe." *Journal of Family History* 3 (1978): 262–96.

Huneycutt, Lois L. "Female Succession and the Language of Power in the Writings of Twelfth-Century Churchmen." In *Medieval Queenship,* edited by John Carmi Parsons, pp. 189–201. New York: St. Martin's, 1996.

———. "Intercession and the High-Medieval Queen: The Esther Topos." In *The Power of the Weak,* edited by Jennifer Carpenter and Sally MacLean, pp. 126–46. Urbana: University of Illinois Press, 1995.

———. *Matilda of Scotland: A Study in Medieval Queenship.* Woodbridge, UK: Boydell Press, 2003.

———. "Public Lives, Private Ties: Royal Mothers in England and Scotland, 1070–1204." In *Medieval Mothering,* edited by John Carmi Parsons and Bonnie Wheeler, pp. 295–312. New York: Garland, 1999.

Hyams, Paul R. "Nastiness and Wrong, Rancor and Reconciliation." In *Conflict in the Middle Ages,* edited by Warren Brown and Piotr Górecki, pp. 195–208. London: Ashgate, 2003.

Innes, Matthew. "Keeping It in the Family: Women and Aristocratic Memory, 700–1200." In *Medieval Memories: Men, Women and the Past, 700–1300,* edited by Elisabeth van Houts, pp. 17–35. Harlow, UK: Longman, 2001.

Iogna-Prat, Dominique. "Évrard de Breteuil et son double. Morphologie de la conversion en milieu aristocratique (v.1070–v.1120)." In *Guerriers et moines: Conversion et sainteté aristocratiques dans l'Occident médiéval,* edited by Michel Lauwers, pp. 537–57. Antibes: Éditions APDCA, 2002.

Jaeger, C. Stephen. *Ennobling Love: In Search of a Lost Sensibility.* Philadelphia: University of Pennsylvania Press, 1999.

———. *The Origins of Courtliness.* Philadelphia: University of Pennsylvania Press, 1985.

Jeanneau, Cédric. "Émergence et affirmation des familles seigneuriales à la frontière des grandes principautés territoriales: Les seigneurs de la Garnache et les vicomtes de Thouars." In *Le médiéviste et la monographie familiale: Sources, méthodes et problématiques,* edited by Martin Aurell, pp. 161–87. Turnhout, Belgium: Brepols, 2004.

———. "Liens adelphes et héritage. Une solution originale en Poitou aux XIe et XIIe siècles: Le droit de viage ou retour." In *Frères et sœurs: Les liens adelphiques dans l'Occident antique et médiéval,* edited by Sophie Cassagnes-Brouquet and Martine Yvernault, 95–105. Turnhout, Belgium: Brepols, 2007.

Jessee, W. Scott. *Robert the Burgundian and the Counts of Anjou.* Washington, DC: Catholic University of America Press, 2000.

Johns, Susan. *Noblewomen, Aristocracy and Power in the Twelfth-Century Anglo-Norman Realm.* Manchester: Manchester University Press, 2003.

Johnson, Penelope. *Equal in Monastic Profession: Religious Women in Medieval France.* Chicago: University of Chicago Press, 1991.

——. *Prayer, Patronage, and Power: The Abbey of la Trinité, Vendôme, 1032–1187.* New York: New York University Press, 1981.

Jordan, Erin L. *Women, Power, and Religious Patronage in the Middle Ages.* New York: Palgrave McMillan, 2006.

Jordan, William Chester. "Isabelle of France and Religious Devotion at the Court of Louis IX." In *Capetian Women,* edited by Kathleen Nolan, pp. 209–24. New York: Palgrave MacMillan, 2003.

Jussen, Bernhard. "Famille et parenté: Comparaison des recherches françaises et allemandes." In *Les tendances actuelles de l'histoire du Moyen Âge en France et en Allemagne,* edited by Otto Gerhard Oexle and Jean-Claude Schmitt, pp. 447–60. Paris: Publications de la Sorbonne, 2002.

Keats-Rohan, K. S. B., ed. *Family Trees and the Roots of Politics: The Prosopography of Britain and France from the Tenth to the Twelfth Century.* Woodbridge, UK: Boydell Press, 1997.

——. "'Un vassal sans histoire'? Count Hugh II (c. 940/955–992) and the Origins of Angevin Overlordship in Maine." In *Family Trees and the Roots of Politics: The Prosopography of Britain and France from the Tenth to the Twelfth Century,* edited by K. S. B. Keats-Rohan, pp. 189–270. Woodbridge, UK: Boydell Press, 1997.

Keller, Kimberly. "For Better and Worse: Women and Marriage in *Piers Plowman.*" In *Medieval Family Roles: A Book of Essays,* edited by Cathy Jorgensen Itnyre, pp. 67–86. New York: Garland, 1996.

Kenny, Gillian. "The Power of Dower: The Importance of Dower in the Lives of Medieval Women in Ireland." In *Pawns or Players? Studies on Medieval and Early Modern Women,* edited by Christine Meek and Catherine Lawless, pp. 59–74. Dublin: Four Courts Press, 2003.

Kirshner, Julius. "Wives' Claims against Insolvent Husbands in Late Medieval Italy." In *Women of the Medieval World,* edited by Julius Kirshner and Suzanne F. Wemple, pp. 256–303. Oxford: Oxford University Press, 1985.

Koziol, Geoffrey. "Baldwin VII of Flanders and the Toll of St. Vaast (1111): Judgment as Ritual." In *Conflict in Medieval Europe: Changing Perspectives on Society,* edited by Warren C. Brown and Piotr Górecki, pp. 151–62. Aldershot, UK: Ashgate, 2003.

——. *Begging Pardon and Favor: Ritual and Political Order in Early Medieval France.* Ithaca, NY: Cornell University Press, 1992.

Laffont, Pierre-Yves. "Réflexions méthodologiques sur un corpus de monographies familiales: L'aristocratie châtelaine de Languedoc septentrional (Xe-XIVe siècle)." In *Le médiéviste et la monographie familiale: Sources, méthodes et problématiques,* edited by Martin Aurell, pp. 227–34. Turnhout, Belgium: Brepols, 2004.

La Monte, John. "The Lords of Le Puiset on Crusade." *Speculum* 17 (1942): 100–18.

Laslett, Peter, ed. *Family Life and Illicit Love in Earlier Generations: Essays in Historical Sociology.* Cambridge: Cambridge University Press, 1997.

——. *Household and Family in Past Time.* Cambridge: Cambridge University Press, 1972.

Lauranson-Rosaz, Christian. "Douaire et *sponsalicium* durant le haut Moyen Âge." In *Veuves et veuvage,* edited by Michel Parisse, pp. 99–104. Paris: Picard, 1993.

Lauwers, Michel, ed. *Guerriers et moines: Conversion et sainteté aristocratiques dans l'Occident médiévale.* Antibes: Éditions APDCA, 2002.

——, ed. *La mémoire des ancêtres, le souci des morts: Morts, rites, et société au Moyen Âge.* Paris: Beauchesne, 1997.

Lefevre, E. "Notice sur la baronnie d'Alluyes." *MSAEL* 5 (1972): 42–88.

Le Jan, Régine. "Continuity and Change in the Tenth-Century Nobility." In *Nobles and Nobility,* edited by Anne Duggan, pp. 53–68. Woodbridge, UK: Boydell Press, 2000.

——. *Famille et pouvoir dans le monde Franc (VIIe-Xe siècle): Essai d'anthropologie sociale.* Paris: Publications de la Sorbonne, 2002.

——. "Personal Names and the Transformations of Kinship in Early Medieval Society." In *Personal Names Studies of Medieval Europe: Social Identity and Familial Structures,* edited by George T. Beech, Monique Bourin, and Pascal Chareille, pp. 31–50. Kalamazoo, MI: Medieval Institute Publications, 2002.

Le Jan-Hennebicque, Régine. "Aux origines du douaire médiévale (VIe-Xe siècles)." In *Veuves et veuvage,* edited by Michel Parisse, 107–21. Paris: Picard, 1993.

Lemaire, André. "Les origines de la communauté de biens entre époux dans le droit coutumier français." *RHDF* 4th series, 1 (1928): 584–641.

Lemarignier, Jean-François. "Political and Monastic Structures in France at the End of the Tenth and Beginning of the Eleventh Century." In *Lordship and Community in Medieval Europe,* edited by Fredric L. Cheyette, pp. 100–27. New York: Holt, Rinehart and Winston, 1968.

Lemesle, Bruno. *La société aristocratique dans le Haut-Maine (XIe–XIIe siècles).* Rennes: Presses Universitaires de Rennes, 1999.

Lesueur, F. *Thibaut le Tricheur, comte de Blois, de Tours et de Chartres au Xème siècle.* Chartres: Mémoires de la société de sciences et lettres de Loir et Cher no. 33, 1963.

Lewis, Andrew. *Royal Succession in Capetian France: Studies on Familial Order and the State.* Cambridge, MA: Harvard University Press, 1981.

Lex, Léonce. *Eudes, comte de Blois, de Tours de Chartres et de Meaux (995–1037) et son frère Thibaut (995–1004).* Troyes: Dufour-Bouquot, 1892.

Leyser, Karl. "The German Aristocracy from the Ninth to the Early Twelfth Century." *Past and Present* 41 (1968): 25–53.

——. "Maternal Kin in Early Medieval Germany." *Past and Present* 49 (1970): 126–34.

——. *Rule and Conflict in Early Medieval Society: Ottonian Saxony.* London: Blackwell, 1979.

Little, Lester. "Anger in Monastic Curses." In *Anger's Past: The Social Uses of an Emotion in the Middle Ages,* edited by Barbara Rosenwein, pp. 9–35. Ithaca, NY: Cornell University Press, 1998.

——. *Benedictine Maledictions: Liturgical Cursing in Romanesque France.* Ithaca, NY: Cornell University Press, 1993.

——. *Religious Poverty and the Profit Economy in Medieval Europe.* Ithaca, NY: Cornell University Press, 1978.

Livingstone, Amy. "Aristocratic Women in the Chartrain." In *Aristocratic Women in Medieval France,* edited by Theodore Evergates, pp. 44–75. Philadelphia: University of Pennsylvania Press, 1999

———. "Brother Monk: Monks and Their Family in the Chartrain, 1000–1200." In *Medieval Monks and Their World: Ideas and Realities; Studies in Honor of Richard E. Sullivan,* edited by David Blanks, Michael Frassetto, and Amy Livingstone, pp. 93–118. Leuven: Brill, 2006.

———. "Diversity and Continuity: Family Structure and Inheritance in the Chartrain, 1000–1200." In *Mondes de l'ouest et villes du monde: Regards sur les sociétés médiévales—mélanges en l'honneur d'André Chédeville,* edited by Catherine Laurent, Bernard Merdrignac, and Daniel Pinchot, pp. 415–30. Rennes: Presses Universitaires de Rennes, 1998.

———. "Kith and Kin: Kinship and Family Structure of Nobility of Eleventh- and Twelfth-Century Blois-Chartres." *French Historical Studies* 20 (1995): 419–58.

———. "Noblewomen's Control of Property in Eleventh- and Early Twelfth-Century Blois-Chartres." *Medieval Prosopography* 18 (1995): 55–72.

———. "Pour une révision du 'mâle' Moyen Âge de Georges Duby." *Clio: Georges Duby et l'histoire des femmes* 8 (1998): 139–54.

———. "Powerful Allies and Dangerous Adversaries: Aristocratic Women and Power in Medieval France." In *Women in Medieval Western European Culture,* edited by Linda E. Mitchell, pp. 12–35. New York: Garland, 1999.

Loengard, Janet Senderwitz. "'Of the Gift of Her Husband': English Dower and Its Consequences in the Year 1200." In *Women of the Medieval World,* edited by Julius Kirshner and Suzanne F. Wemple, pp. 215–55. Oxford: Oxford University, 1985.

LoPrete, Kimberly A. "Adela of Blois as Mother and Countess." In *Medieval Mothering,* edited by John Carmi Parsons and Bonnie Wheeler, pp. 313–34. New York: Garland, 1999.

———. *Adela of Blois, Countess and Lord.* Dublin: Four Courts Press, 2007.

———. "Adela of Blois: Familial Alliances and Female Lordship." In *Aristocratic Women in Medieval France,* edited by Theodore Evergates, pp. 7–43. Philadelphia: University of Pennsylvania Press, 1999.

———. "The Anglo-Norman Card of Adela of Blois." *Albion* 22 (1990): 569–89.

———. "The Gender of Lordly Women: The Case of Adela of Blois." In *Pawns or Players? Studies on Medieval and Early Modern Women,* edited by Christine Meek and Catherine Lawless, pp. 90–110. Dublin: Four Courts Press, 2003.

Lot, Ferdinand. "L'origine de Thibaut le Tricheur." *Le Moyen Âge* 19 (1907): 188.

Lynch, Joseph. *Godparents and Kinship in Early Medieval Europe.* Princeton, NJ: Princeton University Press, 1986.

———. *Simonical Entry into Religious Life from 1000–1200.* Columbus: Ohio State University Press, 1976.

Lyon, Jonathan. "Cooperation, Compromise and Conflict Avoidance: Family Relationships in the House of Andechs, ca. 1100–1204." PhD diss., University of Notre Dame, 2004.

Macé, Laurent. "Les frères au sien du lignage: La logique du lien adelphique chez les seigneurs de Montpellier (XIIe siècle)." In *Frères et sœurs: Les liens adelphiques dans l'Occident antique et médiévale,* edited by Sophie Cassagnes-Brouquet and Martine Yvernault, pp. 127–36. Turnhout, Belgium: Brepols, 2007.

Martindale, Jane. "The French Aristocracy in the Early Middle Ages: A Reappraisal." *Past and Present* 75 (1977): 5–45.

——. "Succession and Politics in the Romance-speaking World." In *England and Her Neighbors, 1066–1453: Essays in Honour of Pierre Chaplais,* edited by Michael Jones and Malcolm Vale, pp. 19–41. London: Hambeldon Press, 1989. Reprinted in *Status, Authority and Regional Power: Aquitaine and France, Ninth to the Twelfth Centuries,* edited by Jane Martindale, pp. 19–41. Aldershot, UK: Variorum Reprints, 1997.

Mazel, Florian. "Monographie familiale aristocratique et analyse historique. Réflexions à partir de l'étude de trois lignages provençaux (Xe-XIVe siècle)." In *Le médiéviste et la monographie familiale: Sources, méthodes et problématiques,* edited by Martin Aurell, pp. 145–60. Turnhout, Belgium: Brepols, 2004.

McLaughlin, Mary. "Survivors and Surrogates: Children and Parents from the Ninth to the Thirteenth Centuries." In *The History of Childhood,* edited by Lloyd DeMause, pp. 101–81. New York: Jason Aronson, 1974.

McLaughlin, Megan. *Consorting with Saints: Prayers for the Dead in Early Medieval France.* Ithaca, NY: Cornell University Press, 1994.

——. "The Woman Warrior: Gender, Warfare and Society in Medieval Europe." *Women's Studies* 17 (1990): 193–209.

McNamara, Jo Ann. "Women and Power through the Family Revisited." In *Gendering the Master Narrative: Women and Power in the Middle Ages,* edited by Mary Erler and Maryanne Kowaleski, pp. 17–30. Ithaca, NY: Cornell University Press, 2003.

McNamara, Jo Ann, and Suzanne Wemple. "The Power of Women through the Family, 500–1100." *Feminist Studies* 1 (1973): 126–42. Reprinted in *Women and Power in the Middle Ages,* edited by Mary Erler and Maryanne Kowaleski, pp. 83–101. Athens: University of Georgia Press, 1988.

Merlet, René. "Les Comtes de Chartres, Châteaudun, et Blois au IXe et Xe siècles." *MSAEL* 12 (1895–1900): 19–59.

Mitchell, Linda E. "The Lady Is a Lord: Noble Widows and Land in Thirteenth-Century Britain." *Historical Reflections/Réflexions historiques* 18 (1992): 71–97.

——. *Portraits of Medieval Women: Family, Marriage and Politics in England, 1225–1350.* New York: Palgrave MacMillan, 2003.

Mollat, Guillaume. "La restitution des églises privées au patrimoine ecclésiastique en France du IXe au XIe siècle." *RHDF* 4th series, 27 (1949): 399–423.

Moore, John S. "The Anglo-Norman Family: Size and Structure." *Anglo-Norman Studies* 14 (1991): 153–95.

Morelle, Laurent. "Mariage et diplomatique: Autour de cinq chartes de douaire dans le Laonnois-Soissonais, 1163–1181." *Bibliothèque de l'École des Chartres* 146 (1988): 225–41.

Morsel, Joseph. "Personal Naming and Representations of Feminine Identity in Franconia in the Later Middle Ages." In *Personal Name Studies of Medieval Europe: Social Identity and Familial Structure,* edited by George T. Beech, Monique Bourin, and Pascal Chareille, pp. 157–81. Kalamazoo, MI: Medieval Institute Publications, 2002.

Murray, Alexander Callender. *Germanic Kinship Structure: Studies in Law and Society in Antiquity and the Early Middle Ages.* Toronto: Pontifical Institute of Medieval Studies, 1983.

Murray, Jacqueline. "Individualism and Consensual Marriage: Some Evidence from Medieval England." In *Women, Marriage and Family in Medieval Christendom:*

Essays in Memory of Michael M. Sheehan, C.S.B., edited by Constance M. Rousseau and Joel T. Rosenthal, pp. 121–51. Kalamazoo, MI: Medieval Institute Publications, 1998.

———. "Thinking about Gender: The Diversity of Medieval Perspectives." In *The Power of the Weak,* edited by Jennifer Carpenter and Sally-Beth MacLean, pp. 1–26. Urbana: University of Illinois Press, 1995.

Nassiet, Michel. "La monographie familiale à la fin du Moyen Âge: Quelques problématiques d'histoire de la parenté." In *Le médiéviste et la monographie familiale: Sources, méthodes et problématiques,* edited by Martin Aurell, pp. 66–78. Turnhout, Belgium: Brepols, 2004.

Nelson, Janet T. "Dispute Settlement in Carolingian West Francia." In *The Settlement of Disputes in Early Medieval Europe,* edited by Paul Fouracre and Wendy Davies, pp. 23–44. Cambridge: Cambridge University Press, 1986.

Nicholas, David. *The Domestic Life of a Medieval City: Women, Children and the Family in Fourteenth-Century Ghent.* Lincoln: University of Nebraska Press: 1985.

Nicholas, Karen. "Countesses as Rulers in Flanders." In *Aristocratic Women in Medieval France,* edited by Theodore Evergates, pp. 111–37. Philadelphia: University of Pennsylvania Press, 1999.

Niermeyer, J. F. *Mediae Latinitatis Lexicon Minus.* Leiden: Brill, 1984.

Nolan, Kathleen, ed. *Capetian Women.* New York: Palgrave MacMillan, 2003.

Noonan, John T. "The Power to Choose." *Viator* 4 (1973): 419–34.

Œillet des Murs, Marc A. P. *Histoire des comtes du Perche de la famille des Rotrou de 943 à 1231.* Nogent-le-Rotrou: A. Gouverneur, 1856.

Oexle, Otto Gerhard, and Jean-Claude Schmitt, eds. *Les tendances actuelles de l'histoire du Moyen Âge en France et en Allemagne.* Paris: Publications de la Sorbonne, 2002.

Pacaut, Marcel. *Louis VII et son royaume.* Paris: École Pratique des Hautes Études, 1964.

Parisse, Michel, ed. *Veuves et veuvage dans le haut Moyen Âge.* Paris: Picard, 1993.

Parsons, John Carmi. *Eleanor of Castile: Queen and Society in Thirteenth-Century England.* New York: St. Martin's, 1995.

———. "Mothers, Daughters, Marriage, Power: Some Plantagenet Evidence, 1150–1500." In *Medieval Queenship,* edited by John Carmi Parsons, pp. 63–78. New York: St. Martin's, 1997.

Parsons, John Carmi, and Bonnie Wheeler, eds. *Eleanor of Aquitaine: Lord and Lady.* New York: Palgrave MacMillan, 2002.

———, eds. *Medieval Mothering.* New York: Routledge, 1999.

Pellaton, Frantz. "La veuve et ses droits de la Basse-Antiquité au haut Moyen Âge." In *Veuves et veuvage dans le haut Moyen Âge,* edited by Michel Parisse, 51–98. Paris: Picard, 1993.

Petot, Pierre. "Le mariage des vassales," *RHDF* 4th series, 56 (1978): 35–38.

Pollock, Linda. *Forgotten Children.* Cambridge: Cambridge University Press, 1984.

Power, Eileen. "The Position of Women." In *The Legacy of the Middle Ages,* edited by C. G. Crump and E. F. Jacob, pp. 403–30. Oxford: Oxford University Press, 1926.

Quirk, Kathleen. "Men, Women and Miracles in Normandy, 1050–1150." In *Medieval Memories: Men, Women and the Past 700–1300,* edited by Elisabeth van Houts, pp. 53–71. Harlow, UK: Longman, 2001.

Rachinet, Philippe, ed. *Archéologie et histoire d'un prieuré bénédictin en Beauce: Nottonville (Eure-et-Loir), Xe-XVIIe siècles.* Paris: Éditions CTHS, 2006.

Réal, Isabelle. "Représentations et pratiques des relations fraternelles dans la société franque du haut Moyen Âge (VIe-IXe siècles)." In *Frères et sœurs: Les liens adelphiques dans l'Occident antique et médiévale,* edited by Sophie Cassagnes-Brouquet and Martine Yvernault, pp. 73–93. Turnhout, Belgium: Brepols, 2007.

Reuter, Timothy. "The Medieval Nobility in Twentieth-Century Historiography." In *Companion to Historiography,* edited by Michael Bentley, pp. 177–202. London: Routledge, 1997.

——. "Nobles and Others: The Social and Cultural Expression of Power Relations in the Middle Ages." In *Nobles and Nobility,* edited by Anne E. Duggan, pp. 85–98. Woodbridge, UK: Boydell Press, 2000.

——. "Property Transactions and Social Relations between Rulers, Bishops and Nobles in Early Eleventh-Century Saxony." In *Property and Power in Early Medieval Europe,* edited by Paul Fouracre and Wendy Davies, pp. 165–99. Cambridge: Cambridge University Press, 2003.

Reuter, Timothy, and Chris Wickam. "Debate: The 'Feudal Revolution.'" *Past and Present* 155 (1997): 177–208.

Riché, Pierre, and Danièle Alexandre-Bidon. *L'enfance au Moyen Âge.* Paris: Bibliothèque de France, 1994.

Ricketts, Philadelphia. "Widows, Religious Patronage and Family Identity: Some Cases from Twelfth-Century Yorkshire." *The Haskins Society Journal* 14 (2004): 117–36.

Riley-Smith, Jonathan. *The First Crusaders, 1095–1131.* Cambridge: Cambridge University Press, 1997.

Rouche, Michel, ed. *Fulbert de Chartres: Précurseur de l'Europe médiévale?* Paris: Presses de l'Université Paris-Sorbonne, 2008.

Röckelien, Hedwig. "Entre société et religion: L'histoire des genres au Moyen Âge en Allemagne." In *Les tendance actuelles de l'histoire du Moyen Âge en France et en Allemagne,* edited by Otto Gerhard Oexle and Jean-Claude Schmitt, pp. 583–93. Paris: Publications de la Sorbonne, 2002.

Rosenthal, Joel T. *Old Age in Late Medieval England.* Philadelphia: University of Pennsylvania Press, 1996.

Rosenwein, Barbara, ed. *Anger's Past: The Social Uses of an Emotion in the Middle Ages.* Ithaca, NY: Cornell University Press, 1998.

——. "Feudal War and Monastic Peace: Cluniac Liturgy as Ritual Aggression." *Viator* 2 (1971): 129–57.

——. *To Be the Neighbor of St. Peter: The Social Meaning of Cluny's Property.* Ithaca, NY: Cornell University Press, 1989.

——. "Worrying about Emotions in History." *AHR* 107 (2002): 821–45.

Rosenwein, Barbara, Thomas Head, and Sharon Farmer. "Monks and Their Enemies: A Comparative Approach." *Speculum* 66 (1991): 764–86.

Rousseau, Constance M. "Kinship Ties, Behavioral Norms, and Family Counseling in the Pontificate of Innocent III." In *Women, Marriage, and Family in Medieval Christendom: Essays in Memory of Michael M. Sheehan, C.S.B,* edited by Constance M. Rousseau and Joel T. Rosenthal, pp. 325–48. Kalamazoo, MI: Medieval Institute Publications, 1998.

Rubenstein, Jay. *Guibert of Nogent: Portrait of a Medieval Mind.* New York: Routledge, 2002.

Santinelli, Emmanuelle. "Ni '*morgengabe*' ni *tertia* mais *dos* et dispositions en faveur du dernier vivant: Les échanges patrimoniaux entre époux dans la Loire moyenne (VIIe–XIe siècle)." In *Dots et douaires dans le haut Moyen Âge,* edited by François Bougard, Laurent Feller, and Régine Le Jan, pp. 245–70. Rome: École Française de Rome, 2002.

Schmid, Karl. "The Structure of Nobility in the Earlier Middle Ages." In *The Medieval Nobility: Studies on the Ruling Classes of France and Germany,* edited by Timothy Reuter, pp. 37–59. Amsterdam: Elsevier Science, 1978.

——. "Zur Problematik von Familie, Sippe und Geschlecht, Haus und Dynastie beim mittelalterlichen Adel: Vorfragen zum Thema 'Adel und Herrschaft im Mittelalter.'" *Zeitschrift für die Geschichte des Oberrheins* 105 (1957): 1–62.

Schowalter, Kathleen. "The Ingeborg Psalter: Queenship, Legitimacy and the Appropriation of Byzantine Art into the West." In *Capetian Women,* edited by Kathleen Nolan, pp. 99–135. New York: Palgrave MacMillan, 2003.

Seidel, Linda. *Legends in Limestone: Lazarus, Gislebertus, and the Cathedral of Autun.* Chicago: University of Chicago Press, 1999.

Shadis, Miriam. "Berenguela of Castile's Political Motherhood: The Management of Sexuality, Marriage and Succession." In *Medieval Mothering,* edited by John Carmi Parsons and Bonnie Wheeler, pp. 335–58. New York: Routledge, 1999.

——. "Blanche of Castile and Facinger's 'Medieval Queenship': Reassessing the Argument." In *Capetian Women,* edited by Kathleen Nolan, pp. 137–61. New York: Palgrave MacMillan, 2003.

——. "Piety, Politics and Power: The Patronage of Leonor of England and Her Daughters Berenguela of Leon and Blanche of Castille." In *The Cultural Patronage of Medieval Women,* edited by June Hall McCash, pp. 202–27. Athens: University of Georgia Press, 1995.

Shahar, Shulamith. *Childhood in the Middle Ages.* Translated by Chaya Galai. New York: Routledge, 1990.

Sheehan, Michael M. "The Bishop of Rome to a Barbarian King on the Rituals of Marriage." In *In iure veritas: Studies in Canon Law in Memory of Schafer Williams,* edited by Steven B. Bowman and Blanche E. Cody, pp. 187–99. Cincinnati: University of Cincinnati Press, 1991.

——. "The Formation and Stability of Marriage in Fourteenth-Century England: Evidence of an Ely Register." *Medieval Studies* 33 (1971): 253–56.

——. "The Influence of Canon Law on the Property Rights of Married Women in England." *Medieval Studies* 25 (1963): 109–24.

Skinner, Patricia. "'And Her Name Was…?' Gender and Naming in Medieval Southern Italy." *Medieval Prosopography* 20 (1999): 133–52.

——. *Family Power in Southern Italy: The Duchy of Gaeta and Its Neighbors, 850–1139.* Cambridge: Cambridge University Press, 1995.

——. *Women in Medieval Italian Society, 500–1200.* Harlow, UK: Longman, 2001.

Soares-Christen, Eliana Magnani. "Alliances matrimoniales et circulation des biens à travers les chartes provençales (Xe–début du XIIe siècle)." In *Dots et douaires dans le haut Moyen Âge,* edited by François Bougard, Laurent Feller, and Régine Le Jan, pp. 131–52. Rome: École Française de Rome, 2002.

Sopena, Pascual Martinez. "Personal Naming and Kinship in the Spanish Aristoc-racy." In *Personal Names Studies of Medieval Europe,* edited by George T. Beech, Monique Bourin, and Pascal Chareille, pp. 67–76. Kalamazoo, MI: Medieval Institute Publications, 2002.

Stafford, Pauline. *Queen Emma and Queen Edith: Queenship and Women's Power in Eleventh-Century England.* Oxford: Oxford University Press, 1997.

———. *Queens, Concubines and Dowagers: The King's Wife in the Early Middle Ages.* Athens: University of Georgia Press, 1983.

Sullivan, Richard E. "The Carolingian Age: Reflections on Its Place in the History of the Middle Ages." *Speculum* 64 (1989): 267–306.

Stuard, Susan Mosher, ed. *Women in Medieval History and Historiography.* Philadelphia: University of Pennsylvania Press, 1987.

Tabuteau, Emily Z. "The Role of Law in the Succession to Normandy and England, 1087." *The Haskins Society Journal* 3 (1991): 141–70.

———. *Transfers of Property in Eleventh-Century Norman Law.* Chapel Hill: University of North Carolina Press, 1988.

Tellenbach, Gerd. "From the Carolingian Imperial Nobility to the German Estate of Imperial Princes." In *The Medieval Nobility: Studies on the Ruling Class of France and Germany from the Sixth to the Twelfth Century,* edited by Timothy Reuter, pp. 203–42. Amsterdam: Elsevier Sciences, 1978.

Tessier, Georges. *Diplomatique royale française.* Paris: Picard, 1962.

Thireau, Jean-Louis. "Les pratiques communautaires entre époux dans l'Anjou feu-dal (Xe-XIIe siècles)." *RHDF* 4th series, 67 (1989): 207–35.

Thompson, Kathleen Hapgood. "Dowry and Inheritance Patterns: Some Examples from the Descendants of King Henry I of England." *Medieval Prosopography* 17 (1996): 45–61.

———. "The Formation of the County of Perche: The Rise and Fall of the House of Gouet." In *Family Trees and the Roots of Politics,* edited by K. S. B. Keats-Rohan, pp. 299–314. Woodbridge, UK: Boydell Press, 1997.

———. *Power and Border Lordship in Medieval France: The County of the Perche, 1000–1226.* Woodbridge, UK: Boydell Press, 2002.

Turner, Ralph V. "The Children of Anglo-Norman Royalty and their Upbringing." *Medieval Prosopography* 11 (1990): 17–49.

———. "Eleanor of Aquitaine and Her Children: An Inquiry into Medieval Family Attachment." *Journal of Medieval History* 14 (1988): 321–35.

Tuten, Belle. "Women and Ordeals." In *Conflict in Medieval Europe: Changing Perspectives on Society and Culture,* edited by Warren C. Brown and Piotr Górecki, pp. 163–74. Aldershot, UK: Ashgate, 2003.

Van Engen, John. "Sacred Sanctions for Lordship." In *Cultures of Power,* edited by Thomas N. Bisson, pp. 203–31. Philadelphia: University of Pennsylvania Press, 1995.

Van de Kieft, C. "Une église privée de l'abbaye de la Trinité de Vendôme au XIe siècle." *Le Moyen Âge* 119 (1963): 157–68.

Van Houts, Elizabeth, ed. *Medieval Memories: Men, Women and the Past, 700–1300.* Harlow, UK: Longman, 2001.

———. *Memory and Gender in Medieval Europe, 900–1200.* London: MacMillan, 1999.

Venarde, Bruce. *Women's Monasticism and Medieval Society: Nunneries in France and England, 890–1215.* Ithaca, NY: Cornell University Press, 1997.

Verdon, Jean. "Les veuves des rois de France aux Xe et XIe siècles." In *Veuves et veuvage dans le haut moyen âge,* edited by Michel Parisse, pp. 187–201. Paris: Picard, 1993.

Walker, Sue Sheridan. "Litigation as Personal Quest: Suing for Dower in the Royal Courts, circa 1272–1350." In *Wife and Widow in Medieval England,* edited by Sue Sheridan Walker, pp. 81–108. Ann Arbor: University of Michigan Press, 1993.

Ward, Jennifer C. "Noblewomen, Family and Identity in Later Medieval Europe." In *Nobles and Nobility in Medieval Europe: Concepts, Origins, Transformations,* edited by Anne J. Duggan, pp. 245–62. Woodbridge, UK: Boydell Press, 2000.

Weinberger, Stephen. "Les conflits entre clercs et laïcs dans la Provence au XIe siècle." *Annales du Midi* 92 (1980): 269–79.

Werner, Karl Ferdinand. "L'apport de la prosopographie à l'histoire social des élites." In *Family Trees and Roots of Politics,* edited by K. S. B. Keats-Rohan, pp. 1–22. Woodbridge, UK: Boydell Press, 1997.

——. "Die Nachkommen Karls des Großen bis um das Jahr 1000 (1.–8. Generation)." In *Karl der Grosse, Lebenswerk und Nachleben,* vol. 4, *Das Nachleben,* edited by Wolfgang Braunfels and Percy E. Schramm, pp. 402–84. Dusseldorf: L. Schwann, 1967.

White, Stephen D. *Custom, Kinship and Gifts to Saints: The "Laudatio Parentum" in Western France, 1050–1150.* Chapel Hill: University of North Carolina Press, 1988.

——. "The Discourse of Inheritance in Twelfth-Century France: Alternative Models of the Fief in *Raoul de Cambrai.*" In *Law and Government in Medieval England and Normandy: Essays in Honor of Sir James Holt,* edited by George Garnett and John Hudson, pp. 173–97. Cambridge: Cambridge University Press, 1994.

——. "Feuding and Peace-Making in the Touraine around the Year 1100." *Traditio* 42 (1986): 195–263.

——. "Inheritances and Legal Arguments in Western France, 1050–1150." *Traditio* 43 (1987): 55–103.

——. "'*Pactum…Legem Vincit et Amor Judicium*': The Settlement of Disputes by Compromise in Eleventh-Century Western France." *American Journal of Legal History* 22 (1978): 218–308.

——. "The Politics of Anger." In *Anger's Past: The Social Uses of an Emotion in the Middle Ages,* edited by Barbara Rosenwein, pp. 127–52. Ithaca, NY: Cornell University Press, 1998.

Wollasch, Joachim. "Parenté noble et monachisme réformateur: Observations sur les 'conversions' à la vie monastique aux XIe et XIIe siècles." *Revue historique* 264 (1980): 3–24.

Ziezulewicz, William. "Abbatial Elections at Saint-Florent de Saumur (ca. 950–1118)." *Church History* 57 (1988): 289–97.

——. "From Serf to Abbot: The Role of the *Familia* in the Career of Frederick of Tours." *The American Benedictine Review* 36 (1985): 278–91.

——. "'Restored' Churches in the Fisc of St. Florent de Saumur (1021–1118)." *Revue bénédictine* 96 (1986): 106–17.

❦ INDEX

Page numbers in *italics* refer to charts, maps and tables.

Abelin the knight, 224, 225
Achard (nephew to Hugo Cadebertus), 219
Ada (daughter of Archembald Occha), 129
Ada of Touraille, 40n59, 81–82, 82n76
Adam (husband of Hildegard), 132
Adam (uncle to Hugh of Mondoubleau), 71, *243*
Adam of Avasiaco, 124
Adam of Brou, 192
Adela (Countess, wife of Count Stephen of
  Chartres, daughter of King William I), 15,
  49n96, 50n104, 172; church reform, support
  of, 18, 19
Adela (daughter of Fulcher Dives), 63, 65;
  dowry, 125–126
Adela de Bezai (wife of Fulcher Dives), 64–65,
  78, 96, 155, 155n40, 228, *243*
Adela of Mantes, 220
Adela of Montigny, 67–68, 103n51, 149, 154,
  240
Adelaide (sister of monk of St. Trinité), 114
Adelaide (wife of King Louis VI the Fat), 33
Adelaide of Espiers, 226
Adelaide of Le Puiset, 196, *239*
Adelard (son of Erchembald), 216
Adelard the Eel Biter (brother to Matthew
  Griponis), 110–111, 110n76
Adelasia of Sicily (Countess), 186
Adeled (wife of Gosbert Boschet), 84
Adelina (daughter of Ingenulf), 44
Adelina (daughter of Landric), 122
Adenord (wife of Simon of Beaugency), 134
adulthood: extended kin, interactions with,
  41–45, 41n60, 53–54, 73–82. *See also*
  Fréteval-Mondoubleau-Dives kindred;
  siblings, adulthood bonds
affinal kin: noblewomen, relationship with,
  41–42, 44–45, 55, 126, 136, 166, 236;
  property claims by, 220–221
affinal kinship, 3n2
Agatha (daughter-in-law of Ursio
  of Fréteval), 79

age of majority, 145n18
agnatic kinship, 2n2
Agnes (Countess of Anjou), 38
Agnes (daughter of Fulcher of Fréteval). *See*
  Comitissa (daughter of Fulcher of Fréteval)
Agnes (wife of the earl of Buckingham), 186
Agnes of Montigny, 68n25, 103, 103n51,
  175, 175n26, *240;* marriages of, 43, 43n68,
  146, 152
Agnes of Vendôme, 199
Agrippa (sister of Matthew Griponis) 94–95,
  110–111, 110n76
Aimery Chenard, 111
Alberic of Montoire, 179
Alburgis (wife of Gaufred Norman), 123,
  123n11, 124n12
Alluyes-Gouet, seigneurial family of, 21–22,
  22n40, 62, 154, *240;* church reform,
  support of, 200–202; marriage, frequency
  of, *151*
Almaric (brother of Robert Michael and Salo-
  mon of Fréteval), 215–216, 215n42
Amboise, seigneurial family of, 36–37. *See also*
  Elizabeth; Gaufred; Lisois; Sibilla; Sulpice I;
  Sulpice II
André of Baudement, 58, 59
Angevin comital family, 13
Anjou, Count of: Geoffrey Martel, 16, 24,
  229n81
Anjou, county of, 10–11
Ansold of Beauvoir, 136
Ansold the Knight, 43
Archembald Occha, 129
aristocracy, 20–26; origins of, 20; twelfth cen-
  tury changes, 76. *See also specific families*
aristocratic family dynamics: inclusivity, 2–3,
  235–236
Arnulf (Count of Boulogne), 87
Arnulf Ceotard, 227
Arnulf Malesherbes, 181
Avelina (daughter of Hugh of Lavardin), 123

271